# family fun in Montana

## Chris Boyd
### (formerly Chris Brewer)

FALCON®

HELENA, MONTANA

**ᴀFALCON**GUIDE®

Falcon® is continually expanding its list of recreational guidebooks. All books include detailed descriptions, accurate maps, and all the information necessary for enjoyable trips. You can order extra copies of this book and get information and prices for other Falcon guidebooks by writing Falcon, P.O. Box 1718, Helena, MT 59624 or calling toll-free 1-800-582-2665. Please ask for a free copy of our current catalog. Visit our website at http://www.falconguide.com.

2 3 4 5 6 7 8 9 0 MG 03 02 01 00 99

Cover photos by Michael Sample, Donnie Sexton, and Spiker Stock Photography.

Library of Congress Cataloging-in-Publication Data
Boyd, Chris, 1953-
   Family fun in Montana / by Chris Boyd Brewer.
     p. cm.
   ISBN 1-56044-554-8 (pbk. : alk. paper)
   1. Montana—Guidebooks. 2. Family recreation—Montana—
Guidebooks. I Title.
F729.3.B74 1998
917.8604'33—dc21                                 98-42834
                                                             CIP

CAUTION

All participants in the recreational activities suggested by this book must assume responsibility for their own actions and safety. The information contained in this guidebook cannot replace sound judgment and good decision-making skills, which help reduce risk exposure; nor does the scope of this book allow for disclosure of all the potential hazards and risks involved in such activities.

    Learn as much as possible about the recreational activities in which you participate, prepare for the unexpected, and be cautious. The reward will be a safer and more enjoyable experience.

This book is dedicated to the memory of Charlie Haddock, my husband and my children's stepfather. Originally a co-author of this book, Charlie died during the early phases of research. His lively spirit, appreciation of nature, and love for Montana are within these pages.

# ACKNOWLEDGMENTS

Personal thank-yous are enthusiastically given to my children, David and May, for helping me find out how to be a Montana explorer with kids; to my mother, Ellen Boyd, and my father, Ted Boyd, for giving me an appreciation of life in its various forms; and to my children's father and my ex-husband, Ken, for helping me gain skills needed for exploring nature. Thanks, also, to friends who accompanied me on some of these journeys and supported the writing of this book: Bob Dombroski, Nancy Rose, Judith Pressmar; and, oh yes, to Zip, my faithful dog-friend who has seen more of Montana than most people.

There are innumerable people from government agencies and private organizations throughout the state who believe that recreation is an essential part of family life. They provided me with helpful information to make this book interesting and effective. Thanks to them for their time and patience. A special thanks also goes to Curt Thompson for sharing his wisdom about Montana rivers.

# CONTENTS

· · · · · · · · · · · · · · · · · · · · · · · · · · · · · · · · · ·

# Montana State Map

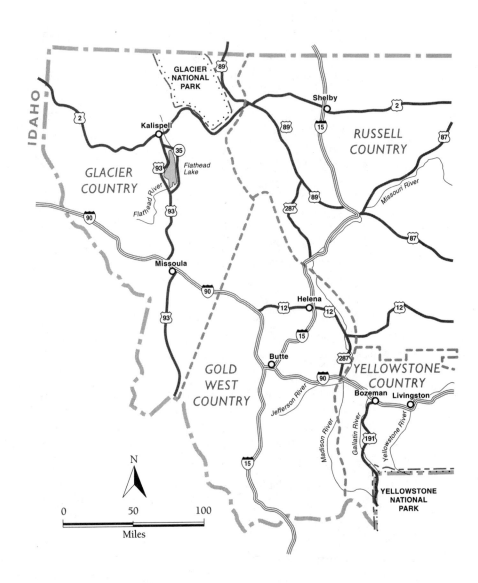

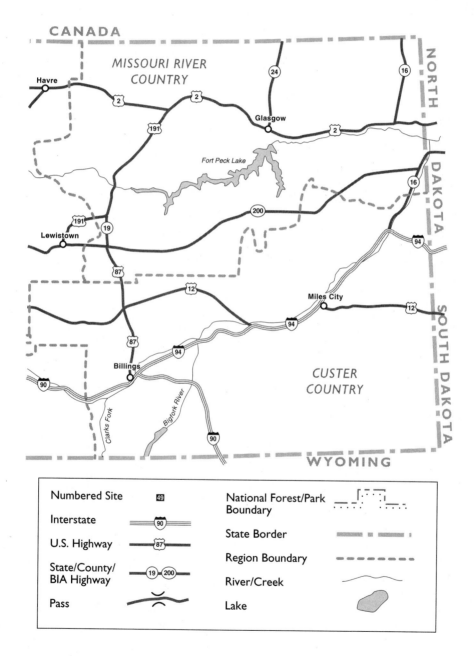

CANADA

MISSOURI RIVER COUNTRY

Havre

NORTH

24

16

2

2

Glasgow

191

2

Fort Peck Lake

16

DAKOTA

200

191

94

Lewistown

19

87

12

Miles City

12

94

87

94

Billings

90

Clarks Fork

Bigfork River

CUSTER COUNTRY

SOUTH DAKOTA

90

WYOMING

| Numbered Site | 49 | National Forest/Park Boundary | |
| Interstate | 90 | State Border | |
| U.S. Highway | 87 | Region Boundary | |
| State/County/BIA Highway | 19  200 | River/Creek | |
| Pass | | Lake | |

# Introduction

As a single parent who enjoys the outdoors and the cultural resources Montana offers, I have been determined not to let my solo status and busy life keep my children and me from having good family fun exploring Montana. However, I have friends who, because of the overwhelming demands of single parenting, are reluctant to go on family outings. Others—both single and two-parent families—simply aren't sure where to go or what to do for fun with their kids. I have actually met children living in Kalispell who have never been to Glacier National Park, only 30 miles away! It is for these people, especially, that this book was written.

Time spent with my kids in family activities has been precious, and I have always viewed it as essential. These experiences create the kind of family bonding that holds families together through trying times. They provide lifelong memories and give children a model of parenting that will become part of a template for their own parenting when their turn comes. Even if there aren't as many outings as I would like, I value each one as I would a gift. Time with my family will be gone before I know it, but I will always have these memories. Family outings give a vitality and pleasure to life that I wouldn't want to miss.

In the big picture, the understanding and appreciation of nature, of community, and of human history that is gained through early, enjoyable exposure to natural, community, and human resources are the nutrients for a healthy society. Opportunities to learn about human history and to love nature should not only be part of the school curriculum, but also be part of the heritage parents pass on to their children. People who have played along the rivers as children grow up wanting to care for and protect these rivers. Kids who have been enthralled by the poignancy of human struggles and achievements, displayed in museums and experienced in community activities, will contribute to the preservation of cultural and historical resources as adults. Children who have positive, caring family experiences most often go on to share these same types of experiences with their own children. Bless and enjoy these experiences!

## How to Use This Book

· · · · · · · · · · · · · · · · · · · · · · · · · · · · · · · · · · ·

This book is designed to make the enjoyment of Montana's natural, historic, and cultural resources more accessible to families. However, Montana is a big state with vast resources, which could not all be included in a single volume. The areas presented in this book have been thoroughly researched to provide a wide variety of potential activities in close proximity. Thus, as families travel along major roads or tourism routes or near significant recreation areas they can have numerous recreational options within a short distance and have less travel time invested in their family outings.

Both highly developed and undeveloped natural sites are listed in the book to provide a range of outdoor recreational opportunities. Undeveloped sites are noted as such and visitors should recognize that these places may not even have toilets and will certainly not have services. Roads and trails are often limited and unmaintained. Go to these places if you want to experience untamed nature and come prepared to take care of your family's needs. The hikes presented in this book are, for the most part, along very easy trails with little or no elevation gain. If a hike is somewhat steep in places it is mentioned in the site description.

In addition to the more rural locations, city and county parks are listed when they are easy to reach from main roads, or are especially interesting for children. These provide areas where kids can play while parents relax, or where families can stop for lunch or snacks. City pools are also listed so that it is easy for families to find a place for a refreshing dip on a hot summer's day.

Each of the state's six tourism regions—Glacier Country, Gold West Country, Russell Country, Yellowstone Country, Missouri River Country, and Custer Country—is covered in a separate chapter; together, these present recreational opportunities throughout the state. Numbered sites, which are keyed to locator maps found within each section, follow a short introduction to the area.

- Site descriptions include what you can expect to find at a site, interesting facts or history about the site, and information of particular interest to kids.
- Detailed directions are provided to make getting to sites as easy as possible (there's nothing quite as frustrating as being lost with hot, tired kids in the car).
- Admission costs and hours of operation are listed under "Important Information" where applicable, though these items are always subject to change.
- Wheelchair accessibility is included under "Important Information."
- Contact phone numbers to obtain more information on sites can be found under "Important Information."

In addition to the numbered sites, interesting stories, facts, and history are found throughout the book in boxed inserts—read them to your kids!

*Special note:* Every effort has been made to provide current information about sites. However, what is true one year may not be true the next. Admission charges, hours of operation, available facilities, contact numbers, and even whether or not a site is open may change. Take advantage of the phone numbers provided and double check on particulars before you go on your family outing. And, if you discover changes or errors, please let us know at:

Falcon Publishing
Attention: Reprint Editor
P.O. Box 1718
Helena, Montana 59624

# PLANNING YOUR TRIP

. . . . . . . . . . . . . . . . . . . . . . . . . . . . . . . .

Family fun can happen anywhere! Sometimes spontaneous activities are the most memorable, but, on the other hand, planned trips can become a highly anticipated event. Either way, here are some thoughts on how to make decisions about where to go on your trips, things to have readily accessible, and how to view your family time together.

## Where Do We Go and How Far Is It?

If you haven't done many family trips, deciding where to start can be mind-boggling. The opportunities for family outings are incredibly abundant in Montana, and I always recommend that people start simply. Read about what is in your local area and go to places that are a short drive away. It's easier to get family activities going when there is less preparation time and not as much investment in driving. This also gives you the opportunity to ask friends in your area for any additional information about the places you want to visit.

Once you have some experience going out on family outings, you can advance to longer trips. Sometimes we go where we have friends we can visit. Other times, it is a particular interest that leads us to an area. Occasionally we just get curious about somewhere we've never been or someone tells us that the area is fun to explore.

If you are used to going on family trips, you may want to jump into longer trips that are farther from home. Since this book is set up to thoroughly explore a particular area, there are numerous activities for any city or region listed in the book. It is possible to plot a course within one area that will keep your family busy for several days. You will also see how loop tours can be created so that you and your family have interesting stops along your entire journey. But keep in mind that the longer the trip, the more involved you will be in planning and preparation.

Although we go out regularly to local sites, I like to plan a couple of long-distance trips in Montana each year with my kids. Usually we do one in the winter or early spring, and one in the summer. The rest of the year we take short jaunts. I have found this to be a nice balance that gets us out frequently and yet includes some new and exciting discoveries in longer outings. Experiment with what works for your family.

# 10 Tips for Family Fun

While there are innumerable benefits to family outings, such outings are not always easy and no one says that every moment will be fun. Certainly life has its challenges and being on the road with your kids presents unique problems. So, don't worry when these come up, just work through them and continue on.

Since it never hurts to avoid problems where you can, here are some tips on ways to make your family outings easier:

**1. Let's Go Out and Play: Make having fun a priority**
I like to remind myself of the days when my childhood friends would come over and say, "let's go out and play" and I would eagerly join them. We didn't always have a plan, or if we did, it might change dramatically if something we saw intrigued us, if someone who joined us had fresh ideas, or if there was a change in the weather. The point was to have fun, and that we did! With this kind of attitude, your chances of having fun are high from the start.

In the end, it doesn't matter *what* you do on a family outing as much as it matters *how* you do it. If your family trip was too rushed, too angry, too cold, or too hungry, the kids will balk at going out again. But if there was laughter and camaraderie, the kids won't really care what they did or whether or not they had the snack they wanted, and they will want to go out again. Keep in mind that it is the process and not necessarily the product that is important in family outings. Kids will remember whether or not they had fun with you long after they forget what they saw at the museum.

**2. Recognize the limits of your children's interests and abilities**
Short legs, even shorter attention spans (for adult topics), constant appetites, and little tolerance for long car rides are pretty universal limits to kids' traveling abilities. While it's important to expand their tolerance for these things, be gentle. It's easier to stretch little by little than it is to repair damage done by over-stretching! Kids will develop the ability to go farther, withstand greater discomfort, and attain more patience as they get older.

So, ask yourself before you choose a family adventure, "What do I want to get out of this, anyway?" If your goal is to get to the top of the hill for the great view—at whatever costs, you may want to rethink your trip. You may have been a long-distance hiker, an avid angler, or a dedicated museumgoer before you had kids, but now that you have a family, your adventure limits have changed. While doing these things is still wonderfully possible with your family, doing it the same way may not be. Trying to fit your kids into adult-style activities is a setup for disaster—the kind of excursion that ends up not being fun for anyone. If the goal of your trip is your personal entertainment, find a way to go without the kids and take them on an outing that is family oriented.

### 3. Enjoy the journey

It sometimes happens that a fair amount of the adventure time is involved in travel. While reaching your destination is important, we need to realize that the whole trip is, too. My kids taught me this on our annual treks from Montana to Washington to visit family. I discovered that my kids had a 2- to 3-hour driving limit on these 10-hour trips. The kids inevitably started fighting and getting antsy and, consequently, so did I. In desperation, I began looking for quick stops along the route to relieve travel pressure. I had passed the sign for Lake Coeur d'Alene numerous times en route, but when the kids were getting travel weary one year, I decided to stop. We discovered a great beach and park only a few blocks from the highway with a wonderful playground and lots of shady trees. This was not only a refreshing stop but also allowed us to go on contentedly for many miles. It became a regular break on ensuing trips. We tried the same tactic in eastern Washington and found a great beach at Moses Lake and another one on the Columbia River before Ellensburg! Sometimes these stops were quick dips in the water for 15 minutes, and other times they were longer lunch or dinner breaks with a leisurely swim, or even kite flying or kickball. The ritual of stopping got to be one of the parts of this trip we looked forward to, and I learned the value of taking some time to enjoy the journey.

### 4. Keep it simple

A family outing doesn't have to be elaborate. In fact, it is usually the case that the more involved the outings are, the more effort it takes to get ready, the more opportunities there are for problems, and the less we enjoy the trip. Some of our best experiences are simple two- or three-hour evening trips to the river or a local park. On the longer trips, not having a laundry list of places you have to go to can actually be more rewarding than checking off numerous "been there, done that" items. A friend of mine just returned from a two-week trip to Hawaii, saying, "we managed to fit one week's worth of sightseeing into two weeks and had a wonderful time!" Now there are some words of wisdom.

### 5. Set yourself up for success

Build a plan for an outing that includes something interesting to do, bring the necessary comfort items with you (see page 8), and leave plenty of time for your activity. Once on the road, be flexible!

When planning, I look for a variety of activities in the immediate area we plan to visit. That way, you can select sites to visit that appeal to you, yet have some options if the weather changes. There is somewhere to go if you have extra time and there are alternatives if something you planned to visit is unexpectedly closed.

Planning for a trip sometimes involves special items or considerations. On a winter trip to Lolo Hot Springs, I decided to stay in the hotel that *didn't* have a television. However, I came prepared. I picked up a book of short stories (this one happened to be science-fiction award-winners). Every night, I would read one or two stories aloud. They were interesting stories, different from what we normally read, and it was really quite fun. Better yet, no one missed the television.

In order to make trips easier, I have a large box which carries all the necessary road-trip items that we need. It stays packed all the time, and in the summer, it sometimes stays in the car all the time. In it are good munchies, extra clothing, toys, first-aid kit, etc. My camping gear is set up the same way. It's all loaded in boxes so I can just pick it up and go when I want to.

## 6. Build upon your successes

If you have success with one family outing, keep it going! Find out what your kids enjoyed the most on your trips and build on it. If it turns out that your children are enamored of the rocks they found, consider adding rockhounding to your next trip. Our family discovered that trips to hot springs made everybody happy, so we began to build on this success and ended up exploring ten delightful hot springs in 14 years by making an annual trip to a new one each year (and going back a couple of times to favorite sites).

On the other hand, you can build a sense of adventure by making a habit of trying something new. Include the kids in this thought: "I've never been sapphire-digging—have you? Let's try it!"

## 7. Keep your eyes open for opportunities to explore

You never know what you will encounter in a new place. Be aware of what is around you and allow time to explore something you hadn't thought of when making a travel plan. On one of our outings for this book my kids and I were camped along the Rocky Mountain Front and I decided to investigate the Sun River area. I pulled off on a bluff above the river to take a look at it. One of the kids discovered a trail to the river, and they were halfway down when I decided I had better join them. From the river's edge we could see an amazing tunnel upriver a ways. Well, a short walk, a quick swim, and a rock scramble later, we were in the tunnel—dog and all. The rest of the trip involved some moderate sightseeing, a fair amount of driving, and a picnic lunch by the river—all fairly lukewarm in comparison to our exciting spontaneous adventure.

## 8. Build the excitement

Talk about your trip if it's one you are planning ahead of time. In fact, you might ask the kids what they are interested in and research it with them. One year I wrote a short curriculum guide on paleontology for an educational press, and I discovered just how much dinosaur stuff there was in Montana. Intrigued by the topic, I planned a spring break vacation around dinosaurs in Montana and we explored a variety of dinosaur doings. Before we went, the kids and I researched some interesting dinosaur facts, found out about the sites we would be visiting, and generally got jazzed about the idea.

## 9. Share the wealth

Some of our best trips go beyond family to include friends. There were a few years where our trips to hot springs always included other families. This was particularly advantageous when the kids were little as it gave them someone to play with and the adults could take turns getting a little time off while some of the other adults played with the kids.

One year we planned a fall potluck in Glacier National Park and invited lots of people for the dinner and campfire. Anyone who wanted to stay overnight and go canoeing the next day just brought his or her tent. We found that this was a great way to expand our repertoire of camping friends.

Now that my kids are older, I inevitably end up with more of their friends than mine on our trips. Teens seem to feel that being with friends is more important than being with parents, so I always ask my kids if they want to bring a friend. In the end, the kids are happier, I get to know their friends, and we still go on family outings together.

## 10. Go with the flow

When the hike to the fishing lake drags on and the kids start playing in the creek along the way, it may be that it's better to stop. Sometimes a few minutes by the water will provide renewed energy for more hiking, too. Or you can use the experience to nudge them upstream by saying, "Let's see what's along the creek up there!" And, of course, it may be that the goal you set for the day's journey was unrealistic and playing in the creek will be the endpoint of your trip. But at least it was fun and you got out. The best memories from the trip may be of time spent exploring the creek.

Be flexible. If time gets short, develop a Plan B that gives you time to explore and have fun at fewer places. If it's too hot, add a dip in the lake along the way, or a stop in a shady park. If it rains, pull out the rain gear and enjoy the puddles along the way, or if it's too cold to be fun, do something indoors instead!

# Travel Essentials

Kids' bodies just don't do well sitting in cars for long. Sometimes even short periods of time don't work well, but if you have certain items in the car, you can help the trip go faster. I always felt these were essential items for the inevitable needs that come up on the road (I keep the non-perishable items in a box in my trunk).

- snacks such as fruit, carrot and celery sticks, beef jerky, crackers and cheese (especially in cans or as pre-packaged sticks), water and other drinks
- paper towels, small plastic bags, and garbage bags
- a first-aid kit that includes sunscreen, mosquito repellent, and plenty of Band Aids®
- a couple of bath-size towels
- warm jackets (I also leave gloves and hats in the car, even in the summer)
- a trowel and toilet paper
- a small bucket
- a pillow and blankets

# Entertainment Supplies

I think these items are just as essential as the travel supplies! The following have helped us get down the road with little arguing and complaining:

- reading books and picture books about the areas you will be in or the topics you are investigating, plus good books on other topics that the kids will like
- a magazine related to each kid's special interests. There are magazines on everything so I often pick one up for each kid, or have them choose one that matches their most recent blossoming interest. We take these along as special trip items.
- a Walkman-style cassette player with headphones (but watch the volume levels!) and cassette tapes of stories or music
- grocery-store books of mazes and other pencil activities
- car toys, such as playing cards, Etch-A-Sketch™, or Game-boy™
- drawing paper and markers, modeling clay (make sure markers and clay are kid-friendly and easy to clean up.)
- a lap-desk or clipboard for each kid so they have a hard surface to write on
- a small keyboard with headphone jack and headphones (the ones that sell for $15 to $25)

# Car Games

When all of the above fails, we play car games. There are books on these entertaining activities, but here are some of our favorites:

- The Alphabet Game. Find letters of the alphabet, starting from A and going to Z, on road signs. The first person to Z wins.
- The Animal Game. Look for animals along the roadway and call out what you see. The first person to call the animal gets points. Cows are 1 point, horses 5, cats and dogs 10, and wild or exotic animals are 20. To avoid competition, you can pick sides of the road to call. In this version "winning" is more a matter of luck than who called first. We sometimes do this in teams so everyone can play.
- Car Colors. Each person picks a color of vehicle to count (parked cars count, too).
- "I See Something . . . ." One person picks out an object inside the car and tells what color it is. The other participants can ask up to 20 yes-or-no questions about the object. The first person to guess the object correctly picks the next object. If no one gets it in 20 questions, the person who picked the object gets to go another round.
- Make up your own song about your journey using the melody of a familiar tune such as "Row, Row, Row Your Boat" or "Mary Had a Little Lamb." These tunes have a way of expanding as you go on your journey.
- Have each person keep track of the license plates they see from different states. The one with the most states at the end of the journey wins.

# SEEING THROUGH KIDS' EYES

Trips can be interesting and entertaining. The trick is to be open to finding things that have interest, which means keeping that sense of wonder that young children have. It also means being in awe of the little things.

Something doesn't have to be front-page news to be interesting. However, in our high-tech society it is easy to lose sight of the simple joys and respond only to the Disneyland sort of scenario. Exciting discoveries are everywhere if we just look. So here are some ideas on ways to enhance looking.

# Hey, Look at This!

Here are some ways to involve kids in finding out what's interesting on your outings.

- Ask questions such as "What's this?" or "How does this work?" Even if you know the answer, having the kids figure it out draws them actively into the discovery process, rather than passively into someone else's verbal description.
- Keep in mind that kids need to be hands-on! Unless it's dangerous or breakable, let the kids put themselves into the experience. Keep in mind that wet clothes dry, dirt comes off, and touching something is a great way to figure it out. (Safety comes first, of course, and sometimes there are rules against touching, too.)
- Remember that phrase, "You get out what you put in"? It applies here. Take time to explore and be curious yourself, for you will find interesting things if you approach activities with a sense of interest. Besides, your attitude will rub off on the kids.
- Capitalize on the moment. When we stopped once at the Choteau city park for lunch, my kids discovered the little creek that runs along its edge. It was knee-deep, warm, and in the shade. They were so interested in playing in it that lunch turned into an event of a couple of hours, but it was fun, and we made a new discovery about Choteau!
- Let the kids decide what to do. Go ahead, ask them what they want to do for the day. Let them pick between a list of choices. It does wonders for their enthusiasm.
- Play, "Look at This!" at museums and art galleries. Everybody gets to explore the facility fully and then share one thing they found particularly interesting with the rest of the family.
- Have respect for family members' interests. While model trains may not be appealing to you, if you look carefully you may discover what it is about them that interests someone else. And if you do this, chances are the other family members will show the same kind of respect for your interests.

# Special Programs for Kids

There are specially designed programs for kids and families operated by state and federal agencies that offer new insights for kids about Montana. These programs provide materials and ideas for making outdoor experiences more interesting. Investigate the National Park Service Junior Naturalist Program. Get involved in the Montana Department of Fish, Wildlife & Parks M*A*Y

Club, which stands for Montana Angling Youth, a program that encourages family fishing activities. Participants receive a free newsletter. The organization also provides a free fishing day with a free license good for a single day at a specific location and time.

The "Just for Kids" Internet program provides information about Montana history, geography, facts, wildlife, and much more. The site is designed specifically for kids. The program was developed by numerous agencies including Travel Montana, the Montana Department of Fish, Wildlife & Parks, the USDA Forest Service, the Bureau of Land Management, and others. The address is http://kids.mt.gov.

# Hiking Hints

• • • • • • • • • • • • • • • • • • • • • • • • • • • • • • • • • • •

When taking kids on hikes, it's important to provide for their needs and interests or you may find that they resist going on hikes in the future. Here are some considerations:

- Keep kids' limits in mind and don't go any farther than you think they can walk back. Be wise about not planning any hikes that are too demanding, if you want them to enjoy hiking.
- Let the kids set the pace. Keep in mind how fast they may have to walk to keep up with you if you lead!
- Take care of your children's feet as you would your own. Make sure they have good walking shoes and check their feet for hot spots where their shoes might be rubbing. Use Band-Aids or moleskin to protect these places before they get too bad.
- Bring hats, layers of clothing, sunscreen, and mosquito repellent. Be sure to use them when they are needed!
- Carry a towel and dry clothing if you think there might be water to play in on the trail.
- Bring a bandana to use for various purposes. Dip it in water and have your child wear it on his or her head when it's hot, wrap things in it, or use it for an emergency bandage if necessary.
- Have plenty of water and stop frequently to drink it.
- Keep nutritious energy food handy for snacks.
- Stop to enjoy things along the trail. Bugs, water, flowers, rocks, and all kinds of little wonders make a hike interesting to kids. Keep your sense of adventure and don't worry too much about reaching a particular destination. Enjoy the walk and they will too.
- Tell kids what to do when lost. Give them a whistle to use if necessary, and have them wear bright clothing so you see them easily. Teach kids survival skills early. Also, it helps if you have taught children to pay attention to

landmarks along the way. If they do get lost, they may be able to find their way back more easily if they are used to remembering what is around them.

- Teach kids about treading lightly on the land and practice these principles yourself.
- When you just have to keep going but the kids are getting weary, make up a game to keep going. My kids actually went from 100 all the way to 1 with the song "100 Bottles of Pop on the Wall" as we hiked a rather strenuous 3 miles. Until we started singing, I wasn't sure we would make it! Be creative and make up your own game to fit the moment.
- Make up games for when you reach your destination, too. We play "Pooh Sticks," a game we got from a Winnie-the-Pooh movie. Everyone grabs a stick and throws it into a creek at the same time (doing this from a bridge works great). We then watch to see which one reaches a pre-determined spot first (the other side of the bridge is best, if you are on one). It's amazing how long you can do this with kids.
- Most of all, have fun and your kids will, too!

# BIG SKY AND LONG ROADS

Beneath the big Montana sky are the long, and we mean long, Montana roads. It's important when you travel around Montana that you look at two things: the highway mileage chart and the road designation legend.

## Montana Road Services

Montana towns are often long distances apart and there is a good chance there will be no services in between. So keep an eye on your gas gauge and an eye on the miles to the next town. And if it's night, be aware that sometimes the gas station in town is not a 24-hour service. Montana has very few rest stops along highways, too. That's why this book contains numerous site listings for city parks convenient to main roadways.

## Montana Roads

When planning a trip, check out the road designations on the highway map. The legend will tell you whether the road you plan to take is a highway, an improved gravel road, or an unsurfaced route. Montana interstates are well-maintained, four-lane highways where you can travel at a good speed. Montana highways are another topic. I often joke when I've been to another state and come back to Montana, that I know why I live here when I get on these two-lane roads that Montanans call highways. These roads are peaceful and uncrowded, and I appreciate that. But, they are often slow. While most of these are good roads, many of them wind through mountainous areas. On some of these, passing is difficult and can be dangerous. You may find yourself traveling at 50 miles per hour for long distances on Montana highways, especially during the high tourist season. Also, since the Montana summer season is short, road construction will sometimes tie up a portion of a highway for a significant part of the tourist season, causing travel delays.

If the road you plan to take is shown on the highway map as improved or unsurfaced road, you may be looking at anything from a good, solid, dirt- or gravel-surfaced road to a pot-holed, slow-going back road. While these routes are inevitably scenic, plan on the possibility of a slow drive. But beware of taking these roads in wet weather, as rain may make the surface literally impassable, and getting stuck in the backcountry of Montana is no joke! Roads in springtime often deteriorate severely with the heaving of the ground. During "spring break-up," as it's called, these potholes and dips are generally marked, but the marking systems vary from a noticeable, diamond-shaped warning sign, to a red ribbon tied on a stick, to nothing at all. Keep your eyes open! If you have a vehicle low to the ground, be extra careful on these roads. Though I only lost one muffler while exploring Montana for this book, there were a number of times I backed out of bad roads.

# Montana Road Signs

Look for large, brown, wooden signs around the state. They provide geographical and historical information and are interesting reading, plus a good reason to stop and get out of the car for a minute. There are pullouts located by the signs.

When traveling the state you will also see white crosses dotting the roadways. These are memorials to people who have died in traffic accidents at these sites. Many are maintained with flowers by family members.

One final road warning deals with the temptation to take alternate back roads along your trip. My experience with these has been that there are usually several intersecting roads not shown on the map and road signs are rare on these routes. I got lost about 50 percent of the time on these back roads due to lack of signage. If you decide to take one, be sure to ask locally for directions and road condition information.

# SAFETY

No trip is fun if someone gets hurt or sick. Take a moment and read the following warnings about potentially dangerous situations you may encounter in Montana.

## Bears

Although they generally fear and avoid humans, both black and grizzly bears can be dangerous. While black bears tend to be in low-elevation forest areas and grizzlies in higher alpine lands, the ranges do mix. Hikers and campers should be aware that you may find either kind of bear in either kind of area. Along the Rocky Mountain Front, grizzly bears can be found in their traditional prairie habitat, too. In the spring, bears move to low-elevation areas to find food; they go to higher areas during summer. Bears are active mostly in early morning or late evening, and these are the hours you are more likely to see them. If you are fortunate enough to spot a bear, you need to realize that you could be in a potentially dangerous situation. Most bears will not attack humans without a reason, however. Food, cubs, and surprise are the primary reasons hikers get into trouble with bears.

Like all wild creatures, bears spend much of their time looking for food. When they smell some luscious food scent, they may decide they want a share. Odorous foods such as meats and fish are particularly appealing, but bears have a very good sense of smell and will be attracted to all kinds of human foods. Normally a bear's diet is about 80 to 90 percent roots, berries, and other plant food, but bears that have come to know what human food is about and become enamored of it can be troublesome. If you are camping, it is essential you leave your food in your car at night and at other times when you aren't preparing meals. Make sure your tent is upwind of where you are cooking so your tent doesn't smell like food.

When backpacking, store food in plastic bags so smells won't rub off onto clothing. When you are camped overnight in the backcountry, put the food in a bag, tie a rope to it, toss the rope over a high tree branch, and haul the food well above reach of bears (15 feet or more is advisable). While this might seem silly, it is also good protection against the numerous small critters that can decimate your food supply.

When handling food, make sure you wash up afterwards and don't get food smells on your clothing, tent, or any items that you plan to have in your tent. Also, avoid strong-smelling perfumes, deodorants, soaps, or lotions. Bears will be drawn to these smells as well.

Sometimes bears that are surprised by hikers along trails will become defensive and dangerous. In some cases, people may have unwittingly stumbled in between a mother and her cub. The best defense against surprising a bear is offense—make plenty of noise on the trail so the bear can hear you coming. Some people wear bells, whistle, or talk loudly as they hike. It's best, too, not to hike alone in bear country.

Most often a bear will move off the trail if it hears you coming, and you won't even see it. If a bear does stay on the trail, talk to it calmly and softly, back away slowly, and keep walking, but don't turn your back on the bear. Find a way to assume a non-threatening posture by turning sideways or bending at the knees to look smaller. Whatever you do, don't run, as this generally gets them running after you. In fact, if the bear charges you, it is better to stand your ground because bears are known to sometimes make a "mock charge" and if you stand your ground they may stop or run past you. For the worst-case scenario, if the bear doesn't stop, roll up in a ball, protecting your stomach and other vital organs. Clasp your hands over the back of your neck and don't make any noise; just play dead. You won't be very interesting in this position and the bear will generally leave you alone. Stay in this position until you are sure the bear is gone.

# Mountain Lions

Mountain lions, or cougars, as they are sometimes called, can be found in most regions of Montana, except for open prairie lands. Though there have been few problems with lions, encounters have been increasing throughout the country. Nationally, there have been only 50 recorded mountain lion attacks on humans during the last 100 years, but the majority of these have occurred in the last 20 years. Unfortunately, nine out of ten victims have been children. Of the 50 attacks, 10 resulted in fatalities.

Though seeing one of these magnificent animals is very rare, it is possible. Lions are generally more active in the morning and evening, but have been seen at all times of day. Most confrontations have involved human food, pet food, or even pets themselves. Dogs don't seem to be much of a deterrent to mountain lions and may even be responsible for bringing them into contact with humans.

Since mountain lions tend to be unpredictable, there is no one right way to handle an encounter. However, there seem to be some behavior patterns that help, and some that don't. Never turn your back, try to hide, or lay down. Don't run. Move slowly and try to back away from the lion. Never approach a lion and be especially careful not to put one in a position where it feels trapped. Speaking to a lion in a calm, confident voice seems to help. If you have small children with you, pick them up off the ground. Older children should stand close to you. First and foremost is to stay standing, face the lion, and fight back with whatever is handy. If the animal behaves aggressively, defend yourself with rocks, sticks, fishing poles, or hands. Speak loudly and firmly if lions are aggressive, as you must somehow convince the animal that you are not prey and could be a danger to them.

# Rattlesnakes

Most rattlesnakes are found in eastern Montana, south of the Missouri River. They frequent rocky hillsides, bluffs, and rock outcrops but can also be found on the open prairie and in hay fields. You'll recognize the tan-colored rattlesnake by the conspicuous rattle on the tail and the squarish, black-bordered, dark brown blotches along its back. A rattlesnake is generally only dangerous when disturbed and will most often (but not always) warn that you are bothering it by shaking the rattles at the end of its tail. Walking away from the snake will usually end the confrontation.

Be on the lookout for snakes in rocky areas, thickets along roadways, and in prairie dog towns. They often come out in early morning and evening time. When hiking in snake country, watch where you put your hands and feet. Long pants and tall boots are good protection against bites if you are in a high-risk area. Carry a walking stick and use it to check grassy areas ahead of you if you are concerned about being in snake territory.

While a rattlesnake bite isn't always fatal, it is painful and can cause serious illness. It's a good idea to carry a snakebite kit and know how to use it. If someone is bitten, keep the victim down and quiet, apply ice if you have it, use your snakebite kit, and get immediate medical attention.

# Other Wildlife Warnings

Nearly any wild animal will defend itself if it feels threatened. Bison and moose are among the Montana animals large enough to cause serious damage to a human. Avoid provoking these animals; it is best to appreciate them from a distance if you see them. Most other mammals are fairly secretive and it would be unusual to see them. We once came across a badger atop a ridge. We just stared at it and it watched us. Since they can be vicious fighters, we gave it plenty of distance and so, by the way, did our dog, who seemed to have a lot of respect for it. Porcupines are another animal to stay away from.

Though you can hardly see a tick, these tiny insects can carry serious diseases such as Rocky Mountain spotted fever and Lyme's disease. Ticks are common in wooded areas in spring and early summer. If you are in a high-tick area, wear clothes that fit tightly around the waist, wrists, and ankles. Check your family for ticks in the scalp and along folds in the skin. If you find any, completely remove the entire tick and disinfect the area. If rashes form around the bite, or flu-like symptoms develop, consult a physician.

# Not-So-Wild Animals

While Montana is home to lots of wild creatures, keep in mind that it is also cattle country. There is still some open range in Montana and sometimes government land is leased to ranchers, so you will find cattle wandering the roads in unexpected places. Be cautious when you see cattle along the roadway, as they may walk out into the road. While they don't harm people, you wouldn't want to hit one.

You may also cross cattle guards on some of the back roads in Montana. These wide metal grates keep cattle from crossing property lines, since they cannot walk over them. Driving over these grates is not dangerous but it will rattle your teeth somewhat as you cross them. Sometimes they are located by highway entrance and exit ramps.

# About Pets

It's great fun to see the family dog enjoying an outing and it can make your time more fun too. However, be aware that dogs might come into contact with bears or other wild animals and end up bringing them back to you! Fido can also get a little carried away chasing wildlife, which is usually against the rules and not a very good idea anyway. Finally, in some places your animal must be leashed or is just not allowed in at all. Your dog may end up waiting in a hot car, a scenario that can actually be fatal if it gets too hot! If you do bring the family dog on your outing, bring a leash, food, and lots of water, too.

# Water Warnings

Despite the crystal clear, tempting appearance of Montana's pristine mountain waters, a naturally occurring parasite, *Giardia lamblia*, is found in many mountain lakes and streams. The single-celled parasite cannot be seen with the human eye, but causes persistent, severe diarrhea, abdominal cramps, and nausea. So before you drink from any of Montana's free-flowing waters, think twice. It is best to bring your own water from a safe source, though you can boil mountain water (rapid boiling for five minutes), or use a filtering device designed to filter out parasites and bacteria. These are available in sporting goods stores.

Besides being wary of drinking Montana's surface water, be aware that, if you choose to get into the waters of Montana, much of this water is only a short distance from snow or ice and is extremely cold. While wading in an alpine lake or creek may not be dangerous, jumping or falling in could be, as the shock of the cold water can be extreme. Watch for slippery rocks, especially around waterfalls. Also be careful if fording a stream as the waters may be swifter than they appear. This could be especially dangerous for children.

# Weather

The landscape is not the only dynamic feature of the northern Rocky Mountains. Weather in Montana is likely to be just as dynamic. Expect warm to hot summer daytime temperatures and cool nights. Temperatures drop significantly in the mountains when the sun goes down, and you can expect to need warm evening clothing. It's also been known to snow during Montana summers, and cold, wet days can be expected too. What may start out as a clear, warm day can turn to a cold one with rain or snow showers within a short period of time. Afternoon summer thunderstorms are quite common and usually dissipate, but not always. Watch the weather patterns and be aware of rain or snow clouds that are quickly moving in.

# Hypothermia

Hypothermia is a significant danger in extreme mountain weather. When the human body loses heat faster than it can produce it, core body temperatures drop, causing hypothermia, which can result in death. Children and elderly people are more susceptible to hypothermia because of body size and physical condition. Lack of water or food can increase the danger of hypothermia, as can wet clothing.

Your best defense against hypothermia is to keep warm, water-repellent clothing with you when camping or hiking. It's wise to dress in layers of clothing that can be removed or added depending on the weather. Hats are a good way to protect yourself from the hot sun and keep body heat in when it's cold. Dry clothes are an important element for hypothermia prevention. Keep a blanket in the car at all times, and use it if necessary. A first-aid kit with waterproof matches is another good idea in case you are unable to get back to the trailhead but can start a warming fire. Even after 20 years of living in the mountains, we were caught recently by a sudden snowstorm in

July in the Jewel Basin. Because of the weather we were just barely able to make a fire and would have been in serious trouble if we hadn't. We also make a point of carrying lightweight snacks such as raisin-nut mixes, candy bars or sucking candy, beef jerky, and apples with us whenever we go hiking.

If you think your kids or other fellow travelers are becoming hypothermic, get them into shelter and put dry clothes on them or wrap them in blankets. Build a fire, give them wrapped, heated rocks to warm their bodies, or use the warmth of your body to help raise their body temperature. Feeding warm liquids is advised but avoid giving victims alcohol, cigarettes, or medications. Seek medical help as soon as possible.

## Sunstroke or Heat Exhaustion

Too much sun can be a problem in any part of Montana. Kids are particularly susceptible. Sunstroke is the result of elevated body temperature, and heat exhaustion is caused from physical exertion in the heat. Symptoms are flushed face, headache, dizziness, weakness, and profusion of sweating (heat exhaustion), or no perspiration (sunstroke). You will need to immediately lower the body temperature by getting the individual into shade and applying cool water to his or her body. Give the person plenty of liquids and keep the victim out of the sun. Prevention includes wearing hats, finding shade, and drinking plenty of liquids.

## Altitude

If you aren't from a high-elevation location, you may find the thin Montana mountain air decreases your energy level, or may even make you feel sick for a bit. Certainly, higher altitudes increase the amount of ultraviolet light you get. Be sure to bring hats and sunscreen when you come to Montana, no matter where you are from, and don't expect to be able to exert yourself as much as normal until you get used to the elevation.

# PUBLIC-USE LANDS AND REGULATIONS

Much of Montana is public land, and the majority of the outdoor sites listed in this book are on public property. Here are some of the regulations for public lands as well as information about resource management.

# Fishing

Montana fishing regulations require that all anglers purchase a $4 conservation license. Nonresidents also need a fishing license, unless they are under age 15 and in the company of an adult with a valid Montana license. In this case, the catch limit for the two anglers combined cannot exceed the limit for one. Nonresidents may purchase an annual fishing license ($45 in 1998) or a two-day license ($10). Resident licenses are $13, although residents between 12 and 14 years of age, or age 62 or older, need only a conservation license. Children under age 12 do not need a license. Residents with disabilities who have been certified by Montana Fish, Wildlife & Parks need only a conservation license.

A fishing license allows the purchaser to fish under the state's fishing regulations. This license is issued for March 1 through February 28 of the following year and is not transferable or refundable. Special permits are required for paddlefish. For rules and regulations on fishing, contact any of the state offices of the Montana Department of Fish, Wildlife & Parks (see page 345).

Special fishing rules apply on Indian reservations, and tribal headquarters (see page 348) should be contacted before fishing on tribal lands. Yellowstone National Park requires anglers to obtain a $5 license. There is no additional license for Glacier National Park, but special regulations must be followed while fishing on park land. Be sure to get these regulations from a visitor center or ranger station.

# Entrance Fees

Entrance fees are assessed for the use of some of Montana's public lands. Fees are required in any Montana state park. Currently, there is usually a daily fee of $4 per vehicle or $1 per person, though fees can vary from park to park. A seasonal passport vehicle sticker, which allows entry into any state park during the year, is available for $20 for residents and $24 for non-residents (1998 rates). Reduced rates are given for purchase between December 1 and February 14. The passport does not cover camping fees.

Entrance fees are also charged at national parks and monuments. Fees vary at each park and it is best to contact the specific park service headquarters for more information (see page 347). An annual pass for Glacier National Park is $20 and an annual entry pass for all national parks in the United States is currently $50.

Fees for other public lands are generally marked at the site.

# Watchable Wildlife Program

The Montana Department of Fish, Wildlife & Parks manages some state public lands, including state parks, with particular emphasis on fishing, hunting, and other outdoor recreational activities. Around the state you will see brown and white signs along the roadway showing a pair of binoculars. These identify a particularly good wildlife viewing area, part of the state Fish, Wildlife & Parks Watchable Wildlife Program. Follow the signs and then take a moment to stop and see what might be there; you will no doubt be rewarded, at least some of the time, with seeing birds and animals in the wild.

# State Wildlife Management Areas

The Montana Department of Fish, Wildlife & Parks manages state wildlife management areas (WMA). These lands differ from state parks in that the primary management goal is protection and development of important wildlife habitat. Waterfowl, upland game, deer, and elk are the primary wildlife served by these areas, though a multitude of small mammals and songbirds take advantage of the prime habitat too.

In most cases, wildlife management areas are available for outdoor recreational activities such as fishing, outdoor photography, hunting, hiking, bird watching, canoeing, and mountain biking. Visitors to these areas should know that they are not developed sites. Don't expect much more than a vault toilet, if that. Some have picnic tables and self-guided auto tours on dirt roads. These roads may be impassable in wet weather. Some management areas have marked trails, but on most you are on your own to explore. An expedition to a wildlife management area will provide good wildlife viewing but families must be prepared to take care of their own needs. Also note that some of these areas have seasonal use restrictions to protect wildlife during critical periods. Check with the individual area headquarters to determine specific closure schedules (see specific WMA site listings for phone numbers).

# U.S. Fish and Wildlife Service Refuges

The U.S. Fish and Wildlife Service provides management of federal lands for protection and development of wildlife habitat. The service operates several wildlife refuges and fish hatcheries. Visitor facilities vary from site to site. Some have picnic areas, auto tour routes, toilets, and even visitor centers. Others have no visitor facilities at all but are still available for public use. Site listings in the book describe what is available at the various locations. Call specific sites for more information.

# Good Neighbor Policy

To keep Montana lands pristine and enjoyable, here are some general rules to follow:

- Pack your garbage out when you are in public places. NEVER leave garbage in anything but a garbage receptacle, both for the sake of safety and for keeping natural sites clean.
- Leave natural features and artifacts as you found them for everyone to enjoy.
- Be careful with fires or matches. Most state forests have signs showing current fire dangers. However, fire always poses a threat. Extinguish all fires completely before leaving the area. Dispose of matches or cigarettes in a fire-safe manner. Report all uncontrolled fires immediately to a local management agency.
- Keep quiet hours in mind at campgrounds.
- Check to see whether dogs are allowed before you bring your pet.
- Be conscious of other people; share public areas. Be courteous on trails and when camping. Be considerate of others' needs.

# Glacier Country

Glacier Country is a place where seasons are dramatic, wildlife is plentiful, and nature is a constant companion. Here, rugged peaks stand majestically above scenic mountain valleys and foothills and pristine lakes; crystal clear rivers flow freely toward the ocean from these high lands. In Glacier National Park, the forces of nature are dynamically apparent as active glaciers continue to scour the landscape.

Within the valleys nestled among the mountains live people dedicated to this vibrant land. These hardy folks withstand the winter hardships for the opportunity to live amid its beauty. For some, the wealth of winter recreational activities is the draw to the area. Whatever the season, outdoor recreation is a highlight for locals and visitors.

Glacier Country residents also occupy themselves with music, art, culture, and festivals. Artists have been lured to the area for its striking beauty, and communities such as Missoula and Kalispell are centers for regional culture. The smaller towns in the area create their own interesting diversions, as well.

Come to Glacier Country to explore the wildness of the mountains and drink in nature's grandeur. You will find yourself among others willing to share in your joy and admiration.

## THE BITTERROOT VALLEY

The Bitterroot Valley, which Lewis and Clark called "Traveler's Rest," is cradled between two scenic mountain ranges, the steep Bitterroot Mountains rising majestically in the west and the rolling Sapphire Mountains in the east. U.S. Highway 93 runs the length of the valley, and provides frequent access to the delightful Bitterroot River along the way. The river flows mostly on the east side of the highway; its river access sites offer travelers fun stop-and-stretch breaks. There are also a wide variety of recreational opportunities along this 80-mile length of highway between the Idaho border and Lolo.

The Bitterroot Valley is a delightful place to fish, boat, ski, raft, swim, bike, hike, and watch wildlife. The Bitterroot National Forest maintains 1,600 miles of trails for hiking and horseback riding and 18 developed campgrounds in this region. The Selway-Bitterroot Wilderness and the Anaconda-Pintler Wilderness add another dimension to the recreational opportunities here.

# GLACIER COUNTRY

· · · · · · · · · · · · · · · · · · · · · · · · · ·

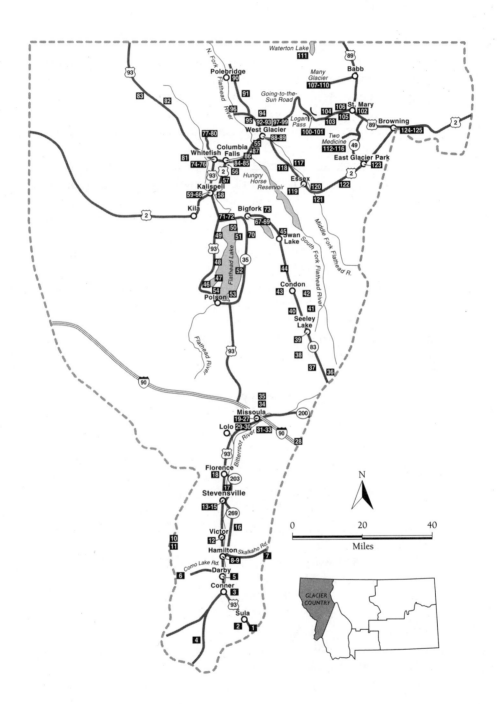

93

Waterton Lake
111

89 Babb

Polebridge
90

91

Going-to-the-
Sun Road

Many
Glacier
107-110

83    82

N. Fork Flathead River

96

94

104 106 St. Mary
102

Logan
Pass

103

105

89 Browning

2

77-80

95  92-93 97-99

West Glacier

100-101

Two
Medicine
112-116

124-125

49

88-89

55

Columbia
Falls       87

86

118    117

East Glacier Park

81

Whitefish Falls

123

74-76

84-85

2

2

93

56

57

Hungry
Horse
Reservoir

Essex

120

122

Kalispell

59-66

58

119

121

2        Kila

Bigfork 73

71-72

67-69

50

45 Swan
Lake

Middle Fork Flathead R.

49

51    70

93

48

35

44

47

52

Condon

Flathead Lake

South Fork Flathead River

46    54

43    42

Polson    53

40    41

Seeley
Lake

Flathead River

39    83

93

38

37    36

90

35

34

Missoula

200

19-27

Lolo    29-30  31-33  90

28

93

Bitterroot River

Florence

18

203

17

Stevensville

13-15    269

Victor    16

10

12

11

Hamilton Skalkaho Rd.

8-9    7

Corno Lake Rd.

6    Darby

5

Conner

3

93

Sula

2    1

4

N

0        20        40

Miles

GLACIER
COUNTRY

There are four USDA Forest Service ranger stations in the valley, and the Supervisor's Office can be found at 1801 North 1st Street in Hamilton, 406-363-7161.

This is an area steeped in Montana's settlement history, and the small valley communities have preserved this history in museums and at historic sites. As you travel the highway, you should also look for roadside chainsaw artists who create wooden sculptures from logs. You'll also see log homes in the making. Those involved in these endeavors often allow visitors to stop and observe construction practices.

The old Eastside Highway (Montana 269) is an interesting alternate travel route between Hamilton and Florence. Although this 32-mile byway is narrow in places, it provides access to the Bitterroot River, views of Blodgett Canyon and the Bitterroot Mountains, and entrance to many of the sites listed below, including the Lee Metcalf Wildlife Refuge, the Marcus Daly Mansion, St. Mary's Mission, and Fort Owen.

For more information about the area, contact the Missoula Convention and Visitors Bureau, 825 East Front Street, Missoula, MT 59807, 800-526-3465, or contact the Hamilton Chamber of Commerce at 406-363-2400.

# The Bitterroot Plant,
## *Lewisia rediviva*

The Bitterroot Valley and river are named after Montana's state flower, a pink-blossomed member of the portulaca family. The plant was an important food source for Montana Indians, who taught explorers Lewis and Clark how to eat the nutritious root. Flathead Indians explain the name in the legend of an old woman crying bitter tears for her starving family. The Creator took pity on her and sent a spirit bird to tell her that a nourishing root would grow where each of her tears fell. So long as her people continued to respect and honor all of creation, the root would come back each spring.

Look for the bitterroot close to the ground in dry, gravelly areas. Just about the same time the delicate pink flower opens, usually in May, the bitterroot's leaves shrivel up and vanish, an unusual feature in the plant world.

# The Southern Bitterroot Valley

From Lost Trail Hot Springs to the Skalkaho Wildlife Preserve, the southern half of the Bitterroot Valley is a recreationist's wonderland. History buffs will also find many stops of interest in the locality, including the Medicine Tree and the Pioneer Museum at Darby. All extremely kid-friendly, the following are recommended stops for families between the Idaho border and Hamilton on U.S. Highway 93.

## 1. Lost Trail Hot Springs

· · · · · · · · · · · · · · · · · · · · · · · · · · · · · · · · · · · · ·

These natural mineral springs have been commercially developed but retain a quiet, rustic feel. The resort provides accommodations in cabins, motel rooms, and camping and RV spaces. A store, restaurant, and casino are also on the grounds. The springs include a large medium-hot pool, a small hot pool, and a sauna, though the facilities are rustic. Indian Trees Campground, a USDA Forest Service facility, is right next door, too.

While in the area you may want to go to the ski area at Lost Trail Pass or to the Big Hole Battlefield National Monument. Lost Trail Pass is 6 miles from the hot springs on U.S. Highway 93. Fourteen miles east of Lost Trail Pass on Montana Highway 43 is the Big Hole Battlefield National Monument, the preserved site of a major conflict between the U.S. infantry and the Nez Perce Indians that took place in 1877.

**Directions:** Turn right (west) off US 93 as you travel south of Sula, just before mile marker 6. A sign for the hot springs will be on the right side of the road.

**Important Information:** Contact Lost Trail Hot Springs Resort at 406-821-3574 for rate information.

## 2. Medicine Tree

· · · · · · · · · · · · · · · · · · · · · · · · · · · · · · · · · · · · ·

Settlers in the 1800s wrote about this Ponderosa pine tree with large ram's horns embedded in the trunk. It has long been sacred to the Indians who even today hang gifts and ribbons on the tree as "good medicine" offerings. Though the ram's horns can no longer be seen, an interpretive sign explains the significance and history of the tree. Look up to see the good medicine tokens hanging from it. My kids enjoyed hearing the Salish Indian legend of the tree and we, too, left gifts to honor it.

**Directions:** The tree is 10 miles south of Darby, just beyond the town of Conner, on the left (east) side of U.S. Highway 93 as you travel south. It stands just a foot or two off the highway next to a rocky embankment.

**Important Information:** It is "bad medicine" to disturb the tree or offerings left there, although you may add your gift to the tree for good medicine.

# The Salish Legend of the Medicine Tree

Old Man Coyote was directed by the Manitou, or Great Spirit of the West, to venture out and destroy all the evils, which prey on human beings. As Old Man Coyote was traveling one day, he accidentally stepped on something that cried out in pain. There at his feet, Coyote saw a small Lark with a broken leg. Using his great powers, he healed the Lark's leg, and in return the Lark warned him of a great but wicked Mountain Sheep that killed everyone who passed by his territory.

Coyote traveled on, and, sure enough, he met the Ram, who asked him: "What right have you to travel on my land? You must know that it will cost you your life."

"Have you already killed many?" asked Old Man Coyote.

"Yes," replied the Ram, "Very many."

At this boasting, Old Man Coyote challenged Ram to demonstrate his strength by charging a large tree. The proud Ram charged the tree so hard that he buried one horn deep in its side. Though he tried to break free, Ram could not, and there the great animal died.

Then Old Man Coyote stood by the tree and proclaimed, "In the future, this tree shall be a medicine tree to all the tribes."

A passing Salish war party chased Coyote away, and on the ram's horns they hung bits of wampum and colorful beads, good medicine tokens to free the scene of evil spirits. Countless successive Indian tribes followed the same practice until about 150 years ago when the tree engulfed the horns. Indians today continue to place offerings on the Medicine Tree's branches, and white people also honor this sacred legend.

## 3. East Fork Bighorn Sheep Herd Viewing Area

The hills and slopes above the East Fork of the Bitterroot River are a favorite hangout for bighorn sheep. Though viewing is best in the winter, you can usually see sheep there year-round.

Across from a prime viewing site is the Broad Axe Lodge and Restaurant where you can enjoy the wildlife watching from the parking lot and from within the dining area. The restaurant employees will even provide binoculars and show you where to look. Other wildlife to look for are golden eagles, elk, and white-tailed deer in the winter, and nighthawks in the summer. Feeders surrounding the restaurant bring hummingbirds into close viewing proximity too.

**Directions:** From U.S. Highway 93 traveling south of Sula, turn east (left) onto the East Fork Road. You will see the lodge and restaurant on the right-hand side of the road 5.5 miles from US 93.

**Important Information:** The restaurant is open year-round for dinner, but only on weekends in the winter. Dinner menu items are priced between $10 and $17. The lodge also has reasonably priced cabins for rent year-round. Call ahead for hours, 406-821-3878.

## 4. Painted Rocks Reservoir

The beautiful coloration of the rocks jutting above the West Fork Road comes from minerals and lichen. The reservoir—a flooded, narrow canyon—provides boating, skiing, swimming, and fishing activities. You will also find the Alta Ranger Station here. The Alta Pine, believed to be the oldest pine in the Bitterroot Valley, is on a short, wheelchair-accessible trail, which starts at the ranger station. This tree was mature when Christopher Columbus landed in the West Indies. The reservoir campground provides tables, fire rings, toilets, trailer space, and potable water.

**Directions:** Three miles south of Darby, take the marked turnoff west at the West Fork Road and continue south about 20 miles. The road to the reservoir is mostly paved, though the road around the reservoir is not.

**Important Information:** For more information, contact the West Fork Ranger District, 406-821-3269.

## 5. Pioneer Museum in Darby

This is the place to enjoy exhibits and memorabilia from bygone eras, including Darby's original telephone switchboard. The old photo albums and stereoscope are kids' favorites.

**Directions:** The museum is on Main Street (U.S. Highway 93), behind the library.

**Important Information:** From Memorial Day to Labor Day, it is open Wednesday through Saturday from 1 to 5 P.M. Contact the museum at 406-821-4503 for winter hours. This is an area resident's phone, as there is no phone in the museum.

# 6. Lake Como Recreation Area

Local Indians called this lake the Lake of the White Moose because of an albino moose that frequented its shores. A white settler named it Lake Como after the Italian lake he thought it resembled.

This 906-acre scenic lake is a popular local recreation site for water skiing, boating, picnicking, swimming, fishing, and hiking. The USDA Forest Service campground has nine units and an equestrian campground with a livestock ramp. Facilities include picnic tables and toilets.

Trail 502, the Lake Como National Recreation Trail, is a 7-mile foot-traffic-only trail that loops around the lake. The trailhead is just below the campground.

**Directions:** The Lake Como Recreation Area turnoff goes west (left) off of U.S. Highway 93, 4 miles north of the town of Darby. The turn is right by the Bitterroot River Bridge. Turn at the Lake Como sign and follow the road for about 4 miles to the recreation area.

**Important Information:** Just before the turnoff to the recreation area, US 93 becomes narrow and winding as it follows the Bitterroot River.

There is a day-use fee and a campground fee. The campground is wheelchair accessible. This is a high-use area. Contact the Darby Ranger District, 406-821-3913, for more information.

# 7. Skalkaho Wildlife Area

*Skalkaho* is the Flathead Indian word meaning "place of the beaver." It is worth the drive on Skalkaho Highway just for the astounding scenery, even if you don't see beaver. Originally a wildlife preserve, the area no longer has this designation, but still offers an opportunity to see wildlife and explore the forest lands.

The 23,000-acre wildlife preserve is a heavily forested mountain area with entrancing meadows. In the fall, large elk herds form and can be heard bugling, especially east of Fool Hen and Kneaves lakes. Dome Shaped Mountain provides habitat for mountain goats. Other animals you might see are moose, mule deer, badgers, wolverines, coyotes, and black bear. You can use mountain bikes in the area, an especially nice way to travel when the roads are closed to motorized vehicles in the fall.

**Directions:** Three miles south of Hamilton, take Montana Highway 38 (Skalkaho Highway) from the junction on U.S. Highway 93. Follow MT 38 to Skalkaho Pass, 27 miles east. Turn north on Forest Road 1352 and within 5 miles you will be in the Skalkaho Basin.

**Important Information:** There are no developed facilities at this site. Forest Road 1352 is closed to all motorized vehicles from mid-October to December 1. For more information, contact the Bitterroot National Forest, 406-363-3131.

# Hamilton

The largest Bitterroot Valley town, Hamilton, was planned and built by Marcus Daly, one of Montana's "Copper Kings." Seeing potential to acquire much-needed timber for his mines and smelters, Daly bought the existing sawmill there and had the town built to support his new timber industry. Daly also loved the climate of the Bitterroot and thought it a good place to raise his thoroughbred horses. Today, Hamilton is the Ravalli County seat and attracts many retirees. The Hamilton Chamber of Commerce is located at 105 East Main, 406-363-2400.

## 8. Ravalli County Museum

The Ravalli County Museum in Hamilton was originally built in 1900 as the Ravalli County Courthouse. The displays in this 14-room museum include extensive Flathead Indian artifacts, a veterans' exhibit, "Apple Boom Days" relics, period rooms, and items from the Rocky Mountain Lab Tick Museum. The Rocky Mountain Lab has been conducting extensive research on spotted fever and the wood ticks responsible for the disease since World War I. Every Sunday at 2 P.M. is a program featuring such things as history, cowboy poetry, or folk music.

**Directions:** The museum is located at the corner of South 3rd Street and Bedford. From U.S. Highway 93, turn west onto Bedford and look for the museum on the left side of the second block.

**Important Information:** The museum is open 1 to 4 P.M. in the winter, 10 A.M. to 4 P.M. in the summer, and is closed every Tuesday and Wednesday. Wheelchair accessible. For more information call 406-363-3338.

## 9. Daly Mansion

This National Historic Site is owned by the state of Montana and operated by the nonprofit Daly Mansion Preservation Trust. The Georgian Revival-style mansion was built in 1890 for Marcus Daly, an Irish immigrant who made his fortune in the Butte mines and founded the Anaconda Mining Company, as well as the towns of Anaconda and Hamilton.

The "Riverside" Mansion, a three-story, 24,000-square-foot estate, was Daly's summer residence. The 42 rooms include 24 bedrooms and 15 baths. There are five Italian marble fireplaces. The mansion has many of the original furnishings and 50 acres of the original 22,000-acre grounds are still beautifully maintained. Once a stock farm, the grounds today still feature gardens of flowers and trees from around the world. This is the site of many valley events, such as an annual doll show, the Bitterroot Valley Good Nations PowWow, and a fall festival.

**Directions:** The mansion is 2 miles north of Hamilton at 251 Eastside Highway. From U.S. Highway 93, turn east at the Main Street intersection. East Main becomes Marcus Street and the Eastside Highway. Just past Fairgrounds Road is a sign marking the left-hand turn into the mansion entrance.

**Important Information:** Only the first floor is wheelchair accessible. There are portable toilets on the grounds. Open April 15 to October 15 daily, from 11 A.M. to 5 P.M. Tours are given each hour. Call 406-363-6004 for current fees and hours.

## 10. Blodgett Canyon Trail

This steep-cliffed canyon is a scenic gem and provides families an easy outdoor experience along a forested trail. An entrance to the Selway-Bitterroot Wilderness, the trail is 20 miles long; the last 9 miles are in Idaho. Families can go in as far as they like on the gently rolling trail, which is rarely steep for any significant amount of time. About an hour in is the first of many nice spots by Blodgett Creek, which is never too far from the trail at any point. By the way, the water does look refreshing but may have the *Giardia lamblia* amoebae, and should not be consumed without special filtering.

When you get far enough in to see the spectacular canyon walls rising nearly 4,000 feet from the valley floor, look for mountain goats on the cliffs. You may also see some "human goats," as climbers frequent the area, scaling the 500- to 600-foot cliff faces that are common in the canyon. There are several waterfalls between 3 and 6 miles up the trail. You can fish in Blodgett Creek with a good chance of being rewarded with small rainbow trout. As you go further up the canyon, your chances of seeing moose, elk, and deer increase.

If you decide on a short hike in, you can fill part of your visit exploring the campground, or a few minutes enjoying Blodgett Creek near the picnic area. In December of a low-snow year we did just that, hiking only the first mile or two before coming back to explore the campground. The trail is passable early in the spring, and the kid consensus was that it was a great place!

**Directions:** Two miles north of Hamilton, by the bridge crossing the Bitterroot River, go left (west) on Bowman Road. Follow this road for approximately

0.5 mile, then go left (south) on Ricketts Road. In 1.7 miles the road bends sharply right (west), and in another 0.2 mile comes to a four-way intersection. Go straight at this intersection, traveling west on Blodgett Camp Road (Forest Road 736), and continue west for another 2 miles to the trailhead. **Important Information:** Camping is permitted anywhere along the trail, with no-trace fire policies. Contact the Darby Ranger District, 406-321-3913, for more information. The campground and picnic area are wheelchair accessible.

## 11. Canyon Falls

Though we did not have a chance to visit Canyon Falls, we have read that it is one of the more accessible waterfalls in the Bitterroot Range. The trail to the falls is about 3 miles long and avoids stream crossings. The total falls elevation drop is nearly 200 feet, in a series of cataracts along the stream. The falls are especially nice during spring runoff in May or June. Watch for slippery rocks.

**Directions:** Two miles north of Hamilton, turn left (west) onto a county road from U.S. Highway 93, just before it crosses the Bitterroot River. Follow this road west for 0.5 mile, south for 1.75 miles, and then west until it intersects Forest Road 735. Go straight at this intersection, traveling west on Blodgett Camp Road (Forest Road 736), and continue west until you see a left turn onto FR 735. This will take you to the trailhead on Canyon Creek.

# Victor and Stevensville

The town of Victor has only a few buildings on the highway frontage, but there is a museum and a nice town park one block west of U.S. Highway 93 behind the gas stations. Originally Montana's state capital, Stevensville also has the distinction of being the oldest town in the state. History abounds in this little burg, named after the 1850s governor of Washington Territory, Isaac Stevens. Stevensville is 1.5 miles east of US 93 on the Eastside Highway (Montana Highway 269).

## 12. Victor Heritage Museum

The Victor museum is housed in an old railroad depot and has many railroad exhibits. The kids will enjoy the hands-on wildlife book there.
**Directions:** Located at the corner of Main and Blake in Victor.

**Important Information:** The museum is open daily, 1 to 4 P.M. from Memorial Day through Labor Day. Wheelchair accessible, no bathroom. For more information call 406-642-3416.

## 13. Stevensville Historical Museum

Photo displays, Indian artifacts, and clothing exhibits from Stevensville, Montana's oldest town, can be viewed at this museum.

**Directions:** From U.S. Highway 93, turn east onto Bell Crossing. Take this to the Eastside Highway (Montana Highway 269). Turn left onto MT 269 and go into Stevensville. The museum is on the left in a large two-story white house. There are signs to point the way.

**Important Information:** Wheelchair accessible. Open 11 A.M. to 5 P.M. Tuesday through Saturday from Memorial Day to Labor Day. For more information call 406-777-3201 or 406-777-5126. (These are home phone numbers of local residents; leave a message if no one answers.)

## 14. St. Mary's Mission

The well-preserved buildings here are from the first permanent white settlement in Montana. Father Pierre DeSmet established St. Mary's Mission in 1841, only 35 years after Lewis and Clark passed through the valley. Even before this expedition, Shining Shirt, a native prophet and medicine man, had predicted to his people that men with long black robes would give the Indians a new strength. Father DeSmet was approached by various tribes to bring his Jesuit priests, the "Black Robes," to Montana. The missionaries created a long list of Montana "firsts" including the first cultivated gardens, the first harvested wheat and oats, the first breeding of cattle, swine, and poultry, the first classes taught, the first church, even the first musical band to play German and Italian music.

The site today has the restored log chapel and priests' quarters, the pharmacy, and a cemetery. The house belonging to Salish Chief Victor, namesake for the town of Victor, is now an Indian museum. We found the cemetery, with headstones for both Indians and settlers, particularly intriguing. Many historically significant people are buried here and you may recognize names on headstones that are also found as place names on local maps. There are picnic tables, bathrooms, and a gift shop.

**Directions:** The mission is in Stevensville at the west end of 4th Street.

**Important Information:** Open daily 10 A.M. to 5 P.M., April 1 to Christmas. Tours 10 A.M. to 4:15 P.M., April 15 to October 15, and by appointment from October 16 through April 14. Admission for adults is $3, and for children is $1. Wheelchair accessible, except bathrooms. For more information call 406-777-5734.

## 15. Fort Owen

This one-acre state monument site makes a nice quick stop or picnic area in Stevensville. When the Jesuit missionaries decided to leave the Bitterroot Valley, they sold their property to Major John Owen for $250. The fort was active as a trading post from 1850–1872, but as travel routes changed, traffic to the fort dwindled. Several of the adobe and wooden structures have been restored. Interpretive displays and a brochure are available for a self-guided tour. The site has picnic tables and vault toilets.

**Directions:** Located west of Stevensville on the Stevensville Cutoff Road. The entrance for Fort Owen and Fort Owen Ranch are the same, but keep to the left for Fort Owen.

**Important Information:** Open daily with no specific hours. Wheelchair accessible.

# The Watchable Wildlife Triangle

This USDA Forest Service and U.S. Fish and Wildlife Service designation includes three wildlife areas: the Willoughby Environmental Education Area, the Lee Metcalf National Wildlife Refuge, and the Charles Waters Memorial Natural Area. These areas are all within 30 miles of each other and provide easy wildlife viewing in riparian streamsides, old-growth forest, sagebrush benchlands, forested bottomlands, meadows, and wetlands. Don't forget the binoculars! For more information, contact the U.S. Fish and Wildlife Service at 406-777-5552.

## 16. Willoughby Environmental Education Area

This 40-acre parcel of National Forest land sits at the base of the Sapphire Range. A 1-mile loop nature trail provides access through each of three habitats. An interpretive brochure describes their ecology. The site has a picnic shelter and toilets.

**Directions:** Two miles north of Victor, turn east from U.S. Highway 93 onto Bell Crossing and go approximately 10 miles on this road, which becomes Willoughby Lane and South Sunset Road. The site is on the south side of the road, about 1 mile past MacIntire Lane. The road is marked with Watchable Wildlife signs.

## 17. Lee Metcalf National Wildlife Refuge

• • • • • • • • • • • • • • • • • • • • • • • • • • • • • •

This 2,800-acre wildlife refuge was established to provide an undisturbed waterfowl habitat area. When Montana Senator Lee Metcalf died, it was named in his memory. Most of the refuge is wetlands and forested river-bottom habitat of the Bitterroot River. It is, indeed, a popular feeding ground and nesting area for resident and migrant waterfowl. Expect to see tundra swans and other waterfowl during the March and April spring migration. Interesting to see are the 20 or so osprey nests, easily spotted in the treetops because of their large size. In early spring you can view Canada geese nesting in them, but in April you will see ospreys trying to reclaim them. Bald eagles are common in winter and spring, and there are owls, woodpeckers, and a myriad of shore and song birds here, including Montana's state bird, the western meadowlark. Look for white-tailed deer, coyotes, skunks, muskrats, beavers, minks, porcupines, red foxes, and, especially, painted turtles. If you are lucky you might catch sight of elk, moose, or bear in the refuge.

Good access by foot or car is possible to most of the refuge. Hiking trails lead to the Bitterroot River and picnic area. Between July 15 and September 15, you can take a 2-mile loop trail near four ponds, where blinds allow close-up observation and photography of waterfowl and shore birds. Year-round access is available to a 140-acre picnic area with two hiking trails, each 0.9-mile long. Bathrooms and parking space are available at the picnic area.

**Directions:** From U.S. Highway 93, turn east onto Montana Highway 269 at the Stevensville junction and go east for approximately 1.5 miles, until you reach Montana Highway 203 (Eastside Highway), just past the USDA Forest Service ranger station. Turn left (north) onto MT 203, and then take the first left onto Wildfowl Lane, which winds through the southern part of the refuge. Take this road 1.5 miles until you see the refuge boundary signs.

**Important Information:** The picnic area is open year-round during daylight hours. Call the Stevensville Ranger District at 406-777-5552 for more information about the refuge.

## 18. Charles Waters Memorial Natural Area

• • • • • • • • • • • • • • • • • • • • • • • • • • • • • •

The natural area includes a campground, nature trail, and fitness trail. A fire ecology trail is set for completion in 1998. The nature trail goes by Bass

Creek and then wanders through the dry, pine forest area. There is also a fitness trail with several fitness stations which kids enjoy jumping and playing on. If you continue up to the campground, Bass Creek Trail begins from the west end. The 2.5-mile interpretive fire ecology loop trail will leave from the main road at the first switchback past the campground.

**Directions:** From U.S. Highway 93, turn west at the signed entrance 3.8 miles north of the Stevensville turnoff. From this turn it is 2.75 miles to the campground. The nature and fitness trails are less than a mile before the campground. Both start near the first parking area, where an interpretive sign describes the natural area. Turn right and drive through the parking area to the road at the north side. Go a short distance on this road to a very small parking area. The fitness trail and nature trail start near here on opposite sides of the road.

# MISSOULA AND THE SURROUNDING AREA

Missoula was named *Nemissodatakoo* by David Thompson in 1812. A Salish Indian word, it is interpreted to mean "river of awe" or "by or near the cold chilling waters." The water referred to is the Clark Fork of the Columbia River, which bisects the city and is the focus of many community activities.

## City of Missoula

Missoula is the third largest city in the state and is home to the University of Montana. The city is often heralded as the "Bicycle Capital" of the United States as it is situated along major bicycle touring routes and is host to national and regional biking events. Enthusiasm for bicycling got started in Missoula when the 25th Infantry Bicycle Corps was housed at Fort Missoula in 1888. For more biking information, contact the City of Missoula Bike Program at 406-523-4626 or the Adventure Cycling Association, 406-721-1776, a nonprofit organization that researches and maps special bicycle routes. For more information about the city of Missoula, contact the Chamber of Commerce at 406-543-6623 or 800-526-3465.

# Fort Missoula

The open fort (no walls) was built in 1877 during the settler-Indian conflicts. U.S. Army troops were involved in an attempt to halt Chief Joseph and the Nez Perce people on their historic journey toward refuge in Canada. In 1888 the 25th Infantry Bicycle Corps was stationed at the fort to test the potential of using bicycles for large-scale troop transportation. Included in the feasibility testing was a 1,900-mile journey by the infantry from Missoula to St. Louis—a remarkable but difficult journey that discouraged the military from using bicycles. Fort Missoula was also used as a prison for military personnel accused of war crimes in World War II. The facility now houses non-military land management agencies.

## 19. Fort Missoula

Fort Missoula provides a great day's adventure or a welcome respite during a quick road stop. The Bitterroot River runs adjacent to the 32-acre site that provides ample space for kids to run and play. A short, self-guided, outdoor interpretive trail describes 13 historic buildings and gives you an interesting excuse for a walk around the fort property.

Among kids' favorite activities is the Sliderlock Lookout, which they waste no time in scaling (they will obligingly count the steps to the top if you ask). You may want to be careful about small children climbing to the lookout unattended. A train engine in which kids can climb offers another intriguing diversion.

The museum contains more than 18,000 artifacts from Missoula County and Western Montana, documenting community history as well as history of the fort and the forestry industry of the area. An exhibit on the bicycling infantry troop is particularly interesting to kids. Many community activities are held at this site, and a schedule of events is available from the museum. The annual Fourth of July activities are a highlight at the fort.

**Directions:** From U.S. Highway 93, entering Missoula from the south, turn left on Reserve Street across from K-Mart, then left onto South Avenue just beyond the Larchmont Golf Course. Watch for the Fort Missoula sign on the left where you turn into the complex.

**Important Information:** Use of the site is free. The museum fee is $2 for adults and $1 for students and seniors. There is no charge for children under 6. Hours from Memorial Day through Labor Day are Monday through Saturday 10 A.M. to 5 P.M., and Sunday noon to 5 P.M.. Winter hours are Tuesday through Sunday noon to 5 P.M. For more information call 406-728-3476.

## 20. Rocky Mountain Elk Foundation Wildlife Visitor Center

• • • • • • • • • • • • • • • • • • • • • • • • • • • • • •

The Rocky Mountain Elk Foundation is dedicated to enhancing and increasing elk habitat. This nonprofit organization has contributed greatly to conservation efforts throughout North America. The foundation's headquarters are in Missoula, and the visitor center features a life-size bull elk bronze, wildlife theater, beautiful wildlife art, and natural history displays.

A wildlife diorama displays wildlife mounts of a grizzly bear, mountain goat, bighorn sheep, wolf, lynx, elk, bison, deer, and numerous small mammals and birds. Kids can see and admire the wildlife of Montana through this fascinating taxidermy exhibit and learn about wildlife ecology through the films available in the 50-seat wildlife theater. Feature films are *Elk of the Northern Herd* and *Montana: Its Seasons and Its Wildlife*. Kids especially enjoy the display of animal furs that invites them to feel the fur and guess which animal it is from.

**Directions:** Turn left from U.S. Highway 93 onto Russell Street. Just after you cross the Clark Fork River, you will reach Broadway. Turn left on Broadway; the visitor center is on the left in less than a mile at 2291 West Broadway.

**Important Information:** The visitor center is supported by donations. Memorial Day through Labor Day it is open 8 A.M. to 6 P.M. on weekdays and 11 A.M. to 4 P.M. Saturday and Sunday. Winter hours are 8:30 A.M. to 5 P.M. weekdays and 11 A.M. to 4 P.M. Saturday and Sunday. For more information call 406-523-4545 or 800-CALL ELK.

### Elk, *Cervus elaphus*

• • • • • • • • • • • • • • • • • • •

Rocky Mountain elk, also known as wapiti, are widespread throughout Montana's forests and meadows. These popular game animals weigh an impressive 500 to 1,000 pounds and stand 4 to 5 feet tall at the shoulder. The huge antler "racks" can be 4 or 5 feet long and there can be as much as 5 feet between the tips! The distinctive, high-pitched whistling and grunting noise they make during the mating season is called bugling and can be heard for great distances.

## 21. Smokejumper Visitor Center and Aerial Fire Depot

• • • • • • • • • • • • • • • • • • • • • • • • • • • • • •

Aerial smokejumping combines two activities naturally fascinating to kids: firefighting and parachuting! This Forest Service base is the largest active smokejumpers' base and training center in the United States. The visitor center displays describe wildland fire ecology, wildland fire suppression, firefighting technology and tools, and the science of fire behavior. Employees say kids always enjoy their visit. Tours are given by smokejumpers who often have exciting tales to tell. If the center is not too busy, the guides will provide a tour of one of the airplanes, so be sure to ask. Visitors can go inside two lookouts to get a feel for what it is like to live in one. Picnic tables are available.

**Directions:** The base is located at 5765 U.S. Highway 10 West. Shortly after entering Missoula from the south, turn left off U.S. Highway 93 onto Reserve Street and travel north. At Broadway, turn left (west) and you will see the base on the left, 0.5 mile beyond the Missoula airport. From Interstate 90 take the Reserve Street exit off the highway and go south until you reach Broadway.

**Important Information:** Free. Open daily from 9 A.M. to 5 P.M. mid-May to mid-September. There are six tours daily from 10 A.M. until 4 P.M. No tour is offered at noon. The site is wheelchair accessible. For more information call 406-329-4934.

## 22. Missoula Museum of the Arts

This museum features changing exhibits of regional, national, and international art with a special emphasis on art of the western states. The museum sponsors informative programs and summer art classes, and has a gift shop.

**Directions:** 335 North Pattee Street across from the post office off Broadway.

**Important Information:** Open year-round, Tuesday through Saturday from noon to 6 P.M. Tuesdays are free; a $2 donation is suggested at other times. The museum is wheelchair accessible on the first floor. For more information call 406-728-0447.

## 23. Clark Fork Northside Riverfront Trail

This riverside trail is 2 miles long and provides a scenic walking, biking, or rollerblading site. The trail is a place where kids can stop to throw rocks and sticks into the water, and is a convenient spot to just enjoy the sights and sounds of the fast-flowing river. Be careful about wading out into the water. Just east of the Higgins Avenue Bridge is Jeffrey Funk's bronze sculpture, *Returning*. Kids love to touch and climb the three large fish in this sculpture.

**Directions:** The trail can be easily accessed from Caras Park (site 25), Bess Reed Park, Kiwanis Park, or the Van Buren footbridge. Parking is best at Caras Park or the Chamber of Commerce on Van Buren and Front streets.

The trail appears to end a couple of times but can be accessed again by taking a jog on the city streets. On the east side of Bess Reed Park go left (north) on Washington Street, then right (east) on Kiwanis Street, which dead-ends at Kiwanis Park. The path starts again on the levee next to the river. When you reach the residential area next to the Madison Street bridge, turn left (north) on Parsons Street to East Front Street. Then turn right (east) on Front Street across Madison and continue until you reach the Van Buren footbridge.

**Important Information:** The Chamber of Commerce Visitor Center, just north of the Van Buren footbridge, has maps of Missoula trails. You can reach them at 406-543-6623 or 800-526-3465. The trail is paved and wheel-chair accessible from Caras Park east to Bess Reed Park.

## 24. Clark Fork Southside Riverfront Trail

The popular Southside Trail runs 1.5 miles from McCormick Park to the University of Montana and connects the Clark Fork Natural Park, John C. Toole Park, the University of Montana River Bowl, and Jacobs Island Park. Each of these parks has something unique to offer. McCormick Park is on the western end of the trail and has a public swimming pool, a children's fishing pond, and a playground. Bring your skates for ice skating in the winter. The Clark Fork Natural Park has a collection of Montana native plants. The large grassy area at John C. Toole Park is a frequent frisbee-tossing site and has restrooms. At the U of M River Bowl Park, the open grassy area is frequently used for soccer or softball. Jacobs Island Park is on a very small river island by the Van Buren Bridge. Here you can bask in the solitude or take the path around the island.

Three additional trails lead off at the east end of the Southside Trail. From the Van Buren footbridge you can get on the Kim Williams Nature Trail (site 27) and go east through Hellgate Canyon, or you can cross the footbridge to get on the Northside Riverfront Trail (site 23). You can also go to the "M" Trail (site 26) by following the sidewalk at the Van Buren foot-bridge one block south to Campus Drive and turning left. About half a mile up Campus Drive you will find the trailhead on your left.

**Directions:** Access the Southside Trail from any of the parks mentioned. To start at McCormick Park on the west end, take Orange street to Cregg Lane. At the intersection of Cregg and Hickory is McCormick Park and a large parking lot.

**Important Information:** The Chamber of Commerce has Missoula Trail maps at the visitor center on Van Buren and Front streets or you can reach them at 406-543-6623 or 800-526-3465.

# 25. Caras Park and the Carousel for Missoula

Fifteen-acre Caras Park is the focus of many community activities. It is the western trailhead for the Northside Riverfront Trail (site 23). The large parking area there makes it an easy starting point for riverfront exploration. You will also find restrooms, picnic tables, and an outdoor amphitheater. The park is one block from downtown Missoula and adjoins the Clark Fork River.

A highlight of the park is the unique and fully operational Carousel for Missoula. The 35 beautifully hand-carved horses are each painted differently, and every one is a work of art. Not only is the Carousel a pleasure to experience visually, but kids appreciate the outside row of ponies moving at a rousing 8 mph. The Carousel organ is designed to replicate the sounds of 23 different instruments as played by 45 musicians. The 400 organ pipes range in size from 2 inches to more than 10 feet. There are two chariots available for riders not interested in galloping up and down (acceptable, too, for wheelchair users). At the Carousel is a gift store and restoration shop with information about the extensive efforts involved in the Carousel's creation.

"Out to Lunch" happens at Caras Park every Wednesday at noon from June through August and is well worth the parking hassles. Numerous food vendors offer a variety of lunches at reasonable prices. Highly talented regional musicians and theater groups of all kinds are featured performers. The popularity of "Out to Lunch" means that up to 2,000 people may be in Caras park at noon on Wednesdays. If the Caras Park lot is full, an off-street parking area is available by North Higgins.

**Directions:** The park is on the north side of the river on both sides of Higgins Avenue. The Carousel is on the northwest corner of the park.

**Important Information:** Carousel hours are noon to 7 P.M., from Memorial Day through Labor Day, and noon to 5:30 P.M. the rest of the year. Rides are 50 cents for everyone. The Carousel is occasionally closed for maintenance and on some holidays. Call 406-549-8382 for more information.

# The Carousel

How many pennies does it take to adopt four carousel ponies? Missoula school children collected more than 1 million pennies to help in the "Carousel for Missoula" efforts. The completion of the first fully hand-carved carousel to be built in America since the Great Depression took thousands of volunteer hours. Donations came from around the United States and from several foreign countries, including Canada, where carvers from Calgary, Alberta, created the "friendship horse" that proudly gallops on Missoula's carousel.

# Missoula's "M"

The first Missoula "M" was built of whitewashed rocks in 1909 by the university's junior class. In 1912, the second "M" was built of wood and equipped with a lighting system and generator so it could be lit up on special occasions. The freshmen of 1915 wanted something more permanent, so they formed a bucket brigade that stretched a quarter of a mile up Mount Sentinel and relayed buckets of shale 200 feet above the site of the previous "M." Today's concrete "M" was completed in 1968 and cost $4,238.01.

## 26. The "M" Hike on Mount Sentinel

Mount Sentinel is a Missoula hallmark and a special landform for students at the University of Montana, which is located at the mountain's base. The hike to the "M" on the mountain is a short 0.75 mile, but it is steep (11 switchbacks), so plan on quite a few stops with or without kids. The view of Missoula and the Clark Fork is excellent, and the accomplishment of reaching Montana's "M" is worth the effort. One more mile gets the hearty to the top of Mount Sentinel where the view is even better. Take water with you as none is available on the trail.

**Directions:** Drive south on Van Buren Street from the Van Buren and Interstate 90 interchange. Go right (east) on Broadway and left across the Madison Street Bridge. Stay on the left fork which turns onto Arthur. Turn left onto 6th at the stoplight, and head toward Harry Adams Field House. Follow the one-way street past the field house to Campus Drive, and then turn right and go around Washington Grizzly Stadium. The trail is behind the campus security building. There is free parking at the trailhead but don't park in other campus lots unless you want a parking ticket.

## 27. Kim Williams Nature Trail and the Hellgate Canyon Trail

The Kim Williams Nature Trail is a wide, flat, 2.5-mile hiking or biking trail that is an easy escape from the hustle and bustle of the city. Made from an abandoned railroad right-of-way, it follows the Clark Fork River through a scenic 134-acre natural area in Hellgate Canyon. On this trail, named for a local naturalist, you stand a good chance of seeing wildlife. Keep an eye out for birds or deer by the river, and look for chipmunks on the talus slopes of Mount Sentinel off to the right.

For a longer loop hike and a route to the top of Mount Sentinel that is less steep than the "M" Trail, you can veer off to the right on the Kim Williams Trail after about a mile and join up with the Crazy Canyon Road. From this junction it's a rigorous 1.4-mile climb to the top of Mount Sentinel. To make the loop complete, take the "M" Trail 1.75 miles down the mountain to the trailhead. Note that the stretch between Kim Williams and Crazy Canyon Road turns into a narrow path about three quarters of a mile from the turnoff on Kim Williams. On this stretch you pass through the 1985 Hellgate Canyon Fire area and have wonderful vistas! The Kim Williams–Crazy Canyon–"M" Trail Loop is 5 miles and gains nearly 2,000 feet in elevation. If you bring little ones, be sure they are ready for action or be prepared to carry them.

**Directions:** The trailhead connects directly to the Clark Fork Southside Trail on the south side of Van Buren footbridge. Parking is readily available in the summer but may be hard to find during the university's fall and spring semesters.

## 28. Beavertail Hill State Park

Fishing, swimming, camping, and good outdoor fun is just a half hour from Missoula at Beavertail Hill State Park. Standing on the banks of the Clark Fork River you can try your hand at bringing in brown, cutthroat, or rainbow trout. The 65-acre campground does not have a boat ramp but does have a restroom. There is no designated picnic area, but there is also no shortage of pleasant places by the river to lay out a blanket. The park is heavily used on weekends.

**Directions:** Take Interstate 90 east of Missoula to the exit at milepost 130. From there the park is 0.25 mile on a gravel road.

**Important Information:** Open May 1 to the end of September. Day-use and camping fee. Contact Montana Department of Fish, Wildlife & Parks at 406-542-5500.

# Blue Mountain Recreation Area

Two miles southwest of Missoula is the 5,500-acre Blue Mountain Recreation Area. The site allows bicycling, hiking, backpacking, horseback riding, and all-terrain vehicles in designated areas. The two hikes below are enjoyable even with fairly young children. For more information contact the Lolo National Forest at 406-329-3814.

# 29. Maclay Flat Interpretive Trail

This 1.8-mile loop trail along the Bitterroot River can be shortened to 1.25 miles by taking a cutoff trail. Interpretive signs along the way explain the river system, wildlife, vegetation, and archaeology of the area. See if you can spot the wood duck and bluebird nest boxes along this trail. Keep your eyes open for hawks, ospreys, bald eagles, blue herons, ducks, and deer, too. A good picnicking spot in a grassy area is 0.3 mile down the trail (clockwise).

A river float popular with locals begins on the Bitterroot River at Maclay Bridge and joins the Clark Fork. A convenient pullout is located 6 miles down at Harper Bridge. This is an enjoyable beginner's float and has the added advantage of good rainbow trout fishing.

**Directions:** Drive south on U.S. Highway 93 one mile from Missoula. Turn right (northwest) onto Blue Mountain County Road at the Western Montana Sports Medicine Center, and go 1.5 miles. The parking lot for Maclay Flat is on the right. To find the Maclay Bridge, continue past Maclay Flat and take the first right, which leads you to the bridge.

**Important Information:** Wheelchair accessible.

# 30. Blue Mountain Lookout

During fire season, generally July and August, you can drive 11 miles to the Blue Mountain Lookout on a Forest Service road. Off-season there is a gate across the road 2.5 miles below the lookout. If the gate is closed when you get there, you can still hike to the top or enjoy the popular nature trail off of Forest Road 365. The lookout provides scenic views of Lolo Peak and the Selway-Bitterroot Wilderness to the south and west. On a clear day you will see the Mission Mountains to the northwest. The lookout itself is in service during the fire season, and if someone is on duty and not too busy, you may be able to get a tour of the building and hear about life as a fire lookout.

A 0.25-mile loop nature trail is a pleasant stopping-off point about 2 miles up FR 365 from Blue Mountain County Road. The mostly level trail has interesting interpretive signs about forest ecology and is a favorite late spring field trip for local schools. Check out the view from the rock outcropping near the start of the trail. Wheelchair access is possible to this point. There is no parking area here but three or four cars can fit along the road. The trailhead sign is a few feet down the path so watch closely for it.

**Directions:** Take Blue Mountain County Road (see directions to Maclay Flat, site 29) about 1.25 miles from U.S. Highway 93 until you reach FR 365. Go west, and after 9.5 miles look for a road to the left, Forest Road 2137. This road takes you to the lookout.

**Important Information:** The Forest Service roads may be closed in early spring due to weather conditions. They are closed in winter except to snowmobiles. For more information contact the Lolo National Forest at 406-329-3814.

# Pattee Canyon Recreation Area

Towering ponderosa pines grace the narrow canyon of the Pattee Canyon Recreation Area, now a part of Lolo National Forest. A well-developed network of foot, horse, bicycle, and cross-country ski trails makes this a favorite Missoula recreation spot. For more information call the Lolo National Forest Office at 406-329-3814. Maps are available at the office.

## 31. Northside Trails: Pattee Canyon Picnic Area

A number of unsigned trails traverse the meadow and forest lands just north of the Pattee Canyon Picnic Area. Most are between 1 and 3 miles and are relatively level. One of the most popular is the 2.2-mile Meadow Loop Trail that skirts the south edge of the meadow and goes north through the woods. This trail is an easy hike or bike ride in the summer and a delightful winter cross-country ski. During snow season it becomes a 3.2-mile maintained ski trail that starts from the Pattee Canyon Trailhead.

The meadow was used as an Army firing range for soldiers at Fort Missoula from the early 1920s to 1940. The mounded-earth firing lines are still visible as is a large mound backed by a wooden wall on which soldiers carved their names. You'll have to look carefully for these as there is no sign indicating their presence.

**Directions:** The Pattee Canyon Picnic Area is just off Pattee Canyon Road 3.6 miles from where it intersects with Southwest Higgins Avenue. The picnic area is closed in the winter, but you can park at the Pattee Canyon Trailhead 1 mile down.

**Important Information:** Open 8 A.M. until dark in the summer. For more information contact the Lolo National Forest office at 406-329-3814.

## 32. Southside Ski (and Hiking) Trails

Though designed for cross-country skiing, these mostly flat trails are nice for hiking or mountain-biking at other times of the year. The main loop is 2.4 miles but three cutoff routes can shorten the distance.

**Directions:** Go straight past the Pattee Canyon Picnic Area (site 31). The parking lot for the Southside Trails is a short distance on the right.

**Important Information:** Contact the Lolo National Forest office at 406-329-3814.

## 33. Sam Braxton National Recreation Trail

This 3.4-mile loop trail through an old homestead area of Pattee Canyon Recreation Area was named after Sam Braxton, a well-known Missoula skier, bicyclist, and outdoorsman. At the beginning of the trail, you will see giant old-growth western larch and ponderosa pine, Montana's state tree. If you look closely you'll see remnants of old homesteads along the way. Numerous old horse-logging trails crisscross the area, which may be confusing. A Pattee Canyon brochure from the Lolo National Forest is helpful for identifying trails.

**Directions:** Go 4 miles up Pattee Canyon Road to the Pattee Canyon Trailhead. Stay to the right after the parking area gate and follow the road to the trailhead.

**Important Information:** Contact the Lolo National Forest office at 406-329-3814.

# Rattlesnake Valley National Recreation Area and Wilderness

Another popular recreation site, the Rattlesnake Valley Recreation Area and Wilderness, extends north from Missoula. The short trails along Rattlesnake Creek provide good biking and walking. No need to worry—the name does not reflect the presence of rattlesnakes! Within the valley is a 61,000-acre recreation and wilderness area, 8 miles northeast of Missoula. The trails are diverse in both length and difficulty. Backpacking is permitted in the high-country wilderness area. Although mountain bikes are not permitted in the wilderness area they are allowed in the recreation areas. Rattlesnake Creek is part of Missoula's water supply, so visitors are asked to be careful about stream pollution. For more information call the Lolo National Forest Office at 406-329-3814. Maps are available at the office.

# 34. Greenough Park Trails

Encircling the 42 acres composing Greenough Park is a 1-mile paved walking and bicycling path. More than 100 bird species have been identified here, and interpretive signs identify the ones seen most often. Keep an eye out for large woodpeckers with red heads—pileated woodpeckers. Or, if you see a little brown bird bobbing up and down on a rock in the creek, you have most likely found a "dipper." There is probably a nest nearby, precariously close to a waterfall or running water. This is the dipper's form of nest protection. Listen for chickadee-dee-dees, watch for hummingbirds, and look for ducks and hawks. On an occasional early fall morning, black bear are seen here though they have not been a problem.

From the main trail, several unpaved paths go through the woods or along the stream. Bicycles are not allowed on these trails. Picnic tables and benches along the creek are located on the south side of the park, just west of the footbridge.

**Directions:** Take the Van Buren Avenue exit from Interstate 90 and go north. At Locust turn left and go two blocks. Turn right on Monroe and look for the Greenough Park sign.

**Important Information:** Wheelchair accessible. Contact the City of Missoula at 406-721-7275 for more information.

# 35. Main Rattlesnake Travel Corridor

This unnamed trail is commonly referred to as the main travel corridor in the Rattlesnake Valley National Recreation Area and Wilderness and is actually an old farm and logging road (Forest Road 99) that is closed to motor vehicles. The gently sloping road is 15 miles long, but you can, of course, go just as far as you feel comfortable. Connecting trails go further into the wilderness area.

If you make it in 8 miles to Franklin Bridge, your reward is a good chance of seeing mountain goats on the cliffs above Rattlesnake Creek.

**Directions:** Take Van Buren Street north from where it intersects Interstate 90. Stay to the right and the road will turn into Rattlesnake Drive. Turn left onto an unmarked road just beyond Wildcat Road. The parking area is at the mouth of Sawmill Gulch, just beyond the bridge about 4 miles from the I-90 interchange.

# THE SEELEY-SWAN VALLEY

For an interesting excursion take the 91-mile drive along Montana Highway 83 that goes through the Seeley-Swan Valley. This route from Missoula to the Flathead Valley is a wonderful alternative to busy U.S. Highway 93. Although it is 24 miles longer, just counting the deer along the Seeley-Swan route can make the trip go quickly. The valley is also a rewarding destination in its own right.

This two-lane forested highway takes you between the Swan Mountain Range and the enchanting Mission Mountains. Here, the Bob Marshall, Great Bear, and Scapegoat wilderness areas come together to form an impressive 1.5 million acres of wilderness, the largest in the lower 48 states. This region supports vast numbers of wildlife; watch carefully and you'll see many wild critters.

The Seeley-Swan Valley is actually two scenic river valleys—the Clearwater and the Swan. On the southern end, the Clearwater River flows south through a "chain of lakes" to its confluence with the Blackfoot River near Clearwater Junction. In the north end, the Swan River flows from the Mission Mountains toward Flathead Lake.

Turn north off Montana Highway 200 east of Missoula, onto MT 83 by a big black-and-white bull statue and you will be on the Seeley-Swan Highway. The highway goes through the towns of Seeley Lake and Swan Lake and ends by Ferndale, where a left turn (west) goes toward Bigfork.

## Common Loon,
### *Gavia immer*

If you hear some eerie sounds while traveling through the Seeley-Swan, you could be in luck—you might be hearing a loon. Along this route is the largest nesting area for common loons in the western states. You'll know it's loon country when you hear one of the four wonderful calls these birds make. A loon wail can pierce the deepest forest while its hoot or yodel will fill the mountains and your spirit. The tremolo, a laughing sound, is actually a loon warning that something is near. If you do see one of these shy creatures, keep your distance, as loons are likely to abandon their nest if people come within 200 yards of them. Adult loons can dive deeper than 200 feet.

# Clearwater River Valley

If you were to take a hot-air balloon ride during Seeley Lake's August balloon festivals, you would see the chain of lakes along the Clearwater River. Of these lakes, Salmon, Placid, and Seeley lakes all have good access with pleasant campgrounds and facilities, making this an enjoyable summertime place to visit. If you're looking for somewhere to play in the winter, this area offers cross-country skiing and dog-sled races, too.

## 36. Blackfoot-Clearwater Wildlife Management Area

This 67,000-acre forest area in the Rocky Mountain foothills is full of bird life—woodpeckers, owls, and eagles, just to mention a few. You'll enjoy this wonderful drive-through area which is also a great place to bike or get out and go for a walk. In the winter you can view large herds of elk and deer from the pullout. Binoculars are useful at this site.

**Directions:** A marked pullout less than 0.5 mile north of the Clearwater Junction is a good wildlife viewing area. Almost 2.5 miles north is a road to the right (east) that takes you through the wildlife area.

**Important Information:** Closed mid-November through mid-May. Contact Montana Department of Fish, Wildlife & Parks, Missoula, at 406-542-5500 for more information.

## 37. Salmon Lake

Salmon Lake provides an enjoyable stop or weekend campsite at the state park located on the east shore. There are 20 camping units, a boat launch, a day use area, and toilets.

**Directions:** Located 5 miles south of the town of Seeley Lake on the west side of Montana Highway 83.

**Important Information:** Open Memorial Day through Labor Day. State fee area. Contact the Montana Department of Fish, Wildlife & Parks, at 406-542-5500 for more information.

# 38. Placid Lake

Most of the lakes in Montana are colder than ice-cold drinking water. Placid Lake, however, is a nice, warm swimming lake with picnic areas. A paved trail around the lake can be used for bicycles, rollerblades, or foot recreation. The camping area has 42 camping units, water, restrooms, a swimming area, and a boat launch.

**Directions:** Turn west onto Placid Lake Road, 3 miles south of the town of Seeley Lake. Follow the signs west for about 3 miles to the campground.

**Important Information:** Wheelchair accessible. The Placid Lake State Park is open Memorial Day through Labor Day. State fee area. Contact the Montana Department of Fish, Wildlife & Parks, at 406-542-5500 for more information.

# Seeley Lake Area

The people who live in the town of Seeley Lake and in the surrounding area have a high degree of appreciation for the land. Their loyalty comes from a rich history in which finding a balance with the environment was essential. The town of Seeley Lake has unique shops and interesting community events that are open to visitors. It is known for its festive Fourth of July celebration, so if you are planning on being in the area then, make your reservations well in advance. In August the hot air balloons come to town, and you can get a breathtaking view of the Chain of Lakes and surrounding wilderness while floating aloft. The Seeley Winter Carnival is held the first week of January and is full of activities—a parade, snow sculptures, dog-sled rides and races, snowmobile races, games, and cross-country skiing.

## 39. Seeley Lake

Seeley Lake is noted for its year-round recreational activities and is a peaceful place for outdoor fun—good fishing, a swimming beach, hiking, boating, horseback riding, and canoeing. There are three National Forest campgrounds located on the lake.

**Directions:** Look for Seeley Lake 54 miles from Missoula and 91 miles from Kalispell, on Montana Highway 83.

**Important Information:** Contact USDA Forest Service, Seeley Lake Ranger District, 406-677-2233, for information.

## 40. Clearwater Canoe Trail

The Clearwater Canoe Trail is a calm one- to two-hour float or canoe trip down the winding Clearwater River. Anticipate seeing beavers, turtles, river otters, loons, ducks, moose, deer, eagles, ospreys, or muskrats. You may even get to see an eagle or osprey diving for fish. The 3-mile river float ends at the lake by the Seeley Lake Ranger Station. From here it is a 1.5-mile hike back to the launching area along the Clearwater River—keep a lookout for wildlife. **Directions:** Put in 1 mile north of Seeley Lake Ranger Station. **Important Information:** Contact the USDA Forest Service, Seeley Lake Ranger District at 406-677-2233.

## 41. Morrell Falls

The hike to Morrell Falls is a fairly easy 5-mile round-trip hike with only a 250-foot elevation gain. This cascading waterfall drops about 100 feet, and the amount of water coming over the falls is overwhelming. If you catch the

# Old Two Toes, What a Bear!

If you haven't already heard of Old Two Toes, then sit back and relax. Here is the true story of a 1,100-pound grizzly bear whose claws were as sharp as a razor and more than 3.5 inches long. He was twice the size of an average grizzly bear and mean. Ranchers said he was a deliberate killer who stalked his prey but often wouldn't even take a bite of his kill. In 1898 an old trapper named Ricks came across bear tracks and set up his traps. Two days later he returned to find one of the traps gone as well as the tree that it was chained to. Ricks followed the bear's trail about a mile down the mountain and found the tree—still attached to the trap. But the only thing left in the trap was—guess what—half a bear foot and two toes. That bear had chewed off part of his own foot to get away. From then on, the bear was known as Two Toes.

For the next eight years, Two Toes roamed the Seeley-Swan area and earned his reputation as a troublemaker by killing more than $8,750 worth of livestock. The ranchers in the area put up a $575 reward for his hide and many a hunter took a shot at the great bear. Rancher Caleb Myres even hired a bounty hunter by the name of Kline, but Kline was later found half-dead on a river bank. Two Toes had almost bitten Kline's leg off in a confrontation. Finally in 1906, a man named Dale was trailing a string of seven pack horses in the Flathead when the huge grizzly startled his horses and attacked. Two Toes was killed by Dale that day. When the infamous bear's hide was examined, it was found to be full of old bullet-hole scars. What a bear!

falls at the right time of year you can see two waterfalls. Before you get to the falls you will come to Morrell Lake, a refreshing place to take a dip. As you can tell, this is a great hike for water play, so bring swimsuits and towels—or at least dry clothes. With all these diversions, time seems to slip away, so you may want to bring snacks and drinking water.

**Directions:** Going north of Seeley Lake, turn east (north) onto Cottonwood Lakes Road, Forest Road 477. Drive for slightly more than 1 mile, then turn left on Morrell-Clearwater Road. After 7 more miles, turn right over the Morrell Creek bridge and take a left at the next junction. One more mile and you are at the trailhead.

**Important Information:** Camping in this area is not recommended by the Forest Service due to overuse. Usually open mid-May through October. Contact Seeley Lake Ranger District at 406-677-2233.

# Swan River Valley

The Swan River gathers water from both the Mission Mountains and the Bob Marshall Wilderness and then flows north to Swan Lake and on to Flathead Lake. The forest areas along the highway that parallel the river are thick and offer wonderful wildlife habitat. The tiny town of Swan Lake goes by in the blink of an eye, but take time to stop at the sites listed, and you will find it well worth your while.

## 42. Holland Lake and Falls Trail

This two-hour hike is about 4 miles round trip and follows the north shore of Holland Lake. There are lots of places for play by the lake, so even if you never make it to the falls you'll have a fun trip. However, the 40-foot waterfalls are spectacular and well worth the short climb. If the little ones fuss about the uphill section, take a snack break before pushing on. Once there, you won't find much room near the falls, so be careful. We hiked this trail in early winter and found an icy wonderland by the falls. If you take a winter hike here, be sure to dress warmly and watch for the ice all around the falls.

Holland Lake is known as one of the doorways into the one-million acre Bob Marshall Wilderness. Known locally as "The Bob," this rugged mountain area is named for Bob Marshall, a famous wilderness advocate. He was once quoted as saying that there was only "one hope of repulsing the tyrannical ambition of civilization to conquer every niche on the whole earth. That hope is the organization of spirited people who will fight for the freedom of the wilderness." Way to go, Bob!

**Directions:** The Holland Lake turnoff to the east is 8.3 miles south of Condon. The turnoff is well marked. The trailhead is just past the campground and lodge. Good parking is available.

**Important Information:** The campground is open Memorial Day through Labor Day. Contact Swan Ranger District at 406-837-5081.

## 43. Cold Lakes

There is an Upper Cold Lake and a Lower Cold Lake. The lower lake trail is an easy 1.5-mile hike with opportunities for fishing and experiencing the splendor of the Mission Mountain Wilderness. There are lots of creeks to cross along the way and a refreshing waterfall about 0.5 mile into the hike. Besides being a good hike for splashing in the water, there is a high probability of seeing wildlife. There is no established trail to Upper Cold Lake.

**Directions:** At 0.7 mile north of mile marker 46, about 23 miles south of Swan Lake on Montana 83, turn right (west) onto Cold Creek Forest Road 903. Drive southwest for 3 miles, then turn right on Forest Road 9568 and left again on Forest Road 9599. From the highway it is 7 miles to the trailhead.

**Important Information:** There is no camping at either lake. Since this is bear country, check with the Forest Service about bear safety. Only experienced hikers should attempt to reach Upper Cold Lake. Contact Swan Ranger District in Big Fork, 406-837-5081, for information.

## 44. Old Squeezer Loop Road

Explore the multitude of trails that crisscross the meadow and forest here, or quietly observe abundant wildlife from viewing benches. Ospreys, eagles, woodpeckers, hummingbirds, flycatchers, warblers, and Swainson's thrushes are among the birds often seen here. Black bear, elk, and deer can be seen as well.

**Directions:** Across from the Swan River State Forest Service headquarters, around mile marker 58, take the Goat Creek Forest Road 554 east for 1.5 miles. At the fork turn right onto Old Squeezer Loop Road and look for a small parking lot on the left in about 2 miles.

**Important Information:** Contact Swan River State Forest Service at 406-754-2301.

## 45. Swan Lake Recreation Area

The Forest Service maintains a campground and beach at Swan Lake. The beach has facilities for picnics and swimming. Across the road are campsites with drinking water and toilets. There is a boat launch just north of the town.

**Directions:** Just north of the community of Swan Lake on either side of the Montana Highway 83.

**Important Information:** This is a Forest Service fee area. Contact Swan Lake Ranger Station for information at 406-837-5081.

# THE FLATHEAD VALLEY

The Flathead Valley, with the Salish and Mission ranges rising on either side, offers a myriad of outdoor opportunities for families. The valley's towns also offer a surprising variety of indoor and outdoor activities. The scenic nature of the surrounding wilderness and forest lands has drawn a number of high-quality artists to the area and spawned equally excellent local artists, so you'll find a healthy arts base in the valley.

Flathead Lake stands out as a prime recreation area in the Flathead Valley due to its large size and purity. The largest natural, freshwater lake west of the Mississippi, Flathead Lake is 125,000 acres with 135 miles of rocky shoreline. Though the land along the shore is mostly privately owned, there are public places at the lake where you can enjoy the clear freshness of the water and the ever-present mountain views. Six state parks provide camping, swimming, picnicking, boat-launching facilities, and vistas. The southern half of the lake is in the Flathead Indian Reservation, and in these waters you will need a tribal license to fish (see page 348.) On the northern end you will find three lake access points with swimming and boat launching facilities: Ben Williams Park in Lakeside, the Somers Fishing Access, and Woods Bay Fishing Access south of Bigfork.

Sailboats, motorboats, canoes, sailboards, and other watercraft are available for rent on the lake. Call the Bayview Resort, 406-837-4843, or Marina Cay, 406-837-5861, in Bigfork; A-1 Fishing Charter, 406-844-3602, or Power Play Water Sports, 406-844-2400, in Lakeside; Flathead Boat Rentals at KwaTaqNuk Resort, 800-358-8046, in Polson; and Big Arm Resort, 406-849-5622, in Big Arm. The Flathead Convention and Visitor Association, 800-543-3105, can help with additional references and more information.

Tour boats are perfect for the relaxed sightseer and families who don't want to rent boats. Short cruises, evening cruises, or day trips are available. The Far West power boat tours, 406-857-3203, leave from the dock at Somers right off U.S. Highway 93. In Bigfork, take a Questa sailboat tour, 406-837-5569, from historic Flathead Lake Lodge. Lake tours are available in Polson out of KwaTaqNuk Resort on the *Port Polson Princess*, 406-882-2448.

If you are in the area between mid-July and early August, check out the famous Flathead Lake sweet cherries. Mild lakeshore weather makes cherry-growing feasible despite the snowy winters (though a heavy frost in 1989 caused the loss of a number of orchards). You can find these delectable items in local supermarkets, at roadside stands, and in U-pick locations on the lake. Or, you can go to the Flathead Lake Cherry Growers plant at Finley Point to buy them, and take a quick tour as well. Call 406-887-2632 for information. To drive to the plant, turn off Montana Highway 35 south of Bigfork at Finley Point Road (around milepost 6) and go 1.5 miles farther, following the signs to Finley Point State Park. For more information contact the Flathead Convention and Visitor Association, 800-543-3105.

# Flathead Valley State Parks and Fishing Access Sites

The management of the six state parks in the Flathead Valley area is under the jurisdiction of Montana Fish, Wildlife & Parks, 406-752-5501. There are camping and day-use fees for the state parks. A yearly permit provides access to any state park in Montana for $20 for residents and $24 for non-residents. You can purchase the permits at sporting goods stores or at the park entrances.

## 46. Big Arm State Park

One of six state parks in the area, this park has few shade trees but a clear view of Wild Horse Island. It functions mostly as a boat-access site and is the closest public launching point for those wishing to get to Wild Horse Island. You can swim or picnic at this park and camp with tents or trailers. We often make a quick stop here for a restroom and driving break when traveling along the western lakeshore. The kids enjoy even a few minutes of play along the shoreline.

**Directions:** The park is 13 miles north of Polson on U.S. Highway 93 at milepost 74.

**Important Information:** This is a fee area for camping or day use. Contact the Montana Fish, Wildlife & Parks Department at 406-752-5501 for more information.

# 47. Wild Horse Island State Park

• • • • • • • • • • • • • • • • • • • • • • • • • • • • • • • • • •

This park provides for a unique Huckleberry Finn–style family adventure. Be prepared to make this a day-long jaunt as you will have to deal with getting there and back, in addition to having fun exploring the island. You can rent a 14-foot aluminum fishing boat at Big Arm Resort and Marina, 406-849-5622, or bring your own craft. Though the distance is short, storms can kick up on the lake, and the Montana Department of Fish, Wildlife & Parks recommends craft at least 18 feet long. There are no public docks on the island. If you go with your own boat, you will have to anchor and have your own transportation to shore, or bring a boat you can pull up on the beach. The *Port Polson Princess*, 406-883-2448, makes a daily Wild Horse Island three-hour cruise, from 1:30 to 4:30 P.M., from Polson, but doesn't stop at the island. A minimum of six passengers is needed. Pointer Scenic Cruises, 406-837-5617, near Bigfork, offers custom charters that can include taking the boat by cliffs at Rollins to look at petroglyphs. Prices vary depending on the number of passengers and length of the trip.

The effort of getting to this 2,134-acre island pays you back with lots of wildlife viewing on the rocky, open, island hills and wooded areas. Bighorn sheep are plentiful. You'll have the best luck looking for the herd of about 100 sheep on the northwest corner which you can access via the unofficial state land trails. You may also see mule deer, white-tailed deer, coyote, mink, or the three wild horses that reside on the island. The name of the island comes from earlier times when the Flathead and Pend Oreille Indians used the island to protect their horses from raids by the Blackfeet Indians.

Parts of the island are steep, but everyone can enjoy some portion of the trails and the excitement of island exploration. Be prepared to wander on your own as there are no interpretive displays or marked trails. Take water, too, as none is available and there are no facilities.

**Directions:** The closest boat ramps are at Big Arm State Park and Walstad Fishing Access (sites 46 and 54).

**Important Information:** Note that much of the island is under private ownership, so visitors must be careful to stay on public land. Private land is well marked. There is no fee for use of this park. No camping, dogs, or fires are permitted. Contact the Montana Department of Fish, Wildlife & Parks at 406-752-5501 for more information.

# 48. West Shore State Park

• • • • • • • • • • • • • • • • • • • • • • • • • • • • • • • • • •

West Shore State Park combines a scenic view of the north end of Flathead Lake with interesting rock outcrops and plentiful trees. There is no designated swimming area, but there are numerous spots along the rocky beach to wade or swim, if you can brave the cold water. There is a day-use picnic area, drinking water, and boat access. A short, signed trail gives interpretive information and a good view of the lake.

**Directions:** Look for the signed entrance about 29 miles north of Polson, and about 16 miles south of Kalispell on U.S. Highway 93.

**Important Information:** The park is open all year. Contact the Montana Department of Fish, Wildlife & Parks at 406-752-5501 for more information.

## 49. Somers Fishing Access

This fishing access site is adjacent to U.S. Highway 93 and has a dock, so lots of people stop by for a quick dip in Flathead Lake's refreshing waters.

**Directions:** The access is just south of the flashing yellow light on US 93 that marks the turn to "downtown" Somers.

## 50. Sportsman Bridge Fishing Access

For a nice view of the river and a quick play-stop, take a break at the Sportsman Bridge Fishing Access.

**Directions:** Turn south into the Sportsman Bridge fishing access just east of the Flathead River Bridge on Montana Highway 82.

## 51. Wayfarers State Park

This park has a rocky shoreline that gives plentiful access to the lake for water play. A nicely wooded campground provides tent and trailer camping with fire rings and grills. An interpretive display and short, unmarked walking trails provide opportunities to explore. A boat ramp and boat rentals, flush toilets, and a telephone are also available.

**Directions:** The park entrance is just south of the town of Bigfork on Montana Highway 35, south of the junction with Montana Highway 208 to Ferndale. The entrance road is well marked on the west side of the highway.

**Important Information:** There are fees for camping and day use. Pay at the entrance station. Call 406-752-5501 for more information.

# 52. Yellow Bay Unit

• • • • • • • • • • • • • • • • • • • • • • • • • • • • • • • • • •

This small, 15-acre park has only two campsites. A designated swimming area is good for small kids, and there is a nicely shaded picnic area with a small shelter. Yellow Bay has showers, flush toilets, water, and electricity. Next door is the Montana Biological Research and Education Station which offers tours of the station.

**Directions:** Look for the park 15 miles south of Bigfork on Montana Highway 35.

**Important Information:** The park is open all year. Open fires are not allowed, and you need both tribal and state fishing licenses to fish here, (see page 348). Call 406-752-5501 for more information.

# 53. Finley Point Unit

• • • • • • • • • • • • • • • • • • • • • • • • • • • • • • • • • •

This is the most developed park in the Flathead Lake state park system. The paved sites have electricity, drinking water, picnic tables, and grills. Boat slips are available for rent.

**Directions:** Turn into Finley Point State Park at the marked entrance, 11 miles north of Polson on Montana Highway 35, and follow this county road 4 miles west to the park.

**Important Information:** State and tribal fishing licenses are necessary here, (see page 348). The fishing area and boat ramp are wheelchair accessible, as are the vault toilets. Call 406-752-5501 for more information.

# 54. Walstad Fishing Access

• • • • • • • • • • • • • • • • • • • • • • • • • • • • • • • • • •

This small fishing access site, just off of U.S. Highway 93, gives you a chance to play for a few minutes on the rocky beach. You can launch your boat from here, or just walk out on the small dock to look across the water to Wild Horse Island. There is a vault toilet.

**Directions:** The site is near mile marker 71 on the western lakeshore.

**Important Information:** Wheelchair accessible.

# Flathead River

Another popular outdoor destination in the Flathead Valley is the Flathead River. Portions of all three forks of the river, each a powerful culmination of numerous small mountain streams, are justifiably designated National Wild, Scenic and Recreational Rivers. Despite dams at Hungry Horse and below Polson, most of the river remains wild and undeveloped, offering pristine nature experiences of fishing, floating, or observing free-flowing waters.

An evening or afternoon spent enjoying the river from one of the fishing access sites can fly by, and this kind of simple entertainment for families is heartily recommended. We make regular visits to our favorite sites, and, at least once a year, we float down one of the Flathead Valley's numerous rivers or streams. This takes some planning and the better part of a day, but these events become special trips to remember. The Flathead River Partnership, 406-752-0081, has a handy map of the river from Columbia Falls to Flathead Lake.

While significant parts of the Flathead River forks are turbulent and wild, in other areas the waters glide smoothly onward. Guided river floats are available on all forks and run the gamut from tumultuous rides to relatively peaceful floats on quieter stretches. You can take your own raft or canoe on various stretches of the river, but be aware that even the flatter portions have swift currents and should be approached cautiously. The South Fork floats are strictly backcountry floats that require packing equipment in on horses or mules. The three forks come together at Columbia Falls. From there the main stem of the Flathead River winds and twists for nearly 40 miles toward Flathead Lake.

All three forks of the Flathead offer productive fishing. There are good-sized west slope cutthroat and mountain whitefish. Don't count your fish before they bite, however. Though fish are plentiful, the fishing is not always easy. Because there is so much natural food here, the fish don't always take the nibble.

## 55. Quarter Circle Bridge, West Glacier to Blankenship Bridge Float

One of our family's favorite floats on the Flathead, this trip leaves from a bridge at the confluence of McDonald Creek and the Middle Fork and takes about three hours to reach Blankenship Bridge, just below the confluence of the North and Middle forks of the Flathead River. This is an easy float that includes a short section through interesting cliffs and opportunities to see wildlife, but has few views of manmade developments. Generally the only fast part is right by the pullout above Blankenship Bridge and a short stretch just below the cliffs section. Take lunch or dinner and find an open area along the shore to eat. Outfitters who float this section often provide the dinner!

**Directions:** To reach Quarter Circle Bridge, turn west from the Glacier National Park entrance road onto the road to the park service horse corrals. Blankenship Bridge, the take-out point, is west from U.S. Highway 2 at the sign for Lake Five, north of Coram.

**Important Information:** Contact Glacier National Park at 406-888-7800 for more information.

## 56. Teakettle Fishing Access to Presentine Bar Fishing Access Float

This is a quiet, 6.8-mile, two-hour float. For a day-long float, go from Teakettle Fishing Access in Columbia Falls to the Old Steel Bridge (site 57).

**Directions:** The Teakettle Access site is found on the east side of Columbia Falls, on U.S. Highway 2 and Montana Highway 40, the main road through Columbia Falls. Presentine Bar Fishing Access is on US 2 south of Columbia Falls between mile markers 128 and 129, across from Costco. Turn east onto Birch Grove Road and follow the signs 1.9 miles to the access point.

## 57. Presentine Bar Fishing Access to the Old Steel Bridge Float

This float is 8 miles and about two hours long. The river floats mentioned here have no real rapids, though floaters should steer clear of log jams. Go prepared with food and extra clothing. Frequent stops to swim, eat, or explore make the trip more interesting. When fall colors peak, this stretch of river is particularly colorful.

**Directions:** From U.S. Highway 2 south of Columbia Falls between mile markers 128 and 129, across from Costco, turn east onto Birch Grove Road and follow the signs 1.9 miles to the Presentine Bar Fishing Access point. To get to the west side of the Old Steel Bridge Fishing Access, take Kalispell's 2nd Street East off Main Street (U.S. Highway 93). This becomes Conrad Drive by Woodland Park in 0.6 mile. Follow Conrad Drive about 2 miles and veer right just past the trailer court. Drive a little farther on this road and the access area will be on your right.

## 58. Old Steel Bridge Fishing Access

· · · · · · · · · · · · · · · · · · · · · · · · · · · · · · · ·

The "Old Steel Bridge" fishing access is a nice spot close to Kalispell where families can enjoy the river. There are vault toilets on the west side. A boat launch on this side provides river access. You can play along the river on either side. Unmarked trails on the west shore, north of the bridge, lead nowhere in particular but make a nice walk in the riparian woodlands.

**Directions:** To get to the west side of the Old Steel Bridge Fishing Access, take Kalispell's 2nd Street East off Main Street (U.S. Highway 93). This becomes Conrad Drive by Woodland Park in 0.6 mile. Follow Conrad Drive about 2 miles and veer right just past the trailer court. Drive a little farther on this road and the access area will be on your right.

**Important Information:** Wheelchair accessible on the east side.

# Kalispell

· · · · · · · · · · · · · · · · · · · · · · · · · · · · · · · ·

Kalispell is the largest city in the Flathead Valley and offers the most services. The Kalispell Chamber of Commerce is adjacent to Depot Park (site 59) and can be reached by calling 406-758-2800. Kalispell's central valley location puts it within easy reach of Flathead Lake, Glacier Park, and the Jewel Basin Wilderness Area.

## 59. Depot Park

· · · · · · · · · · · · · · · · · · · · · · · · · · · · · · · ·

This used to be the old train depot and is in downtown Kalispell. The park is a perfect quick-stop as you pass through town. The Kalispell Chamber of Commerce office, 406-758-2800, is in the remodeled train depot on the north side of the park. Let the kids play in the park while you gather local visitor information. The park includes a shaded, grassy area with benches and a fish sculpture by Montana artist Jeffrey Funk. The gazebo there is used for lunchtime concerts at Depot Park Picnics in the Park, held each Wednesday from noon to 1 P.M., mid-June to mid-August. Concerts are also held on an occasional Wednesday. Food vendors are in the park for all of these events.

**Directions:** The park is at the corner of Center Street and U.S. Highway 93, which is also Main Street. Look for the shaded park just south of the US 93 junction with U.S. Highway 2.

**Important Information:** Call Kalispell City Parks and Recreation Department at 406-758-7718 for a schedule of summer concerts.

# 60. Lawrence Park

Nestled between the Buffalo Hills Golf Course and the Stillwater River is this large urban park that local outdoor enthusiasts have pitched in to develop. The park has a sheltered picnic area and restrooms. Drive up the road from the shelter a half mile and you will find a children's playground, picnic area, and some short trails that meander through the woods and by the river. This is a nice quiet park with plenty of room to play.

**Directions:** Take U.S. Highway 93 through Kalispell and go three blocks from the US 93 and U.S. Highway 2 intersection, then go straight onto North Main Street where US 93 veers to the left. This will be marked for Buffalo Hills Golf Course. In a few blocks, you will see a sign to the right for the park. If you end up at the golf course, you've missed this turn.

**Important Information:** For information contact Kalispell City Parks and Recreation, 406-758-7718.

# 61. Lone Pine State Park

This extensive park is just outside the Kalispell city limits, and offers a panoramic view of the valley and mountains. A self-guided interpretive trail has three overlooks, and there is a small interpretive display in the parks building. The park also has picnic tables, a shelter, vault toilets, a volleyball net, and horseshoe pits. There are several easy trails in the wooded areas on park lands. The simplest to find starts by the first parking lot, at the bottom of the grassy area below the picnic area. This trail eventually goes down to Foy's Lake Road and ends at Learn Lane. The hike is steep but makes a nice trip down a ways and back up. When our children were little, we would frequently hike on this trail and I still enjoy it.

**Directions:** The park is 5 miles from downtown Kalispell. Turn west off Main Street (U.S. Highway 93) on either 5th Street West or Center Street. Turn left at the T intersection and follow Meridian Road. This street becomes Foy's Lake Road when it veers to the right by 7th Street West. There is a sign to the park here. Go up the long hill to the top by the lake. The park entrance is on the left at the top of the hill.

**Important Information:** The interpretive trail is designed for wheelchair access. This is a state park fee area open from 10 A.M. to 7 P.M. Call 406-755-2706 for information.

# 62. Foy's Lake Park

Foy's Lake lies in the basin at the top of the hill on Foy's Lake Road, just beyond the turn for Lone Pine State Park. The lake is slightly warmer than some of the others in the area, due to its small size. If you want a quick cool-off dip, this spot will work. The bank is sandy but steep. The facilities provided vary, depending on the money available to support the park and the amount of recent vandalism. There is a boat ramp here and sometimes a dock.

**Directions:** The county-managed park is about 0.5 mile beyond the Lone Pine State Park turnoff (site 61).

# 63. Smith Lake Fishing Access

Smith Lake, near Kila, has a waterfowl production area with fishing access. The extensive marshes and small open water areas are nice for family boating or fishing. This is a good place to see shorebirds and waterfowl—great blue herons, bald eagles, ospreys, black terns, red-necked grebes, and ring-necked ducks to mention a few. You may also see the brilliant mountain bluebirds in the fields along the way. In late March and early April tundra swans are often seen here. Sandhill cranes can be observed in the spring and fall in the grassy meadows. The site includes a small dock and a vault toilet. You can put your boat in at the bridge and paddle along slow-moving Ashley Creek, too.

**Directions:** From Kalispell, take U.S. Highway 2 west for 9 miles, then turn south off the highway, toward Kila, at the fishing access sign. It is 1.6 miles to the left-hand turn that takes you to the lake. The fishing access is 1 mile past the bridge.

**Important Information:** Open year-round at the fishing access. Some parts of the lake are closed for nesting from March 1 to July 1. Contact the Montana Department of Fish, Wildlife & Parks at 406-752-5501 for information about the fishing access, or the U.S. Fish and Wildlife Service, 406-755-7870, for information about waterfowl protection.

# 64. Woodland Park and Bruckhauser Pool

This is a wonderful family park with a pool, playground, rose garden, running-jogging-walking course, horseshoe pits, playing fields, picnic gazebos, barbecue pits, tables, and lots of birds. There is a paved path around a large pond that is good for biking, walking, or rollerblading. The black swans in the pond have been a long-time favorite attraction at the park. Bruckhauser

Pool has a waterslide, a deep-water swimming area, a shallow area for small children, and a kiddie wading pool.

**Directions:** The main Woodland Park entrance is on Conrad Drive. From Main Street (U.S. Highway 93) turn east onto 2nd Street East. As the street goes down the first hill it becomes Conrad Drive. The park entrance is the first left at the bottom of the hill, 0.6 mile from Main Street.

**Important Information:** Bruckhauser pools are all outdoor pools, generally open Memorial Day through Labor Day. There is a small fee for swimming, and some hours are reserved for swimming lessons. Call Kalispell City Parks and Recreation Department at 406-758-7718 for information.

## 65. Hockaday Center for the Arts

The Hockaday is the primary art center for the Flathead Valley. It offers five galleries with a permanent collection of regional artwork, plus rotating exhibits. Children's classes are offered year-round. The center coordinates a large three-day arts fair in Depot Park every year toward the end of July.

**Directions:** The art center is located at the corner of 2nd Avenue East and 3rd Street East, just across from the public library. Turn east on 3rd Street East from Main Street (U.S. Highway 93). The center is on the right in two blocks.

**Important Information:** The art center is open Tuesday through Friday from 10 A.M. to 5 P.M., and Saturday from 10 A.M. to 3 P.M. Admission is $2 for adults, $1 for seniors, and free for kids under 18. The center has wheelchair access at a special side-entrance elevator. Call the center at 406-755-5268 for information.

## 66. Conrad Mansion

If Montana history is a family interest, the Conrad Mansion is an excellent site for a visit. The beautifully maintained flower gardens are another reason. This Norman-style mansion is listed on the National Register of Historic Places and further honored as the most authentic turn-of-the-century home in the Pacific Northwest by the National Register of Historic Places. The mansion was built in 1895 as the home of Charles Conrad, founder of Kalispell. This pioneer was also a Missouri River trader, freighter, and the man responsible for a substantial amount of the valley's development. Tours of the three-level home are given by guides dressed in period costume. On the tour you will find out about the life of the wealthy in early Montana and learn about Kalispell's history. The Conrads used to own extensive areas in the city, including nearby Woodland Park, and Buffalo Hills Golf Course was once Conrad's horse pasture.

There is also an old carriage on display and a gazebo in the gardens. In the winter, a life-sized crèche scene is lit up in the gazebo. You can easily make this a pleasant rest stop with a short walk around the grounds, even if you don't take the tour. From here, Woodland Park (site 64) is only a few blocks.

**Directions:** The mansion is located on Woodland Avenue and 6th Avenue East, between 3rd and 4th Streets. The building and grounds take up an entire city block. From Main Street (U.S. Highway 93) turn east on 3rd or 4th street and you will arrive at the mansion in 6 blocks.

**Important Information:** Open May 15 to October 15. Guided tours are given throughout the day, with the last tour one hour before closing. Summer hours, June 15 to September 15, are 9 A.M. to 8 P.M. For a month before and after the summer season, hours are 10 A.M. to 5:30 P.M. Cost for the tour is $7 for adults and $1 for children under 12. Visiting the grounds is free. For more information, call 406-755-2166.

# Bigfork

The small community of Bigfork has a high interest in and dedication to the arts, as you will see by the number of art galleries on its primary street. Numerous potters and artists reside nearby, and the community hosts a summer arts festival. The Bigfork Playhouse is acclaimed for its professional summer performances (406-837-4886), and local restaurants are touted for their exceptional menus. For more information about Bigfork contact the Bigfork Chamber of Commerce at 406-837-5888.

## 67. Everitt L. Sliter Memorial Park

You can stop by Sliter Memorial Park and enjoy use of the picnic tables, restrooms, and playground equipment at any time, but the highlight at this park happens every Sunday evening from late June to late August. Here, in an open amphitheater called Riverbend Stage, musicians from around the state perform each summer Sunday at 8 P.M. Bring your own lawn chairs or blankets.

**Directions:** The park is located by the Swan River. Turn east from Montana Highway 35 onto Grand Avenue, which leads into the town of Bigfork at the flashing yellow light across from the bowling alley. In 0.5 mile you will see the Bigfork Inn on the left. Electric Avenue turns right here. Take Electric

Avenue through town, stay right, and cross the bridge at Bigfork Bay. This is called Bridge Street and will take you directly to Sliter Memorial Park, which is on the left side just after the bridge. If you continue on Bridge Street past Sliter Park, you will be back at MT 35.

**Important Information:** Mosquito repellent is a good idea during moist summer months. Cost for concerts is $3 for adults and $1 for children under 12. Call 406-837-4848 for the performance schedule.

## 68. The Wild Mile and the Swan River Nature Trail

The Swan River is appropriately named the Wild Mile at this stretch just below an electrical dam. This portion of the river here is designated a class V river, and the frolicking water is the site of an annual springtime whitewater festival. A gravel road above the river on the north side provides viewing access during the festival, and is a favorite place for biking or walking. Stop and look down at the river, but be careful not to let kids get too close to the steep road edge.

There is a metal gate about halfway along this trail. On the river side by the gate is a short spur trail that leads down to the river just below the spillway. It's nice to get down by the water and see the rapids, though wading is obviously not a good idea. The pool behind the spillway is most often still and reflective, in nice contrast to the whitewater. There is another metal gate at the end of the trail, and just beyond is a bridge across the Swan River, under reconstruction in 1998.

**Directions:** Turn east from Montana Highway 35 onto Grand Avenue, which leads into the town of Bigfork at the flashing yellow light across from the bowling alley. In 0.5 mile you will see the Bigfork Inn on the left. Electric Avenue turns right into town, but continue straight up the hill on Grand Avenue. Stay on this road and you will come to a parking area and a metal gate. The Swan River Nature Trail is signed at the trailhead, but not in town.

**Important Information:** Be careful of the fast-flowing water if you take the little ones onto the spillway access trail, and, of course, swimming is not an option.

## 69. Kehoe's Agate Shop

History, rocks, jewelry, and Indian artifacts can be found in this rustic shop, built in 1932, in what was once the community of Holt. The town was a steamboat stop along the Flathead River, the main thoroughfare through the valley. The road now ends near Kehoe's, which has a collection of fossils, petrified wood, minerals, gems, and thunder eggs collected from around the world.

**Directions:** There are three well-marked routes to Kehoe's: two from Montana Highway 35 and one off of Montana Highway 82. Kehoe's is on Holt Drive. From the town of Bigfork, where Grand Avenue goes into Bigfork, turn west onto Holt Drive at the flashing yellow light. (This is a right-hand turn if you are headed south toward Flathead Lake.) Stay on winding Holt Drive for 2.3 miles. Signs will lead you to the agate shop.

**Important Information:** Summer hours are 10 A.M. to 6 P.M. daily. In winter the shop is closed on Mondays, but open from 10 A.M. to 5 P.M. Tuesday through Saturday, and noon to 5 P.M. on Sunday. The USDA Forest Service Swan Lake District Office is on the right, just after the turn onto Holt Drive in Bigfork. Local trail and campground information can be picked up here.

## 70. Royal Tine Elk Farm

If you missed seeing elk in the area and have a desire to do so, here's a sure thing! Drive by the Royal Tine Elk Farm to see these majestic animals from the road. This 600-acre ranch has 100 elk, which are easily viewed through the elk-proof fence. You may see calves in June. The ranch is owned by Justin Haveman.

**Directions:** The farm is on Montana Highway 35, 3 miles south of Bigfork and just north of Woods Bay, by mile marker 28. You will know you are at the elk farm when you see the tall fence on the west side of the highway. Small signs are posted on the fence.

**Important Information:** Cost for the farm tours varies depending on group size. To schedule a tour, call the owner at 406-837-3557. Drive-by viewing is free. Look for a wide spot to pull over as there is no parking area along the highway.

## 71. Gatiss Gardens

This may be one of the prettiest 1.25-mile walks you ever take! Few gardens have the love and attention bestowed upon this 4-acre garden, originally developed by the Gatiss family. Two families of Sibleruds have owned and maintained it since 1990, continuing the tradition of sharing the gardens with the public. You will see flowers here all season, mainly perennials. In fact, there are more than 2,000 varieties of flowers, most identified with signs. A self-guided walk takes you through the gardens, along tiny Mill Creek. You can enjoy the mountain views around you as well as the classical music that often plays from the tool shed. There is also a small (very small) gift shop here. Families can make this a stop on the way to the Creston Fish Hatchery (site 72), which is nearby.

**Directions:** You can find the gardens at Creston on Montana Highway 35 between Kalispell and Bigfork. The gardens are almost exactly 10 miles from Kalispell.

**Important Information:** The gardens are open during the summer season from 9 A.M. to 9 P.M. A free parking area is provided off Broeder Loop Road, just west of the gardens. For more information call 406-755-2418.

## 72. Creston Fish Hatchery

• • • • • • • • • • • • • • • • • • • • • • • • • • • • • • • • •

At one time this federal hatchery supplied fish to Glacier National Park. Today, it provides rainbow trout for Montana's Indian reservations and kokanee salmon for Flathead Lake. The hatchery building has an interpretive display on development of fish eggs and egg hatching. Outside are the raceways where the fish mature. Across the road is Jessup Mill Pond, which is too small for motor boats but where fishing is allowed. This spring-fed pond can hold over one million fish. You may also get to see the fish-eating birds that hang out here—ospreys, great blue herons, kingfishers, magpies, Canada geese, and more. There is a single picnic table by the pond.

**Directions:** From the junction of U.S. Highway 93 and U.S. Highway 2 in Kalispell, take US 2 east to the light by K-Mart where US 2 turns north. Go straight (east) here on Montana Highway 35 toward Bigfork, about 10 miles, until you see the sign for Creston Fish Hatchery on your left. Turn left (north) on Fish Hatchery Road. It is 0.9 mile to the hatchery and Mill Pond.

**Important Information:** The hatchery is open daily from 7:30 A.M. to 4 P.M. Tours are available on weekdays with advance arrangements. For more information call 406-758-6868. There is a wheelchair-accessible restroom in the hatchery building.

## 73. Jewel Basin Hiking Area

• • • • • • • • • • • • • • • • • • • • • • • • • • • • • • • •

The majesty of nearby Glacier National Park eclipses many other hiking areas, but the Jewel Basin, with its sparkling alpine lakes and panoramic mountain vistas, manages to hold its own. The 15,349-acre designated hiking area is tucked away in the Swan Mountains, a rugged range that flanks the Bob Marshall and towers above the Flathead, Swan, and Clearwater river valleys. Jewel Basin has more than 35 miles of hiking trails where horses and motorized vehicles are not allowed. The basin is a grizzly bear corridor for bear migration to the Mission Mountains and provides habitat for wildlife of all kinds. Those who like to fish will be interested to know that many of the 25 lakes in Jewel Basin offer successful fishing opportunities. Check with the Montana Department of Fish, Wildlife & Parks, 406-752-5501, for information on which lakes have been stocked. Also, there's no telling when the huckleberries will be ripe in this basin, but when they are, you can experience a little piece of heaven!

Our first family backpacking trip was into the Jewel Basin and is a good memory. Because it is easily accessible, this is a wonderful day-hiking area, too. During the long summer days, you can actually start hiking in the afternoon and plan an evening hike that gets you out before nightfall. It stays light until 10 P.M. in June, until about 9 P.M. in July, and until 8:30 P.M. in August! The two best family hikes are Picnic Lakes and Birch Lake. If you decide to backpack overnight, set up a base camp at either of these places, and then hike to other areas from camp.

The two Picnic Lakes are 2.5 miles from the trailhead at Camp Misery (don't let this name scare you, it's not miserable there). Begin the hike on Forest Trail 8. You will change trails more than once as you take switchbacks to the "notch," the pass above the trailhead. Picnic Lakes are nestled in the basin at the top within a mile from the pass. The trail to Birch Lake is Forest Trail 717 which is actually an old road. Halfway to Birch Lake, switch to Forest Trail 7.

If you are adventurous, and have the time and energy to coax your kids to mountaintops, you can take the trail to the top of Mount Aeneas, elevation 7,530 feet. The trail from Picnic Lakes is a relatively short, but steep, hike that rewards you with a 360-degree view of the Flathead Valley, the Bob Marshall, the Great Bear Wilderness, Glacier National Park, the Mission Mountains, and the Swan Range. We have often seen mountain goats on the trail by the microwave station and once saw a badger at the top! The peak can be reached from the Birch Lake Trail junction of Forest Trails 717 and 7. **Directions:** From Kalispell, take U.S. Highway 93 south 7 miles and turn east toward Bigfork on Montana Highway 82. Take this to Montana Highway 35 and turn right. Go to the flashing light and turn left onto Montana Highway 83. Follow MT 83 about 3 miles to the flashing light at Echo Lake and turn left, north, onto Echo Lake Road. There is a sign here to Jewel Basin. From this turn it is about 2 miles to a right turn onto Foothill Road. Just about where the pavement ends, in 0.9 mile, is Forest Road 5392. This road goes straight ahead, while Foothill Road turns left. Unfortunately, signs here seem to be frequently stolen, so it will probably not be marked. If you come to the road for Strawberry Lake, you have gone too far. You can also access Foothill Road from MT 35 out of Kalispell, but Foothill Road is long and winding. It is simpler to come in from Echo Lake Road. Once on FR 5392, it is 6.5 miles to the parking lot, called Camp Misery. The trailheads take off from here.

**Important Information:** Be aware that Jewel Basin receives high visitor use and you may see numerous people on the trail. Also, with recreation dollars tight, the Forest Service has difficulty maintaining trails or staffing busy trailheads. Low-impact, clean use of the Jewel Basin area is a must. Maps are available from the Flathead National Forest Supervisor's Office at 1935 Third Avenue East in Kalispell, or from Hungry Lake Ranger District in Hungry Horse at 406-387-4253. A quad map from a sporting goods store may be useful, too.

# Whitefish

The town of Whitefish is known as a recreation center in the valley, in part because of the Big Mountain downhill ski area, but also because of other developed outdoor activities: cross-country skiing, boating, biking, hiking, and horseback riding. Forest land was originally cleared to build the town, from whence came the nickname, "Stumptown." The town has a history with railway lines and Amtrak still maintains a stop here. For more information contact the Whitefish Chamber of Commerce at 406-862-3501.

## 74. Whitefish Lake City Beach

This free-use city beach has picnic tables and shelters, swimming docks, a boat launch, and food concessions. Paddle boats, sea cycles, and kayaks are available for rent.

**Directions:** To get to the beach, turn north off U.S. Highway 93 in Whitefish onto Baker Avenue. Cross the viaduct a couple of blocks away, and stay to the left on Edgewood Drive at the other side of the viaduct. Edgewood leads to the beach.

**Important Information:** Open 11 A.M. to 7 P.M. with lifeguards during summertime only. Contact Whitefish Parks and Recreation at 406-863-2470.

## 75. Whitefish Lake State Park

This pretty park, set amongst woodland hills, is large enough to offer good boating activities, and is a pleasant place for a brief nature encounter. This 10-acre facility is located on the west shore of the lake just 3 miles from Whitefish. The wooded park has a swimming area, boat launch, picnic tables, camping, and toilets. There are no lifeguards here, but the swimming area is marked, and there is a beach. Anglers usually go for the northern pike and whitefish in the lake, but there are also trout. Fall is particularly colorful along the lakeshore.

**Directions:** Drive 1 mile west of Whitefish on U.S. Highway 93. Turn right (north) just past the golf course at the state park sign, and you will reach the park a mile down the road.

**Important Information:** Wheelchair accessible. Open year-round. Call the park at 406-862-3991.

## 76. Whitefish Museum

The Stumptown Historical Society bought the old Burlington Northern Railroad depot for $1 in 1990 when the railroad built a new depot and no longer needed the old one. The old depot now holds an interesting museum of local history, including photographs of the town of Whitefish when the streets were literally filled with tree stumps. The area was once a forest but the trees were cut down to create the town. The town got its nickname "Stumptown" from these early days. Also in the museum are numerous railroad artifacts, a telegraph operator's desk, and period clothing. A 1942 locomotive has been restored and can be found in the adjoining parking area.

**Directions:** The museum is one block from downtown Whitefish at the north end of Central Avenue and is open 11 A.M. to 3 P.M., Monday through Saturday. Admission is free; donations are accepted. Call 406-862-0067 for information.

## 77. Big Mountain Ski and Summer Resort

Look down to see strikingly colorful mountain wildflowers, and look around for spectacular panoramic vistas of the Flathead Valley and Rocky Mountain wilderness. From a high mountain perch in the Whitefish Range, Big Mountain Ski Resort and the USDA Forest Service offer an array of summer activities attractive to families. Regardless of your budget, a trip to the mountain is entertaining and refreshing.

A mountain bike ride or hike can be found on Big Mountain for any age and all ability levels. A specially designed trail system has mountain bike trails from 0.7 mile to 8 miles long, with varying degrees of difficulty. The recently founded Mountain Bike Academy offers lessons and guided mountain bike tours for a fee. Call for information about free weekend guided bicycle tours and special kids programs, 406-862-1995. Families can bring their own bicycles and helmets or rent them at Big Mountain. In fact, even hiking boots can be rented at the mountain. Hiking trails at the mountain include a 0.75-mile path atop the summit, the 3.4-mile Flower Point Hike, and the 5.6-mile Danny On Trail. Many people hike up the Danny On Trail to get to the summit, which also avoids the lift charge. See separate site listings for information on these hikes.

The Glacier Chaser gondola ride takes riders up 2,000 feet of vertical gain in about 10 minutes. The Summit House at the top has food, restrooms, and a deck with tables. A restaurant at the summit offers cafeteria-style lunches and snacks, along with great views. Tables, both inside and outside the building, are available for picnicking. There are other restaurants in the resort area below.

The USDA Forest Service operates an Environmental Education Center with interpretive displays that include wildlife, nests, skins, skulls, wildflowers, birds, maps, and a children's corner with interactive skill stations. There is also a historic photo display of Forest Service lands. Forest Service personnel are on hand daily and give guided 20-minute wildflower walks at 11 A.M. and 3 P.M. A slide show is presented at 2 P.M. Call the Big Mountain, 406-862-2900, for additional summer hiking offerings and to check on hours.

If these activities don't suit you, there are many others to choose from, including guided horseback rides for ages 7 and up, corral rides for younger children, wagon rides, barbecues, telescope stargazing, fly-casting in a catch-and-release pond, concerts, festivals, tennis, and golf. Lodging can be had in the resort area for deluxe or economy rates.

**Directions:** To get to Big Mountain, take U.S. Highway 93 north into Whitefish and follow the highway where it turns left (west) in Whitefish. Turn right (north) onto Wisconsin Avenue, two blocks away, and cross the viaduct. Stay on Wisconsin Avenue all the way to the right turn onto the Big Mountain Road by the flashing yellow light. From here the road gets narrower and steep, but is paved and in good condition.

**Important Information:** Helmets are mandatory for all bikers using the biking trails. The Forest Service center is open 10 A.M. to 5 P.M. every day during the summer season, which is the end of May to the end of September. The chairlift operates between 10 A.M. and 6:30 P.M. during the same dates. In July and August, lift hours are extended to 9 P.M. Round-trip tickets for the chairlift are $9.50 for adults and $7.25 for senior riders and young people ages 7 to 18. Kids 6 and under ride free. After 6 P.M. the chairlift rates go down to $6.25. Season passes are available for $80, $40 for ski passholders. The chairlift charge for bicycle and rider is $17.75 for an all-day pass. A one-way ride costs $12.75.

Call 800-862-2900 or 406-862-2900 for information about activities, events, and prices. An information and ticket center is located in the octagonal building near the chairlift. For lodging information call 406-862-1960 or 800-859-3526. Check the Internet at www.bigmtn.com/resort for information, too.

## 78. East Rim Trail—Big Mountain

• • • • • • • • • • • • • • • • • • • • • • • • • • • • • • • •

This 0.75-mile hike atop the summit area of Big Mountain is short, but the sweeping panorama makes it sweet. The marked trail begins at the Summit House and follows a portion of the Danny On Trail (site 80), then swings around the eastern edge of the summit and returns.

**Directions:** The journey begins with the chairlift ride to the summit of Big Mountain (see previous listing for rate and time information). Begin the rim trail at the signed trailhead for the Danny On Trail, about 100 yards from the Summit House.

**Important Information:** Make sure you bring a warm jacket, as it is sometimes cold and windy on top and mountain weather can change quickly.

## 79. Flower Point Trail—Big Mountain

• • • • • • • • • • • • • • • • • • • • • • • • • • • • • • • •

After feasting on the view up the Big Mountain chairlift, you can go on to dessert. Scenic vistas of the Flathead Valley from a 7,000-foot elevation and views into Glacier National Park can be enjoyed on the 2.4-mile-round-trip hike. Along the way, you will see numerous wildflowers, especially Indian paintbrush.

**Directions:** See directions for the Danny On Trail (site 80).

**Important Information:** Make sure you bring a warm jacket, as it is sometimes cold and windy on top, and mountain weather can change quickly.

## 80. Danny On Trail—Big Mountain

• • • • • • • • • • • • • • • • • • • • • • • • • • • • • • • •

Danny On was a popular Montana nature photographer and a silviculturist with the Forest Service. When he died in a skiing accident on Big Mountain, the Forest Service decided to name this trail in his memory. Nothing could be more appropriate, for the views from this trail, like Danny's photos, cover expansive mountain vistas as well as the minute detail of colorful Rocky Mountain wildflowers. For years I hiked this trail with a group of mothers who all had small children. We would hike together, herding our kids on the ridge trail. I will never forget the year I had a two-and-a-half-year-old in a backpack and a newborn in a frontpack! This 5.6-mile hike has the advantage of having a chairlift to the top that eliminates any steep uphill climb. However, the hike to Flower Point makes the trip a shorter 3.8-mile hike with a ride back down the lift. Trail maps are available at the chairlift and at the Summit House at the top.

**Directions:** Catch a ride on the Big Mountain Glacier Chaser chairlift. The trail starts about 100 yards from the Summit House and ends up back at the chairlift area at the bottom of the hill.

**Important Information:** Make sure you bring a warm jacket, as it is sometimes cold and windy on top, and mountain weather can change quickly. See site 77 for chairlift information.

## 81. Tally Lake State Park

This is reputed to be Montana's deepest natural lake and is a good place to see birds. Look for ospreys, bald eagles, and common loons which all nest here. The lake viewpoints on the road to Tally Lake Campground near mile markers 6 and 7 are good viewing areas. You may see dipper birds and warblers along Logan Creek, which flows by the campground. Listen for great horned owls and northern saw-whet owls, too. A 1-mile hike starts from the campground and gently climbs up a hill above the lake. It has nice views of Tally Lake along the way and at the end. Look for a sign identifying the hiking trail on the way to the north shore sites of the campground. There is a small parking area by the sign.

**Directions:** From Kalispell take U.S. Highway 93 north 1 mile to Reserve Street (there is a stoplight here). Turn west and go 4 miles to Farm-to-Market Road. Turn right (north) and the Tally Lake Road, Forest Road 913, is in 9 miles, signed Tally Lake Campground. Turn left and follow this gravel road to the campground.

**Important Information:** Look out for traffic along the forest road. Overnight camping is $9 and there is a $3-per-vehicle fee for day use. For information contact Tally Lake Ranger District in Whitefish, 406-862-2508.

## 82. Beaver Lake Area

This out-of-the-way area actually has several little lakes: Murray, Rainbow, Beaver, Little Beaver, Woods, and Dollar. It is an undeveloped day-use area operated by the Montana Department of Fish, Wildlife & Parks. Some of the lakes have boat access and vault toilets while others have no facilities. Beaches are undeveloped and road access may be difficult to some of the lakes. Beaver Lake is the easiest to reach and the road is not bad. During our visit, a bear with two cubs were seen in the area. Deer and bird life are commonly observed.

**Directions:** Go north of Whitefish on U.S. Highway 93 about 20 miles, and turn right (east) at the sign near mile marker 135. In 1.7 miles there is a large sign and map of the area.

**Important Information:** The roads to the lakes vary in accessibility. Our experience is that, when the road begins to get rutted, it is best to turn around, unless you have four-wheel drive. We recommend that you make a simple drawing of the map near the entrance as you go in. There are no signs along the roads and you might wander some (though wandering can be interesting). Mosquito repellent is not a bad idea.

# 83. LeBeau Roadless Area and Finger Lake

The LeBeau Roadless Area is not only roadless, but mostly trail-less as well. In this 5000-acre protected area, there are only two lowland lake trails. Those who want to explore more of the area must go in armed with topographic maps and a sense of adventure.

However, Finger Lake is 1.7 miles from the trailhead and is a delightful lake. The trail is easy and will take you to a small ridge, then down to a cliff area just above the lake. From here you can go down to the lake itself. There is ony about 100 feet of an uphill climb over a ridge and down the other side to the lake. My kids enjoyed this lake a great deal and made me promise to bring them back. There is a spur trail at Finger Lake that goes from the cliffs down to the lake and along the lakeshore for a ways.

**Directions:** Take U.S. Highway 93 about 22 miles north of Whitefish. The left hand turnoff to the west is marked Legoni Lake. We found it easiest to turn at the third dirt road, which is about 100 feet from the sign on the highway. Follow this road across a creek and the railroad tracks. About 0.1 mile after the tracks, the road makes a hairpin turn to the left. The campground is 0.4 mile from this point. A couple of roads turn off along the way, but stay on the main road. The parking area is on the right just before the Upper Stillwater Campground. When you see the trailhead sign on the road, park and walk along the logging road until you reach the trail sign for Finger Lake. Follow the logging road to the right here, and within a few feet you will see the trail lead off to the left. A little more than halfway to the lake, the trail forks. Take the trail to the ridge top rather than the one down to the meadow.

**Important Information:** Mosquito repellent is a must, and you should bring your own drinking water. There are 50- to 60-foot bluffs here, so hang on to little ones, and be sure you give older kids rules about the cliffs. Despite the sound of this, the lake is great fun!

# Columbia Falls and Hungry Horse

Two other towns in the Flathead Valley, Columbia Falls and Hungry Horse, are great places to visit on your way to Glacier National Park. Columbia Falls is at the north end of the Flathead Valley and has one of the world's largest aluminum extrusion plants. Hungry Horse is 5 miles beyond Glacier Park and through narrow Badrock Canyon.

If you need a break en route to Glacier National Park or just want some entertainment, there are varied roadside attractions on U.S. Highway 2 between Columbia Falls and West Glacier. Look for go-cart tracks, gift shops featuring Indian art and nature items, a maze with bumper boats and other activities, and a trout pond, to name a few. The town of Columbia Falls also has some imagination for different tourist attractions—you'll find the multi-activity Just for Fun attraction on the west end of town as well as the Montana Wildlife Museum. There is a water slide park just west of the junction of Montana Highway 206 and US 2. For more information contact the Columbia Falls Chamber of Commerce at 406-892-2072.

## 84. Pinewood Park

This park is in downtown Columbia Falls and has a swimming pool, picnic tables, and restrooms.

**Directions:** Take Montana Highway 40 (also marked U.S. Highway 2) right (east) into Columbia Falls at the light by the Blue Moon Nite Club at the northern end of US 2. Go into town and turn right (south) onto 4th Street. The park is at the corner and can be seen from the highway.

**Important Information:** Call 406-892-3500 for information about the pool.

## 85. Maranette Park

Maranette Park is at the eastside city limits of Columbia Falls on Montana Highway 40 (also marked U.S. Highway 2). It has picnic tables, a shelter, vault toilets, and grills. The Chamber of Commerce and a visitor center are located by the entrance.

**Directions:** Turn south from MT 40 (US 2) at the east side of town, directly at the "Welcome to Columbia Falls" sign. This is 1.5 miles west toward Columbia Falls from the US 2 and MT 206 junction.

# 86. House of Mystery

One of the more unusual U.S. Highway 2 attractions is the House of Mystery. The enigma is explained as a gravitational vortex that causes trees in a small area to grow at an angle. Families can play with the phenomenon in a leaning house that sits in the vortex. The angle of the building, and possibly "The Force," creates a different perspective on life that kids of all ages have fun exploring. Whether optical illusion or gravitational mystery, the perceptual phenomenon is a different experience. The facility has a small gift shop, picnic area, and a two-story outhouse, used for pictures only.

**Directions:** This mysterious house sits at the edge of Badrock Canyon around mile marker 140. It is about halfway between Columbia Falls and Hungry Horse on US 2, 13 miles from West Glacier.

**Important Information:** Open April to November 9 A.M. to 9 P.M. Entry prices are $4 for adults and $3 for children ages 6–12. Kids under 6 are admitted free. Call 406-892-1210 for more information.

## Huckleberries, *Vaccinium membranaceum*

Few things in life compare to fresh, wild huckleberries. You are in huckleberry country and you'll know it when you go through the town of Hungry Horse, a self-proclaimed center for the small purple treasures. Check out the offerings at the Huckleberry Patch restaurant and gift shop on U.S. Highway 2—you can get huckleberry everything there. You'll find these delightful berries in other areas of the state too. If you decide to try huckleberry-picking on your own, stop by a Forest Service ranger station to check out what they look like and find out where they can be picked. July and August are good months but the pickin's vary depending on the weather and the altitude. Keep in mind that bears love these things, too, so sing a joyful tune or make noise while you're picking.

# 87. North American Wildlife Museum

If you missed seeing any wildlife in Glacier National Park or want to know what to look for before you enter, this museum will prove an educational, fun encounter for kids and adults. The one-room exhibit area has 85 animal and bird mounts artistically arranged to simulate an outdoor setting. The exhibit includes mostly native species, but also a few unusual ones not found in the area. An eerie loon call sets the tone for the exhibit, and you can hear an elk bugle, too. The museum has unique gift shop items, a teepee, an outdoor barbecue, and an RV park and campground.

**Directions:** The museum is on U.S. Highway 2, between Coram and West Glacier, 5 miles from Glacier National Park. Look for it between mile markers 147 and 148.

**Important Information:** Open May 1 to October 31, 9 A.M. to 9 P.M., seven days a week. Cost for the museum is $3 for adults and $2 for kids ages 6 to 14; kids under 6 enter free. Group and family rates are available. Call 406-387-4018 for more information.

# GLACIER NATIONAL PARK

. . . . . . . . . . . . . . . . . . . . . . . . . . . . . . .

Glacier National Park is a spectacular national treasure, truly a gift to experience. In this rugged landscape, we are taken into a world that touches us deeply. There are many places in the Rocky Mountains of Montana where the inspiration of nature fills us in this way, but few places that have this kind of accessibility for families. Glacier National Park offers ringside seats for an exquisite performance. Take the time to bring your family to this phenomenal park. And then, take the time to enjoy being there. Bask in the view, appreciate nature's rhythms, and place importance on simple acts of joy. Allow play to be your destination, for every place here is magnificent in its own way.

**General Information:** There are both entrance and campground fees for Glacier National Park. The main park entrance stations are at both ends of Going-to-the-Sun Road—West Glacier and St. Mary. Other entrance stations are found at Many Glacier, Two Medicine, Camas Creek, and Polebridge. Week-long passes are $10 per vehicle, and $5 for entrance by foot, motorcycle, or bicycle. An annual Glacier National Park Pass is $20, and allows entry as often as you like. Golden Eagle Passes, good for any national park in the United States, are $50. All listed costs were effective in 1998, and may have since been raised.

Check carefully through the park materials given to you at the entrance station for important information about facilities or warnings. Be sure to read the section on bears in the introductory chapter of this book, for you are now in their territory. Also, be aware of the rapid weather changes possible in the mountains, and the real threat hypothermia poses, especially to small bodies. Remember that the glacial waters here are truly one step from ice, and can be a serious danger. Wading in a creek can be fun on a hot day, but an unplanned immersion can result in disaster. You are responsible here for the safety of your family—be alert.

Families will find facilities and activities to meet varying degrees of comfort in Glacier National Park. If you are new to the outdoors, consider staying in one of the lodges, cabins, or motels. If you want to camp, bring along your tent. For maximum success, think through the limitations of your children's abilities and plan activities to match them.

There are thirteen park service campgrounds in the park. Most campgrounds are available on a "first come, first served" basis, and are generally $12 per night. Sites at Fish Creek and St. Mary campgrounds may be reserved ahead of time through the National Park Service Reservation System by calling 800-365-CAMP. Campsites are limited to eight people and two vehicles per site. Most campgrounds have drinking water, restrooms with flush toilets, and cold running water. Utility hook-ups are not provided.

Back in the early 1900s, the Great Northern Railroad developed a tourism circuit in Glacier National Park for East Coast vacationers. This included the building of several impressive lodges. Tourists were taken from lodge to lodge via train or horse. Most of these phenomenal lodges are still in full operation. Glacier Park, Inc. (GPI) operates all but one of the lodges in the park, plus the Prince of Wales Hotel in Waterton, Alberta, and the Glacier Park Lodge in East Glacier. GPI also maintains other lodging in the park. Call 602-207-6000 for information and reservations. Suggestions for lodging outside the park can be obtained through the Glacier Country Tourism Commission at 800-338-5072 or Flathead Convention and Visitors Association, 800-543-3105.

Most of the hotels and visitor centers in Glacier National Park, a few trails, and three campgrounds are wheelchair accessible. The park service provides a complete listing of accessible facilities and services in the free brochure, *Accessibility for Disabled Visitors.*

Call 406-888-7800 for any information about Glacier National Park, or research the park website at http://www.nps.gov/glac/.

**Activity Information:** To gain a deeper appreciation of the park's natural systems, participate in guided educational programs, or pick up one of the many natural history books on Glacier. The National Park Service offers regularly scheduled interpretive programs and guided hikes. Contact park headquarters, 406-888-7800, for information. Another exceptional learning resource is the Glacier Institute, a nonprofit environmental education organization, which offers excellent field courses on various cultural and natural resource topics in the park. Special one-day family courses can be attended for a reasonable rate, and longer courses are available. Contact the Glacier Institute at 406-888-5215, June through August, or 406-755-1211, year-round, and check the web site at http://www.nps.gov/glac/inst.htm. The Glacier Natural History Association provides trail guides and other publications via a catalog, which can be obtained by calling 406-888-5756; their website can be found at http://www.nps.gov/glac/gnha1.htm.

An outdoor experience can be especially memorable when we look around us in a new way. Viewing Glacier National Park from a boat is one such opportunity. A variety of water-oriented trips are available in the park, from calm lake canoe paddles to wild class IV river runs. Tour boat rides are available through Glacier Park, Inc. on Lake McDonald, St. Mary Lake, Two Medicine Lake, and in Many Glacier. Fares vary but are under $10 per person, half-price for children ages 4 to 12, and free for kids under 4. GPI also has small boat rentals at Apgar, Lake McDonald, Two Medicine, and Many Glacier. For more information on boat tours, you can call the sites directly during the summer: 406-888-5727 for Lake McDonald, 406-732-4480 for Many Glacier, and 406-732-4430 for the St. Mary and Two Medicine areas. Winter contact may be made at 406-257-2426. Also, there is e-mail (gpboats@montanaweb.com) and a website (www.montanaweb.com/gpboats).

There are more than 700 miles of trails in Glacier National Park. The trails listed here are selected as introductory hikes suitable for families with young children. However, they are delightful hikes that all ages will enjoy. Anyone planning to hike in the backcountry overnight must obtain a permit within 24 hours of the trip. Permits may be reserved in advance by mail or in person. Pets must be on a leash in the park, and are not allowed on roads closed to motor vehicles or trails.

Bicycles are not allowed on trails, except for the Apgar Bicycle Trail. Cyclists may bike the roads, but should know that park roads are narrow and summer traffic is heavy. Biking can be done in campgrounds, and there are some quieter roads where a cycling family would feel safe.

Contact the Glacier Country Tourism Commission, 800-338-5072, or Flathead Convention and Visitors Association, 800-543-3105, for other information on outfitters, guided river float trips, and backcountry guide services in the national park.

# The West Entrance

The heavily forested west side of Glacier Park has five glacial valleys, each with a good-sized glacial lake and opportunities for camping, hiking, and fishing. Lake McDonald, the largest lake in the park, is the most used and developed. Logging, Quartz, Bowman, and Kintla lakes are north of Lake McDonald and are referred to as "the North Fork." Logging and Quartz lakes are accessible only by trail. A ranger station at Polebridge services these northern areas. The main west entrance station is at West Glacier, and the west side visitor center is located at Apgar.

# 88. West Glacier

Stock up on last-minute items at this park-entrance town where you can find the bare necessities. Park maps and information are provided at the entrance station just up the road, or at the headquarters offices, to the right shortly after you cross the Flathead River. Belton Chalet, a historic building that is officially the area's first hotel, is in West Glacier, and is currently under renovation. The Alberta Visitor Centre (site 89) is very informative.

**Directions:** West Glacier straddles the railroad tracks 32 miles northeast of Kalispell on U.S. Highway 2. The Belton Chalet is on the right-hand side of US 2 just past the train trestle (don't go under the trestle). To get to the main part of West Glacier and head toward Glacier National Park, turn left off US 2 at the sign for the park, and go through the train trestle underpass.

# 89. Alberta Visitor Centre

The Alberta Visitor Centre is a good place to find out about Canada's Waterton National Park, which borders Glacier National Park. The two parks are jointly designated as a World Heritage Site. This classification recognizes the outstanding natural and cultural value of these parks and provides resource protection across political boundaries. Naturalists from both countries are on hand to answer questions. The Centre has excellent interpretive exhibits for children and adults. After being greeted at the door by a *Tyrannosaurus rex* replica, our kids discovered the interactive bobsled exhibit and we could hardly pull them away. The nicely done taxidermy display of wildlife creates both interest in and excitement for the upcoming park explorations.

**Directions:** Alberta Visitor Centre is in West Glacier, immediately to your right after you turn off U.S. Highway 2 and go through the train trestle underpass.

**Important Information:** Open from mid-May until late September, 9 A.M. to 6 P.M. For more information call 406-888-5743.

# The North Fork

For a quiet experience in Glacier Park, explore the northwest area, where the north fork of the Flathead River marks the western boundary of the park. Here you can enjoy this wild stretch of river and appreciate the land much as it was before the settlers came. The Polebridge Ranger Station services the North Fork, and is about halfway from West Glacier to the Canadian border.

Mountain biking makes sense in the North Fork, for you could consider yourself lucky to see cars here. The roads are unpaved except for short stretches at the south end and up around Polebridge. You can start a bike trip at Polebridge on either of the two dirt roads that go out from the town. The Bowman Lake ride is a hilly 6 miles, one way. The Kintla Lake road is much easier, though it is 14 miles to the lake.

Canoeing and fishing are possible on both Bowman and Kintla lakes, though there are no facilities for boat rentals. Bowman Lake has the best day-use facilities and is less of a drive. Family activities can include playing on the lakeshore and hiking up the lake trail. Primitive campgrounds are located at Bowman and Kintla lakes.

The Polebridge Mercantile is a historic building worth stopping at, if not for the last minute items it provides, then just for the fun of seeing it. It won't be hard to find on the North Fork Road, for there isn't much else up there. For lodging, one facility is the North Fork Hostel. If you are interested, call 406-756-4780 well ahead of time to reserve bunks. The kitchen, washrooms, and other facilities are shared. The Polebridge Mercantile has cabins available, as well; call 406-888-5105.

There are two routes through the North Fork. The Outside North Fork Road, or Forest Road 210, is in the Flathead National Forest. It parallels the park boundary for 33 miles to the Canadian border. The more rugged Inside North Fork Road, sometimes referred to as Glacier Route Seven, is on park service land and ends at Kintla Lake. It is aptly described as a 15-miles-per-hour, remote, scenic, wildlife-viewing road. The two roads converge near Polebridge. The Polebridge Mercantile and Polebridge Ranger Station can be reached easily from either the Inside or Outside North Fork Road.

To reach the Outside North Fork Road from the West Glacier park entrance, go straight to the T intersection and turn left (west) onto Camas Road. This connects with the Outside Road with a right-hand turn north, in 11 miles. Eleven miles farther turn right (east) to reach Polebridge.

To take the Inside North Fork Road, turn left (west) at the T intersection just beyond the West Glacier park entrance. Follow Camas Road 1.3 miles and turn right (east) and then head north toward Fish Creek Campground. Go past the campground road turnoff, and the road becomes the Inside North Fork Road. A small red sign indicates the transition and reminds you that this scenic road is rugged. It is 28 miles to Polebridge Ranger Station via the Inside Road.

Folks in the North Fork trade civilization for solitude, so don't expect to see too many people there, and don't rely on having access to many facilities in this area. The North Fork may have more bears than people, and, in fact, has one of the densest populations of grizzlies in the contiguous 48 states. All bear precautions apply (see page 14).

The North Fork of the Flathead River is both wild and pristine. Be careful if wading, as the river runs fast and cold. This is definitely a river for rafts and not canoes. Only experienced rafters should attempt floating this river. Guided floats are available. Call Glacier Country Tourism Commission at 800-338-5072 for names of rafting companies.

Polebridge Ranger Station is generally open from 9 A.M. to 5:30 P.M., June through Labor Day. Call park headquarters, 406-888-7800, for information about the North Fork area.

## 90. Covey Trail

This 1.5-mile loop trail by the Polebridge Ranger Station was built in 1997. It begins right by the station and wanders through a meadow, primarily so that visitors can enjoy mountain flowers and views.

**Directions:** Take either the Inside or Outside North Fork Road to the Polebridge Ranger Station. The trail begins right by the station.

## 91. Hidden Meadow Trail

This is a pleasant, short, family hike through a peaceful meadow and an area burned in the Red Bench Fire of 1988. The 1.2-mile hike (2.4 miles round trip) passes by an old homestead and ends at two ponds that provide good waterfowl viewing.

**Directions:** Hidden Meadow Trail is on the Inside North Fork Road. It can also be reached via the Outside North Fork Road by turning east at Polebridge,

# Bear Grass, *Xerophyllum tenax*

What's bear grass got to do with bears? Nothing, really, except that early explorers saw it in the same ecosystems where they frequently saw bears. The explorers named the plant bear grass, though it has also been called bear lily, elk grass, and Indian basket grass. The plant has more to do with elk, which eat the whole thing, and mountain goats, which only eat the parts of it that are around in winter when not much else is. Indians wove clothing and made baskets with the leaves.

The Glacier National Park hallmark flower has a fist-sized bunch of white flowers on stalks that can be as tall as 5 feet. The narrow grasslike leaves stand in bunches on the ground. These are slick to walk on, and more than one hiker has been sent sliding down a hill after stepping on the leaves growing on a slope!

and taking the road north to the ranger station. Here you access the Inside road and follow it south for 3.5 miles. You will see a sign marked Lone Pine Prairie and a small parking lot. The trailhead here is marked.

# Lake McDonald Valley

Lake McDonald is the longest and deepest lake in the park, carved 472 feet deep in places and 10 miles long by glaciers. Kootenai Indians called this the *Yakilahkwilnamki*, "The Sacred Dancing Place," and held ceremonies on the lakeshore. The sparkling clear waters and prominent mountain views no doubt contribute to the lake's continued popularity.

This well-used area has been developed with four campgrounds, the west side visitor center, visitor services at Apgar Village, and an amphitheater. Historic Lake McDonald Lodge is near the head of the lake, where a boat tour is available.

Going-to-the-Sun Road traverses the southern boundary of the lake. This road provides easy access to the lakeshore and banks of McDonald Creek, which empties into the lake. There are easy woodland trails to be pursued in this valley, including paved trails at Apgar Village and Avalanche Creek. The National Park Service conducts interpretive programs and guided hikes in the area.

The Lake McDonald Valley sits just beyond the West Glacier entrance station and can be reached from the east, via the Going-to-the-Sun Road over Logan Pass.

Park rangers from headquarters and the Apgar Visitor Center are available for visitor assistance. There is a ranger station at the head of Lake McDonald. Contact park headquarters at 406-888-7800 for more information about west side activities.

## 92. Apgar Village, Visitor Center, and Campground

The pristine beauty of 10-mile-long Lake McDonald and opportunities for simple fun make Apgar a fulfilling experience in the Rocky Mountain wilderness. The area includes a campground, picnic facilities, visitor center, amphitheater, restaurant, and motels. Families can entertain themselves with biking, hiking, camping, water play, and interpretive displays. The Apgar Visitor Center features exhibits on Glacier's plants and animals. Because Apgar is one of the lowest elevations in the park, it is one of the most easily accessible areas year-round. This makes it a good location for fall and spring activities when the volume of visitors drops.

One of my favorite ways to enjoy Apgar is to simply soak up the inspiring vista from the lake's edge, looking to the distant north at some of the most stunning peaks in the Rocky Mountains. Over the years I have done this innumerable times. While I sit my children do kid things—toss rocks into the lake, explore the shore, and always (no matter what the age) end up in the water, giggling as they manage to get soaking wet. Somehow they don't seem to notice that the water is icy cold. These are truly shining moments in the spirit of family play. Many of our visits to "The Park," as locals say, include a picnic on the lakeshore just for this reason. We usually bring our bikes, too, and ride along the Apgar Bicycle Trail (site 93). Regularly scheduled interpretive programs are held in the amphitheater.

**Directions:** Enter the park at West Glacier, go through the entrance station, and turn left where the road comes to a T, then turn right at the sign for Apgar. The Apgar Visitor Center is located at the edge of Apgar Village, on the left. If you keep going on this road you will come to the lake. The road veers right here toward the campground, picnic area, and amphitheater.

**Important Information:** The visitor center is open from early May through October and on winter weekends. Hours from late June to early September are 8 A.M. to 8 P.M. At other times the center closes at 4:30 P.M. Almost every place is wheelchair accessible here, including the bike path.

## 93. Apgar Bicycle Trail

Here's a very useful path through park woodlands. Hike, bike, or roller blade along this 1.5-mile paved trail that ends up near the West Glacier entrance station. There are no scenic mountain vistas along the way, but exercise is easy to get and family-friendly. After 0.2 mile, the trail crosses the road and the Apgar Bridge over McDonald Creek is to the right. Take a quick side trip to the bridge to enjoy looking at the creek. Back on the trail, when you reach what appears to be the end of the trail, it actually crosses the road. This part of the trail goes into the park housing and maintenance area and is generally used by park employees only.

You can extend your Apgar biking experience by riding around the four Apgar campground loops. Much of this is paved and there is very little traffic. The campground is a short distance from the Apgar Bicycle Trail on the Apgar loop road. Bring a lunch and picnic along the lake.

**Directions:** The trail begins in Apgar Village just before the visitor center and is marked with a small, brown trail sign. There is a convenient parking lot next to the Red Schoolhouse Gift Shop, or you can park in the boat launch area and ride to the entrance.

**Important Information:** This is the only Glacier National Park trail where biking is permitted. Every year on this trail, there is at least one black bear siting, or report of a bicyclist being followed by a bear. These haven't ever ended negatively, but it is a good idea to be aware that you are in bear country. Wheelchair accessible.

## 94. Rocky Point Hike and McDonald Lake Trail

The Rocky Point Hike Trail is an easy hike through the forest and has the added advantage of frequent access to Lake McDonald. This 0.7-mile hike (1.4 miles round trip) can be extended to a longer hike if you want to walk up McDonald Lake Trail.

**Directions:** There are two ways to start the Rocky Point Hike Trail. You can begin at a trailhead for McDonald Lake Trail on the Inside North Fork Road, which avoids going through the campground. Go past the entrance to Fish Creek Campground, and look for the trailhead right before the bridge over Fish Creek. There is a parking lot here. There is also an unsigned trailhead at campsite 174, in loop "D" of Fish Creek Campground. Rocky Point Hike Trail begins at the left side of the campsite, as you face the lake. We discovered that you can also pick up the trail next to campsite 112 by walking down the closed road to the old boathouse and turning left onto the trail. To follow the McDonald Lake Trail, take the signed left fork just before you reach Rocky Point. The trail goes 4.1 miles.

**Important Information:** The trailheads are not well marked but can be found fairly easily with the directions given here.

## 95. Camas Creek Road

The forest and meadowlands along Camas Creek Road are good habitat for moose, deer, elk, grizzly bear, and black bear. We often drive this road at dusk just to look for bears, but our success rate is probably 20 percent or less. I still remember the bear we saw sitting by the side of the road, eating a McDonalds paper cup. No one has ever been hurt by bears on this road, but bears do frequent the area and are wise to the fact that people may have food with them.

**Directions:** Enter the park at West Glacier, go through the entrance station, and turn left where the road comes to a T intersection. Stay to the left on this road. After you pass the right turn to Lake McDonald campground, you are officially on Camas Creek Road.

**Important Information:** Keep in mind that all bears can be dangerous. Stay in your car if you see a bear and don't attempt to feed it.

## 96. Huckleberry Mountain Hike

This 1-mile loop trail is an easy hike through an area burned in the massive 1967 fire. Tree snags stand starkly as a reminder of the fire, but the vast array of colorful wildflowers that grow in the burned areas brighten the scene. An interpretive leaflet, available at the trailhead, explains the events of the lightning-caused fire, principles of fire ecology, and forest succession. The trail descends for 100 feet and then begins the loop section. Stay to the left here, and you'll return to this spot in 0.9 mile. There is some up-and-down walking on this path, but nothing excessively steep.

**Directions:** From the T junction just beyond the West Glacier Entrance Station, turn left (west). Go 0.3 mile past the Camas Creek entrance station, which is no longer in use, and turn left onto the paved trailhead access road. The road is found before you cross the river at the park boundary and goes to a parking area where you will see the trailhead.

## 97. Lake McDonald Lodge

Built in 1895, this lodge was the first of a series of lodges constructed in the park. The huge timbers used to build this magnificent hotel are awesome. You are welcome to come into the lodge and gift shop areas just to look. The hunting trophies throughout the lobby and the ice cream available at the local store are additional reasons to stop. This is also where you catch the Lake McDonald tour boat. A walkway from the lodge goes to the lakeshore. The complex includes a restaurant, gift shop, camp store, post office, and service station. Horse and small boat rentals are available here, as well.

**Directions:** Follow Going-to-the-Sun Road and take the marked turn left (north) for Lake McDonald Lodge. The turn is about 9 miles from the T intersection beyond the West Glacier entrance station.

**Important Information:** The lodge is open from late May to late September. Wheelchair accessible. Call 406-888-5431 in the summer, or 602-207-6000 for year-round reservations and information.

# 98. Sacred Dancing Cascades

There are numerous pullouts along Going-to-the-Sun Road where you can stop and get out of the car for a breath of clear mountain air. The day's journey will be enhanced by pausing periodically to appreciate the lake or McDonald Creek. One such stop is the Sacred Dancing Cascades. The two overlooks here provide a close-up view of fast-flowing McDonald Creek.
**Directions:** This pullout is about 4 miles beyond Lake McDonald Lodge going toward Logan Pass.

# 99. Trail of the Cedars and Avalanche Lake Trail

Trail of the Cedars is perhaps the best interpretive trail on the west side. The fully wheelchair-accessible path makes a 1-mile loop around a portion of Avalanche Creek, on paved trail and wooden boardwalk. On this memorable nature walk, you can enjoy the sights, sounds, and smells of a wise old forest as you walk amongst trees 4 to 7 feet in diameter. Listen for the bubbling voice of Avalanche Creek, and take in the smell of moist woodland soil. An interpretive leaflet identifies notable natural features.

Not long into the hike, the trail passes by a picturesque waterfall that is one of the most photographed spots in the park. To extend your adventure, take the spur trail (not wheelchair accessible) which follows the creek beyond the waterfall. Here you can enjoy the interesting, water-molded rocks and look for "dipper birds," which make their nests by fast-running water. Keep a close watch on your children, however, as they might be tempted to run and play here; the rocks can be slippery, and the water runs fast during high-water season!

By the Avalanche Creek footbridge is the trail to Avalanche Lake. While not wheelchair accessible, the 2-mile trail (4 miles round trip) makes a nice day hike for families. The wooded trail gains some elevation on its way to a serene glacial lake. Rocky shore and icy water make swimming difficult here so plan to just wander the shoreline and enjoy the view. Mosquito repellent is a good idea.
**Directions:** Take the Going-to-the-Sun Road toward Logan Pass, about 16 miles from West Glacier and 5 miles from Lake McDonald Lodge. You will see the Avalanche Picnic Area to the left and the Avalanche Campground a little farther up to your right. You can begin the trail at the campground or just north of the picnic area beyond the bridge on Going-to-the-Sun Road. The trail here goes to the right. Parking is best in the picnic area. Parking for wheelchair access is in Avalanche Campground across from the ranger's residence. At times,

the parking areas are full and visitors park along the roadway. Future plans call for a new parking lot which may change some trailhead locations.

**Important Information:** The trail is a wonderful spot for little children and elderly visitors who may want only a short, enjoyable hike. The portion on the southwest side of the creek follows a paved road on a no-longer-used loop of Avalanche Campground. This road joins with the Going-to-the-Sun Road. Wheelchair accessible restrooms and a spur trail to Avalanche Creek are along this road.

# Going-to-the-Sun Road

This road is rightfully a National Civil Engineering Landmark, and the construction details will boggle your mind. The two-lane highway was finished in 1933, after 12 years of effort and $3 million. All bridges, walls, and guardrails were constructed from native rock. The job of constructing this road was not easy, and crew turnover was 300 percent! The masterpiece, 52-mile road leads travelers through various park ecosystems on the winding path between West Glacier and St. Mary. The section over Logan Pass crosses the Continental Divide at 6,680 feet and is a drive you won't forget. The experience is one of sheer cliffs, vistas beyond description, and a recognition of the awesome power of nature. Your enjoyment of the ride will greatly increase if you leave time to stop frequently, and soak up the magnitude of the area.

There are several highlights en route. The "Loop" viewing area is on the west side and marks the first big hairpin turn. From here it is another 7.9 miles to Logan Pass. Stop at the large parking area at the Loop for a clear view of Heaven's Peak or to use a vault toilet. From this point on, the road is narrow with sheer cliffs on both sides, though the right side is sheer down several hundred feet. DRIVE SLOWLY.

About 4 miles above the Loop is the Big Bend parking lot, which is not marked. It is the only other big parking lot until the top, though there are numerous small pullouts. The Weeping Wall is on the way to Big Bend. This rock wall usually seeps water from the mountainside to the road and over cars, sometimes significantly.

There is a good chance of encountering snow on this road, even throughout the summer. One mile east of Logan Pass, toward St. Mary, is the infamous "Big Drift." Though not marked, this snow pile generally stays until August. At its peak, the drift has measured at 80 feet deep. Kids love playing in the snow, so take a moment to indulge.

Logan Pass has a visitor center and interpretive trail worth exploring. Two miles east of the pass is Jackson Glacier Overlook, where you can see remnants of glaciers still actively scouring the terrain, at the breakneck speed

# Hoary Marmot,
## *Marmota caligata*

· · · · · · · · · · · · · · · · · · · · · · · · · · · · · · · ·

Ever seen a "slinky with fur"? That's a fairly accurate description of the hoary marmot. These 20-pound, wiggly creatures live year-round in the severe alpine elements. You may catch sight of a marmot in the high country as it scrambles over and through rock piles. Or you may hear its characteristic whistle of surprise and warning. The largest member of the squirrel family in Montana, the marmot is an endearing critter to observe. Marmots burrow into the hard ground and hibernate during the harsh, high-mountain winters. During hibernation, marmots' bodies slow down so much that they breathe only 3 times a minute. They tunnel back out through the snow in early spring.

of an inch a year. As you descend the east side there is a pullout where you can appreciate the views of St. Mary Lake. Notice the difference in plants on the drier east side of the park.

Approaching from the west, you are on Going-to-the-Sun Road when you turn right at the T intersection beyond the West Glacier entrance station. On the east side at St. Mary, turn left (west) off U.S. Highway 89 to get on Going-to-the-Sun Road.

Vehicles longer than 21 feet or wider than 8 feet, including mirrors, are not allowed between Avalanche Campground and Sun Point. Shuttle service may be available between West Glacier and St. Mary with a stop at Logan Pass. Bicycles are restricted on portions of Going-to-the-Sun Road between 11 A.M. and 4 P.M. during the summer.

Note that the 52-mile trip from West Glacier to St. Mary is not a one-hour jaunt. The narrow, and often crowded, road is slow going and you will want to leave plenty of time to take in the scenery. On a good day, with no stops, the trip takes a minimum of one and a half hours. Plan for 3 hours, but allow longer for a leisurely trip.

It is rare to have a summer when there isn't any snow at the pass, and in some years it is considerable. Weather changes quickly in these parts, so be prepared for everything from hot, sunny, sunburned-skin kind of weather to windy, cold, and wet weather. It is possible to encounter all of the above on the same day when you cross the pass. If the mountains are shrouded in clouds, visibility may be limited at Logan Pass, and you may want to pick another day for this trip.

# 100. Logan Pass Visitor Center and Hidden Lake Nature Trail

Alpine ecosystems are accessible by car in only a few places in the United States, and Logan Pass is one of these spots. The visitor center, located just east of the Continental Divide, has interpretive materials, restrooms, and park personnel on hand to answer questions. An exhibit here identifies alpine plants and animals. The 1.5-mile (3 miles round trip) boardwalk trail to Hidden Lake Overlook provides an opportunity to see this unique alpine habitat without damaging the delicate ecosystem. Interpretive leaflets are available at the visitor center, and there are regularly scheduled guided walks. If you hike the entire trail to the overlook, you will cross the Continental Divide three times. The steady, uphill climb to 7,140 feet at the overlook is a 500-foot elevation gain and a moderate effort that many young children can handle. If you don't make it to the top, it's still worth going as far as little legs will let you. The panoramic views of Glacier's mountains and the alpine plants and animals are a treat. So is the opportunity to be in snow during the summer, which is frequently the case here. A light snowfall in July is not unusual.

While at the pass, look for Columbian ground squirrels, gophers, pikas, and chipmunks. You may also see the larger hoary marmots, or hear their sharp whistle of alarm. Mountain goats and sheep are often seen on the road, the Hidden Lake Nature Trail, or on the surrounding cliffs. The best time to see goats or sheep is early morning, late afternoon, or early evening. Occasionally a grizzly bear will wander through Logan Pass, but park personnel are careful to monitor for bears and advise visitors of their presence. You may see ptarmigans, bluebirds, and rosy finches too. Depending on the time of year, the delicate alpine flowers may be in bloom, especially the bright yellow glacier lilies.

**Directions:** Once on the Going-to-the-Sun Road, you have no option but to end up at Logan Pass. On a good day in July, the busiest month in the park, 20,000 people might stop at Logan Pass. Parking can be a problem and the park closes the parking lot when it is full. If this is the case, you can always take a quick jaunt to one of the turnouts nearby and try again after a bit.

**Important Information:** Bring warm clothes, observe animals at a distance, and stay on the trails! For current weather information at Logan Pass, or guided hike schedules, call park headquarters at 406-888-7880.

# 101. Highline Trail

It is rare to have this opportunity to hike in alpine terrain without having to expend the effort to get up to the high country first. The Highline Trail starts at 6,680 feet on Logan Pass and, for the most part, is relatively level. That makes this hike a possibility for families with young children, who can realistically walk a short distance or be carried if necessary. It is 7.5 miles to the Granite Park Chalet on this trail, but you can hike in even a short distance and have a powerful experience in the alpine ecosystem. We frequently take visitors halfway in to the short climb up Haystack Butte, and return. If you have children old enough to make the 7.5-mile journey in to Granite Park, there is a shorter route out. The "Loop" Trail is only 3 miles, and ends at the Loop parking area mentioned in the description of the Going-to-the-Sun Road. On these rocky trails, however, even those in good shape feel the effects of a 10.5-mile hike! Another option which might make a trip to Granite Park Chalet kid-friendly is to make arrangements to stay overnight at the rustic chalet. Recent controversy about human use of the area and funding issues have challenged maintenance of the chalet, so check to make sure it is open.

One of the most special aspects of this trip is the wildlife to be seen. I have found that it is rare not to see mountain goats on this hike. We often meet them right on the trail. They are generally harmless, but give them room, and don't approach them too closely. Keep an eye out for hoary marmots, too. Feeding animals is strictly against park policies.

**Directions:** Park at the Logan Pass Visitor Center or on the side of Going-to-the-Sun Road just below the pass on the west side. Cross the road at the pass, and you will find the marked trailhead. The trail is visible all the way to Haystack Butte on the mountainside below the ridge.

**Important Information:** Good shoes and extra clothes are a must. The weather can make the difference between a fun family outing and a miserable trip everyone would like to forget. This trail generally opens the first weekend after the Fourth of July weekend. Check with park headquarters, 406-888-7800, about trail conditions. For information on Granite Park Chalet, call 406-387-5555 or 800-521-7238. Reservations for the chalet need to be made months in advance.

Grizzly bears are sometimes in the mountain meadows and frequent Bear Valley, just before Granite Park Chalet. Look for park signs at the start of the trail to indicate if bears have been seen in the area recently, and follow park advice about traveling on the trail.

# Bears

Montana, with its wild lands and rugged mountains, is home to both black and grizzly bears. In fact, Montanans have recognized the grizzly as the official state animal. Bears live primarily in wooded and mountainous areas now, though they once made their home on the plains. You will most likely see grizzlies in the higher alpine areas along the Continental Divide, while black bears will be found mostly at lower elevations. An estimated 600 to 800 grizzlies live in Montana; black bears are much more common. Both types of bears are generally vegetarian and spend most of their time eating bulbs, berries, grasses, and flowers. About 10 percent of a bear's diet is meat, usually carrion or rodents.

## Grizzly Bears,
### *Ursus horibilis*

These beautiful animals come in large sizes and a variety of colors. The 200- to 600-pound animals can be blonde, brown, or nearly black. Some even have a silvery look caused by a grayish color at the tip of the hairs of their fur coats. The massive animals have exceptionally strong muscles in their forequarters, used for digging up dinner. These powerful muscles actually form a hump on their back, which is one of the ways you can identify a griz. Grizzly bears have long, curved claws that help them dig. Another distinctive grizzly trait is the "dished" profile. Grizzly faces have a flattened appearance, with broader faces and shorter noses than a black bear.

## Black Bears,
### *Ursus americanus*

Black bears are not always black but actually come in a variety of colors from black to brown to reddish-brown, or even golden-brown. In Montana, black bears average around 200 pounds. They are not the diggers that grizzlies are, but instead have short, curved claws. These allow them to tear up stumps and logs to look for insects to eat and to climb trees (grizzlies can't climb trees). Black bears have straight, Roman-style noses.

# St. Mary Valley

The dry, east side of Glacier National Park offers Rocky Mountain magic equal to, but nicely different from, the moister west side. Ecosystems and plant life change as you go over Logan Pass toward plains country. The mountainous areas still have forests, but support species that thrive on drier soils. As you enter valley areas, prairie ecosystems take over. There will be more sun and wind on the east side, though weather patterns will still be as variable here as they are anywhere in the mountains.

There are four major glacial valleys to visit in Glacier National Park's east side, each with spectacular mountain scenery and crystal clear lakes. The St. Mary Lake area, with Going-to-the-Sun Road passing through the valley, is the most developed.

## 102. St. Mary Lake

St. Mary Lake is 9.6 miles long and varies in width from a quarter of a mile to 1 mile. The turquoise lake is 292 feet deep in places and bow-shaped. There are lowland trails that access the lakeshore and waterfalls at the head of the lake. High-country trails lead to ridges and alpine lakes. From St. Mary Valley, enthusiastic hikers can access the Many Glacier, Lake McDonald, and Two Medicine areas via trails.

The National Park Service maintains an entrance station, ranger station, and the main east side visitor center near St. Mary. The visitor center highlights the geology and life zones of Glacier. Interpretive programs and guided hikes are also available. St. Mary Townsite has food, camping, lodging, showers, gift shops, and gasoline services. There are additional visitor facilities 6 miles up the lake at Rising Sun, including a boat tour of St. Mary Lake.

**Directions:** St. Mary Townsite is located at the junction of Going-to-the-Sun Road and U.S. Highway 89. From here, Going-to-the-Sun Road follows the valley west 18.2 miles to Logan Pass.

**Important Information:** The visitor center is about a mile west of the townsite, north of the entrance station. It is open late June through early September, from 8 A.M. to 9 P.M. From late May to late June, and from early September to September 30, the center is open 8 A.M. to 5 P.M. For information, call 406-732-7750.

# 103. St. Mary Falls and Virginia Falls

Two impressive falls can be reached in the span of this 1.5 or 2.3-mile hike, with the option of also seeing Baring Falls. The miles vary depending on where you catch the trail.

You will be rewarded for the walk to St. Mary Falls by experiencing the sight, sound, and presence of this dramatic force of nature. This is really two falls that pound into St. Mary River, causing quite a disturbance in the water below. The falls trail is moderately steep for a bit in the beginning as you climb to a small ridge, then it levels out and climbs again between the two sets of falls. Total elevation gain is 240 feet. Virginia Falls is a nice place to relax or eat lunch while you enjoy the picturesque cascade into Virginia Creek. In case you don't make it to Virginia Falls, you can get a glimpse of them back at the trailhead, through the trees, just south of the parking area.

The hike is shortest, 1.5 miles one-way, if started from the pullout signed for St. Mary Falls. However, you can begin on a trail across from Sunrift Gorge, which adds another 0.8 mile to the hike, but allows you to see Baring Falls along the way, too. If you start from the St. Mary Falls pullout, though, you can still catch Baring Falls by stopping at Sunrift Gorge when you drive by. Either way, families can easily hike to St. Mary Falls and then determine whether the kids have the endurance to go the remaining 0.7 mile to Virginia Falls.

**Directions:** The St. Mary Falls pullout is on the south side of Going-to-the-Sun Road, 6.5 miles east of Logan Pass and about a mile west of Sunrift Gorge.

**Important Information:** About halfway along the trail to St. Mary Falls, the Piegan Pass Trail joins St. Mary Falls Trail from the right and shortly after continues on to the left. The trail is signed, but be sure to stay on the falls trail. You will cross a bridge at both waterfall sites. Since these bridges may be slippery due to spray from the falls, hold hands with little ones while crossing.

# 104. Sunrift Gorge and Baring Falls

Sunrift Gorge is a narrow, long gorge that can be seen at a quick stop along Going-to-the-Sun Road. A 143-foot uphill jaunt goes to the spot where you can look at Baring Creek as it slips through the tiny gorge. At the right time of day, streams of sunlight highlight the shaded gorge.

On the south side of Going-to-the-Sun Road is a 0.3-mile trail which leads to Baring Falls and then connects with the trail to St. Mary and Virginia Falls. The St. Mary Falls hike is 1.7 miles one-way from Baring Falls, and Virginia Falls is another 0.7 mile beyond. The short trail to Baring Falls is an enjoyable hike, though a bit steep at the beginning, and the misty falls are appealing. If it's a hot day, take the trail from the road to the shady area beneath the creek bridge, and partake in the pleasant coolness by the creek. **Directions:** On Going-to-the-Sun Road, pull over at the pullout signed "Sunrift Gorge" on the south side of the road, which is the right side as you travel from Logan Pass east to St. Mary Townsite.

## 105. Sun Point and Baring Falls

The trail to Sun Point is only 80 yards long and offers majestic mountain vistas and a scenic view of St. Mary Lake. But hold on to your hat, for Sun Point is nearly always windy. Take a look at the mountain-finder interpretive display at the point to identify the surrounding glacial peaks.

The trail forks shortly after you begin the Sun Point hike from the parking lot. Go straight ahead, staying left, for the short trek to Sun Point. The right fork is the 0.7-mile trail to Baring Falls, which follows above the lakeshore and provides nice views of the lake. If you decide to take this jaunt, you will reach a fork in the trail just before the falls. Go straight ahead and you will cross Baring Creek shortly. The roaring sound of 30-foot Baring Falls will lead you to the impressive cascade via a short trail that turns sharply to the right just after the bridge. Note the brightly colored lichen growing on the rocks. These primitive plants, made up of algae and fungus, are also responsible for the chartreuse color on the cliffs above St. Mary Lake. If you turn right at the fork, the 0.3 mile trail goes back up to Going-to-the-Sun Road at Sunrift Gorge.

The round-trip distance from Sun Point to Baring Falls is 1.6 miles, but 2.2 miles includes the side trip to Sunrift Gorge. With older children, you could continue from Baring Falls to St. Mary Falls (4.8 miles round trip) or even on to Virginia Falls (6.2 miles round trip). With younger children, driving to Sunrift Gorge and hiking to the falls cuts down trail miles. **Directions:** The Sun Point trailhead is on a side road that turns south off Going-to-the-Sun Road. It is marked Going-to-the-Sun Point. This turnoff is 0.6 mile from Sunrift Gorge, and about 4 miles west of the Rising Sun Campground Road. The trailhead sign is at the end of the parking lot where there is also an interpretive leaflet about St. Mary Valley. There are picnic tables in the campground. **Important Information:** This area is significantly windy, as you see from the way the tree branches grow. Sun Point drops off steeply on the east side, and there is no barrier or fence. Keep track of kids here!

## 106. Rising Sun

• • • • • • • • • • • • • • • • • • • • • • • • • • • • • • • •

Located near St. Mary Lake, Rising Sun has a campground, picnic area, dining facilities, a general store, gift shop, and restrooms. Rising Sun Motor Inn, 602-207-6000, has rooms, cabins, and showers. An evening National Park Service campfire program is held here regularly. Boat tours, one and a half hours in length, cruise narrow St. Mary Lake and begin from Rising Sun.
**Directions:** Take Going-to-the-Sun Road from St. Mary toward Logan Pass. The complex is 6 miles west of St. Mary Townsite.
**Important Information:** Contact the National Park Service for campfire program information at 406-732-7750. For cruise information call 406-732-4430.

# Many Glacier Valley

• • • • • • • • • • • • • • • • • • • • • • • • • • • • • • •

The east side is the place to observe waterfalls! In fact, the Blackfeet name for the Many Glacier area is *Óhpskunakáxi*, meaning waterfalls. In addition to the numerous waterfall hikes listed in this section, there are many other east-side hikes which follow ridges and go over passes to the glacial valleys. Some of these could certainly be handled by older children. For more information, call park headquarters.

The Many Glacier Valley reveals some of Glacier National Park's most spectacular scenery. A 4,200-foot cliff wall towers majestically above the valley. Nearby is one of the largest glaciers in the park, Grinnell Glacier. Trails lead in three directions from Many Glacier, into areas of outstanding alpine beauty. Most of these hikes are strenuous uphill climbs, which require some stamina and determination. However, the lake and falls trails listed here are excellent, easy trips that allow families to enjoy nature's powerful presence without paying for it with difficult hikes.

There are boat tours on Swiftcurrent and Josephine lakes. Rowboats, canoes, and horses are available for rent.

## 107. Many Glacier Hotel

• • • • • • • • • • • • • • • • • • • • • • • • • • • • • • •

Many Glacier Hotel, the largest lodge in the park, looks out over Swiftcurrent Lake toward Grinnell Glacier. A unique aspect of this hotel is the regular entertainment by staff who have been carefully selected for their musical and dramatic abilities. Other valley services include camping, dining, gas, groceries, and gift shops.

# Rocky Mountain Sheep,
## *Ovis canadensis*

Rocky Mountain Sheep are known as bighorn sheep. The curled horns on either side of their heads can be as heavy as 30 to 40 pounds. A male will weigh up to 250 pounds. In late autumn, if you hear a hollow crashing sound in the park, it may be the result of two males butting heads in their annual dominance rituals. Bighorns are often seen in Many Glacier Valley, sometimes on the roadways, and especially around Red Rock Canyon.

There is no visitor center in Many Glacier, but you may want to stop by the ranger station, where maps and publications are for sale.

**Directions:** Enter Many Glacier Valley from U.S. Highway 89 by turning west at Babb onto Many Glacier Road. This junction is 9 miles north of St. Mary. The park entrance station is about halfway up Lake Sherburne. The ranger station, campground, and picnic area are at the end of the road. Many Glacier Hotel is a short ways from the end of the road and 12 miles from Babb.

**Important Information:** The ranger station is open mid-June to mid-September, 8 A.M. to 4:30 P.M. Contact Many Glacier Hotel at 406-732-4411 during summer months or 602-207-6000 year-round. Swiftcurrent Motor Inn also has rooms and cabins; call 406-732-5531.

## 108. Apikuni Falls

From the grassy meadow where this 0.7-mile hike begins, the trail climbs 542 feet to a pleasing view of Apikuni Falls. At various points, hikers are treated to spectacular mountain views. Look for lupine, purple geranium, and harebell wildflowers in the meadow, where you will also see great numbers of Columbian ground squirrels. The trail goes on through a tightly packed lodgepole pine forest and into a subalpine area. The path continues a short ways beyond the falls into a steep, rocky area where you may see small, furry pikas.

**Directions:** Take Many Glacier Road about 1 mile east of the Many Glacier Hotel entrance to the trailhead parking lot on the north side of the road. This is 0.1 mile east of the Apikuni Creek bridge. The trailhead is in the parking area.

**Important Information:** Portions of this trail climb steeply, but only for short distances.

# 109. Swiftcurrent Lake

Here's an easy hike around Swiftcurrent Lake that is a total of 2.5 miles. An interpretive leaflet is available at two trailhead areas. Along the way, you'll cross Swiftcurrent and Grinnell Creeks and go close to the edge of the lake. This hike can give you an opportunity to explore Many Glacier Hotel, as one of the trailheads begins there.

**Directions:** Pick up the trail at the Swiftcurrent Lake Picnic area, just off Many Glacier Road between the lake and the Many Glacier Campground. You can also begin from the signed trailhead on the Many Glacier Hotel loop road at the south end of the loop.

**Important Information:** Other trails lead off from the Swiftcurrent Lake Hike. At one point, the trail to Grinnell Glacier heads up the moraine, while another trail goes down to the boat dock. Continue straight around the lake. The trail forks again later and goes to a residential area. Stay on the trail that follows the lakeshore.

# 110. Redrock Falls

A waterfall, mountain views, and interesting red rocks make this trail an enjoyable hike for kids of all ages. It is 1.8 miles to the falls, and along the way you can appreciate the geology of the red Grinnell mudstone for which Redrock Lake and the falls are named. Look for large, flat rocks along the path, where centuries-old mud cracks have been preserved. Notice the distinctive sedimentary rock

## *Ninaiistako,* Chief Mountain

You can't miss *Ninaiistako*, Chief Mountain, the rocky, monolithic mountain you will see to the west when traveling north of Babb. The klippe, in geologic terms, was, at one time, a part of a giant slab of ancient rock that was thrust above younger rock some 60 million years ago during the Lewis Overthrust. Chief Mountain was separated from the rest of the rock by erosion. It stands 9,066 feet, like a sentinel above the valley, and is one of the 50 to 60 vision quest sites still used by local native peoples. The Blackfeet people say that Dream Person lives there, and that *Ninaiistako* is the home of Thunderbird, a member of the Up Above People, who gave the first medicine pipe to the People. If you wish to go closer to *Ninaiistako*, inquire at the Blackfeet Tribal Office, 406-338-7207, for permission and regulations, or contact the St. Mary Visitor Center, 406-732-7750.

layers in Mount Henkel, to the north, and in the weathered cliffs near the beginning of the trail. You will also see remains of the 1936 fire on this hike. The trail forks at the head of Redrock Lake. Redrock Falls are a short distance to the left, and the trail to the right is a long grind to Swiftcurrent Pass.

**Directions:** Go to the parking area at the end of Many Glacier Road, near the Swiftcurrent Coffee Shop and Campstore. The trailhead is on the right side of the parking lot.

**Important Information:** A short distance from the start of the hike, the trail crosses a three-way junction. Stay on the trail to the left, and you will cross Wilbur Creek shortly. At Redrock Falls there are a number of refreshing pools which may seem like a good place for a dip. However, this icy creek is not good for swimming or wading as there are strong and unpredictable water currents, and the rocks may be slick.

# Upper Waterton Lake Area

Waterton Lake, which straddles the Canada-United States border, is accessible from the U.S. side by trail, and by boat or trail from Canada. Only half of this lake is in the United States. The other half is part of Canada's Waterton Lakes National Park. The northern border of Glacier National Park is where the two parks meet, forming the International Peace Park. The Canadian park service maintains trails and interpretive programs on the Canadian side of the lake, so you could spend significant time enjoying a bit of Canada here, too.

The easiest access to the U.S. National Park Service ranger station on Waterton Lake, called Goat Haunt, is by tour boat from Waterton Townsite in Alberta, Canada. This is an interesting town with numerous services. Mountain sheep and goats regularly roam the streets. The Prince of Wales Hotel sits majestically at the north end of the lake. A favorite short hike at Waterton Townsite is the Bear's Hump Trail, located near the Canadian Visitor Centre.

There is a Lakeshore Trail, which skirts Waterton Lake for 7.5 miles on the way from Waterton Townsite to Goat Haunt Ranger Station. If your kids have the endurance for this long of a hike, you can ride the boat one direction and hike the other way. Once at Goat Haunt, the Rainbow Falls Trail is a short, wooded nature trail that ends at a picturesque waterfall (see site 111).

To reach Waterton, take Montana 17, Chief Mountain International Highway, 4 miles north of Babb. It is 26 miles from St. Mary Townsite to the Port of Chief Mountain customs. This border station is open June 1 to September 14, 7 A.M. to 10 P.M., but only from 9 A.M. to 6 P.M. mid-May to June 1 and September 15 to 30. The Piegan/Carway Crossing on U.S. Highway 89, open 7 A.M. to 11 P.M. year-round, is the alternate Canadian border crossing. This route goes 16 miles north to Cardston, and then 28 miles farther to the Waterton National Park entrance.

There is a fee for entrance to Waterton Lakes National Park. For more information call 403-859-2224. You might also ask about border-crossing information. For boat schedules, call 403-859-2362.

## 111. Rainbow Falls

Unless you have taken the last boat of the day from Waterton, you can get off the tour boat and stay at Goat Haunt to enjoy this 1-mile hike or play along the lakeshore until the next boat arrives. The park maintains only a small facility here, but rangers can direct you to the falls trailhead by the station. The trail is an easy hike with only a little climb. About halfway, the Waterton Lake Trail turns right and goes over a suspension bridge. This is a fun diversion. Continue on the Rainbow Falls Trail, and you will arrive at the falls in another half mile. Along the way, enjoy the wooded walk, and look for beargrass and other woodland flowers.

**Directions:** From the boat launch, walk 0.2 mile around the lake to the ranger station. The trailhead is 44 yards up the path by the station. The trail follows the Waterton Lake Trail, which forks to the right shortly. The suspension bridge is at the second fork, a short distance ahead.

# Two Medicine Valley

Three small lakes are held in the southernmost glacial valley on Glacier's east side, Two Medicine. The crooked valley twists between sentinel-like peaks, which surround crystal clear Two Medicine Lake on three sides. A hiking companion, who teaches high school English, poetically says these mountain create, for her, an "embracing serenity." Historically the area has always been considered by Native Americans a special place with great medicine, hence the name.

Visitors to the area will find that the towering mountains provide plentiful opportunities for play. The Two Medicine area offers families a magnificent getaway, with enough outdoor activities to keep kids entertained. Five family-style trails lead to dramatic waterfalls or picturesque panoramas of the colorful landforms. The lake and creeks offer water play for the young, though the glacial water is icy cold. During my most recent stay at Two Medicine, I was delighted by the number of families fishing from small boats or along the lakeshore. The fishing must be rewarding here, whether or not the catching is any good.

The National Park Service here operates an entrance station, ranger station, picnic area, and a 99-site campground with flush toilets. A small, historic chalet offers groceries, gas, gifts, and a hamburger-type snack bar, but no lodging. There are also boat rentals, a boat tour, and interpretive programs. The picnic area, located by the ranger station, has nice views of Two Medicine Lake and the surrounding mountains.

To reach Two Medicine, turn north from U.S. Highway 2 at East Glacier onto Montana Highway 49, at the sign marked Glacier National Park. This goes under the "Glacier Park Gateway" train trestle, and past the Glacier Park Lodge. Continue 4.2 miles to the Two Medicine junction. Turn left (west) and you will be at the complex in 7.5 miles. From St. Mary, travel 19 miles south to Browning on US 89, then take MT 49 south for 9 miles to the Two Medicine junction. Turn right at the sign for Two Medicine. The entrance station is at the head of Lower Two Medicine Lake. The park road continues 3 miles to the foot of Two Medicine Lake, where you will find the area facilities.

For information on the boat trip, call 406-732-4430. The ranger station is open early June to mid-September. A nice, comprehensive trail map is available free at the station. This is grizzly bear habitat, so follow suggested guidelines for camping and hiking (see page 14).

## 112. Running Eagle Falls

This 0.3-mile hike is an easy one that any family can do. It is extra fun because of the natural phenomenon which makes this falls into a "double falls." Some of the water from Two Medicine Creek slips into a cave before the edge of the falls. It re-emerges part-way down the falls and forms a second waterfall behind the first. For a while, the waterfalls were called "Trick Falls" because of this. When the water is low, it mostly goes into the cave and forms only the lower waterfall, with the appearance that the water emerges from solid rock. When the water is too high, you can't tell one waterfall from the other. In any configuration, the falls are an interesting sight, and kids will enjoy playing in the creek before the falls or clambering amongst the large rocks on the trail near the falls.

**Directions:** Follow Two Medicine Road 0.9 mile past the entrance station toward the park service complex. The well-marked parking lot is on the right-hand side of the road. The trail leaves from here.

# 113. Appistoki Falls

One of the stories about the name of this waterfall, and the peak above it, is that a surveyor named Evans thought Appistoki Peak looked out over everything. He asked his Indian guide for a term that meant "overseer" and was given the word *appistotoki*, which means God. The word apparently lost a syllable, but the 8,164-foot peak does indeed oversee the land below.

The 0.6-mile trail travels gently uphill and is a good hike for any family. The trail ends rather abruptly with no viewing platform. You can see from the trail up the narrow gorge toward the pretty 65-foot falls. My friend's 8-year-old daughter was less impressed than I with this hike, but became extremely interested when we found the little side trail to Appistoki Creek, 50 feet or so back down the trail. We spent a full 20 minutes playing by the small creek, after which she informed us that "this was the best trail ever." Though the creek in August was only a few inches deep, it probably runs considerably higher in spring runoff, and if so, will not be a good place for play.

**Directions:** The trailhead is west 2.8 miles from the entrance station and 0.3 mile east from the campground entrance. Turn at the sign for Scenic Point and park. The trail begins right by the turnoff. When you are almost to the falls, the trail reaches a junction. The trail to the left is a steep hike that leads to Scenic Point. Take the right fork a short distance farther to the falls.

**Important Information:** A trail goes on beyond the falls overlook. However, it is marked with a warning sign to indicate that it is not a safe trail. Make sure your little ones don't stray beyond the overlook.

# 114. Twin Falls

If you decide to take the Two Medicine Lake boat tour, you have the option of staying at the west end of the lake till the next boat comes. This provides time to hike the 0.9-mile trail to Twin Falls. The trail goes gently up and down through the forest to reach a double set of falls that plummets into Two Medicine Creek. Taking the boat and the hike make a nice day's activity. Consider bringing a picnic lunch along, too.

**Directions:** Catch the boat ride from the lower end of Two Medicine Lake, beyond the historic chalet at the end of Two Medicine Road. The boat runs four times every day and may fill up, so get to the dock ahead of time. The Twin Falls trail starts from the boat shelter at the upper end of the lake. A guide is available at certain times to lead the hike.

If you go on your own, stay right at the first junction, only 250 feet from the beginning of the trail. The trail to the left returns to the boat dock area at the other end of the lake and is a fairly long trail. About halfway to the falls, you will cross a bridge over Two Medicine Creek, and 0.2 mile later take the left fork, as the right fork is the North Shore Trail which goes back to Two Medicine Campground. Soon the trail comes to another bridge. The falls trail turns sharply to the right for a short walk to the falls. If you go straight here, the trail takes you 1.3 miles to the foot of Upper Two Medicine Lake.

You can also get to Twin Falls by taking the North Shore Trail from a parking area by Pray Lake (site 116) in the B and C campground loop, 0.5 mile from the ranger station. The lake trail is 2.9 up-and-down miles. If your kids are older and good hikers, you can consider hiking the lake trail one way and taking the boat the other way. Total miles one way, combining the North Shore and Twin Falls trails, is 3.8 miles.

**Important Information:** If you take the boat ride and choose to stay to hike the lake trail, check times carefully to make sure you will be able to catch another boat back down the lake. Otherwise, you may get a little more exercise than you expected!

## 115. Aster Falls and Paradise Point

• • • • • • • • • • • • • • • • • • • • • • • • • • • • • • • • •

Aster Falls is a nice 1.3-mile falls hike with the option of adding 0.6 uphill miles to hike to Aster Park for a view of the valley. The trail to Paradise Point leaves from the Aster Falls Trail, 0.2 mile from the trailhead. It is a 0.6-mile woodland hike to a pleasant gravel beach on Two Medicine Lake. This short walk and the opportunity to play along the lakeshore make a simple and enjoyable family activity. From the gravel beach, you can walk along the water's edge toward the head of the lake or just appreciate the peacefulness.

The trail goes uphill from the trailhead for a short distance and then levels out. The Paradise Point trail veers to the right in 0.2 mile, and continues 0.4 mile to the point. The Aster Falls Trail goes up and down through the woods and a meadow, passing by beaver ponds along the way. After 1.2 miles, the trail goes left 0.1 mile toward the cascading waterfall. From the falls it is 0.6 mile to the Aster Park Overlook. The overlook has a good view of the lake and immediate valley area.

**Directions:** Take Two Medicine Road to the boat dock area beyond the Two Medicine store. The trail for both hikes begins by the boat rental facility.

**Important Information:** The trailhead sign indicates that Aster Park Overlook is 1.9 miles up the trail but does not mention Aster Falls. The falls is 1.3 miles on this trail.

# 116. Pray Lake

Pray Lake is a small lake at the campground end of Two Medicine Lake. The two lakes are linked by a short creek. Kids seem to gravitate to this little creek to play while parents watch along the shore. The creek is often shallow, so kids can wade in safely. Be aware that Pray Lake gets deep quickly not far from shore, however. **Directions:** To find this spot, look for the first small parking area to the left after the Two Medicine campground entrance.

# U.S. Highway 2: West Glacier to East Glacier

This is the only route, besides Going-to-the-Sun Road, that takes you from the east side of the Rocky Mountains to the west side through Glacier National Park. U.S. Highway 2 is a good, two-lane highway that follows the southern edge of Glacier National Park. In the 56 miles from East Glacier to West Glacier are a few stops to make the trip fun.

## 117. Flathead River: the Middle Fork

There are three river access points on U.S. Highway 2 where you can get out and enjoy the Middle Fork of the Flathead River: Moccasin Creek, Cascadilla Creek, and Paola Creek. We will sometimes just stop for a few minutes to look at the river and walk along the rocky shore. The kids like to toss rocks in the river, but be *very* careful not to let them wander into the fast river current.

If the river is enticing to you, exciting whitewater river floats are available which shoot down rapids with names like "Jaws," "Pinball," and "Bonecrusher." Generally, you can invest a full day or a half day on a whitewater float, or take a "supper" float in late afternoon. A family-oriented whitewater float trip is a wonderful memory in family history! **Directions:** The highway follows the river for 30 miles between West Glacier and Essex. From West Glacier it is 6.4 road miles to Moccasin Creek (mile markers 153 and 154), 12.6 road miles to Cascadilla Creek (mile markers 160 and 161), and 21.8 road miles to Cascadilla River Access (mile markers 166 and 167). **Important Information:** Beware of fast river currents. Contact the Glacier Country Tourism Commission for names of whitewater guides. Some are capable of assisting people in wheelchairs.

# 118. Stanton Lake Trail

. . . . . . . . . . . . . . . . . . . . . . . . . . . . .

This trail is in the Great Bear Wilderness and offers entry into a remote area via a relatively easy trail. The lake hike is a gradual uphill walk, gaining 318 feet of elevation in 2 miles. There are few bears in this area, but there are numerous mosquitoes during wet seasons. Look for moose and beavers and enjoy the wildflowers! Like most trails in this area, you will be rewarded with glorious views along the way. The notable mountain to the south is Great Northern Mountain. If you feel like carrying fishing poles in, you may have luck with small cutthroat from the shore—or if you bring along a rubber raft, you can go after the larger rainbow and cutthroat trout.

**Directions:** The trail begins just east of Stanton Creek Lodge on U.S. Highway 2. It is 17 miles east of West Glacier and 38 miles west of East Glacier on US 2 between mile markers 169 and 170.

**Important Information:** There is no water along the way so bring your own, and don't forget the mosquito repellent.

# 119. Izaak Walton Inn

. . . . . . . . . . . . . . . . . . . . . . . . . . . . .

Just off U.S. Highway 2 is the Izaak Walton Inn, a lodge built in 1939 by the Great Northern Railroad to house its workers. This historic inn is listed on the National Register of Historic Places and has photos and information about the railroad days. Stop by for a quick look at the historical information and the quaint lobby area, or to have a bite to eat. The inn operates year-round with a lodge and restaurant. There are 19 miles of groomed cross-country ski trails here for winter fun.

The lodge is nestled between Glacier National Park and the Bob Marshall Wilderness. There are short hikes in the area; check at the lodge for information.

**Directions:** Take the marked turn on the south side of US 2, 27 miles from West Glacier and 29 miles from East Glacier Park.

**Important Information:** Contact the Izaak Walton Inn at 406-888-5700.

# 120. Walton Ranger Station

. . . . . . . . . . . . . . . . . . . . . . . . . . . . .

This station has a small picnic area. Trails head up river valleys to the mountains from here. None are specifically designed for families, but could be taken for a short distance just to get out and walk. If you need a place for a quick lunch along the road, there are picnic tables and pit toilets just off the highway.

**Directions:** The station is just east of a bridge across the Flathead River, between milemarkers 180 and 181 on U.S. Highway 2. Turn north off the highway.

## 121. Goat Lick Overlook

Families can stop here briefly to stretch or eat lunch and also have a chance to see mountain goats, elk, and deer licking minerals from the exposed river bank cliffs above the Middle Fork of the Flathead River. Chances are good that you will see billy goats and nannies with kids. Binoculars are helpful. The best viewing is April through mid-July. A record count is 89 goats seen at one time.

**Directions:** Three miles east of Essex, at mile marker 183, turn south from U.S. Highway 2 and drive to the end of the parking lot. Here you will see the trail to the overlook.

**Important Information:** The short trail is wheelchair accessible.

## 122. Marias Pass

This is the lowest crossing of the Continental Divide in Montana. At the 5,216-foot pass is a rest stop area with interpretive information about Marias Pass and "Slippery" Bill Morrison. This frontier philosopher and mountain man willed the surrounding land to the government. The National Forest Service operates Summit Campground here.

**Directions:** Marias Pass is 44 miles from West Glacier and 11 miles from East Glacier Park on U.S. Highway 2. The turn is on the southeast side of the highway.

## 123. East Glacier Park and The Glacier Park Lodge

This town is outside of park boundaries but has trails leading into the park from Glacier Park Lodge. This historic lodge was known as "The Big Tree Lodge" by the Blackfeet because of the large Douglas-fir pillars in the lobby area. The structure was built between 1912 and 1914. Stop to see the lodge and the beautiful flower gardens at the entrance. Services include a restaurant, coffee shop, nightly entertainment, gift shop, heated pool, service station, and horseback tours.

**Directions:** East Glacier Park is located at the junction of U.S. Highway 2 and Montana Highway 49. To get to Glacier Park Lodge, turn west from US 2 onto MT 49 at the train trestle, marked "Glacier Park Gateway."

**Important Information:** For information about Glacier Park Lodge, call 406-226-9311 in summer or 602-207-6000 for year-round reservations or information.

# The Blackfeet Reservation and Browning

The Blackfeet Indians believed that the Rocky Mountains were the "backbone of the world." Numerous Indian tribes used what is now Glacier National Park, but the Blackfeet dominated the area long before European explorers ever saw the spectacular peaks. Consider a visit to the nearby 1.5-million-acre Blackfeet reservation that borders the east side of Glacier Park, for a glimpse into native life.

Browning, the largest town on the Blackfeet Reservation, is 13 miles northeast of East Glacier Park on U.S. Highway 2 and 31 miles south of St. Mary on U.S. Highway 89. The greatest recorded temperature swing in the nation occurred here in a 24-hour period on January 23 and 24, 1916 in Browning, the temperature shifted 100 degrees, dropping from 44 degrees to 56 degrees below zero! For information about the Blackfeet Reservation call the tribal office at 406-338-7276.

An interesting addition to National Park Service guided interpretive programs is the privately owned Sun Tours, led by Blackfeet guides, who share Indian cultural history related to Glacier National Park's natural features. For more information call 406-226-9220 or 800-SUN-9220.

## 124. Museum of the Plains Indians

A visit to this museum in Browning, on the Blackfeet reservation, will give your family insight into the history of the Northern Great Plains tribes. Take time to see the multimedia show, *Winds of Change*. The small museum also has a wonderful collection of Indian beadwork and art, plus a fine collection of contemporary native products for sale. Check out the Medicine Rock and the footprints of those who attended the 1930 conference for the preservation of Indian sign language. Both are located outside by the front of the museum.

**Directions:** From East Glacier Park, go east on U.S. Highway 2. When you come to the T intersection in Browning, go right and look for the museum on your left in a short distance.
**Important Information:** Call 406-338-2230.

## 125. Bob Scriver Montana Museum of Wildlife and Hall of Bronze

Kids will enjoy seeing the taxidermy displays of wildlife, and Scriver's bronze work is some of the best.
**Directions:** From East Glacier Park, go east on U.S. Highway 2. When you come to the T intersection in Browning, turn right toward town. The museum will be on your left.
**Important Information:** There is a small fee for this museum. Open every day 9 A.M. to 5 P.M. June through September, and weekdays 10 A.M. to 4:30 P.M. the rest of the year.

**I-90 and Outskirts of Missoula**
Frenchtown Pond
Ninemile Remount Station
Blackfoot River
Lolo Hot Springs

**The Mission Valley**
The Mule Palace
Swartz Lake
Twin Lakes
Mission Falls
Mud Lake
St. Ignatius Mission
Ninepipe National Wildlife Refuge
Pablo National Wildlife Refuge
Pablo Reservoir
Kicking Horse Reservoir
The People's Center: *Sqelix'u/Aqlismaknik* Cultural Center
National Bison Range
Garden of the Rockies Museum
Flathead Historic Museum
Kerr Dam

**Clark Fork River Area**
KooKooSint Sheep Viewing Area
Cabinet Gorge Dam and Reservoir
Hub Lake
Heart and Pearl Lakes
Stateline Trails
Clark Fork River Floats
Grahmrick Trails
Thompson Falls State Park

**Libby-Yaak Area**
Kootenai Falls
Libby Creek Gold Panning
Old Libby–Troy Road
Heritage Museum
Murr Canyon Hike
Libby Dam
Lake Koocanusa
Ross Creek Cedars
The Yaak River and Purcell Mountains

### Highway 2: Libby to Kalispell
Thompson Lakes
Logan State Park
McGregor Lake
Little Bitterroot Lake
Ashley Lake

### Eureka
Ten Lakes Scenic Area
Murray Springs Fish Hatchery
Murphy Lake
Ant Flat Natural Resource Education Center
Tobacco Valley Historical Village

# GOLD WEST COUNTRY

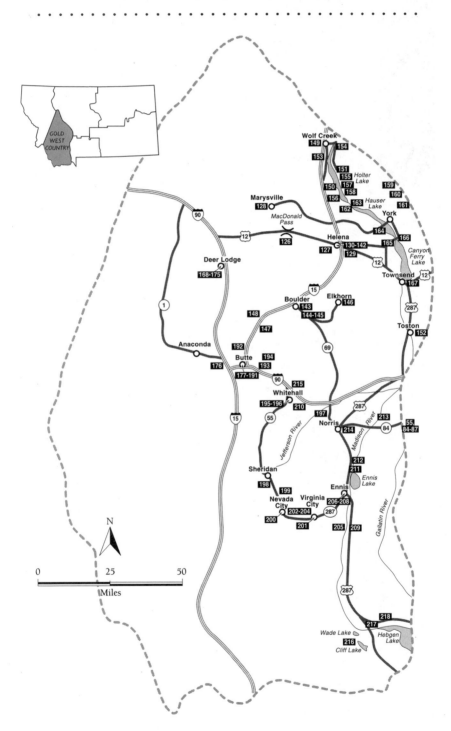

Wolf Creek
149 154
153
151
155 Holter
157 Lake
150 158 159
156 160
163 Hauser
162 Lake 161

Marysville
128

MacDonald
Pass

York
164

Helena 166
130-142 165
127 129 Canyon
12 Ferry
Lake

Deer Lodge
168-175 Townsend
12
167

15 287

Boulder Elkhorn
143 146
148 144-145
147 Toston
152

Anaconda
192
Butte 194 69
176 193
177-191
90 215
Whitehall
195-196 210
197 287
55 Norris 213
Jefferson River 214 55,
84 84-87
Sheridan
212
211
198 Ennis
Ennis Lake
199 206-208
Nevada Virginia 287
City City 205 209
200 202-204
201

15

Madison River

Gallatin River

N

0        25        50
Miles

287

218
217
Wade Lake 216 Hebgen
Cliff Lake Lake

112

# Gold West Country

Here's the heart of Montana's mining lands, nestled in some of the prettiest mountains you could ever hope to see. Deep within these striking hills are some of the world's largest deposits of gold and copper. A number of other minerals and gems offer rockhounds a reason to explore the area. Sapphires are a much sought-after gem found in Gold West Country and there are other interesting rocks such as quartz, petrified wood, fossils, and a variety of crystals.

Much of Montana's history is centered on the boom-and-bust mining days in Helena, Anaconda, Butte, Virginia City, and numerous other cities that are only ghost towns today. Many historical features, including whole towns, have been preserved or restored to share with visitors. Since much of early state commerce was based on mining and a lot of people lived in this region, it's no surprise that state government has also been focused in this area. Virginia City once functioned as the territorial capital, and Helena is the state capital.

Gold West is a region with plenty of character—and characters, for that matter. The mining days brought people from afar, some hard-working, treasure-seeking sorts and others like renegade Sheriff Henry Plummer, whose livelihood was robbing successful miners. The region had its share of entrepreneurs who built the towns, cities, and businesses, too. You'll find the story of Montana intertwined with people like Marcus Daly and William Clark, the "Copper Kings" of Butte.

Of course, one of the best treasures in this area is the land itself. Mountains and streams offer excellent recreation here. There is no lack of opportunities to hike in the mountains and wilderness areas, fish for famous Montana trout, or explore rivers and lakes. There is treasure throughout Gold West Country, both above and below the surface of this rich land!

# THE HELENA VALLEY AND SURROUNDING AREA

Gold may have brought people to Helena originally, but those who have stayed do so in part because of what the town has to offer as a beautiful place to live. Take a ride up MacDonald Pass and stop at the vista point at the top or at the pullout part way down the pass. As you look out over the wide, grassy plains of the Helena Valley you will see why this area is so appealing. Surrounded by four mountain ranges, the city offers plentiful and accessible recreation. Fishing, boating, and playing along the mighty Missouri River, which courses to the east, provide more reasons to visit the area.

# The Continental Divide Area

The Continental Divide bisects Montana, running through the Gold West region near Helena, Butte, and Anaconda. In the region outside of Helena, MacDonald Pass, at 6,320 feet, allows a view of the surrounding land from atop the world. Other sites in this vicinity open doors to mining history or offer high-mountain recreation.

## 126. MacDonald Pass Vista Point and Cromwell-Dixon Campground

The vista point is a quick stop at the pass with an excellent view of Helena and the surrounding area. The campground makes a nice picnic spot and has picnic tables, water, and vault toilets (not open in winter). MacDonald Pass is on the Continental Divide, elevation 6,320 feet. It is also a historic site marking the general area where Cromwell Dixon became the first aviator to cross the Continental Divide in 1911. In addition to the acclaim for his accomplishment, Dixon also won $10,000 for the feat.
**Directions:** Follow U.S. Highway 12 to the top of MacDonald Pass. The campground and vista point are on the south side of the highway.

## 127. Ten Mile Picnic Area and Environmental Trail

Take a break to enjoy a picnic in the woods and a walk along a ridgeline trail at the Ten Mile Picnic Area west of Helena. The Environmental Trail explains a variety of ecological principles on a pleasant 0.8-mile hike. It begins by heading briefly up a steep hill, but then levels out to complete a loop which ends up back at the parking area. Because of sign vandalism, the environmental education information is now presented through pamphlets available from the USDA Forest Service, Helena District Office at 406-449-5490, or from the Helena Chamber of Commerce at 406-447-1532. The Moose

Creek Campground is immediately south of the picnic area. If you continue up Rimini Road you will find the mining ghost town of Rimini (some folks still live here), which served as a World War II training camp for dog-sled teams used for rescue missions of flyers downed in the Arctic.

**Directions:** Take U.S. Highway 12 west from Helena about 8 miles. Turn left (south) at the sign for Rimini and continue south on the graveled Rimini Road. The picnic area will be on your left. The trail begins from the northwest corner of the picnic area, at the base of the hill that is across from the vault toilets.

**Important Information:** Contact the USDA Forest Service, Helena District Office, at 406-449-5490 for more information or to obtain copies of the environmental education pamphlet.

## 128. Marysville

No one knows whether to call this a ghost town or not, since the 80 people living there don't feel like ghosts. However, the town used to have 7,000 residents and was home to the Drumlummon Mine, a famous underground mine that produced $50 million worth of gold and silver between 1885 and 1910. When silver prices declined in 1893, the town began to decline, too, and mostly gave up when the entire business district burned in 1908. The town has numerous (mostly brick) buildings left which are identified with historic markers. There is a little business action here and in nearby Silver City, so you might be able to get a meal. The local history includes interesting stories about "Irish Tommy" Cruse, a town character whom gold made wealthy, and Lady Luck from "silk-stocking row." One mile from Marysville is the Great Divide ski area, 406-449-3746. Locals cross-country ski on the road that goes north out of Marysville and up Trinity Hill. You may see some husky dog-sled teams here in the winter, too.

**Directions:** Drive north from Helena on Interstate 15. Take Exit 200 and get onto Lewis and Clark County 279. Follow CR 279 for 9.25 miles, and turn left onto Marysville Road about a quarter of a mile past Silver City (this turn is signed). It is 5 miles to Marysville. Marysville is 22 miles from Helena.

# City of Helena

Helena was once one of the wealthiest cities in Montana, and it is rich in history and recreational opportunities. Helena serves as the state capital, and historical resources include the outstanding Montana Historical Society Museum and the state capitol building. You will find the arts expressed in many places, including museums and galleries, and in the sculptures along the Last Chance Gulch Pedestrian Mall. The city has enjoyable parks and within easy reach are the Helena Valley and the area to the south of Helena, both wonderlands of recreational opportunities.

Contact the Helena Chamber of Commerce at 800-743-5362 for more information about Helena, the Helena Valley, and the surrounding area.

## 129. Kleffner Ranch

The Kleffner Ranch history goes back 110 years to when the octagonal stone ranch house and three-story barn were built. It is still a working ranch. Tours are given regularly which include interesting details about life during Montana's pioneering days. The tour lasts between an hour and an hour and a half.

**Directions:** Go to East Helena on U.S. Highway 12 (also called Euclid Avenue and Lyndale Avenue at various points), then take Montana 518 south toward Montana City. Go 1 mile and you will see the ranch.

**Important Information:** Open all year. $5 per person; free for kids under 10. Call for hours at 406-227-6645.

## 130. Montana State Capitol

Montana's capitol building is not only a place to explore the working space of state government, but also offers insights into Montana's frontier times. Historical paintings by Montana artists portray the lives of miners, cowboys, and Indians. The most spectacular is a 25-foot-by-25-foot Charlie Russell painting in the chambers of the House of Representatives.

There is a self-guided tour brochure of the building and guided tours are available at regularly scheduled times. If you take the guided tour, be sure to ask about the secret passageway. The building was completed in 1902 and is of Greek neoclassical design. Across the street is the Montana Historical Society Museum, definitely worth a stop.

**Directions:** Take Exit 192, the capitol area exit, into Helena from Interstate 15. If you are going north, the exit will be 192B. Once off the interstate, you will be on Prospect Avenue. Follow Prospect Avenue west to Roberts Street. Turn left (south) and you will be at the capitol building in 4 blocks. Entering Helena on U.S. Highway 12 from the west, continue east through town on the highway, which is called Euclid Avenue and later becomes Lyndale Avenue. Turn right (south) at Montana Avenue and follow the State Capitol signs to 6th Avenue. Turn left and go one block to 1301 6th Avenue.

# Montana's Jeanette Rankin: First Woman in the House

The year was 1917, and 36-year-old Jeanette Rankin, from Missoula, Montana, sat as the first woman to serve in the U.S. House of Representatives. Jeanette would leave her mark that year as a staunch supporter of peaceful conflict resolution. She and 55 other members of Congress voted against declaring war on Germany. The vote cost Jeanette the opportunity for re-election.

Not one to give up, Jeanette was back in national politics at the age of 60, again in the House of Representatives. The Montanan voted again for peace, as the only legislator in either house to cast a ballot against entering World War II. Jeanette left office in 1942 but was active in Vietnam anti-war protests and continued her political support of issues involving women, children, and peace. She died in 1973 at the age of 92. A statue by Terri Mimnaugh commemorates her bravery, accomplishments, and peaceful ideals. It stands on the second floor of the Montana State Capitol.

**Important Information:** Open from 8 A.M. to 6 P.M. daily from May 28 to September 15. Guided tours are on the hour from 9 A.M. through 4 P.M., Memorial Day to Labor Day. Admission is free. Wheelchair accessible. Call 406-444-4789 for more information.

## 131. Montana Historical Society Museum

A visit to this museum is a must. Montana's largest, and perhaps finest, museum displays artifacts covering 12,000 years of history. Kids and adults will find the exhibits interesting and informative. Paintings of Montana people and landscape provide a view of Montana life through the eyes of Montana artists. Kids especially like to ride the two wooden horses in the entry area. **Directions:** Take Exit 192, the capitol area exit, into Helena from Interstate 15. If you are going north, the exit will be 192B. Once off the interstate, you will be on Prospect Avenue. Follow Prospect Avenue west to Roberts Street. Turn left (south) and go 4 blocks.

To reach the museum entering Helena on U.S. Highway 12 from the west, continue east through town on the highway, which is also called Euclid Avenue and later becomes Lyndale Avenue. Turn right (south) at Montana Avenue and follow the State Capitol signs to 6th Avenue. Turn left and you will be at Roberts Avenue in 2 blocks. The museum is across from the east side of the capitol building at 225 North Roberts.

**Important Information:** Open between Memorial Day and Labor Day from 8 A.M. to 6 P.M. weekdays and from 9 A.M. to 5 P.M. weekends and holidays. Winter hours, from Labor Day through Memorial Day, are 8 A.M. to 5 P.M. weekdays, and 9 A.M. to 5 P.M. on Saturdays; the museum is closed Sundays and holidays. Group tours are available by reservation only. Wheelchair accessible. Entrance is free; donations are accepted. Call for information at 406-444-2694.

## 132. Last Chance Tour Train

The Last Chance Tour Train is a fun way to find out about Helena's colorful history. The hour-long tour takes riders by magnificent mansions, humble miners' cabins, the historic downtown area, and the state capitol complex.
**Directions:** Tours leave from the Montana Historical Society Museum, 6th Avenue and Roberts Street (see site 131 for directions).
**Important Information:** Daily tours from May 15 through September 30. Between June 1 and Labor Day, tours leave on the hour from 9 through 11 A.M., 1 through 4 P.M., and at 6 P.M. For two weeks before and after these holidays, tours leave at 10 A.M., 11 A.M., 1 P.M., and 2 P.M. Fees are $4.50 for adults, $3.50 for children 12 and under, and $4 for riders 65 and older. Call 406-442-1023 or look on the web at http://www.lctours.com for more information or to check on hours.

## 133. Original Governor's Mansion

Stop by the original Governor's Mansion and participate in a guided tour of the Victorian mansion that served as home for nine Montana governors from 1888 to 1959. The building is authentically furnished.
**Directions:** The mansion is on the same street as the state capitol building, 6th Avenue (see site 130). From the capitol, go 1 mile (12 blocks) west on 6th Avenue to 304 North Ewing.
**Important Information:** Guided tours only, on the hour, from noon through 4 P.M. daily, except Sundays and Mondays. Memorial Day through Labor Day the mansion is also open on Sundays, noon to 5 P.M. Closed January through March. No admission charge. The mansion is operated by the Montana Historical Society, 406-444-2694.

# Landmarks on the
# Helena Skyline

What's that unusual-looking white tower rising high above the buildings of old Helena? You are looking at the 175-foot minaret of what was originally an Algerian Shrine temple. Built with one million bricks in 1921, the tower was damaged in the 1935 earthquake after which the Shriners sold the building to the City of Helena. It is located at the intersection of Benton and Neill avenues and is now the Civic Center.

About a half-dozen blocks from the Civic Center, the twin spires of the Cathedral of St. Helena tower majestically above the city skyline. The cathedral was modeled after the Vienna Votive Church and the German Cologne Cathedral. The building features 46 beautiful stained glass windows, 21 carved marble statues of scientists and statesmen, and other fine appointments. It is located at Lawrence Street and North Warren Avenue.

Less obvious on the skyline but equally prominent in historical stature is the "Guardian of the Gulch," as the old fire tower is called. The tower stood guard against fire during mining days from its location atop a hill on the west side of Last Chance Gulch. Fires were indeed a problem as the fire of 1874 proved, when most of downtown Helena was engulfed in flames. This tower was built in 1876 and it is one of only five of its kind left standing in the United States. Look for it near the south end of the Last Chance Gulch Pedestrian Mall, near Broadway Street.

The "Sleeping Giant" landform rests far to the north of Helena. From the second floor of the State Capitol and other locations in the city, you can see the resemblance that the mountain ridgeline has to a dozing person. Look for features of the head. The Sleeping Giant lies in the Holter Lake area west of the Beartooth Wildlife Management Area.

## 134. Holter Museum of Art

The Holter Museum displays local artists' works and traveling shows. The art center also holds classes and educational programs and has a gift shop. **Directions:** Go south on the street called Last Chance Gulch, almost to the pedestrian mall. Turn left (east) onto Lawrence Street. The museum is at 12 Lawrence, between Last Chance Gulch and the Cathedral of St. Helena. **Important Information:** Hours from Memorial Day through Labor Day are 10 A.M. to 5:30 P.M. Tuesday through Friday, 10 A.M. to 5 P.M. Saturday, and noon to 5 P.M. Sunday. Labor Day to Memorial Day the center is open 11:30 A.M. to 5 P.M. Tuesday through Friday, and noon to 5 P.M. Saturday and Sunday. Closed Mondays and major holidays. Donations are accepted. For more information, call 406-442-6400.

# 135. Museum of Gold in Norwest Bank

When you are exploring the Gold West region, here's a chance to see some of the stuff that made the region famous. This "museum" is actually in the lobby of Norwest Bank. It includes a gold collection worth more than $600,000. Here you can see gold flakes, wires, nuggets, coins, and "character" nuggets. "Character" nuggets are gold hunks in interesting shapes, such as the "Cowboy Boot" nugget.

**Directions:** The main branch of Norwest Bank, where the museum is located, is at 350 N. Last Chance Gulch. This is south of the pedestrian mall across from Bert and Ernie's Restaurant.

**Important Information:** The bank is open Monday through Friday from 9 A.M. to 4 P.M., but is closed weekends and holidays. No charge. Wheelchair accessible. For more information, call the bank at 406-447-2000.

# 136. Last Chance Gulch Pedestrian Mall

Helena's gold rush days were played out in Last Chance Gulch. Some of the history of this era is still preserved in what is now a pedestrian mall. Markers note historic buildings of interest and there are statues and unique play areas that reflect mining history too. Features along the mall sidewalks which entertain children are the small log cabin play area, the old trolley, and the tiny creek which flows down part of the southernmost mall area. You might also want to stop to look at the memorial for the USS *Helena*, or view the "Women's Wall" honoring Montana pioneer women. And, of course, there are always interesting shops along the way. A favorite kid-stop is the Parrot Confectionary, known for its variety and quality of candy. On the east side of the mall at the southern end, near the USS *Helena* Memorial, is the historic fire tower, actually used in mining days. At the southern end of the mall is Pioneer Park (site 138) and across the street is Reeder's Alley (site 137).

**Directions:** The pedestrian mall is located on the southernmost portion of the street called Last Chance Gulch and runs between 6th Avenue and Pioneer Park. From the state capitol building, take Montana Avenue north to Eleventh Avenue, turn left (west) and continue till you come to Last Chance Gulch. Turn left to get to the pedestrian mall. From U.S. Highway 12 on the west side of town, follow the highway as Euclid Avenue and Lyndale Avenue. Turn right (south) onto the road called Last Chance Gulch and drive to where the road closes to vehicles and becomes the pedestrian mall.

**Important Information:** When you get to the point where Last Chance Gulch closes to vehicles and becomes the pedestrian mall, you will be in

# Why is Last Chance Gulch the Last Chance?

Well, Last Chance Gulch is where four miners from Georgia, having tried their luck at mining in Virginia City for some period of time, decided to give gold mining one last chance up a remote gulch in Prickly Pear Valley. Lo and behold, in 1864 they struck it rich! The miners named the gulch Last Chance in honor of how they had felt about mining, and this was the beginning of Helena's boom days.

A year later, there were 100 new houses built, 100 more under construction, and rent was $200 a month. In 1970, when Helena underwent its urban renewal project, the excavated downtown building sites were successfully sluiced for gold. People say that when the prominent buildings (like the Atlas and Broadwater) were built in 1988, construction workers found nuggets in the excavation dirt. The placer gold strike in this area ultimately produced close to $35 million before it played out. Silver, lead, and sapphires lent their riches to the mineral wealth of the Helena Valley, too. Within 20 years of the Last Chance Gulch discovery, Helena was the leading financial and industrial center of the region. By the time placer mine production slowed down—in 30 years—the city had plenty else to do.

downtown Helena. You may have to drive around a bit to find a parking place on the street. The mall sidewalks are wheelchair accessible.

## 137. Reeder's Alley and the Pioneer Cabin Museum

Reeder's Alley has some of the few remaining original buildings from the Last Chance Gulch mining era. In the 1970s urban renewal hit downtown Helena and 228 undesirable buildings were removed. Federal aid rebuilt the downtown to be the attractive area you see today. Many of the most prominent buildings from the wealthy 1880s have been preserved and are in use, but most of the ragtag mining buildings are now gone. Along cobblestone Reeder's Alley is a handful of stores operating in a few of the only preserved and renovated buildings of the 1860s. This area was one of the wilder portions of Helena in its time and, though the buildings don't reflect the grandeur of the downtown area, Reeder's Alley is an important piece of mining history. The Pioneer Cabin, the oldest house in Helena, sits at the entrance to the alley. This small building has been authentically reconstructed and is now a museum of Montana's pioneering days. The museum grounds have a picnic table set in a quiet garden.

**Directions:** Entering Helena on U.S. Highway 12 from the west, turn right (south) on Benton Avenue. At the stoplight by the Civic Center (the building with the tall white spire) Benton Avenue veers off to the right. Continue straight through the light and you will be on Park Avenue. Go less than a mile. Reeder's Alley will be on your right just before the Reeder's Village Subdivision.

**Important Information:** Museum hours are 10:30 A.M. to noon and 1 to 3 P.M. during June, July, and August. Call for an appointment to see the museum during other months. For more information, call 406-443-7641.

## 138. Pioneer Park

This park has a nice playground for small children. It is situated at the south end of Last Chance Gulch Pedestrian Mall and across from Reeder's Alley, so it makes a nice resting spot while visiting one or both of these locations.

**Directions:** Entering Helena on U.S. Highway 12 from the west, turn right (south) on Benton Avenue. At the stoplight by the Civic Center (the building with the tall white spire) Benton Avenue veers off to the right. Continue straight through the light and you will be on Park Avenue. The park is on the left about a mile south on Park Avenue.

## 139. Hill/Women's Park

This city park, near the historic district, has a picnic area. Last Chance Gulch pedestrian mall is only a couple of blocks away on 6th Avenue.

**Directions:** Entering Helena on U.S. Highway 12 from the west, turn right (south) onto Benton Avenue. At the Civic Center, easily recognized by the tall white spire, turn left and go down the hill. Take the first right and park on Fuller Avenue. Women's Park is on the left side of the street; Hill Park is on the right.

## 140. Memorial Park and the Helena Municipal Swimming Pool

Memorial Park has numerous sports facilities including baseball fields, soccer fields, an ice skating area, and basketball courts. There is a picnic area, a playground, restrooms, and two war memorials here also. The Helena Municipal swimming pool is across the street from the park.

**Directions:** Entering Helena on U.S. Highway 12 from the west, continue east through town. The highway is also called Euclid Avenue and becomes Lyndale Avenue. Turn left on Last Chance Gulch and then take the first right. The park is at 1203 North Main, which is what Last Chance Gulch is called on the north side of Lyndale Avenue.

**Important Information:** Generally the pool is open the week after school is out and closes at the end of August. Pool hours for open swim are usually 1 to 4 P.M. and 5:30 to 8:30 P.M., Monday through Friday, and Saturdays 1 to 4 P.M. Call City Parks, 406-447-8463, for information or to check open swim hours. June through August you can call the pool directly at 406-447-1559. Admission for kids is $1 during the day and 50 cents at night; adult admission is $1.50 during the day and $1 at night.

## 141. Mount Helena City Park

● ● ● ● ● ● ● ● ● ● ● ● ● ● ● ● ● ● ● ● ● ● ● ● ● ● ● ● ● ● ● ●

An 800-acre city park, Mount Helena stands out as a rewarding, yet easily accessible, urban outdoor area. The mountain rises 1,300 feet above Last Chance Gulch and offers panoramic views of Helena and the surrounding area. Twenty miles of hiking trails, some easier than others, are accessed from downtown Helena, which makes the park a perfect place for a walk in the evening or other short window of time. A map of the trails can be found on a sign in the parking area. You hardly have to keep your eyes open for mule deer on Mount Helena because there are so many. Kids love to explore what locals call the "Devil's Kitchen," a fire-blackened cave in the limestone cliffs of the mountain.

**Directions:** Take Exit 192, the Capitol Area exit, into Helena from Interstate 15. If you are going north, the exit will be 192B. Once off the interstate, you will be on Prospect Avenue. Follow Prospect Avenue west to Montana Avenue and turn left (south). Take Montana Avenue to Broadway and turn right (west). Follow this to Park Avenue and turn left (south). Reeder's Village subdivision will be on your right in 0.2 mile. Turn into the subdivision. The road winds uphill but stay on the entry road, Village Road, to its endpoint. Then turn left, going uphill to the Mount Helena parking area.

Entering Helena on U.S. Highway 12 from the west, continue east through town on the highway, which is also called Euclid Avenue and later becomes Lyndale Avenue. Turn right (south) onto Benton Avenue. Go straight onto Park Avenue at the light by the Civic Center, and drive for about 1 mile. At the Reeder's Village subdivision, follow the directions above to the trailhead parking area.

## 142. Spring Meadow Lake

Here is a great place to enjoy outdoor play without going very far from Helena. Spring Meadow Lake is a 30-acre, spring-fed, manmade lake just outside the city limits. Nonmotorized boats are allowed, and both the swimming and the fishing are good. An 0.8-mile, self-guided nature trail follows the lakeshore and is nice for running, rollerblading, or walking. Look for shorebirds and other wildlife. The south end of the lake has been intentionally left undeveloped, but you'll find restrooms, picnic tables, a sandy beach, and boat docks at the north end.

**Directions:** From Helena take Euclid Avenue (U.S. Highway 12) west to Joslyn Street. Turn right (north) if you are traveling west, and go 0.1 mile. Here the road veers to the left and becomes Country Club Avenue. It is 0.7 mile to the park.

**Important Information:** There is a user's fee of $1 for people over 11 years old, and 50 cents for everyone else. Pets are not allowed between April 15 and October 1. The trail is wheelchair accessible. Contact Montana Department of Fish, Wildlife & Parks at 406-444-4720 for information.

# The Butte Batholith: Helena to Butte

The 64-mile stretch of road between Helena and Butte goes through some mighty pretty country as Interstate 15 crosses over the Butte Batholith. This volcanic formation was created some 70 million years ago when lava shot up from the earth's core. This phenomenon is responsible for the wealth of minerals in the area. At one time numerous mining towns flourished. Today a handful of small towns are located along the route, some only ghost towns.

The small town of Boulder is situated in an area that had successful mining operations at one time, including gold, silver, lead, and uranium. The large boulders in the area surrounding town explain how Boulder got its name. Several ghost towns remain in the area, the most well known being Elkhorn, now a state park (site 146). Boulder also has hot springs and radon mines, touted by many for having positive health benefits. There are facilities in Boulder where visitors can enjoy these offerings (see sites 144 and 145).

For more information about Boulder, contact the Boulder-Basin Chamber of Commerce at P.O. Box 68, Boulder, Montana 59632.

# 143. Boulder City Park

This park is just off the interstate and has picnic tables and some shade. It is a great place for a quick snack and a chance to get out of the car for a few minutes.

**Directions:** From Interstate 15, take the Boulder exit. The park is on the left side of the road just as you enter the town.

# 144. Boulder Hot Springs

This facility has a history going back to 1880 when the hot springs entertained the rich from Helena and Butte. The impressive lodge has changed hands and been remodeled over time and is an interesting building with wonderful pools. There is an indoor area for men with hot plunges and a steam room. The women's indoor area has a steam room with hot and cold plunges. A large outdoor pool is not segregated.

**Directions:** Exit Interstate 90 on Montana Highway 69 to Boulder. Go 3 miles south on MT 69 and turn right at the signed entrance for the hot springs.

**Important Information:** April 1 through October 31, the hot springs are open Monday through Thursday from 2 to 7:30 P.M., and Friday through Sunday from noon to 9 P.M. The rest of the year the hot springs are open Friday through Sunday from noon to 7:30 P.M. Pool rates are $4 for adults and $2 for children. Bed and breakfast rooms run between $45 and $90. Wheelchair accessible. Call 406-225-4339 for more information.

# 145. Free Enterprise Health Mine

The effects of low-level radiation from the radon gas that is released by uranium have not been clearly determined, but hundreds of people have testified to their positive health effects. People flock to Boulder to reap the reputed benefits of this exposure in mines such as the Free Enterprise Mine. The trip 85 feet down the old uranium mine shaft is interesting, and at the bottom health seekers can be found calmly playing cards and chatting as they sit in the old mine tunnel. On the walls are testimonials to radon treatment for arthritis, psoriasis, carpal tunnel syndrome, and numerous other maladies. Being inside the mine tunnel is really quite interesting but parents must decide if they feel the radiation is a health benefit or health risk before taking their children into the mine.

**Directions:** Exit Interstate 90 on Montana Highway 69 to Boulder. Turn onto Depot Hill Road and go 2 miles west of Boulder to the mine.

**Important Information:** Open March through November daily from 8 A.M. to 6 P.M. Natural ionizing radiation therapy, as the radon gas treatment is called, is not an accepted practice by the American Medical Association. Consult your physician for advice before entering the mines. Call the mine at 406-225-3383 for rates and other information.

## 146. Elkhorn Ghost Town State Park

Once a thriving silver-mining town with a population of 2,500, Elkhorn now has only a few residents. The town boomed in 1870 when silver ore was discovered, but declined with the silver prices in 1896. In its heyday, Elkhorn had all the businesses needed to keep a town going, plus maybe a few extra saloons—14 in all! Many of the original buildings are still standing, but most are privately owned. You can go into two buildings, the Fraternity Hall and Gillian Hall, which have not been renovated. Boxing matches, theater performances, dances, and meetings used to happen in the Fraternity Hall, but today it stands quiet and empty. Visitors can wander through the town, though they are asked not to go into any buildings except the Fraternity and Gillian halls.

One of the most interesting features here is the old cemetery, located on the hill above the town. An epidemic of diphtheria swept Elkhorn in 1888 and 1889. Children suffered most from the disease. A walk through the cemetery reveals an alarming number of graves for young people.

A picnic area and toilets are located on the right just before you enter the town. Primitive camping facilities are provided just outside the town by the USDA Forest Service.

**Directions:** From Interstate 15, take the Boulder exit and go south on Montana Highway 69 for 7 miles. Turn left (east) at the sign for Elkhorn. Continue straight ahead 12 miles on this county gravel road, Elkhorn Road. You will encounter numerous small offshoot roads and two more established roads, which may be confusing. Take the left road (straight) at the fork you will encounter 2.4 miles from MT 69, and stay left at the fork 0.7 mile beyond this.

To get to the cemetery in Elkhorn, go to the end of town on the road that has the Fraternity Hall on it. Turn right at the end of town and go 0.1 mile, then turn right again 0.5 mile up the cemetery road. This road ends at a turnaround. Park and walk up the hill.

**Important Information:** Only two buildings in the town are owned by the Montana State Department of Fish, Wildlife & Parks; it is important not to

# Where Does Gold West Gold Go?

Civilizations everywhere have sought after the glitter of gold. People use it as money for trading and have adorned their most loved with the precious metal. In fact, even today, two-thirds of the world's gold goes to make jewelry. But the rest has found an important role in our everyday lives and, if you didn't think you had any gold, guess again. Gold is everywhere. One ounce of gold makes 5 miles of wire, which is used in our electronic equipment, cameras, videocassette recorders, camcorders, fax machines, televisions, and compact discs. Contact points in our telephones are covered with gold, and microchips in computers use it too. Though this gold may never be seen, it is essential to the effective functioning of much of our electronics. More than other metals, gold doesn't tarnish or corrode and is an excellent transmitter of electricity and heat. Gold is even a healer, for it has been found to help retard certain types of cancer and is being tested for use in an AIDS treatment. In the Gold West region, it has built cities, towns, and history.

enter any of the other buildings, which are privately owned. Call 406-994-4042 for more information about the state park, and the USDA Forest Service. Call 406-444-4720 for information on nearby campgrounds.

## 147. Bear Gulch Trail 123

This 4-mile trail follows Bear Gulch to Bear Meadows. It is an easy hike that is on an old jeep trail for the first mile. The trail follows a small creek and, during wildflower season, the meadow at the end offers an array of colors. **Directions:** Take Interstate 15 to Bernice, Exit 151. Go east 0.1 mile and turn right (south) onto Forest Road 8481, the Bear Gulch access road. This is a narrow, but passable, dirt road that runs parallel to the interstate. The trailhead is 1.8 miles from the interstate, just after FS 8481 goes through a wooded "subdivision."
**Important Information:** For more information call the USDA Forest Service, 406-494-2147.

## 148. Cottonwood Lake Trail

Here is a nice lake trail in a remote mountain area. Though the drive in to the trailhead takes a while, the trail itself is an easy 2.5 miles and the lake fishing is good. There are trails from the lake to Thunderbolt Mountain and Electric

Peak. The trailhead is near Whitehouse Campground, a primitive campground. There are two other campgrounds on the road into the area as well.

**Directions:** Take Interstate 15 to Bernice, Exit 151. Go to the access road on the west side of the highway. Follow Boulder River Road 0.2 mile north to a signed road junction. Go straight at the sign onto the dirt road (don't go right). You will reach Mormon Gulch Campground in 0.9 mile. Ladysmith Campground is about 2 miles beyond, and just past the campground there is a Y junction. Turn right here onto Forest Road 82. (The left turn goes to Sheepshead Recreation area.) It is 4 miles on FR 82 to Whitehouse Campground. The Cottonwood Lake trail is a right turn by the campground onto Forest Road 65. It is 3 miles further to the lake. The trailhead is not well marked, but the road ends in an open area.

**Important Information:** The drive to the trailhead is slow-going on a dirt road, so plan for 20 to 30 minutes of travel time each way. The road is narrow in places and it is surprising how many people come back in here, so watch carefully for other vehicles.

# THE UPPER MISSOURI RIVER

Lewis and Clark followed the Upper Missouri River in their journeys and had much to say about its spectacular beauty and prolific wildlife. These unique features are still impressive to visitors today. The Missouri River is the longest river in the state, flowing 734 miles within state boundaries. The headwaters are at Three Forks, where the Madison, Gallatin, and Jefferson rivers converge. From there the river flows north to Great Falls and then east across Montana. On its way, the Missouri passes to the east of Helena. The upper Missouri River is considered to be the 200-mile section from the Three Forks confluence to Morony Dam, north of Great Falls.

The power of this mighty river has been harnessed by hydroelectric dams in four places within the Gold West region. These impoundments create a chain of three lakes. Going downstream from south to north, the reservoirs are Canyon Ferry Lake, Hauser Lake, Upper Holter Lake, and Holter Lake. Recreational opportunities abound at these sites and along the unfettered stretches of the river.

# Missouri River Float Trips and Recreation Areas

• • • • • • • • • • • • • • • • • • • • • • • • • • • • • • •

The upper Missouri River offers easy family floats as it flows through narrow canyons and Rocky Mountain landscapes. Floaters on the upper Missouri will pass by some homes and subdivisions while occasionally glimpsing the Missouri River Recreation Road. Despite these glimpses of civilization, wildlife may still be seen and river floating on the upper Missouri is pleasant. Four picturesque lakes formed by hydroelectric dams are good places to learn the art of canoeing or rafting. An extra benefit of the upper Missouri River is its reputation as a blue-ribbon fishing area with plentiful brown and rainbow trout.

Numerous public river-access points allow considerable variation in the potential lengths of river trips. The Montana Department of Fish, Wildlife & Parks has a good map of floating opportunities for this stretch; it's available through the Region 4 Headquarters in Great Falls at a cost of $3.50. Call 406-454-5840 to inquire about the "Montana Afloat" maps.

The only rapids which may challenge beginning floaters between Holter Dam and Great Falls are the Half Breed Rapids just below Prewett Creek Recreation Area. The rapids are class II or III, depending on water volume, but can easily be avoided. Also, the river moves quickly through a narrow channel just below Craig and there are small rapids above and below the Dearborn access site.

When planning a float trip, consider shuttle times for vehicles and remember how short the attention span of children can be. This will help you decide how long a stretch of river you want to float and which put-in and take-out sites are best. The upper Missouri River flow rate averages about 4 miles per hour, although the river runs slower where it approaches dams.

## 149. Holter Dam Access Site to Prewett Creek Fishing Access Site Float

• • • • • • • • • • • • • • • • • • • • • • • • • • • • • • •

This float is 23 miles and ends above Half Breed Rapids. This entire segment is about a 6-hour float (river time only). If you do not want to float this long, select any of the ten public access points before Prewett Creek for your put-in or take-out locations and shorten the float length. Two nice half-day trips in this stretch are Holter Dam Access Site to Spite Hill Access Site (12 miles or three to four hours of river time) or from there to Prewett Creek Access Site (11 miles or three to four hours of river time).

**Directions:** To get to Holter Dam Access Site, take Interstate 15 north of Helena to the Wolf Creek exit and go through the town of Wolf Creek. Just before the Wolf Creek bridge, turn south (upriver) and go 2 miles on the Holter Dam Road to the Holter Dam Access Site. A gravel road about 0.1 mile from the bridge will take you to the Holter Dam access site and campground, just down river of the dam. Spite Hill and Prewett Creek access sites can all be reached from the Missouri River Recreation Road, as can any of the other public access points.

## 150. Gates of the Mountains Boat Club to Departure Point Campground River Float

This float is 13.5 miles and involves about 5 or 6 hours of floating time. The trip includes the scenic section traveled by the Gates of the Mountains boat tour. Majestic cliffs border the river as it flows by Meriwether Canyon and Mann Gulch. The river slows down after Mann Gulch. Plan a full-day trip as there are no options for making the float shorter.

**Directions:** Follow directions to the Gates of the Mountains Boat Tour (site 157) to put in at the boat club launch. The launch area is signed and marina attendants can direct you to the put-in location.

**Important Information:** There is a launch fee of $2 on weekdays and $3 on weekends. Log Gulch Recreation Site directions are found in the Holter Lake Recreation Area description (site 154). Meriwether Picnic Area has restrooms and docks and makes a nice stopping point along the way. Look for it on the right (east) riverbank.

## 151. Holter Lake Departure Point Campground to Holter Lake Recreation Site Float

This is a flat lake float across Holter Lake with no current, so it's a paddle all the way. The scenic journey is 4.5 miles.

**Directions:** See directions to Holter Lake Recreation Area (site 154) to find the campgrounds.

## 152. Toston Bridge to Indian Road Access Site Float

This stretch has no rapids and is a good beginning float for families. This 27-mile stretch makes a full-day float. Two shorter floats can be made along this segment: from Toston Bridge to Deepdale Access (15 miles or about 4 hours from Toston) or Deepdale Access to Indian Road Access Site (12 miles or about 3 to 4 hours). The Deep Dale to Indian Road segment is more interesting than the one beginning at Toston, as the river above Deep Dale goes through a great deal of agricultural land.

**Directions:** To get to Toston Bridge, take U.S. Highway 287 south from Townsend to Toston and turn west on U.S. Highway 285. Toston Bridge is at this junction. Deep Dale Access Site is about 5 miles south of Townsend on the west side of US 287. The Indian Road access is north of Townsend at the junction of US 287 and Centerville Road at the Indian Road campground.

**Important Information:** The take-out point is just past the Missouri River bridge on the right side of the river and is actually at the campground. When floating, don't go past this take-out point as there isn't a good take-out after Indian Road campground until the lake.

## 153. Missouri River Recreation Road

The Missouri River Recreation Road meanders through canyons of the Missouri River, often collectively called Wolf Creek Canyon. There are 12 maintained fishing access sites on the 35-mile stretch of winding canyon road that provide opportunities to play or picnic. Adults will marvel at the beauty of the canyon, and a couple of stops at river access points along the way will make the trip memorable in the minds of children. A number of family-style river floats can be made along the gentle stretch of the Missouri below Holter Dam. There are four points along the 35-mile stretch to access Interstate 15.

**Directions:** Take Interstate 15 north of Helena for 25 miles. Exit at Recreation Road. Continue north from the exit and you will see an interpretive sign on the right side of the road which provides a map of the Missouri River Recreation Road route. From this sign, it is 7 miles to Wolf Creek, 16 miles to Craig, 27 miles to the Canyon interchange, and 33 miles to the Hardy interchange.

**Important Information:** Contact the Great Falls office of the Montana Department of Fish, Wildlife & Parks at 406-454-5840 for a map of the area and more information.

## 154. Holter Lake Recreation Area

The U.S. Bureau of Land Management (BLM) recreation sites at both ends of lower Holter Lake are the only public access spots on this pretty lake nestled in the Big Belt Mountains. This is good fishing territory, with or without a boat, for trout, walleye, perch, or salmon. Hikers use the recreation sites as access points for nearby Gates of the Mountains Wilderness, Beartooth Wildlife Management Area, and Sleeping Giant Wilderness Study Area. The lake itself is a nice place to play. BLM facilities at Holter Lake and Log Gulch recreation sites include a beach, restrooms, picnic area, water, and campgrounds. There is a private marina on the lake and the BLM provides boat ramps and boat docks at the Holter Lake and Log Gulch recreation sites. The Log Gulch Recreation Site, located at the south end of the lake, has about 100 camping units with water, toilets, docks, a boat ramp, and a swimming beach area. Beyond Log Gulch is the Departure Point Recreation Site, a primitive campground.

Keep a lookout on the rock outcrops above the lake for bighorn sheep and mountain goats. On the lake you may see peregrine falcons, American white pelicans, great blue herons, common loons, and other waterfowl. The state-operated Beartooth Wildlife Management Area (site 155) and the BLM Sleeping Giant Wilderness Study Area south of the lake offers additional wildlife viewing, hiking, mountain biking, horseback riding, boat-in camping, and picnicking opportunities.

**Directions:** Go north of Helena on Interstate 15 about 30 miles. Take the Wolf Creek exit and go through the town of Wolf Creek. Cross the Wolf Creek bridge and take an immediate right onto Beartooth Road. In 3 miles you will come to the park. Log Gulch and Departure Point recreation sites are further up the lake on Beartooth Road.

**Important Information:** This is a high-use area, particularly in July. There is a use fee. Contact the Bureau of Land Management at 406-494-5059 for more information.

## 155. Beartooth Wildlife Management Area

Looking for bighorn sheep? The Beartooth Wildlife Management Area is a good place to start. The rugged rock outcroppings in the area are excellent habitat for these critters. The management area is also home to a large elk population. A thriving prairie dog town can be found on Bureau of Land Management land on the road to Beartooth Wildlife Management Area. A gravel road runs through the area and unimproved roads on Elkhorn Creek and Willow Creek are suitable for hiking or mountain biking. Camping is permitted in the Cottonwood Creek, Elkhorn Creek, and Willow Creek designated campgrounds and in designated parking areas from May 15 through December 1. More camping is available at the U.S. Bureau of Land Management sites along Holter Lake (see site 154).

**Directions:** Go north of Helena on Interstate 15 about 30 miles. Take the Wolf Creek exit and go through the town of Wolf Creek. Cross the Wolf Creek bridge and take an immediate right onto Beartooth Road. Follow this road along the east shore of Holter Lake for about 6 miles to the Beartooth Wildlife Management Area. Look for the prairie dog town to the left (north) before you enter the area. There is an informational sign at the prairie dog town.

**Important Information:** Call Montana State Department of Fish, Wildlife & Parks in Great Falls at 406-454-5840 for a map and more information.

# Gates of the Mountains Wilderness

Lewis and Clark wrote about a stretch of the Missouri River where 1,200-foot sheer cliffs on either side of the river seemed to close like "gates" behind them. The explorers named this area Gates of the Mountains and there is now a 28,560-acre wilderness area which includes the "gates" mentioned in the journals of Lewis and Clark. Located at the north end of the Big Belt Mountains, the Gates of the Mountains is Montana's smallest wilderness area.

The wilderness trails here are mostly too long and rugged for families with young children. However, any family can make the 0.25-mile jaunt to Refrigerator Canyon. Older children experienced with hiking can enjoy the trails up wilderness peaks, which are comparatively easy Rocky Mountain peaks to climb. People of all ages enjoy the boat tour from Upper Holter Lake along the Missouri River. From the boat landing at Meriwether Picnic Area, families can take the Missouri River Canyon Trail to Coulter Campground or walk to Vista Point. The wilderness area is also the site of the 1949 Mann Gulch fire where 13 firefighters died. Norman Maclean's book *Young Men and Fire* describes the event. An on-site memorial can be visited by the hearty who want to walk the 2-mile, steep trail.

## 156. Gates of the Mountains Boat Tour

The Gates of the Mountains boat cruise has been in operation for more than 100 years, leading visitors up a spectacular stretch of the Missouri River traveled by Lewis and Clark in 1805. The tour begins on Upper Holter Lake and passes through majestic limestone cliffs where wildlife sightings are common. Chances are you'll see some critters, which could include bighorn sheep, mountain goats, waterfowl, red-tailed hawks, ospreys, bald eagles, deer, and possibly black bear and mountain lions.

Tour guides on the boat provide interesting information about the area and its history. The tour stops briefly at Meriwether Picnic Area, where riders can get off the boat for a few minutes or choose to stay ashore to explore the area until the next boat arrives. If you take the first boat of the day (10 or 11 A.M., depending on the time of year) and return on the last boat back (4 or 5 P.M.), there is ample time for a hike to the Vista Point Overlook, to Coulter Campground, or to simply enjoy the beach and picnic area. The 12-mile, round-trip boat tour takes a little less than two hours including the 10-minute stop at Meriwether Picnic Area.

**Directions:** Take Interstate 15 north of Helena toward Great Falls for 18 miles. Exit the highway at Exit 209, marked Gates of the Mountains. Go right (east) and follow this road 3.1 miles to the boat tour center. The Gates of the Mountains tour docks are 68 miles from Great Falls and 21 miles from Helena.

**Important Information:** Boat tours begin on Memorial Day weekend and end in late September. Departure times vary during the summer, so call for a schedule at 406-458-5241. Cost is $7.50 for adults and $4.50 for seniors 60 and over and children 4 to 14. Kids under 4 travel free. There is no wheelchair ramp but tour operators will assist people with wheelchairs into the boat.

## 157. Meriwether Picnic Area: Vista Point Trail

This 0.5-mile trail leads to an overlook of the Missouri River where you can get a nice view. It is steep in parts but most kids can make it to the viewpoint.

**Directions:** Take the Gates of the Mountains boat tour to Meriwether Picnic Area. From the picnic shelter, follow the trail that goes up Meriwether Canyon and turn left immediately after the old Forest Service building where a sign indicates the start of Vista Point Trail. The trail forks soon; the right side goes to the Mann Gulch fire site while the left side goes the short distance to the overlook.

**Important Information:** Even this trail takes longer to hike than the allotted time allowed for shore leave on the boat tour. Plan on returning to the tour docks on a later boat if you hike this trail, and make sure you are there before the last boat leaves! Though no one has been hurt to date, the mountain lion population in the area has grown and these wild cats have been seen in the area. If you choose to stay and hike at Meriwether Picnic Area, be aware that, although it's unlikely, you may see one of these cats.

## 158. Missouri River Canyon Trail 257 to Coulter Campground

If you choose to make a layover at Meriwether Picnic Area during the Gates of the Mountains boat tour (or have come in on your own boat), this is a pleasant short hike that is possible to take between boats. Even if you only walk part of the trail, you will enjoy the views of the river and spectacular limestone cliffs. The trail is mostly flat and goes through the woods by the river for 1 mile to Coulter Campground. It then continues another easy mile to Fields Gulch. From here, the trail goes southeast for 3.5 miles to Spring Gulch. This part of the trail is steeper and can be difficult to find, and would require more time than the layover between boats.

**Directions:** The trail begins from Meriwether Picnic Area and goes upriver to the campground. Unless you've brought your own boat, the trail is accessible only if you have taken the Gates of the Mountains boat tour or if you have come in from other trails in the Gates of the Mountains Wilderness. The trailhead at Meriwether Picnic Area is behind the vault toilet, which is just beyond the picnic shelter.

**Important Information:** You will need to schedule your time carefully to make sure you don't miss the last boat of the day back to the tour docks. Ask the boat company for scheduled pick-up times and plan your hike appropriately.

## 159. Refrigerator Canyon Trail 259

Refrigerator Canyon is an intriguing place to explore and, even if you only walk the 0.25 mile to the canyon, the trip is enjoyable. The trail climbs gradually through lush, shaded forest to a narrow limestone canyon. The canyon is only 10 feet wide in places and 200-foot cliffs tower impressively above the trail. The cliffs help create the "refrigerator" effect of being 10 to 20 degrees cooler inside the canyon than it is outside. This is a result of evaporative cooling from breezes blowing over the stream and through the cliffs.

After winding through the canyon 200 yards or so, the trail slips through a tall slit in the rock walls and continues 18 miles across the Gates of the Mountains Wilderness to Meriwether Picnic Area. If your family is ready for an uphill hike, you may want to continue from the end of the canyon to a viewpoint of the surrounding area. This is about a mile or a mile and a half from the end of the canyon.

**Directions:** Follow the directions to York from Interstate 15 as described in the Trout Creek Canyon Trail (site 161). At York, turn left (north) toward Nelson. At Nelson, turn right (east) toward Hogback Mountain Lookout. The Refrigerator Canyon Trail is about 5 miles from Nelson. The large trailhead sign can easily be seen from the road. To reach York from the Canyon Ferry Visitor Center (site 167) go 0.1 mile east from the center and turn left (north) at the sign for Riverside Campground. Go down this paved road 0.8 mile and turn right toward York. Follow the directions above to reach the trailhead.

**Important Information:** The Refrigerator Canyon trailhead is a 21-mile, one-hour drive from Canyon Ferry Visitor Center on graveled road. The route to York from I-15 is mostly on paved road and takes less time. If you take the route from Canyon Ferry, plan a short play stop to break up the driving time. You can stop briefly at the Riverside Picnic Area (site 166) or at any of the numerous pullouts along Canyon Ferry Lake.

Consider going another 13 road miles beyond Refrigerator Canyon trailhead to Hogback Lookout (site 160). This will add another hour of driving time to get up and back, but you'll enjoy the view and the opportunity to see the lookout. Keep your eyes open for logging trucks on the road after Nelson. For more information call the USDA Forest Service, Helena Ranger District, at 406-449-5490.

## 160. Hogback Lookout

A trip to Hogback Lookout requires a time commitment to driving, but offers interesting geology and good wildlife viewing in exchange. The panorama from the top (7,813 feet) is breathtaking. So is the drive. Between Nelson and the lookout, you will find yourself among 1,500-foot limestone cliffs and picturesque rock spires. At the top you will have a 360-degree view of spectacular scenery. If you're lucky, the Forest Service fire guard will be at the lookout and can tell you about the area. Bring your binoculars and look for deer, elk, mountain goats, black bear, and coyotes along the roadway.

There are several opportunities for quick stops to break up the long drive and make the trip interesting in other ways. Stop for water play at pullouts along Canyon Ferry Lake, at the Riverside Picnic Area, or at the York Bridge Fishing Access Site. The 0.25-mile hike into Refrigerator Canyon (site 159), about 13 miles before the lookout, is easy enough for most hikers and is impressive.

**Directions:** There are two routes to the lookout. The route via Canyon Ferry Lake involves more travel on dirt roads than does the route from Interstate 15 to York. As there are different things to see each way, you might want to take one route in and the other route back.

Follow the directions to Refrigerator Canyon (site 159) to take either the I-15 or the Canyon Ferry Lake route. After you pass the trailhead sign for the Refrigerator Canyon Trail, drive another 10 miles to an open saddle, Indian Flats, which is the divide between the Trout Creek and Beaver Creek drainages. Take the right fork at the saddle and drive about 3 miles to the Hogback Mountain Lookout. The 36-mile drive from the Canyon Ferry Visitor Center to Hogback Mountain Lookout is a slow drive, so plan on an hour and a half each way. You can explore Canyon Ferry Lake sites and Refrigerator Canyon on this route.

If you take the route from I-15, you will cross the York Bridge on the Missouri River, where you can stop and enjoy the river at the York Bridge Fishing Access Site. Follow the directions from the Refrigerator Canyon trailhead (see site 159) to Hogback Lookout.

**Important Information:** The gravel road to the lookout is in good shape, though the last section has sharp rocks. Make sure your tires are not too worn. Most cars won't have trouble on these roads, though very low vehicles should perhaps go slower and may take longer to reach the top.

# Hauser Lake Area

Hauser Lake is the middle of the three lakes formed by impoundment of the Missouri River in this area. York Road crosses the river just below the lake and leads into the Big Belt Mountains, a remote and picturesque back road getaway.

## 161. Trout Creek Canyon Trail

If you want to experience the outdoors from the heart of Montana mountains, this sojourn will provide you with all the trimmings. The long drive to the trailhead at Vigilante Campground is on good gravel road, but leaves no question that you are removing yourself from civilization. At the end of your drive is a quiet campground and a magnificent hike into the Big Belt Mountains.

Trout Creek Canyon Trail winds through an impressive, narrow canyon. Yellow and gray limestone cliffs tower above you for most of the hike. Keep your eyes on the cliffs for you will see some interesting rock configurations. At times, the rock striations are vertical and elsewhere swirl in circles. This geologic shaping is caused by the uplifting of layers of rock over thousands of years. You can also see large, hanging rock ledges and interesting formations at the top of the rock cliffs. This is a good place to play "I see a . . . in the rock" game with children as you imagine with them what the shapes resemble.

Trout Creek Canyon Trail was designed by the USDA Forest Service for people needing special access. The first mile is an extra-wide trail with interpretive signs. It is not quite wheelchair accessible, however. There is a steady, but gentle, uphill grade along most of the trail. After the first mile, the trail becomes as wide as a road, but at times it becomes a narrow footpath. At high water, the creek may be fast and deep but during much of the summer will be only a small trickle.

The trail connects with Hogback Lookout Road in 3 miles and you can continue the walk up the road. Although you can start the trail from

Hogback Lookout Road, the trailhead at this end is not signed. The most spectacular section of the trail is in the canyon above Vigilante Campground.

**Directions:** From Interstate 15 at Helena, go 8 miles north to the Lincoln Road turnoff at Exit 200. Go right (east) 5.2 miles and turn right onto Lake Helena Drive at the stop sign where the road comes to a T. You will reach Helena Causeway Fishing Access Site in 0.4 mile. Go across the causeway and continue for 1.8 miles to a left-hand turn. This is Deal Lane but there are no signs to that effect at this point. In slightly less than 3 miles on Deal Lane, you will come to York Road. To the left (northeast) 0.5 mile is a small community on Hauser Lake called Lakeside. Turn left from Deal Lane onto York Road, and continue beyond Lakeside 3 miles to the York Bridge across the Missouri River. Three miles beyond the river is the town of York which can be recognized by the big sign on the York Bar. Vigilante Campground is 6 miles farther. The road to Vigilante Campground past York is paved about half of the way and hard-packed ground the rest of the way. In rainy weather, the road surface could be slippery.

Trout Creek Canyon Trail begins from the upstream end of the parking lot or you can start it in the campground. Neither trailhead is signed but you will know if you are on the right trail as it follows Trout Creek. The trail starting from the upstream end of the parking lot enters Trout Creek Canyon immediately.

**Important Information:** For more information call the USDA Forest Service, Helena Ranger District, at 406-449-5490.

## 162. Black Sandy State Park on Hauser Lake

Some of the popularity of this state park is due to the fact that it is the closest to Helena of the three Upper Missouri River reservoirs. It is also the middle lake and this central location makes it convenient to reach the other two. Hauser Lake is a good boating lake and has Kokanee salmon and trout fishing. It is also a good site for viewing eagles during the fall migration.

Black Sandy State Park offers a boat ramp, day-use parking, vault toilets, and campground facilities for motor homes, trailers, and tents. There is a wheelchair-accessible picnic spot with a viewpoint and fishing dock. Nearby is the Lakeside Resort, which has a marina and other recreational facilities.

**Directions:** From Interstate 15 at Helena, go 8 miles north to the Lincoln Road turnoff at Exit 200. Go right (east) 5.2 miles and turn left onto Lake Helena Drive where the road comes to a T intersection. It is 3 miles to the state park.

**Important Information:** This is a high-use area with day-use and campground fees. Wheelchair accessible. 406-444-4720.

# 163. Missouri–Beaver Creek Trail

The Missouri–Beaver Creek Trail is a favorite hike with local families who have discovered that it is a beautiful walk along the river and also quite suitable for children. Don't be put off by the slightly rugged half-mile at the start of the trail, as this is as bad as it gets. The trail is rocky in places but large, level rocks have been hand-laid in the rough spots to make stepping stones—kids love this! The trail is 1.8 miles one way from Hauser Dam to the Beaver Creek Trail. Plan for three hours hiking time round trip, but allow four if you want to picnic.

As you hike, watch for short spur trails down to the river, especially if you want to fish or enjoy the water first-hand. A big bend in the river is about two-thirds of the way to the campground, the endpoint of the trail. Once you go around the bend you can see the trailhead in the distance. Just beyond the bend is a small, sandy spot on the right side of the trail where you can have a nice picnic with a panoramic view. The tall, impressive cliffs along the river are limestone, quartzite, and colorful red shale.

The trailhead is at the south, upstream end of the trailhead parking lot, where Beaver Creek joins the Missouri River. Look for the interpretive signs with information about salmon, cliff geology, and more. Follow the short trails along the river by the trailhead and look for beavers, Canada geese, ducks, loons, American white pelicans, great blue herons, ospreys, eagles, river otters, and deer. Anglers dot the riverbanks, mostly catching walleye and brown trout. The trailhead is a day-use area with a vault toilet.

**Directions:** From Interstate 15 at Helena, go 8 miles north to the Lincoln Road turnoff at Exit 200. Go right (east) 5.2 miles and, at the stop sign at the T intersection in the road, turn left toward Black Sandy State Park. Follow this road (Lake Helena Drive) 3 miles. Veer left just before the park entrance and continue 1.5 miles to Hauser Dam. Park in the small parking area before you cross the dam. The trailhead is across the dam and immediately to the left. A sign saying Public Access Trail is where the Missouri–Beaver Creek Trail begins.

The trail can be accessed from Beaver Creek Trailhead, although this is a long drive. To begin the trail from the Beaver Creek Trailhead, go 0.1 mile east of the Canyon Ferry Visitor Center (site 165) and turn left (north) onto Jim Town Road toward Riverside Campground. At Riverside Campground take the right-hand road toward York and go 7 miles on this dirt road. Turn right (east) on York Road and go 1 mile to the York Bar, then turn left (north). It is about 10 miles from this point to Nelson. Turn left (west) at Nelson and follow this to Beaver Creek Campground. The road is narrow and sometimes bumpy but passable in passenger cars. Keep in mind that this drive is slow going and plan your time accordingly.

**Important Information:** It is possible to encounter rattlesnakes in this area, though this is not a frequent occurrence (see page 16 for information about snakes).

## 164. Spokane Bar Sapphire Mine

There's more than gold in them thar hills. There's sapphires! The Helena area is well known for Montana sapphires and there are several sites close to the city where visitors can sift for these precious gems. Among these is the Spokane Bar Sapphire Mine. Most people find at least a few small gems at the mines, and finding good-sized ones is not altogether unusual. Either way, kids of all ages enjoy the activity and the excitement of finding a gemstone in the rough. At the Spokane Bar Sapphire Mine is the Gold Fever Rock Shop which has an interesting collection of rocks and minerals.

**Directions:** Take Montana Avenue north from Helena and turn right (east) on Custer Avenue. Take Custer Avenue to York Road and turn left (north). Follow York Road to mile marker 8 and turn right onto Hart Lane. Just after the road makes a 90-degree bend, turn left onto Castles Road. Follow this road to the sapphire mine. York Road can also be accessed via Interstate 15 by taking the Cedar Street exit and going east to Custer Avenue. Turn right on Custer and then left onto York Road. Turn right by mile marker 8 onto Hart Lane and left onto Castles Road.

**Important Information:** Wear your diggin' clothes, as this is dirty work. Open 9 A.M. to 5 P.M. daily; hours vary in winter. Prices depend on the size of the gravel bags you decide to sift, but there is an inexpensive option that gives you a taste of the excitement. Call 877-DIG-GEMS or 406-227-8989, or see "get mine" information on the Worldwide web at http://www.crom.net/~gemking. There are other mines in the area, too. Contact the Helena Chamber of Commerce, 800-743-5362, to find out which ones are currently in operation.

# Canyon Ferry Recreation Area

To the south on the Missouri River, Canyon Ferry Reservoir is one of the most popular local recreation areas for Helena residents. In fact, because of its high use, Canyon Ferry is considered Montana's most popular recreation site. Once you see the lake you will understand why it's a favorite spot. This is an easy place to spend a rewarding day or longer vacation.

Three marinas support boating for anglers, water skiers, and sailors and provide groceries. There is also a visitor center and restaurant. Along the 76-mile shoreline are numerous places to easily access the lake for a picnic or an afternoon of play near the water. More than 20 recreational areas around the lake include seven developed fee campgrounds, four dispersed camping areas, and 11 free day-use areas. Although the majority of the recreational facilities are clustered at the northern end of the lake, access areas and campgrounds are also available at the south end. A few access areas are maintained at the southern end for boaters. Anglers will be rewarded at Canyon Ferry Lake with brown and rainbow trout, yellow perch, and mountain whitefish. Kokanee salmon make a run each fall below the dam.

The recreational area is managed through a cooperative effort between the U.S. Bureau of Reclamation (USBR) and the U.S. Bureau of Land Management (BLM). Seven agencies participate in the Bald Eagle-Kokanee Salmon Outdoor program. For current information about recreational facilities, contact the USBR at 406-475-3310 or the BLM at 406-475-3319. Canyon Ferry Visitor Center also provides recreational information and has excellent interpretive displays; call them at 406-475-3128. A packet of recreation and fishing information is available through the BLM.

Keep your eyes open for wildlife around the lake and surrounding area as you have a good chance of seeing bighorn sheep, mountain goats, deer, beavers, geese, waterfowl, American white pelicans, ospreys, and shorebirds. In the fall, you will see migratory eagles which congregate here to feed on spawning kokanee salmon. Other interesting Canyon Ferry features are the petrified wood, agate, and fossils which can be found on the lake's beaches.

## 165. Canyon Ferry Visitor Center

Take time to stop at the visitor center, where you will enjoy learning from the informative and well-presented exhibits. Displays vary seasonally but include live fish, taxidermy mounts, hands-on interactive exhibits, and videos. All are presented in an intriguing manner and appeal to visitors of all ages. Summer exhibits focus on Lewis and Clark, wildlife, tree species, and fish. Fall displays feature eagles, which come to Canyon Ferry in large numbers to feed on spawning salmon. Eagle biology, myths, legends, and bird habits are highlighted. Though the exhibit area is small, there's a lot to see! The visitor center grounds have picnic tables, restrooms, and an outdoor interpretive display.

**Directions:** Take Exit 192A from Interstate 15. Go southeast on U.S. Highway 12 for 10 miles. At the flashing yellow light, which marks the turn for Canyon Ferry, turn northeast onto Broadwater County 284 and stay on this

# The Bald Eagle,
## *Haliaeetus leucocephalus*

What bird, with a 9-foot wingspan, flies at an average speed of 30 miles per hour and dives at speeds up to 90 miles per hour? Which bird can spot other birds of its kind 4 miles away? It is our national emblem, the bald eagle. But the amazing facts don't stop there. Eagles weigh only 7 to 13 pounds, yet can lift half their own weight. And, in the weight of an eagle, the feathers are twice as heavy as the skeleton! Females, by the way, are generally one-third larger than males. The eagle has great aviation skills, not only in speed, but also in the ability to gain altitude, for they have been spotted flying at 18,000 feet. Though they fly fast and far, when they land during nesting season, they are impressive homemakers. The largest recorded eagle nest was 9.5 feet in diameter and 20 feet deep. It weighed two tons. Now that's a nest! Bald eagles, by the way, were moved in 1995 from the federal endangered species list to the list of threatened species.

road for 10.3 miles. Turn right into the visitor center, which is located in an historic schoolhouse.

**Important Information:** The visitor center is generally open from mid-May to Labor Day, 11 A.M. to 5 P.M. Wednesday through Sunday. The center closes after Labor Day but reopens for eagle season, which is generally the last week of October through the first week December. During this time, the center is open weekends from 8 A.M. to 4 P.M., and weekdays from 9 A.M. to 3 P.M. The Canyon Ferry Recreation Area receives very high use. Call 406-475-3128 to check hours.

## 166. Riverside Campground and Eagle Viewing Area

Just a mile from the Canyon Ferry Visitor Center, the Riverside Campground provides access to the Missouri River as it flows from Canyon Ferry Dam. Fishing is often productive here and up the adjoining road that follows the river to the dam. There is a wheelchair-accessible fishing platform in the picnic area. The campground has vault toilets and a beach.

During the bald eagle migration season, generally October 15 through December 31, Kokanee salmon swim upriver, lay their eggs, and die. Bald eagles flock to the Missouri River in the Canyon Ferry area to feast on the dying salmon. For the eagles, this stop is a short pause in their migratory journey south. As many as 302 bald eagles have been counted in the area between Canyon Ferry and Hauser lakes and researchers estimate that more than 1,000 eagles migrate through this area during the fall and winter. The river corridor is closed to visitors during the migration season to protect the eagles, but Riverside Campground is a designated eagle-viewing area. During peak migration times, it's not unusual to see 30 to 40 eagles at the viewing area. A fall trip to the Canyon Ferry Visitor Center, with a stop at the eagle-viewing area, makes an interesting, informative day. Other birds you may see are ospreys, American white pelicans, Canada geese, and other waterfowl. **Directions:** From the Canyon Ferry Visitor Center (site 165) go 0.1 mile east and turn left (north) at the sign for Riverside Campground. Go down this paved road 0.8 mile and turn left into the Riverside Campground and picnic area.

**Important Information:** If you plan to do some eagle watching, bring warm clothes, binoculars, and cameras with long lenses (200 mm or better). As you will see a variety of other birds, a field guide is a good idea, too. Dogs may frighten the birds away, so it's best to leave them home. The best sighting time is early in the day. At dusk the birds move to secluded roosting spots and you may not see them. Wheelchair accessible. Call 406-475-3128 for more information.

## 167. Canyon Ferry Wildlife Management Area

This 5,000-acre management area is located on the south end of Canyon Ferry Lake where the Missouri River enters the reservoir. The wetland serves as a landing spot for various species of migrating birds and is home to numerous others. Birds frequently observed include ospreys, American white pelicans, double-crested cormorants, Caspian terns, Canada geese and various species of waterfowl. Large congregations of common loons are often seen here during spring and fall migrations, and tundra swans stay awhile during their March migration. Beavers, raccoons, otters, deer, and rabbits are sometimes observed, especially in the delta area. Dike Three is a prime place to catch views of waterfowl. The back roads and dikes around Dikes Two and Three are excellent locations for riding bikes as you look for wildlife.

**Directions:** Take U.S. Highway 12 about 3 miles east from Townsend and turn left (north) onto Harrison Road, Montana Highway 284. Ray Creek Road is about 5 miles north on Harrison Road, and leads to a parking lot between Ponds Two and Three. The road is signed; it is about 1 mile west of Harrison to the parking lot. You can reach other areas of the wildlife management area by going west on Delger Road, Riley Road, Meyer Road, or Dry Gulch Road, all of which can be accessed from Harrison Road.

**Important Information:** Take mosquito repellent during moist, warm weather. Maps are available at the Montana Department of Fish, Wildlife &

Parks in Townsend. Future plans call for a wheelchair-accessible trail to one of the wildlife viewing areas. Call 406-266-3367 for information.

# DEER LODGE AND THE SURROUNDING AREA

The Deer Lodge valley was historically a site for gold mining and cattle grazing and has been home to the Montana State Prison for over a century. Historic preservation is a community pastime. There are six museums on the city's Main Street and the Grant-Kohrs Ranch, now a national historic site, portrays cowboy life as it was in the early 1800s. A rewarding visit to the Deer Lodge area includes time to explore these historic resources.

## City of Deer Lodge

The city of Deer Lodge is surrounded by mountain ranges and the Clark Fork River traverses the valley, providing ample trout fishing opportunities. Half of the 6,700 valley residents live in the city of Deer Lodge, the second oldest city in Montana. A visit to Deer Lodge could easily be a two-day trip. Contact the Powell County Chamber of Commerce, located at 1171 Main Street in Deer Lodge, 406-846-2094, or check the Worldwide Web at http://www.chamber@powellpost.com for more information.

### 168. Old Montana Prison and the Montana Law Enforcement Museum

The Old Montana Prison was built in 1871 in an attempt to tame the Wild West by confining the outlaws who once roamed Montana Territory. It remained in use until 1979. A tour will give you an interesting mixture of architecture and prison history. Visitors can walk through most of the prison on a self-guided tour. An explanatory brochure details prison life and security and tells noteworthy prison stories. Kids will find the experience interesting and thought-provoking.

The Montana Law Enforcement Museum is located in the Old Montana Prison. It includes displays from the Montana Highway Patrol, Sheriff and Peace Officers Association, law enforcement agencies across the state, and the Royal Canadian Mounted Police. Across the street is the Montana

State Prison Hobby Store which features hand-crafted gift items made by inmates in the new prison 4 miles west of town. Check out the Lil' Joe Engine, an electric railroad engine on display in the Old Montana Prison Museum parking lot.

**Directions:** The prison is located at 1106 Main Street. From Interstate 90, take either of the two Deer Lodge exits and go toward town. Both roads take you through town on Main Street where the museum is located. The Montana Law Enforcement Museum is inside the prison complex up the metal stairs in the 1912 Cell House lobby. The Hobby Store is on the corner of Main Street and Texas Avenue.

**Important Information:** The prison is open all year. Memorial Day to Labor Day hours are 10 A.M. to 4 P.M., Wednesday through Saturday, and noon to 4 P.M., Sunday through Tuesday. The Old Montana Prison is closed for some holidays. Winter hours are Sunday through Tuesday from noon to 4 P.M., and Wednesday through Saturday from 10 A.M. to 4 P.M. Montana Law Enforcement Museum hours are the same.

The entrance fee for the prison and law enforcement museum is $5 for adults, $2.50 for ages 10 to 15, and $1 for ages 7 to 9. There is no charge for children under 7. Combined passes can be purchased for the five fee museums on Main Street, operated by the Powell County Museum and Arts Foundation. These are the Old Montana Prison, the Montana Auto Museum, Frontier Montana Museum, the Montana Law Enforcement Museum, and Yesterday's Playthings. Pass rates for Memorial Day through Labor Day are $7.95 for adults, $4 for ages 10 to 15, and $1 for ages 7 to 9. Children under 7 are free. Prices go down in the winter. Wheelchair accessible. Call 406-846-3111 for information on the Old Montana Prison or 406-846-3777 for the Montana Law Enforcement Museum.

## 169. Montana Auto Museum

If car history is a family interest, you will enjoy this museum. About 130 vehicles are on display, including a 1917 camping trailer that shows "luxury" camping of bygone years. There is also a gas station and a photo exhibit.

**Directions:** From Interstate 90, take either of the two Deer Lodge exits and go toward town. Both roads take you through town on Main Street where the museum is located at 1106 Main Street. Entrance to the car museum is through the Old Montana Prison Visitor Center.

**Important Information:** The Montana Auto Museum is open all year. Memorial Day to Labor Day, hours are Wednesday through Saturday from 10 A.M. to 4 P.M., and Sunday through Tuesday from noon to 4 P.M. You can also enter this museum with a combined pass for the five fee museums on

Main Street operated by the Powell County Museum and Arts Foundation (see site 172). Wheelchair accessible. For futher information, call 406-846-3111.

# 170. Frontier Montana Museum

Bottles, guns, and other western memorabilia tell the story of an era at the Frontier Montana Museum. Various Old West firearms are on display here and the historical information about who used them and how they were used hints at tales of bandits and desperadoes. While you're at the museum, belly up to Desert John's Saloon bar from the 1800s and take a look at hundreds of antique liquor bottles, some dating as far back as the Civil War. Other memorabilia includes cowboy gear and Native American artifacts.

**Directions:** The museum is located at 1153 Main Street across from the Montana Auto Museum. From Interstate 90, take either of the two Deer Lodge exits and go toward town. Both roads take you through town on Main Street where the museum is located between Texas and Conley avenues.

**Important Information:** The Frontier Montana Museum is open 7 days a week, mid-May to Labor Day, from 9 A.M. to 5 P.M. Call for winter hours. You can enter with a combined pass for the five fee museums on Main Street operated by the Powell County Museum and Arts Foundation (see site 172). Wheelchair accessible. For more information, call 406-846-0026.

# 171. Yesterday's Playthings

Yes, kids, we played with dolls and toys just like these! Here's where your age shows. See china dolls, Barbies, even John Wayne and Princess Diana dolls. A thousand dolls from around the world provide an interesting view of human diversity. There are also other types of toys spanning the last century.

**Directions:** The museum is located at 1017 Main Street across from the Old Montana Prison Visitor Center entrance. From Interstate 90, take either of the two Deer Lodge exits and go toward town. Both roads take you through town on Main Street.

**Important Information:** Open mid-May through September 30 from 9 A.M. to 5 P.M. Enter with a combined pass for the five fee museums on Main Street operated by the Powell County Museum and Arts Foundation. Museum fees and pass rates are the same as those listed for the Old Prison Museum (site 168). Wheelchair accessible. Call 406-846-1480 for more information.

# 172. Powell County Museum

This museum looks at the history of the Deer Lodge valley through a varied collection of historical photos and artifacts from bygone days. Included are antique slot machines, juke boxes, guns, swords, photo equipment, and autographed photos of movie stars.

**Directions:** The museum is located on Main Street and Conley Avenue. It is the farthest south of the museums in Deer Lodge. From Interstate 90, take either of the two Deer Lodge exits and go toward town. Both roads lead to Main Street. The museum is on the left.

**Important Information:** Generally open Memorial Day through Labor Day, 9 A.M. to 5 P.M., and noon to 4 P.M. the rest of the year. Entrance is free. Wheelchair accessible. Call 406-846-3111 or 406-846-1694 for information.

# 173. Cottonwood City

Back in the 1800s, Deer Lodge was called Cottonwood City. A few buildings from the era have been brought in to depict what the town would have looked like back then. You'll find a couple of furnished cabins, a school house, and the inevitable outhouse.

**Directions:** Cottonwood City is on Main Street between the Powell County Museum and the Frontier Montana Museum. From Interstate 90, take either of the two Deer Lodge exits and go toward town. Both roads lead to Main Street.

**Important Information:** From Memorial Day to Labor Day visitors can wander among the buildings. No set hours or fee.

# 174. J.C. (Jaycee) Park

This city park has picnic tables and trees and makes a convenient stop for a rest or lunch. There are restrooms, a playground, drinking water, and horseshoe pits.

**Directions:** From the north Deer Lodge exit, follow Main Street and turn left (east) on Higgins Avenue just beyond the Safeway store. Go 6 blocks to the park. From the south Deer Lodge exit, follow Main Street and turn right (east) just before Safeway.

**Important Information:** Contact the Chamber of Commerce, 406-846-2094.

# 175. Grant-Kohrs National Historic Site and Cottonwood Creek Nature Trail

● ● ● ● ● ● ● ● ● ● ● ● ● ● ● ● ● ● ● ● ● ● ● ● ● ● ● ● ● ● ● ● ●

If there is anywhere in Montana to explore the lifestyle of the cowboy, the Grant-Kohrs Ranch is the place. The ranch was once the largest in Montana, with cattle grazing on more than 10 million acres. The ranch itself is comprised of 1 million acres. Grant-Kohrs is now a national historic site of 1,500 acres. The National Park Service preserves the era of the cowboy at the ranch through a visitor center, 90 historic structures, and 37,000 artifacts covering 130 years of ranch history. Visitors can take a self-guided or ranger-led tour of the facility. In the summer months, the National Park Service operates a living history program with demonstrations of ranch activities. The Cottonwood Creek Nature Trail is a 0.5-mile trail, one way, with an interpretive brochure about ranching, cattle grazing, and riparian ecosystems.

**Directions:** The historic site is found on Main Street at the north end of town, across from the county fairgrounds. From the north Deer Lodge exit, follow Main Street and turn right (west) at the sign for the ranch. From the south Deer Lodge exit, follow Main Street through town and turn left (west) at the sign.

**Important Information:** Open from 8 A.M. to 5:30 P.M., May 1 to October 1, and 9 A.M. to 4 P.M. the rest of the year. The entrance fee of $2 (or $4 per carload) is charged from May to October only. Children 16 and under enter free. No picnic facilities. Wheelchair accessible. Call 406-846-3388 for more information.

# 176. Fairmont Hot Springs

● ● ● ● ● ● ● ● ● ● ● ● ● ● ● ● ● ● ● ● ● ● ● ● ● ● ● ● ● ● ● ● ●

This hot springs is one of the most elaborate in the state. There are two Olympic-sized natural mineral pools, one inside and one outside, plus two smaller, hotter pools. A waterslide into the large, outdoor pool provides another level of excitement and interest for kids. The resort also has hotel rooms, a gift shop, dining facilities, and a lounge. Ski packages can be arranged in the winter and plenty of summer activities are available nearby, too.

**Directions:** Fairmont Hot Springs is 3 miles off Interstate 90 between Butte and Deer Lodge. Take Exit 211, which is 8 miles north of the I-90 and Interstate 15 interchange. Go west from the exit to Fairmont Road, following the signs for the resort. The resort is about 30 miles south of Deer Lodge.

**Important Information:** Rates for the pools are $6.50 for those 11 and older, and $3.50 for kids 10 and under. This is a one-time admission for one-day unlimited use. Hotel guests have 24-hour access at no additional charge. Room rates begin around $70 per night. Call for information on room rates or hotel reservations at 800-332-3272.

# BUTTE AND THE SURROUNDING AREA

. . . . . . . . . . . . . . . . . . . . . . . . . . . . . .

You may notice as you drive to Butte that it is uphill. The elevation of Butte varies but is between 5,500 and 6,500 feet. That's enough to get you a good sunburn, so don't forget the sunscreen.

Butte became known in the mining industry as "The Richest Hill on Earth," for the city is built upon richly laden mineral fields and owes its existence to the copper, gold, lead, and silver found there. It was at one time the country's largest source of silver and copper. The booming mineral town had a population of 100,000 in 1917. Though the population is down to 35,000 today, Butte remains a thriving city that offers visitors some unusual history and activities. Here is a town where the majority of laborers worked below ground, and saloons stayed open 24 hours a day to accommodate three shifts of miners. An exploration of the city brings visitors to interesting mining-related sites, and historic sites with a unique mining-town character. The town is surrounded by mountains and is near five of the state's ten national forests. The Butte Batholith geologic activity has produced intriguing natural landforms.

# City of Butte

. . . . . . . . . . . . . . . . . . . . . . . . . . . . . . . . . . . . . . . .

The city began with a diverse cultural representation of miners, including a high percentage of Irish people. Even today, Butte has a statewide reputation for its celebration of St. Patrick's Day. Local restaurants feature an interesting assortment of ethnic foods. This includes the Cornish-Welsh pasty (PAST-ee) that miners favored because of the food's heartiness and portability. Chinese noodles were introduced in Butte by the Asian community. Other ethnic groups that settled in Butte include Italians, Serbs, Scandinavians, Mexicans, Germans, and African-Americans, to name a few.

## 177. Butte Visitor Center and Walking Trail

. . . . . . . . . . . . . . . . . . . . . . . . . . . . . . . . . . . .

The Butte Visitor Center is conveniently located just off Interstate 90 and has an interesting collection of fly-fishing flies. The Old No. 1 Tour Train leaves from here. The center is also an access point for a walking trail that is under construction and will someday go all the way—about 35 miles—to Warm Springs. "Project Green" funding for the walking, biking, and rollerblading trail is from the ARCO Superfund monies. The trail gets a little longer every year as it is expanded, so you may want to check it out. In 1998 it will be blacktopped from George Street to Harrison Avenue.

**Directions:** From Interstate 90 or Interstate 15, take Exit 126 and go north. One block north of the overpass is George Street. Turn left (east) onto George Street, where a sign directs you to the visitor center at 1000 George Street.

**Important Information:** Open May through Labor Day from 8 A.M. to 8 P.M. daily. Closes at 5 P.M. Labor Day through September 30. October through May the center is open from 9 A.M. to 5 P.M. weekdays. Wheelchair accessible. For more information, call 800-735-6814 or 406-723-3177.

## 178. Berkeley Pit

You can't really miss the Berkeley Pit, once the largest truck-operated open pit copper mine in the United States. Mining ceased at Berkeley Pit in 1982 after 27 years of operation, and the hole is now filled with water. An overlook provides a view of the pit, which is 7,000 feet long, 5,600 feet wide, and 1,600 feet deep. A small visitor center and gift shop are also on-site. Visitors walk through a mock mineshaft tunnel to get to the overlook. Seeing the pit is a good quick-stop that helps visitors appreciate the magnitude of the mining industry in Butte.

**Directions:** Take the Harrison Avenue Exit 127 from Interstate 90. Go north on Harrison 1.6 miles to Utah Street. Note that Harrison makes a 90-degree bend to the left just past the Civic Center. Turn right on Utah just beyond the bend, and follow Utah to Mercury Street. The entrance to the visitor center and the overlook is at the end of Mercury Street in 0.6 mile.

**Important Information:** Visitors can view the pit during daylight hours from March to November. The visitor center and gift shop are open June through October from 9 A.M. to 7 P.M. The viewing stand and visitor center are wheelchair accessible. Call 800-735-3177 or 406-723-3177 for more information.

## 179. Granite Mountain Memorial

In June of 1917, 168 men were killed in a fire at Speculator Mine, the worst disaster in the history of hardrock mining. The miners' memorial sits at the top of the hill Butte is built around. It looks out over the mine site with the Highland Mountains as a backdrop. Interpretive plaques at the memorial describe the events of the disaster and are informative about mining life and the mining industry. An interesting construction feature of the memorial is the display of mining core samples, which have been artistically incorporated into the platform and walls. These samples are long rock cylinders obtained by drilling into rocky areas under consideration for mining. The samples allow geologists to see the mineral composition of rock far below the surface.

**Directions:** Follow the directions to the St. Lawrence O'Toole Church (site 181). Turn right just past the church and follow the road, which becomes dirt, as it meanders to the memorial.

**Important Information:** The road to the memorial site is in poor condition, though driveable, and the road is poorly signed. However, there are small red arrows and signs along the way and the site sits by an electrical station, which serves as a landmark for locating the memorial. Plans for road improvement and better signage are underway. For further information, call 406-723-7211.

## 180. St. Lawrence O'Toole Church

This church was built in 1897 from $25,000 worth of donations made by miners and local families. In 1907, a European artist painted 40 frescoes on the ceilings and numerous paintings elsewhere in the church. The church makes an interesting visit. It is currently not used for services.

**Directions:** Take Exit 126 from Interstate 15 and go north on Montana Street to Front Street, then turn right (east). Take Front to Main Street and turn left on Main. Drive to the top of the hill. Look for the white church on the right at 1308 N. Main.

**Important Information:** The church is only open on Fridays and Sundays from noon to 5 P.M. No admission charge. No restrooms.

# The Gallows

Most cities have landmarks that stand out on the skyline: spires, buildings, churches, and natural landforms. The mining town of Butte has landmarks that are different. Tall, stark structures, they are called headframes, and are like elevators. At one time, they lowered miners and equipment down into mines, and then hauled ore back up. Once busy and active, these days the headframes have earned the nickname of the "gallows," standing as silent memorials to the bygone boomtown days of copper mining. Visitors can check out the Orphan Girl headframe at close range at the World Museum of Mining (site 182).

# 181. Old Number 1 Tour Train

Electric trolleys provided public transportation for Butte residents at one time and Old No. 1 is a replica of one of these trolleys. It is now used for providing daily one-and-a-half-hour tours of Butte's mining features and historic buildings.

**Directions:** Tours leave from 1000 George Street, the location of the Butte Chamber of Commerce (see Butte Visitor Center, site 177).

**Important Information:** Tours run from late May through Labor Day and start at 10:30 A.M., and 1:30, 3:30, and 7 P.M. Cost is $4 for riders 13 and older and $2.50 for kids ages 4 to 12. Children under 4 ride free. For information or reservations call 800-735-6814 or 604-723-3177.

# 182. World Museum of Mining and 1899 Mining Camp

What minerals glow in ultraviolet light? What's it like inside a real mine tunnel? How did miners live in 1899? The extensive Mining Museum and the reconstructed 1899 Mining Camp provide some answers to these questions plus a mother lode of additional information. The 24-acre museum and camp is built on the original Orphan Girl Mine site and has an extensive collection of real-life mining equipment. The museum has fun interactive exhibits, too. Kids will enjoy the comprehensive mineral collection with a special room for viewing fluorescent minerals. Bring small change for the coin-operated machines which do everything from running a model of an underground mine to playing pianos. A self-guiding tour flyer describes the artifacts.

The outdoor mining village has more than three dozen structures to walk through. Some are functioning businesses and others are barricaded but are set up to allow visitors to peek into mining town life. A small picnic area is located on the site. Gold panning is offered on specific days; call for dates.

**Directions:** From Interstate 90, take the Montana Street Exit 126 and go north to Park Street. Turn left (west) on Park Street and go to Montana Tech. Continue straight on Park Street past the Marcus Daly statue. The road veers to the left just before the museum entrance.

**Important Information:** Open 9 A.M. to 9 P.M. every day from mid-June through Labor Day. The museum is closed late November through March. Call for spring and fall hours at 406-723-7211. Children under 12 enter free; adults are charged $3. For a $25 fee, retired miners will guide you through the museum and camp with interesting stories and information. Call two weeks ahead if you want a tour guide.

# 183. Montana Tech Mineral Museum

• • • • • • • • • • • • • • • • • • • • • • • • • • • • • • • • • • •

The mineral museum displays a comprehensive collection of more than 1,500 mineral specimens. The museum is on the campus of Montana Tech of the University of Montana, previously the College of Mineral Science and Technology. Here you can see fluorescent minerals illuminated by ultraviolet light and unique specimens such as a 27.5-ounce gold nugget. The museum is only about a half mile from the World Museum of Mining and it is an easy, quick stop.

**Directions:** From Interstate 90, take the Montana Street Exit 126 and go north to Park Street. Turn left (west) on Park Street and go to Montana Tech. Signs to the museum at the entrance to Montana Tech will lead you around the buildings to the parking lot. Stairs up the hill go to the museum.

**Important Information:** Open from 8 A.M. to 5 P.M. every day from Memorial Day through Labor Day. The remainder of the year, open 8 A.M. to 5 P.M. Monday through Friday, and 1 to 5 P.M. on Sundays. No fee. Call 406-496-4414 or 406-496-4506 for information.

# 184. "M" Trail

• • • • • • • • • • • • • • • • • • • • • • • • • • • • • • • • • •

The "M" painted on a Butte hillside acknowledges the Montana College of Mineral Science and Technology, now Montana Tech. It was constructed by students in 1910 and has been wired for lights, so you'll see it even at night. You can actually drive to a few feet below the landmark, or hike to it from unmarked trails near the college. The vista from the observation point below the "M" provides a good view of the city below.

**Directions:** Take the Montana Street exit from Interstate 90 and go to Park Avenue. Turn left and follow Park Avenue to Excelsior Street, then turn right. From Excelsior, turn left onto Hornet Street and follow it to the J. F. Kennedy Elementary School on the corner of Emmet and Hornet streets. Continue up the hill past the school, to an unmarked dirt road which turns to the left in 0.3 mile. From here it is about a half mile to a turnaround just a few yards below the "M." Park here.

# 185. Copper King Mansion

• • • • • • • • • • • • • • • • • • • • • • • • • • • • • • • • • •

The Copper King Mansion offers tours of the home of copper magnate William A. Clark, once one of the world's richest men. The millionaire spent lavish amounts to embellish his home with beveled glass, stained glass windows, chandeliers, and more.

# Copper Wars

When Thomas Edison invented the light bulb, he thought little of the effects of this event in Butte, Montana. But suddenly the world needed miles and miles of copper wire. Butte, known for its silver mines, was put on the map when the largest copper mine in the world was built there by Marcus Daly. Daly was an Irish immigrant who had worked his way up from the mines and eventually became the wealthy owner of the Anaconda Company. Also in Butte was William A. Clark, a banker from Deer Lodge who established Butte's first fortune in silver mines. The two men became bitter rivals in nearly every aspect, drawing the city and mining business into the feud as well. Politics became involved when Clark put in his bid for the United States Senate and Daly went to great lengths to keep him out of office. The feud even impacted state government as the two men battled over whether the state capital should be located in Helena or Anaconda. When Clark's choice of Helena came out on top, the discouraged Daly retreated to his home and lands in the Bitterroot Valley. Augustus Heinze was a latecomer to the war of the Copper Kings. He began manipulating mining laws in 1900 to grab mining claims already developed by Daly. The battle for Butte mining money got downright nasty and even after Daly's death in 1899, the politics surrounding the War of the Copper Kings continued.

**Directions:** Take Exit 126 from Interstate 90 and go north on Montana Street to Granite Street and turn left. The mansion is at the end of the block on the right at 219 West Granite Street.

**Important Information:** Open 9:30 A.M. to 4:30 P.M. daily. Admission is $4.50 for adults, $4 for seniors, $3 for students, and free for kids under 6. Call 406-782-7580 for information.

## 186. Arts Chateau

The historic home of Charles Clark, son of Copper King William Clark, serves as a living museum for the Butte-Silver Bow Art Foundation. The home displays period furniture and historical exhibits. Rotating monthly exhibits of local and regional artists are featured in the art galleries.

**Directions:** From Interstate 90, take exit 126 and go north on Montana Street to Broadway. Turn left (west) and go 2 blocks to 321 West Broadway.

**Important Information:** Open from 10 A.M. to 6 P.M. Tuesday through Saturday, and noon to 5 P.M. on Sunday from mid-June to early September. Closed Mondays. Open 11 A.M. to 4 P.M. Tuesday through Saturday the rest of the year. Admission is $3.75 for adults, $3 for senior citizens, and $1.25 for children 16 and under. Call 406-723-7600 for more information.

# 187. The Mai Wah Noodle Parlor and Wah Chong Tai Buildings

∙ ∙ ∙ ∙ ∙ ∙ ∙ ∙ ∙ ∙ ∙ ∙ ∙ ∙ ∙ ∙ ∙ ∙ ∙ ∙ ∙ ∙ ∙ ∙ ∙ ∙ ∙ ∙ ∙ ∙ ∙ ∙ ∙ ∙

The Chinese have a history in Butte that goes back to when Chinese miners came to work the placer mines that others had abandoned. The Mai Wah Noodle Parlor can be seen on what little is left of China Alley, between Galena and Mercury streets. Originally, the main floor was a mercantile while the second floor was a noodle parlor where hungry folks would go for a taste of good homemade noodles. Exhibits in the building describe Asian history in Butte and the Rocky Mountain west.

**Directions:** Take the Harrison Avenue Exit 127 from Interstate 90. Go north on Harrison 1.6 miles to Utah Street. Note that Harrison makes a 90-degree bend to the left just past the Civic Center. Turn right on Utah just beyond the bend. Follow Utah to Mercury Street, turn right, and go to 17 West Mercury.

**Important Information:** Open June through August, Tuesday through Saturday from 11 A.M. to 3 P.M. Admission is $1. Call 406-723-6669 for more information or check the Worldwide Web at http://www.montana.com/maiwah.

# 188. Our Lady of the Rockies

∙ ∙ ∙ ∙ ∙ ∙ ∙ ∙ ∙ ∙ ∙ ∙ ∙ ∙ ∙ ∙ ∙ ∙ ∙ ∙ ∙ ∙ ∙ ∙ ∙ ∙ ∙ ∙ ∙ ∙ ∙ ∙ ∙ ∙

Set atop a rugged Rocky Mountain ridge, this 90-foot statue stands as a tribute to human tenacity. Our Lady of the Rockies was built in the likeness of Mary, Mother of Jesus, but is intended to be a representation that honors all women, regardless of religion. The statue was built entirely by volunteers over a six-year period and required a helicopter crane to complete the elaborate construction process. The structure weighs 51 tons. A video showing the construction process can be seen at the visitor center for the statue.

Our Lady is perched at 8,510 feet on the east ridge above Butte with a view that extends 100 miles to the south and west. The statue is lit at night and can be seen glowing on Butte's skyline. Donations to light and maintain the statue are gathered by a nonprofit organization, Our Lady of the Rockies, Inc.

Access to the statue is currently by bus tour only, though a gondola ride to the statue is under consideration. The 2.5-hour round-trip tour currently requires a 45-minute drive each way. Tour riders can go inside the statue and can enjoy the view from outside as well. During the summer the tour leaves several times a day from the Butte Plaza Mall, which has an information center. A gift shop and another information center are located in what was previously St. Mary's Church in Butte. The church has construction information and a panoramic mural of the statue.

**Directions:** The church gift shop and visitor center are located at 434 North Main. Take Montana Street Exit 126 from Interstate 15 and go north on Montana to Front Street, then turn right (east). Take Front to Main Street and turn left on Main. Drive up the hill and look for the stone church on the right.

The information center in the Butte Plaza Mall is on the outside of the mall between JC Penney and Jo-Ann Fabrics and Crafts, facing Harrison Avenue. To find the mall, take Exit 127 and go south on Harrison Avenue. The mall will be on your left.

**Important Information:** Tour reservations are recommended and may be made by calling 800-800-LADY or 406-782-1221. Our Lady of the Rockies Information Center at St. Mary's Church is open from 10 A.M. to 4 P.M. weekdays all year long and closed weekends. The Butte Plaza Information Center is open 9 A.M. to 5 P.M., Monday through Saturday, and noon to 5 P.M. on Sundays. October 1 to Thanksgiving, hours are noon to 4 P.M. Tour fees are $10 for adults, $9 for teens 13 to 17 and senior citizens 55 and older, and $5 for children 5 to 12. Children under 5 ride free.

## 189. Clarks Park

This grassy park covers a full city block and has a few shade trees, playground equipment, a 0.16-mile walking track, and restrooms. The playground equipment includes a 5-foot-tall miniature house that is a fun diversion.

**Directions:** Take the Harrison Avenue Exit 127 from Interstate 15 and go north 0.8 mile to George Street. Turn right on George Street and go one block. Clarks Park is on the left.

## 190. Stodden Park and Public Pool

The city pool is located at Stodden Park, which also has tennis courts, a baseball diamond, and horseshoe pits. The large park provides a picnic area, playground, and restrooms.

**Directions:** From Interstate 90, take the Montana Street Exit 126 and go south on Montana. Just beyond the highway overpass, turn left (east) onto Rowe Road and follow it for 0.7 mile to Dewey Boulevard. Turn left and go four blocks to Utah Street (you will go by the U.S. Post Office). Turn right into the park on Utah Street.

**Important Information:** The park is open from 1 to 5 P.M., seven days a week, and from 6 to 8 P.M. on Wednesday evenings. Children's admission is $1, adults' $2, and senior citizens' $1.50. The pool is open as weather permits, usually mid-June to Labor Day. Call 406-494-3686 to reach the pool in summer or 406-782-1266 during other times of year.

## 191. Father Sheehan Park

You can see this park from the highway, so it's a good quick stop even if you aren't planning on looking around Butte at all. There is a small playground here, a covered picnic area, restrooms, and a baseball diamond.
**Directions:** Take the Harrison Avenue Exit 127 from Interstate 90 and go north one block, then turn right on Cornell Street which runs between the Days Inn and the War Bonnet Lodge. Turn right in one block on Holiday Park Street.

# Butte Area Lakes

The lakes around Butte have been developed to be wonderful family-oriented recreational areas. There is almost nothing as enticing to kids as water to jump, play, and swim in. These sites are all very close to Butte and would be good for a day trip or short visit.

## 192. Sheepshead Mountain Recreation Area and Maney Lake

Sheepshead Mountain Recreation Area was designed so that all people, regardless of physical challenges or age, could enjoy nature. The project involved numerous agencies and organizations, and after 12 years of effort the dream became reality. The designed accessibility has made Sheepshead a pleasant outdoor experience with a wide variety of activities. A volleyball court, softball fields, and horseshoe pits provide for group sports activities. A wheelchair-accessible fishing pier makes access to the cutthroat and brook trout easier for everyone.

A 4.5-mile system of paved trails is also wheelchair accessible. The trails traverse grassy meadows, pass through a lodgepole pine forest, and go around Maney Lake. There is an interpretive nature trail which takes about an hour to complete. Signs and audio messages along the trail communicate information about plants, animals, and the forest ecosystem. This nature trail begins at Freedom Point and is universally accessible. The complex also has picnic pavilions, tables, and barbecue grills. Lowland and Freedom Point campgrounds are wheelchair accessible. You'll have a good chance of seeing deer, squirrels, chipmunks, and rabbits here as well as mountain bluebirds and woodpeckers. On occasion, a moose wanders into the area, too.

**Directions:** From Interstate 15 between Helena and Butte, take the Elk Park Exit 138. This is 13 miles north of Butte and 51 miles south of Helena. The exit is marked with a sign for the recreation area. From the highway, head west to the stop sign. A sign here points you straight ahead 6 miles to Sheepshead Mountain Recreation Area and 7 miles to Maney Lake. To get to the Freedom Point Nature Trail, take the Freedom Point Entrance from the main road. The trail leads off from the parking area. At the trail fork, go right and you will reach the trailhead beyond the picnic pavilion.

**Important Information:** Contact the USDA Forest Service, Deerlodge Ranger District in Butte, 406-494-2147, for more information.

## 193. Homestake Lake

· · · · · · · · · · · · · · · · · · · · · · · · · · · · · · · ·

This pleasant lake offers weary travelers a delightful opportunity to get off the highway and play by the lake. It is also pleasant enough to entertain families for an enjoyable afternoon. The small lake has fishing, swimming areas (no lifeguards), picnic tables, and vault toilets.

**Directions:** From Interstate 90, 5 miles south of Butte, get off the highway at Homestake Exit 233. Go north 1.5 miles to the right-hand turn marked Homestake Lake. It is a quarter of a mile to the lake.

**Important Information:** This is a day-use only area with hours from 7 A.M. to 10 P.M.

## 194. Delmoe Lake

· · · · · · · · · · · · · · · · · · · · · · · · · · · · · · · ·

Here is a little piece of paradise, tucked back in Montana mountains. The lake is big enough to boat on and features the unique landforms which are also prominent along Homestake Pass. The oblong and roundish boulders make the area appear magical and kids find climbing on them irresistible. Though there is no trail around the lake, you could walk along the lakeshore for quite a ways. This lake has a campground, boat access, picnic tables, and vault toilets.

**Directions:** From Interstate 90, 5 miles south of Butte, exit the highway at Homestake Exit 233. Go north 1.5 miles and continue straight ahead another 8.5 miles on Forest Road 222 where the road becomes a good dirt road, just beyond the Homestake Lake turn. The winding road is a 25-miles-per-hour so be prepared for a 20- or 30-minute ride. Stay on the main road, which is not always signed. A few spur roads take off but are fairly recognizable as spur roads. Just in case, however, stay right at the first fork, and then left at the next three. If in doubt, stay on what looks most like the main road.

# THE MADISON RIVER AREA AND THE VIRGINIA CITY LOOP

This 115-mile loop off of Interstate 90 provides a wealth of varied activities. You can walk through two of Montana's best-preserved ghost towns, float scenic rivers, enjoy museums, and explore natural features. Just make sure you leave enough time to fully enjoy this route.

# Whitehall

A small Montana town, Whitehall is located near a number of interesting tourist areas: Butte, Virginia City, and the Lewis and Clark Caverns State Park. There are places in the city itself worth stopping at too. For more information, contact the Butte Chamber of Commerce, 800-735-6814 or 406-723-3177.

## 195. Whitehall City Park

There's no problem finding a place for a picnic in Whitehall. City Park runs the entire length of the main business section. The park has picnic tables and shade trees.

**Directions:** Enter Whitehall at the only Whitehall exit on Interstate 90. The exit leads you onto Whitehall Street. Follow this to Legion Street, where you can't miss the park.

## 196. Jefferson Valley Museum: The Barn

This museum has history built right into the building. The bright red barn was built in 1914 and was donated for use as the local museum in 1992. Inside are artifacts and pictures from local history depicting pioneer days and ranching life in the Jefferson Valley.

**Directions:** Enter the town from Interstate 90 on the only Whitehall exit. You will be on Whitehall Street which comes to a T intersection at Legion Street. Turn left and go two blocks to South Division, then turn right. It is three blocks to the red barn at 303 South Division.

**Important Information:** Museum hours are from noon to 4 P.M. Tuesday through Sunday, Memorial Day through Labor Day. There is no admission charge, though donations are appreciated.

## 197. The Jefferson River

This river has some interesting history which adds to the beauty of the canyons and flat lands it flows through. The Jefferson River is one of the three rivers that form the headwaters of the Missouri River at Three Forks. Lewis and Clark explored the entire 83.5 miles of the Jefferson. They wrote of the 6-mile-wide plains through which the upper river courses and noted the picturesque mountains rising on either side of the valley. Floaters see the Tobacco Root Mountains to the east and the Highland Mountains in the west as they float the upper river. The entire river can be floated by beginners, although care should be taken in the lower section by Three Forks where the river is brushy and the braided channels can be confusing.

The most scenic float is along the 15.2 miles from Cardwell Fishing Access Site to Sappington Bridge. This stretch takes floaters through the canyons around Lewis and Clark Caverns State Park, and it is a 5- to 6-hour trip. The river enters the canyon just below LaHood Park launch area and flows through tall limestone cliffs and colorful rock formations for the next several miles. There are numerous deep river pools, and a few fast riffles that beginners can easily handle.

For a shorter trip that still includes the impressive canyon float, put in at the LaHood Park access site and float to Sappington Bridge. This float is 12.6 miles and can be done in around 4 hours.

**Directions:** Cardwell Fishing Access Site is 1 mile south of Cardwell on Jefferson County 359. The site has camping and toilets. Take out at Sappington Bridge where U.S. Highway 287 crosses the Jefferson River. You can get to this bridge by taking CR 359 east toward Lewis and Clark Caverns to the junction of Montana 2 and US 287. Then go south on US 287 for 1 mile. This site has easy launch facilities and parking, but no toilets.

The LaHood access is harder to find than Cardwell. Take CR 359 from Cardwell to LaHood. This is the road from Cardwell to Lewis and Clark Caverns. LaHood is no longer inhabited but you will see some white buildings and a sign marking the old town. A trail, visible from the road, leads down to the river.

# The John Colter Story

Run for your life or die! And so John Colter ran, and swam, and hiked 250 miles of Rocky Mountain wilderness with no clothes, shoes, or food. At one time a part of the Lewis and Clark expedition, Colter had stayed in southwest Montana to trap beavers and act as a guide and interpreter for fur traders in their dealings with the Indians. This day, he was surprised by Blackfeet Indians as he trapped beaver along the Jefferson River. The Indians took exception to his being there. The white settlement of the West met with varied responses from Native American tribes, and the Blackfeet actively resisted the encroachment of white people on their land and lifestyles.

The Indians stripped Colter of his clothes and shoes, and then asked him how fast he could run. Since the warriors had already killed Colter's hunting companion when the man balked at their demand that he come ashore, Colter must have known what was coming. He cleverly told the Indians that he was a poor runner, although he fortunately was very fast. The chief gave Colter a few hundred yards head start and then set his fleetest warriors after him. So run Colter did! Luckily, he held his lead. Unable to lose one particularly speedy warrior, Colter finally turned to face his armed foe and dodged the spear the Blackfeet warrior threw at him. Quickly picking up the spear, Colter returned it to the warrior with a deadly throw. But the other Indian warriors were not far behind and Colter could not keep running forever. There was little place to hide but in the cold Jefferson River (some say it was the Madison). Colter dove into the icy water and managed to find a way to hide beneath a log jam, using a reed to breathe through. Though the Indians searched extensively for him, Colter remained safe in his watery hideout until the next day when the Indians gave up. He had escaped the Indians, but now he was some 250 miles from shelter at Fort Lisa. It took the naked, hungry, and cold John Colter 11 days to walk the distance. When he arrived at the fort, he was nearly dead but his run for life was successful.

# Nevada City to Virginia City

Explore life in boom-and-bust mining camps along this route. The history of this area is fascinating and sites here are numerous and extensive, so be sure to leave plenty of time to stop and enjoy everything.

## 198. Robber's Roost

Many a stagecoach stopped here in the 1860s loaded with gold from the mines of Alder Gulch and Bannack. Of course, many an outlaw stopped here too, looking for plunder and fortune. Henry Plummer's gang is most

# What is a Vigilante?

The gold rush in Virginia City brought many a fortune seeker to the Alder Gulch fields of gold. With those who were willing to work for their money came the inevitable outlaws who preferred to steal the gold others worked for. Southwest Montana was a wild place in the 1860s, with robbers, gunfights, and hangings regular occurrences. So the good townspeople hired sheriffs to maintain law and order. Back in 1865, Virginia City hired a sheriff who would make the city famous. It turned out that handsome Sheriff Henry Plummer was actually the leader of a band of 75 to 100 renegades who were responsible for a fair amount of thievery and killing. The gambling, woman-chasing Plummer came to them with credentials. He had first got himself the job of sheriff in nearby Bannack, a mining town on the stagecoach route that saw the transport of large amounts of gold. But Plummer wasn't satisfied there and it wasn't long before he decided to capture the job of sheriff in the wealthier Virginia City. Here Plummer's plunders became more and more frequent, and the outlaw sheriff had difficulty hiding his shady activities.

Meanwhile, one story says that the townspeople in Bannack, Nevada City, and Virginia City got plum tired of the robbers' shenanigans and formed their own group to uphold the rights of honest people. Other accounts say the Vigilantes were more political—composed of Masonic Democrats who sympathized with Northerners in the ongoing Civil War. Some claim that the Vigilantes' self-appointed lawmaking was generally aimed at non-Masonic Republicans with southern sympathies. The story has still not been fully unraveled, but the Vigilantes did manage to clear out a high number of men they felt to be undesirable. Hanging was the primary method of citizen justice. However, the Vigilantes were known to sometimes write the numbers 3-7-77 on the door of their next target, and give the identified outlaw time to clear out alive. Rumor has it that these numbers stood for the dimensions of a grave: 3 feet by 7 feet by 77 inches. Others say that these numbers represented the length of time the bad guys had to get out of town: 3 hours, 7 minutes, and 77 seconds. The Vigilantes also put these numbers on the bodies of their victims.

At any rate, the Vigilantes caught and tried Plummer and two of his deputies, found them guilty of murder and theft, and hung them on gallows Plummer had ordered made for a prisoner in his jail. Twenty-two outlaws were reportedly hung in a couple of months. Some met their end on the main street of Virginia City, in an unfinished building which is still standing. Five outlaw graves are still up on Boot Hill above Virginia City. Plummer's grave was plundered more than once and his skull reportedly rested in the Bank Exchange Saloon for a considerable amount of time. The Vigilantes ultimately faded back into hometown daily life, especially when the gold rush ended and Virginia City, Nevada City, and Bannack moved into obscurity.

noted for using the log tavern. Originally called Pete Daly's Place, the name Robber's Roost took over after vigilantes lynched two outlaws in a nearby tree. The building now houses an antique store and gift shop and makes an interesting stop along the highway. Look for bullet holes in the walls put there in the outlaw days.

**Directions:** The outlaw hideout is located about 5 miles south of Sheridan on Montana 287. It is on the southwest side of the highway.

**Important Information:** The building is a privately owned antique store and museum. Visitors are invited in. Call 406-842-5304 for more information or hours.

## 199. Red Rock Mine

When gold mining became a booming business in the Virginia City area, gold dredges mostly replaced gold panning. More efficient and less labor intensive, the dredges were responsible for increasing the amount of gold taken out of the rich land. Dredges also left mining ponds along the landscape. The Red Rock Mine is situated on one such pond, reworking a gravel beach for garnets. The mine is easy to get to from Montana 287 and offers visitors the chance to screen for gems just like the early prospectors. Also available for sifting are gold and sapphire gravel from other mines. There is a KOA campground 1 mile west of the mine.

**Directions:** The mine is 1.5 miles east of Alder on MT 287, and 7 miles from Ennis.

**Important Information:** Open early May through early October from 9 A.M. to 5 P.M., Monday through Saturday, and 1 to 5 P.M. on Sunday. Cost for gem screening is $10 per bucket, $25.00 for 3 buckets, or $3 for a small sample bag. There are day rates as well. Contact Red Rock Mine at P.O. Box 173, Alder, Montana 59710.

## 200. Nevada City

The mining camp at Nevada City has been recreated so well that it has been the set for many western movies, including *Little Big Man* and *Return to Lonesome Dove*. The town is only 1 mile downstream from Virginia City. The original town was mostly destroyed when large gold dredges were brought up Alder Gulch to mine gold. Buildings have been brought to the town from around the state to create five streets of open displays, including shops, homes, a schoolhouse, and Chinatown. A popular exhibit is the Music Hall, which has one of the world's largest collections of mechanical music machines. For a little pocket change to run the machines, kids will find delight in watching these machines play.

**Directions:** Drive to Nevada City on Montana Highway 287 by following directions for Virginia City (site 202). Nevada City is only 1.25 miles west of Virginia City on MT 287. You can take the Alder Gulch Short Line railroad to or from Virginia City.

**Important Information:** The town of Nevada City is open Memorial Day to Labor Day. Cost is $5 for adults, $4 for seniors, and $3 for students ages 5 to 11. There's no charge for children under 5.

# 201. Virginia City

Thar's gold in them thar hills! The cry rallied from town to town, sending gold diggers racing to find the mother lode in Alder Gulch. Since there actually was one, Virginia City was soon a bustling, successful gold rush city. Thousands of people worked in the gold mines and more than 40,000 people lived in the area. The town was Montana's first incorporated town and became the state's second territorial capital in 1864, the year after gold was discovered. When the state capital was moved to Helena in 1894, the city still managed to maintain some life as a county seat. Gold mining continued into the twentieth century at a somewhat slower pace than the gold rush of the 1860's. Charles and Sue Bovey began historical restoration in the mid-1900's, and the area is now maintained by the Montana Historical Society.

The town is a National Historic Landmark that gives visitors a realistic idea of what an honest-to-goodness western mining town was like more than 100 years ago. Most buildings are original, looking pretty much as they did in the 1860s. Walk the boardwalks, peer into preserved buildings, visit the saloon, or wander through shops and buildings set up as they might have been when gold flowed from Alder Gulch. It's easy to spend the day exploring the town and sites, especially if you venture into area museums or take the Alder Gulch Short Line Train (site 202) to Nevada City (site 200).

The Madison County Museum and the Thompson-Hickman Memorial Museum have photographs and artifacts from the era. Both are located on Wallace Street, the main road in Virginia City. If you stop by the Thompson-Hickman Memorial Museum, ask about Club Foot George. The museum has an interesting, if somewhat gruesome, artifact that once belonged to George, the first of Henry Plummer's outlaw band to die at the hands of the Vigilantes. Atop famous Boot Hill, overlooking Virginia City, are the graves of five road agents hanged by Vigilantes in 1864. Down in the town, you can visit the room where some of the outlaws met their end. On Jackson Street is the Alder Gulch Discovery Monument, commemorating the original gold strike of 1863.

There are local accommodations, 1800s style, in motels and cabins. The Virginia City Campground, 406-843-5515, is a private campground located at the edge of town.

**Directions:** The town is located on Montana Highway 287. To reach Virginia City from Butte, take Harrison Avenue south past the airport. The road becomes Montana Highway 2 and goes across the Continental Divide at Pipestone Pass. At the junction with Montana Highway 41, turn south and head for Twin Bridges. Turn left (southeast) onto MT 287. You can also take Interstate 90 east from Butte and exit into Whitehall. Go south on Madison County 55. This becomes Madison County 41. Turn left onto MT 287 at Twin Bridges and follow this road to Virginia City. If you are coming from Ennis, head west for 13 miles on MT 287.

The Thompson-Hickman Memorial Museum is at 218 East Wallace Street, and the Madison County Museum is up the street at 219 West Wallace Street. Go north on Fairweather Street about half a mile to see Boot Hill Cemetery (it's up on the bluff). Catch the Alder Gulch Short Line (site 202) from the west end of Virginia City.

**Important Information:** Walk the streets for free. A walking-tour brochure is available from numerous Virginia City merchants for $1 (it's worth having). Contact the Virginia City Area Chamber of Commerce, 800-829-2969 or 406-843-5321, for more information. The Thompson-Hickman Memorial Museum, 406-843-5346, and the Madison County Museum are open daily from Memorial Day to Labor Day, 9 A.M. to 5 P.M. For information about lodging, call 406-843-5377.

## 202. Alder Gulch Short Line

For a fun excursion, take the narrow-gauge railroad, the Alder Gulch Short Line, between Virginia City and Nevada City. Kids, of course, love the train ride. It is 1.25 miles between the cities and the time goes quickly as riders are entertained by the engineer's running narrative of area history. Originally a gas-powered train, a new steam engine has been purchased for future use.

**Directions:** Follow directions to Virginia City (site 201). The railroad is located at West Wallace and Main Streets and runs between the Northern Pacific Depot on the west end of Virginia City, and Nevada City. The train can also be taken from Nevada City (site 200).

**Important Information:** The train runs from early June to late August. Cost of the round-trip ride is $5 for adults ($3.50 one-way), $4 for seniors 65 and older and students ages 13 to 18 ($2.50 one-way), and $3 for kids ages 4 to 12 ($2 one-way). For kids age 3 and under, the ride is free. Call 800-829-2969 or 406-843-5377 for more information or reservations.

# Boom and Bust: Alder Gulch Gold, 1863 to the early 1900s

Day after day, pan after pan is filled with water and gravel, sloshed and turned, while eager eyes search for glittering gold. Will the dedicated miners find enough gold to buy tomorrow's food and tobacco? Will today be the day they hit paydirt? Countless prospectors tried their hand at gold mining and left Montana hungry, poor, and discouraged, but a few found the gold of a lifetime!

Such was the case for six men living in makeshift shelters while they turned their eyes to the pans for gold. Up a creek in the Tobacco Root Mountains, they found the gold that would create Virginia City! The first successful day's take was $12.30, equal to a few days' supplies, and enough to encourage the miners to keep looking. The Alder Gulch gold mining operations brought in more than $30 million worth of gold in three years, the richest placer gold discovery in history. Overall, Alder Gulch brought miners more than $130 million of nuggets, flakes, and gold dust. At one time, there was a 14-mile stretch of towns and tents along the gulch. Significant amounts of gold continued to be removed from the gulch area even after the boom in Virginia City was over.

## 203. Alder Gulch River of Gold

Alder Gulch River of Gold offers a mining museum, gift store, and gold panning experience. The outdoor mining museum holds historic dredging equipment and other mining artifacts. Visitors can pan for gold and garnets with the equipment and expertise provided. Making a find is guaranteed and fun.

**Directions:** The museum is on the road between Nevada City and Virginia City (see directions for Virginia City, site 201).

**Important Information:** A walk through the outdoor museum is free. A bucket of gravel for panning is $12. Each bucket is guaranteed to have gold and garnets. Call 406-843-5526 or 406-843-5402 for more information.

## 204. Kids' Fish Pond

This old dredging pond on the road between Virginia City and Nevada City has been stocked with trout and is free fishin' for kids 12 and under. There are picnic tables here too.

**Directions:** Follow directions to Virginia City (site 201). Take the mile-long road from Virginia City to Nevada City and you will see the trout pond.

# Ennis

On the map, Ennis appears to be one of Montana's more out-of-the-way towns, but the small village of 800 people has a lot to offer, including the 11 million trout it boasts. Ennis is en route to Yellowstone National Park, if you travel via Hebgen Lake, and only 13 miles from Virginia City, a preserved ghost town. You could miss Ennis if you blink, but the town still manages to provide two interesting wildlife museums, and has a nice city park for a rest stop. Note the sculptures in the yard behind the wrought-iron fence on the south end of town (west side), across from the Valley Western Store. You'll see metal depictions of bear, horses, and Cowboy Jake, whose history is a curious tale. The town also has a variety of interesting stores, art galleries, fly shops, restaurants, and cowboys. For more information, contact the Ennis Chamber of Commerce, 406-682-4388, open Monday through Saturday 10 A.M. to 3 P.M. Check out their website at http://ennischamber.com.

## 205. Ennis National Fish Hatchery

Here's where fishing starts for 22 states! The U.S. Fish and Wildlife Service operates this fish hatchery to produce trout eggs for hatcheries which don't

## Trout, *Salmonidae*

Few fish have the reputation of a trout and even fewer are as sought after as the trout of Montana. Every year, eager anglers capture trout in Montana's clear mountain streams and lakes. For some anglers, fishing from a stream bank is an excellent excuse for solitude; for others it is a chance to test their fishing skills.

There are a number of different kinds of trout in Montana. The rainbow is perhaps the most well known, but anglers are just as interested in Montana's state fish, the cutthroat trout, and probably won't turn down a brook, bull, or brown trout, either. The rainbow is easily identified by the brilliant pink or red line running along its midline and the black spots dotting its head and body. The silvery cutthroat has just a hint of pink on its mid-line and keeps most of its spots on its tail. Brown trout, brookies, and bull trout (also known as Dolly Varden), have an unusual "halo" of color around their spots. Most varieties of trout are particular about living in cold mountain waters, but some will settle for somewhat warmer lakes and reservoirs, too.

Whether you see these fish or not, you will be sure to see the not-so-rare American angler standing in his or her stream-bank habitat, pole in hand, reveling in the joy of fishing.

have brood stock. Each year the Ennis Hatchery sends 20 million eggs to nearly half the states in the U.S. Most of the fish you'll see here are quite large. A small visitor center has interpretive displays of egg development and hatchery operation. There is a self-guided tour of the building and raceways, the staff will give you a guided tour on request. Though there are no picnic tables, the shade trees and lawn make an acceptable picnic spot if you bring a snack to eat. Restrooms are available.

**Directions:** From Ennis, take Montana 287 west 2 miles toward Virginia City. Turn left (south) onto Gravelly Range/Varney Road. The road forks in 8 miles. Stay right at the fork and all the way to the hatchery, which is about 3 miles down the road. The hatchery road is signed.

**Important Information:** No fee. Hours are 8 A.M. to 4:30 P.M., seven days a week. Wheelchair accessible. Call the hatchery at 406-682-4847.

## 206. Wildlife Museum of the West

Have you wondered what a Dall ram looks like or imagined how it would feel to be face to face with a seven-point bull elk? You can experience these things and more at this wildlife museum, owned by a taxidermist who has been collecting specimens for more than 20 years. The museum has some 50 mounts from Montana and other states in beautiful dioramas with photographs and realistic displays. Descriptions of the animals and habitat are provided. See if you can find the hidden gopher and rattlesnake mounts in the exhibit while you are there. You can go into the adjacent taxidermy shop and talk to the owners about taxidermy, too. Summer kids' craft classes are scheduled, usually on Mondays, in the craft shop. Call for specifics.

**Directions:** The museum is in the G and J Artwork gift and craft shop. It is one block north of First Street at 121 West Main Street, behind the Town Pump. This is just south of the U.S. Highway 287 and the alternate US 287 turnoffs on the north end of town.

**Important Information:** Museum hours are 10 A.M. to 5 P.M. Monday through Saturday, and noon to 5 P.M. on Sunday. Museum entrance fees are $3 for adults, $2.50 for seniors, and $1.50 for kids ages 6 to 18. Children under 6 enter free. There is a $10 family rate. Call 406-682-5400 or 406-682-7141 for museum information and 406-682-7141 for taxidermy studio information.

## 207. Antler Designs and Museum

What you'll notice when you enter this store and museum are antlers, antlers, and more antlers. It's actually hard to believe that anyone could collect

as many antlers as you'll see here, but Antler Designs not only makes everything from knives to chandeliers out of antlers, but they also export them to
Korea where they are ground and used in teas and medicines. The antler
museum also has one of the largest collections of big game trophy heads in
the country. Consider a photo under one of the two large antler arches in the
front yard of the store because otherwise they might not believe you back home!
**Directions:** Located on the north end of town on Main Street, which is also
U.S. Highway 287. The museum is across from the police station on "the
hill" at 117 West Main.
**Important Information:** Open 8 A.M. to 5 P.M., and other times by appointment. No charge. Call 406-682-7153 for more information.

## 208. Lion's Club Park

The Lion's Club was thinking about kids when they built this park. Kids
under 12 can bring a fishing pole and fish in a small trout pond for free, but
each child is limited to a catch of three fish. A small, fenced play area allows
young children to play without parents having to worry about them wandering. Playground equipment, picnic tables, barbecue grills, and a covered picnic shelter round off the scene and make this a great place to stop and have
lunch. No swimming is allowed in the pond, however. The park is clean and
well kept; restrooms are available. If you haven't guessed, the trout in the
pond are "retired" brood stock from the Ennis Fish Hatchery (site 205).
**Directions:** This park is on the south end of town. Take U.S. Highway 287
through town, and as the road veers left, look for the Rainbow Motel on the
left. Go straight past it. Note the "Fly Fisherman Crossing" sign!
**Important Information:** Wheelchair accessible.

# Madison River

Anglers say that the words Madison River are nearly synonymous with trout.
The Madison River Valley is likely the most heavily used fishing area in the
state. The river has one of the highest densities of trout per square inch of
river found anywhere in Montana.

There are plenty of fishing shops and outfitters in the Madison River
area to help you get started if you are interested in trying out some of the
famous Madison River trout fishing. Check on fishing regulations if you do,
as the limits and rules vary greatly from one stretch of this river to another
(see page 345).

But you may choose to explore the river purely as a floating opportunity. Whether you go after the coveted trout or not, there are a couple of stretches along the Madison River that suit family floating needs.

The Madison River forms in Yellowstone National Park and flows north 133 miles to join the Missouri River at Headwaters State Park, near Three Forks. On its way, the Madison passes through three dams and Quake Lake. The short stretches above Hebgen Reservoir and between Hebgen Dam and Quake Lake are floatable by beginners and both of these reservoirs are good for a flat-water paddle. But don't try the section just below "Quake Dam" where the sharp boulders that formed Quake Lake create water hazards to boaters. The spectacular Bear Trap Canyon stretch above Ennis is a notorious whitewater area with outstanding rapids that can be floated with a guide company for a really exciting experience. It is definitely not to be tackled on your own, however. The canyon is in the Lee Metcalf Wilderness area, which offers spectacular scenery.

## 209. Madison River Campground to Varney Bridge Float

The river flows swiftly in this 30-mile stretch, looking like one continuous riffle in the shallow water. There are no rapids in this stretch though, and the river is rated at a beginner to intermediate skill level. You can take out at any of three points and make this trip from three hours long to a full-day float. If you take out at the South Madison River Access, the trip is a half-day, 12-mile float. Go 4 miles farther to West Madison or 6 miles beyond to the McAtee Bridge for a longer trip. You can also begin at South or West Madison access sites and go to Varney Bridge for a half-day float.

Below Bear Trap Canyon the river calms down and is good family fun all the way to Headwaters State Park, 31 miles downstream. The river flow becomes slower as it approaches the state park. The 11-mile stretch from the Montana Highway 84 bridge to Grey Cliff Access is a fairly relaxed segment that beginners can enjoy. The access site at the bridge on MT 84 is popular with swimmers and is often used for recreation. The Bear Trap Canyon Trail begins upriver (see site 213). Nearby is Red Mountain Campground, a Bureau of Land Management (BLM) site that has launch access. Above this point the river is whitewater and not advisable for families unless the trip is guided by an outfitter.

If you float from the MT 84 Bridge or Red Mountain Campground launch areas, you may want to take out at the Montana State Department of Fish, Wildlife & Parks access site at Grey Cliff. The next take-out, Cobblestone Fishing Access, is a walk-in site, and taking out at Blackbird or Missouri

River Headwaters State Park access sites makes this a very long day trip. There are additional Bureau of Land Management sites where you can take out as well.

**Directions:** The Madison River Campground access site is 32 miles south of Ennis and 1 mile west from U.S. Highway 287. All of the other access sites can be reached from US 287 south of Ennis.

**Important Information:** Contact the BLM, Dillon Resource Area office at 406-683-2337 for more information.

## 210. Lewis and Clark Caverns State Park

Children and adults seem to have a fascination for these underground caverns, decorated by nature with intriguing and colorful limestone formations. The largest limestone caves in Montana, these caverns also have a national reputation. A labyrinth of narrow passages were carved in subterranean limestone eons ago when acidic water slowly leached away layers of limestone over thousands of years. The glistening limestone is still growing stalactites and stalagmites.

Visitors can find out more about the caverns and area geology at a visitor center. A two-hour tour of the caverns begins with a 0.75-mile moderate walk from the visitor center up to the cavern entrance on a paved trail. Once in the limestone fairyland, it is another 0.75 mile down through the underground chambers and a 0.5-mile walk back to the exit by the visitor center. Guides provide information about cave history and will point out unique formations. Be ready for action on this hike as there are more than 600 steps and some areas are close quarters. At times, visitors find themselves in cathedral-size chambers such as the majestic Paradise Room at the end of the tour. Look carefully in these places for, if you are lucky, you may see the western big-eared bat, a rare Montana mammal, as it whisks overhead.

Stop at the vista point on your drive back down from the visitor center for breathtaking panoramas of the Tobacco Root Mountains and the Jefferson River valley. Camping and rental cabins are available at the state park. There is a picnic area, vault toilets, and showers. Interpretive programs are presented by park staff at the campground amphitheater during the summer. A 0.25-mile, self-guided nature trail provides interpretive information about native plants. Two-mile Greer Gulch Trail leaves from the same trailhead and is a nice family hike as well.

**Directions:** Take Montana Highway 2 from Exit 256 on Interstate 90 and go 13 miles east of Cardwell. You can also take the Lewis and Clark Caverns exit from I-90 near Three Forks and go 19 miles west on MT 2. On this route, you will turn right at the MT 2 and I-90 junction at the edge of Three Forks and travel west. The cavern facilities border MT 2.

A steep, winding, paved road leads 3 miles from the state park entrance to the visitor center and cavern entrance. Tour tickets are purchased at the cavern entrance. The self-guided nature trail leaves from the upper picnic area, about 2 miles up the road from the campground to the caverns.

**Important Information:** The caverns are open daily, May through September, and on weekends from April through October. Tours start at 9:15 A.M. and run on a regular basis. Generally, the wait for a tour is no longer than 30 minutes. Last tour of the day, from June 15 to Labor Day, starts at 6:30 P.M. May 1 to June 15 and from Labor Day until September 30, the last tour begins at 4:30 P.M. Picnic facilities, camping, and rental cabins are open year-round though water is available only from April 15 to October 15. The guided tour is $7 for adults and $4 for children ages 6 to 11. A $4 day-use fee is charged per vehicle. Summer camping fees are $12 a night and include the day-use fee. Cabins are available for rent, call 406-287-3541 for information.

The tour requires some moderate physical exertion and the temperature in the caverns is a constant 50 degrees. Bring a jacket and good walking shoes, preferably with rubber soles, as these will help keep you from slipping on the wet limestone surfaces.

The visitor center is wheelchair accessible, as is the campground. When staffing allows, a special tour for wheelchair-users is provided to the Paradise Room. This tour follows a 0.5-mile level trail and includes a naturalist presentation in the cavern.

Be aware that there are snakes in this region and you may see some in the campground or picnic area (see page 16). This is a high-use area in the summer. Call for information at 406-287-3541.

## 211. Kobayashi Beach on Ennis Lake

Hot and tired? This small lake is a favorite local hangout on hot summer days and is easy enough to find, so it makes a refreshing travel stop. The sandy beach is managed by the U.S. Bureau of Land Management for the Montana Power Company. A nice swimming feature is the warm temperature of the water. The reservoir acts like a giant solar collector and sometimes heats the water up to 85 degrees. While this has caused fishery problems downstream, it does make swimming a pleasure. There are vault toilets at the beach but no picnic tables, and you need to pack out your own garbage. American white pelicans are a common sight on the lake.

**Directions:** Take U.S. Highway 287 north 7 miles from Ennis to McAllister, turn right (east) at this tiny town, and go 3.2 miles. You will pass through a housing area. The beach is signed.

**Important Information:** Contact the Dillon Resource Area, U.S. Bureau of Land Management at 406-683-2337.

## 212. Trail Creek Wheelchair Fishing Access on the Madison River

On your trip to Ennis Lake, go by this U.S. Bureau of Land Management fishing access spot. There are picnic tables here and a wheelchair-accessible path to the Madison River. There is also a fishing pad, constructed to allow fishing from wheelchairs. This is a nice stop just to enjoy the river and there are restrooms here.

**Directions:** Follow the directions to Kobayashi Beach (site 211) and continue past it until you cross the Madison River, then turn left (north) and follow this road about half a mile. The access site is on your left.

## 213. Bear Trap Canyon Trail

This spectacular canyon is on the north end of Bear Trap Canyon Wilderness, one of the four Lee Metcalf Wilderness Area units. The canyon was formed by erosion of the Madison River and is beautiful and dramatic. The U.S. Bureau of Land Management has developed this trail that follows the Madison River through the rugged Bear Trap Canyon.

The trail is a 9-mile hike up the canyon one-way. The Madison River is a wild, whitewater river at this point. The first 3.5 miles of the trail are very easy, but the trail becomes progressively steeper as it rises above the river in the last section. Many people go as far as the point where Bear Trap Creek enters the Madison for a 9-mile round-trip hike. Above Bear Trap Creek the trail is a much more rugged, wilderness trail. Families can enjoy the walk for however long the kids can hike. The trail is a rewarding experience.

**Directions:** Follow U.S. Highway 287 north of Ennis 16 miles and then go east for 6 miles on Montana Highway 84. Turn right onto Bear Trap Road, which follows the river 3.2 miles to the wilderness trailhead and parking area. This is a good gravel road that turns off MT 84 across from the Red Mountain Campground.

**Important Information:** There is no way to leave a vehicle at both ends of this trail, so you will have to retrace your steps. Bring water and remember a garbage bag, as this is a pack-in and pack-out area.

Rattlesnakes have been seen in the area, so follow the safety practices on page 16. The area may also have ticks during tick season. Contact the Dillon Resource Area of the U.S. Bureau of Land Management at 406-682-4253 for information.

# 214. Norris Hot Springs

This small hot springs offers a pleasant pool which is generally around 112 degrees. There is a campground and picnic tables, but few shade trees, so in the summer it can be pretty hot. This makes a nice stop for water play.
**Directions:** The hot springs are located 0.25 mile east of Norris on Montana Highway 84. To get to Norris from Ennis, go 16 miles north on U.S. Highway 287. From Interstate 90, take the Whitehall exit and go south on Madison County 359 to the junction with US 287. Continue south on US 287 to Norris.
**Important Information:** Open Sunday through Thursday from 10 A.M. to 10 P.M., and Friday and Saturday from 10 A.M. to 11 P.M. Winter hours are 2 P.M. to 10 P.M. Tuesday through Sunday. The cost is $5 for adults, $2.50 for seniors, $2 for kids ages 5 to 15, and $1 for kids under 5. Call 406-685-3303 for more information.

# 215. Golden Sunlight Mine Tour

This site offers free tours of an operational gold mine.
**Directions:** From Interstate 90 take the Montana Highway 2 exit at Cardwell and follow the highway for 2.75 miles. Turn right (north) at Mine Road and follow this to the mine.
**Important Information:** Tours are offered Monday through Friday from June 15 to September 15 on Wednesdays at 10 A.M. Reservations need to be made at least 24 hours in advance. Call 406-287-2018 for information.

# 216. Cliff and Wade Lakes and Interpretive Trail

Some billions of years ago a geologic shift caused a chasm where these two lakes now sit, surrounded by tall cliffs. The cliffs provide protection for the nests of numerous raptors: prairie falcons, bald eagles, and ospreys. Waterfowl flock to the lakes and you may also see trumpeter swans. Deer, elk, and moose are frequently observed in the area.

Human visitors find the lakes appealing too. The canoeing is great and canoes can be rented at Wade Lake Resort. Motor boats are allowed, but the no-wake speed limit puts the boating focus on fishing and canoeing. Swimming is possible at the lakes if you don't mind cold water. There are three Forest Service campgrounds here: Wade Lake, Cliff Lake, and Hilltop. A signed interpretive trail connects Cliff and Wade lakes between Wade Lake Campground and Hilltop Campground. The trail is 1.4 miles round-trip, and it gains 400 feet of elevation going uphill from Wade Lake Campground to Hilltop. If your little ones don't want to walk uphill, start the trail at Hilltop and have someone pick you up at Wade Lake.

**Directions:** Follow U.S. Highway 287 south of Ennis about 40 miles. Turn right (west) and go about 6 miles on Forest Road 8381, signed for the lakes. Trailheads are located at the back of Hilltop Campground and on the road just before Wade Lake Campground. The interpretive sign at the trailhead reads "Nature Builds and Destroys."

**Important Information:** There is a parking lot at Wade Lake trailhead, but no designated parking for the Hilltop trailhead. For more information contact the USDA Forest Service, Madison Ranger District at 406-682-4253.

## 217. Madison Canyon Earthquake Area and Visitor Center

Viewing the impact of natural forces reminds us of the potential power of Mother Nature and the fragility of life. Even young children will understand the intensity of this earthquake from the exhibits at the Madison Canyon Earthquake Visitor Center. Photos and an interpretive presentation describe the massive 1959 quake that measured 7.5 on the Richter scale. Twenty-eight people were killed and the Madison River Canyon landforms were significantly rearranged. From the visitor center you can see Quake Lake, created when 80 million tons of rock slid from the mountains in one minute's time. The slide reached a speed of 100 mph and dammed the Madison River. Three weeks later there was a new 6-mile-long, 190-foot-deep lake, which was appropriately named Quake Lake.

The visitor center, operated by the USDA Forest Service, Gallatin Ranger District, displays photos and provides a presentation that portrays the destruction of the landslide and earthquake. The Memorial Boulder, on a hill above the parking lot, lists the names of the people who perished as a result of the natural catastrophe. You can see evidence of the destruction on the drive from the visitor center south along Hebgen Lake.

**Directions:** Go 41 miles south of Ennis on U.S. Highway 287 to reach the visitor center. From West Yellowstone, take U.S. Highway 191 north for 8 miles, then turn left (west) onto US 287. From this junction it is 17 miles to the visitor center. The center is well marked.

**Important Information:** Open daily from Memorial Day through late September from 8:30 A.M. to 6:30 P.M. Wheelchair accessible. Call 406-646-7369 for more information.

# 218. Cabin Creek Campground and Scarp Day-Use Area

● ● ● ● ● ● ● ● ● ● ● ● ● ● ● ● ● ● ● ● ● ● ● ● ● ● ● ● ● ● ● ● ● ●

The clifflike break at this day-use area is the result of a full scarp: a geologic action that occurs when two blocks of earth slide past one another. On August 17, 1959, an earthquake awakened campers at 11:37 P.M. The 21-foot tear in the ground trapped campers until rescue teams could reach them. The campsite was split in half and the scarp also dammed Cabin Creek and created a cascade over the scarp. An interpretive sign in the parking lot of the day-use area explains the events. A 250-yard trail leads to the cascade.

A trail once led from the campground to the scarp area. Recent high water took the bridge out so visitors must now walk along U.S. Highway 287 to get from the campground to the scarp. The first 0.5 mile of the Cabin Creek trail is being renovated in 1998 to accommodate easy walking conditions and will be a nice family hike.

**Directions:** The 16-site campground and day-use area are located on US 287 across the dam from Hebgen Lake (it's not right on the lake). The Cabin Creek Trail begins from the far end of the campground.

**Important Information:** Wheelchair accessible. For more information, contact the USDA Forest Service, Hebgen Lake Ranger District, 406-646-7369.

### Rocky Mountain Front: Blackfoot Valley
Nilan Reservoir
Bean Lake
Little Blackfoot Meadows
Blackfoot River

### Pintler Region
Anaconda Smelter Stack State Park
Georgetown Lake
Lost Creek State Park
Mount Haggin Wildlife Management Area
Phillipsburg:
Ghost Town Hall of Fame
Sapphire Gallery
Garnet Ghost Town
Rock Creek Trail
Babcock Mountain
Bighorn SheepViewing Area

### The Big Hole River Country
Humbug Spires Primitive Area
Big Hole Battlefield National Monument
Sacajawea Historical Area
Pioneer Loop National Recreational Trail
Pintler Lake
Crystal Park
Elkhorn Hot Springs
Jackson Hot Springs
Bannack State Park
Beaverhead County Museum
Beaverhead Rock State Monument
Clark Canyon Reservoir
Cattail Marsh Nature Trail
Red Rock Lakes National Wildlife Refuge

# Russell Country

This region of Montana gets its name from beloved Western artist, Charlie Russell, who lived and worked in this area. Russell Country is as grand as the massive dinosaurs that once roamed its land. This was dinosaur territory, and more *Tyrannosaurus rex* fossils have been found here than anywhere else in the country.

The rugged Bob Marshall Wilderness borders the western edge, where towns like Choteau and Augusta nestle up against the towering peaks in the Rocky Mountain Front. To the east, the mountains drop to flat prairie lands, home of the buffalo and prairie grass.

Crossing this multifaceted land are some of the most unique miles of the mighty Missouri River. Designated a National Wild, Scenic, and Recreational River, the Missouri in this country has 149 miles that cut through spectacular limestone cliffs and rugged breaks. Here you can follow the path along the river that Lewis and Clark took on their journey to the "Great Falls" of the Missouri, a title that truly suits the inspiring cascades.

## THE HI-LINE: SHELBY TO FORT BELKNAP INDIAN RESERVATION

U.S. Highway 2, called the "Hi-Line" in this part of Montana, bisects the northern reaches of the state, parallel to the route of the railroad. There are three Indian reservations near US 2: the Blackfeet reservation, the Assiniboine and Gros Ventre Fort Belknap Reservation, and the Rocky Boy Reservation for the Chippewa-Cree tribes. Powwows and rodeos are commonplace in the region. Fishing in area reservoirs is a favorite activity of visitors and locals alike.

### Shelby

Shelby sits at the crossroads of U.S. Highway 2 (the Hi-Line) and Interstate 15. A grain- and gold-producing area, Shelby has about 3,000 people. For more information, contact the Shelby Chamber of Commerce at 406-434-7184.

# RUSSELL COUNTRY

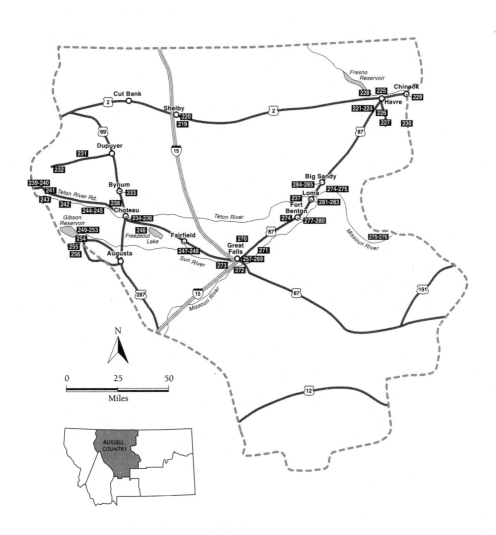

## 219. Marias Museum of History and Art

This ten-room museum has more than 10,000 items, including the largest known collection of memorabilia from the celebrated Heavyweight Championship fight between Jack Dempsey and Tommy Gibbons held in Shelby on July 4, 1923. More than 25,000 spectators gathered in this small town to watch the match in which Dempsey held off Gibbons for 15 rounds.
**Directions:** 206 12th Avenue.
**Important Information:** Free. Open daily, Memorial Day to Labor Day, from 1 to 5 P.M. and 7 to 9 P.M. During the rest of the year, the museum is only open on Tuesday afternoons. To check on hours contact the museum at 406-434-2551.

# Hutterite Colonies

Simple lifestyles and hard work speak for themselves in the Hutterite colonies in Montana. Hutterites are part of an Anabaptist religious movement from Germany that was persecuted during the reformation of the 1500s, left Europe, and eventually ended up in North America. About 4,000 Hutterites live in Montana colonies, and other colonies exist in the Dakotas, Minnesota, Washington, and Canada.

Hutterites choose not to accept the ways of the modern world, but instead live apart in their own communities around the Hi-Line and Rocky Mountain Front areas of Montana. There are colonies near Sunburst, Sweetgrass, Galata, Dupuyer, and Bynum. Hutterites do come to town for supplies and to sell their wonderfully fresh food products. You'll recognize them by their characteristic clothing: women wear long skirts, vests, and scarves while the men dress in black pants, hats, and jackets.

They are excellent farmers and produce about 60 percent of the state's pork, half of the eggs, and around 17 percent of the milk. While they do not give "tours" of the colonies, if you see signs advertising produce for sale at a colony, you are welcome to drive in to make a purchase.

## 220. Williamson Park

Shelby's Williamson Park is tucked away in the woods along the Marias River. The park has picnic tables, fire grills, and vault toilets. There is camping here, but no RV services. Locals like to float the river with inner tubes, starting by the golf course and following the winding river as it meanders by the course. It's easy to get out at Williamson Park as the Marias River at Williamson is quite shallow by the banks. It's nice for swimming, too.

**Directions:** Go south on Interstate 15 for 5 miles and take the signed golf course exit. Turn right onto the Frontage Road and go south for 4 miles to the park.

**Important Information:** The park is open in early May (depending on weather) and closes around the end of September. There is a camping fee of $7 per night, but no RV services. The park is operated by the City of Shelby, 406-434-5222.

# Havre

Havre is the largest town on Russell Country's Hi-Line route. Montana State University-Northern is located here. Ranching provides a livelihood for many of Havre's 10,500 residents. Locals have made a concerted effort to preserve cultural and historic sites, offering visitors some unusual exploration opportunities.

Thinking that Bull Hook Bottoms (the name of the railroad siding) might not look so good on a map, railroad tycoon James Hill suggested that the founding fathers select a new name. The first meeting ended in a brawl. There are two stories of how the town's name finally came about. The most likely is that one of the founding father's families originated from Havre, France, and since many of the original homesteaders were French, they chose to honor the French city with a namesake. Another version suggests that the name came from a tussle between two gentlemen for the affections of a charming woman. When it became clear to one of the two that he was losing the fight, he gave up and said, "you can have her." Either way, Havre stuck. It is pronounced HAVE-er.

Contact the Havre Area Chamber of Commerce at 406-265-4383 for more information.

## 221. Wahkpa Chu'gn National Historic Site

Roughly translated, *Wahkpa Chu'gn* (pronounced WALK-pa-CHEW-gun) means "too close for comfort" in the Assiniboine language. The name refers to the position held by Indian buffalo hunters whose job it was to keep stampeding buffalo lined up so they would end up leaping over a buffalo jump cliff.

The Wahkpa Chu'gn archaeological site has been determined to be both a kill site and a buffalo jump. Though it was used as a *pishkun*, or jump, there is also evidence that it was also a *pound*, or kill site, where the Indians set traps to catch buffalo and used upward-pointing sticks to impale the

# What Makes a Buffalo Jump?

Thousands of year ago, getting food was a different proposition than visiting the local grocery store of today. Buffalo were the mainstay of Indian life on the plains. Before horses appeared in the 1700s, Indians had to cleverly find a way to capture these massive animals on foot. So Indian tribes sought out plains areas where the long, flat lands came to an abrupt ending and dropped off at a steep cliff. Once they found a pishkun, or jump site, such as this, the trick was to somehow convince a herd of buffalo to jump over the cliff, plunging to certain death below. While buffalo may not be very wily creatures, convincing any animal to choose death goes against the grain of Mother Nature. But the Indians had observed herds of buffalo stampeding and knew that once some of the buffalo got started, the rest were likely to follow out of fear and instinct. Getting the great animals to stampede in just the right direction, however, was not easy.

Believe it or not, that's just what the Indians did. Many tribes used these tactics and would travel great distances to the plains each year to hunt buffalo. At some sites, the tribes would "share" a buffalo jump, taking turns using the jump, even having somewhat established times they would return each year.

Before the hunt, the medicine men sang, danced, and prayed to their great spirit for the luck of the hunt. During the hunt, highly skilled young warriors, wearing animal skins, would lure the bison toward the pishkun. This required lining up the bison with "drive lanes" or established pathways that the buffalo would need to be in if they were to end up in the right place. It took some planning to keep the buffalo on track and then to get them to travel at a fast enough pace at just the right time so the lead buffalo wouldn't turn back at the cliff's edge. "Hazers" would hide along the drive lane edges, ready to leap up if the buffalo strayed out of the drive lanes and herd the animals back onto the correct path. One difficult role in particular was that of the decoy, a fast runner who, wearing a complete buffalo robe, caught the lead animal's attention and got them to follow him, going faster and faster all the way to the brink of the cliff. Once there, the decoy had to leap into a specially prepared hole or side area set up to protect him, while the buffalo fell to their deaths.

If for some reason a buffalo survived the fall, hunters below were ready to kill the animal. It was believed that if a bison escaped, it would go back and tell the rest of the herd about the trap, making next year's hunt harder.

Of course, once the animals had made the death leap, there was a significant amount of time and effort involved in processing the meat and hides. So the whole tribe usually came along on these adventures, setting up camp nearby. They made a major outing of gathering and drying the meat and tanning the hides. The Blackfeet, for example, made more than 80 items from the buffalo. Among these were tools, utensils, clothing, and tepee covers. The Indians depended on the buffalo for survival. They used the bones, hides, and horns and wasted little, but the Indians' traditional lifestyle was brought to an abrupt halt when the white men's widespread slaughter of the buffalo began in the late 1800s.

huge animals. Thousands of buffalo bones lie under the soil here and the archaelogical digs, housed in small buildings on the site, reveal 2,000 years of history in bones. There is a guided tour available at the site, the only way you can see the area. The tour requires about a 0.25-mile walk which goes downhill and then back up. The site operators hope to put in a tram and elevator and to develop a self-guided tour. Currently, the hour-long tour includes an opportunity to see and maybe even throw an atalatal, an Indian weapon often used to kill bison.

**Directions:** The buffalo kill site is located behind the Holiday Village Shopping Center on U.S. Highway 2 on the west end of Havre. Tour participants gather inside the mall at the small office by the south entrance. Check at the site if you don't find the tour operations in the mall, as future plans call for the development of a self-guided tour which would begin at the site. This could happen as early as 1998.

**Important Information:** Regularly scheduled tours are given from June 1 to Labor Day, but tours are also available by appointment at other times of the year, weather permitting. During the summer season, tours leave as needed between 10 A.M. and 5 P.M., Tuesday through Sunday. An evening tour leaves at 7 P.M., Tuesday through Saturday. Fees are $3.50 for adults, $3 for seniors, and $2 for children ages 6 and over. Younger children are admitted free. Call for information on group rates, 406-265-6417 or 406-265-7550.

## 222. Havre Beneath the Streets

Beneath the serene streets of downtown Havre, a mysterious tangle of passageways and tunnels were found in 1990 that dated back nearly 100 years. Apparently, numerous Havre businesses at one time actually operated "down under" the city. Havre Beneath the Streets is believed to have housed a bakery, bar, butcher shops, mercantile, drug store, tack and blacksmith shop, Chinese laundry, barber shop, post office, and mortuary. Shadier operations included an Asian opium den and a bordello.

It is speculated that, after the fire of 1904, many businesses operated from basement level while rebuilding. Another thought is that the summer heat and winter cold may have made the ground-insulated areas appealing. Other stories about the underground city reflect the racial tension of the multicultural town. Some say the tunnels were an Asian innovation, intended to help Japanese and Chinese railway workers to escape the persecution that sometimes existed above ground.

Whatever the reason, local history buffs have dedicated endless hours to recreate underground Havre. Tons of rubble and rock had to be removed by community volunteers to begin the project. The facility has been renovated with as much accuracy as possible. The underground businesses had cement floors, wood-covered ceilings, and walls of sandstone and mortar.

The guided underground tour is about one hour long and is the only way to go through Havre Beneath the Streets. A lot of interesting and entertaining history is imparted on this tour.

**Directions:** Tickets are purchased at the Havre Beneath the Streets office located at 3rd Avenue and U.S. Highway 2 (1st Street) in Havre. The tour entrance is at US 2 and 2nd Avenue.

**Important Information:** The underground tour is $6 for adults, $4 for children 6 to 12, and free for children under 6. Seniors 55 and older pay $5. Special group rates are available. Summer hours are 9 A.M. to 5 P.M. daily, with tours beginning at 9:30 A.M. and running every 15 or 30 minutes, as needed. The last tour of the day begins at 3:30 P.M. Winter hours are noon to 4 P.M., Monday through Saturday with tours at 1:30 and 3:30 P.M. Reservations are required; call 406-265-8888.

## 223. H. Earl Clack Memorial Museum

The H. Earl Clack Memorial Museum has exhibits and dioramas relating to western migration, and a gift shop. Dioramas of early western days were created by sculptors Bob Scriver and Jim Plasma. The museum also has Indian artifacts and an art gallery. A Great Northern Railroad caboose is here, too, a relic from the days when Havre was a railroad siding known as "Bull Hook Bottoms."

**Directions:** The museum was relocated in 1998 to downtown Havre and is now located in the Heritage Center at 306 3rd Avenue.

**Important Information:** There is a minimal admission charge. The museum is open all year. Call for hours and costs, 406-265-4000.

## 224. Pepin Park and Havre Community Pool

Pepin Park is a few blocks from U.S. Highway 2 and offers plenty of shade, picnic tables, a restroom, and playground equipment. The community swimming pool is two blocks away.

**Directions:** From U.S. Highway 2 (1st Street) in Havre, turn south on 7th Avenue. Go four blocks to the park, which will be on your left. Turn right on 4th street and go a block to 420 6th Avenue to find the pool.

**Important Information:** The indoor pool is open year-round. Open swim hours in the summer, from early June to late August, are 2 to 3:30 P.M., and 7 to 9 P.M. Monday through Friday. Saturdays and Sundays open swims are

1 to 3 P.M. and 7 to 9 P.M., with a 3 to 5 P.M. session just on Saturdays. Winter hours are in two-hour sessions from 1 to 3 P.M., 3 to 5 P.M., and 7 to 9 P.M. Monday through Saturday and 3 to 5 P.M. on Sunday. Cost is $1.50 for students and $1 for adults. For information, contact Havre City Parks and Recreation at 406-265-8161.

## 225. Rookery Wildlife Management Area and the Milk River

This site is easy to reach from the town of Havre and gets you out onto the Milk River. The management area has 2,500 acres of river bottomlands and includes some upland grass and sagebrush land. You can walk anywhere on the grounds though there are no marked trails. The area is used for fishing, hunting, and wildlife watching. This is an undeveloped site that families who just want to be out in nature will enjoy.

You can canoe the 4- to 5-mile stretch of river within the management area as there are boat launches at both the upper and lower boundaries of the facility. The Milk is a winding river at this point, so this could be a 4- or 5-hour float.

**Directions:** From U.S. 2 (1st Street) in Havre, take 7th Avenue north at the bridge that crosses the railroad tracks and the Milk River. Turn left (west) on North Fifth Street and follow the paved road for about 5 miles. When the paved road goes uphill, turn left onto Badlands County Road. There are signs for the boat launch and management area as well as a parking area.

**Important Information:** The Milk River is well known for its refreshing tree-lined banks, its milky color caused by silt, AND for mosquitoes, so bring mosquito repellent just in case. Downstream from the management area is a water weir which is dangerous to canoeists, so do not float below the management area boundaries. The area is open to hunting in season and a portion of it is leased to the local rifle and pistol club for a shooting range. Contact the Havre Office of the Montana Department of Fish, Wildlife, & Parks at 406-228-6177 for more information.

## 226. Fort Assiniboine

After General Custer's defeat at the Battle of the Little Bighorn, this fort was set up to protect settlers against potential Indian attacks. The fort was established in 1879 and was one of the largest forts in the country. It was strategically located at the north-south and east-west junction of the Indian trails which later became the route of our highway system. No attacks

ever occurred at the fort. The fort was manned in 1896 by the Tenth Cavalry, an all-Black unit led by "Black Jack" Pershing. Sixteen of the original 100 buildings are still standing. The fort is now an agricultural research center and is open for visitors at established tour times only. Tours last about an hour.
**Directions:** Go west of Havre on U.S. Highway 2 for 6 miles, then turn left (south) on Montana Highway 87. You will see signs for the fort on the left-hand side of the road on MT 87.
**Important Information:** Guided tours of the fort are run at 5 P.M. daily, from Memorial Day to Labor Day, weather permitting. Group tours are available. Tour fees are $3 for adults, and $1.50 for students. Children under 6 are admitted free. Contact the H. Earl Clack Memorial Museum, 406-265-4000, or the Havre Area Chamber of Commerce, 406-265-4383, for information about the tours.

## 227. Beaver Creek Park

Here's a prairie jewel. This 10,000-acre park is one of the largest county-owned parks in the nation. The park sits at the northern edge of the Bear's Paw Mountains and has grasslands, pine woods, and cottonwood groves to appreciate. The 16-mile strip of park land follows Beaver Creek and includes two lakes. Both lakes and the creek are well stocked with trout. You can have an enjoyable time in this park simply playing by the water and watching the multitude of birds which frequent the area. There are numerous picnic areas and camping sites, but no electrical hookups. Most campground areas have tables, fire grates, and vault toilets. Some campgrounds require reservations.
**Directions:** From U.S. Highway 2 (1st Street) in Havre, go south on 5th Avenue, also marked as Hill County 234. It is about 10 miles to the Beaver Creek Park boundary.
**Important Information:** There is a campground fee of $5 per night for each household (or tenthold). Contact the park office at 406-395-4565 for more information.

## 228. Fresno Lake

This lake gets a fair amount of local use for fishing, camping, and swimming. The lake, which is actually a reservoir, is 25 miles long so there is also room to boat and water-ski. There is a boat launch area and, to the west, a swimming and picnic area. There are four campgrounds on the lake, but only the one at Kremlin Bay, also called Fresno Bay, has much in the way of facilities. Here there are picnic tables, vault toilets, and a boat ramp. There is no potable water or electricity. The swimming area has restrooms but little else. Below the dam is a nicely developed Bureau of Reclamation access site which is wheelchair accessible.

**Directions:** Go 13 miles west of Havre on U.S. Highway 2. Turn right (north) at a sign for Fresno Lake, across from Blackie's Tavern. Take the first left to get to the beach area and the second left for the boat launch. Follow the signs straight ahead to get to the dam and the Bureau of Reclamation site below the dam.

To get to Kremlin Bay campground, take US 2 west beyond the Fresno Lake turnoff. Turn right at the grain elevators and stay on the good gravel road. About a half mile from the lake turn right (east) at the signed campground road.

**Important Information:** The Fresno Lake turn is marked on the highway but the roads to the picnic area and boat ramp are not well marked. There is a road to the picnic area from the boat launch, but you are better off going back up the road and catching the westerly turn on the entrance road.

The lake is managed through a cooperative effort by Walleyes Unlimited, Montana Department of the Fish, Wildlife & Parks, and the Bureau of Reclamation. For information contact Fish, Wildlife & Parks Havre Area Resource Office at 406-265-6177 from 10 A.M. to 2 P.M., or Walleyes Unlimited at the local sporting goods store, E-fish-hunt Sports, during normal business hours. The number is 406-265-3441.

# Chinook

This small town is named after an Indian word meaning "warm wind." Every winter in this region, warm winds blow through the area, melting away the winter snow and exposing the grasses below. A winter chinook can increase the temperature some 50 degrees in a few minutes. One of Charlie Russell's most famous works of art is called *Waiting for a Chinook*, or *The Last of the Five Thousand*. It shows a lone, emaciated cow standing in the hard winter weather, waiting for the belated chinook that would expose the grasses needed to keep cattle alive through the winter. Charlie made the sketch one long, cold winter when he was caretaker of a ranch. When the ranch owner wrote to inquire about the condition of his herd, Charlie responded with the telling sketch.

## 229. Blaine County Museum

The focus of this museum is the story of the Nez Perce journey toward freedom in Canada and their surrender at the Bear's Paw Battlefield just 16 miles

# "I Will Fight No More Forever"

In 1877, a band of 700 Nez Perce women, children, and the elderly, led by Chief Joseph, fled their homelands in the Wallowa Valley of Oregon. The story began when the U.S. Government demanded that the Nez Perce leave their ancient homelands and move to a reservation. The Indians were reluctant to obey the ultimatum when a skirmish broke out and several white settlers were killed. Rather than suffer the revenge of the military or abandon their way of life and move to the reservation, the Nez Perce began a historic journey toward Canada, where Sitting Bull had offered asylum and freedom.

The tribe traveled nearly 1,300 miles, brilliantly eluding the U.S. Cavalry for 112 days, and were within 40 miles of safety in Canada when the Indians were surrounded in the Bear's Paw Mountains of Montana Territory. The Indians valiantly fought for their freedom but the Nez Perce flight ended in surrender.

The band crossed the Rocky Mountains three times to elude the pursuing cavalry, a clever military strategy that surprised the cavalry and allowed the Nez Perce to maintain their lead. In late September, they had nearly reached refuge with Sitting Bull when the weary tribe stopped to rest. Little did they know that cavalry troops had been approaching from the east and they were now surrounded, only a long day's march from the Canadian border. Some of the Nez Perce escaped, but Chief Joseph would not leave behind the sick and old to be killed. A battle ensued, but the Indians had little chance.

On October 5, 1877, Chief Joseph spoke these words, "It is cold and we have no blankets. The little children are freezing to death. I want to look for my children and see how many of them I can find. Maybe I shall find them among the dead. Hear me, my chiefs! I am tired. My heart is sick and sad. From where the sun now stands, I will fight no more forever." With this, Chief Joseph surrendered to the U.S. Army with the remaining 87 warriors and 147 women and children. Members of the weary band were sent to various reservations and holding areas. The government had promised the Nez Perce that they would be returned to their homeland, and some of the Nez Perce did indeed return. Chief Joseph, however, died in 1904 on the Colville Reservation in Washington State. Legends say his heart was broken, for he had witnessed the destruction of his people's traditional way of life, and he never again saw his people's land.

south of Chinook. A small theater shows an excellent, and very touching, 20-minute multimedia production entitled *40 Miles to Freedom*. Other exhibits in this museum include a paleontology display, Indian artifacts, and a homestead exhibit.

**Directions:** The museum is located on 501 Indiana Street, the main north-south road through Chinook.

**Important Information:** No admission fee. The museum is open June through August, Monday through Saturday from 8 A.M. to 5 P.M., and Sundays from noon to 5 P.M. Hours during May and September are Monday through Friday, 8 A.M. to 5 P.M. From October through April the museum is open Monday through Friday from 1 to 5 P.M. Closed during the lunch hour all year. Contact the museum at 406-357-2590.

## 230. Bear's Paw Battleground

This is the site of the 1877 battle where Chief Joseph of the Nez Perce gave his famous surrender speech to Colonel Nelson A. Miles. A short trail follows the edge of the encampment area and the story of the battle unfolds through interpretive displays. Tepee sites, rifle pits, and battle areas are marked. There are picnic tables and vault toilets here, but no camping. The battlefield is part of the Nez Perce National Historical Park, which comprises thirty-eight sites along the 1,300-mile trail of the Chief Joseph and the Nez Perce. It is managed by the National Park Service.

**Directions:** The battlefield is 16 miles south of Chinook on Blaine County 240. Follow the signs from Chinook.

**Important Information:** There is no fee. A National Park Service ranger is often present and will provide interpretive information.

# ROCKY MOUNTAIN FRONT: U.S. HIGHWAY 89 AND U.S. HIGHWAY 287

The Rocky Mountain Front is the land where the rugged Rocky Mountains of the Bob Marshall Wilderness meet the open prairie of eastern Montana. In this area are several small towns, a number of wildlife management areas, lots of Montana farms and ranches, and some downright pretty country. To the east is the flat, wild prairie. To the west, the Bob Marshall Wilderness complex rises majestically with 1.5 million acres of lakes, rivers, and 10,000-foot peaks.

Wildlife, wildflowers, and wild lands abound. The ranges of plains flowers and alpine flowers intermingle here. There are chokecherries, prairie roses, arrowleaf balsamroot, daisies, wild relatives of the sweet pea, and many other colorful wildflowers. Look for trumpeter swans, white pelicans, sandhill cranes, eagles, and numerous other bird species at the wildlife management areas. The Rocky Mountain Front is also one of the last strongholds of grizzly bear prairie habitat.

One of the most unusual aspects of the Rocky Mountain Front is the area's importance in the field of paleontology. Though humans have been here for more than 11,000 years, dinosaurs ruled the land for eons before humans appeared on the scene. This section of Montana is one of the most significant regions in the world for excavation and research of the ancient reptiles. Visitors to the area can explore the world of dinosaur fossils in museums and at on-site archaeological digs.

The Rocky Mountain Front is an experience of diversity and abundance of life in dynamic and beautiful forms.

# Northern Rocky Mountain Front: Valier to Choteau

North of Choteau are four small prairie towns: Valier, Dupuyer, Pendroy, and Bynum. Farm and ranch communities, these areas enjoyed some growth when the railroad was nearby. Today, the railroad is gone and the towns serve as community centers for locals. There are some interesting natural features along the way as well as some true small-town flavor.

## 231. Theodore Roosevelt Memorial Ranch Wildlife Trail

This 1.4-mile, round-trip interpretive foot trail is privately maintained. The trail climbs to the top of a ridge with a panoramic view, looking north as far as Chief Mountain and south to the mountains near Augusta on a clear day. Along the trail is interpretive information about the wildlife and wild lands of the Rocky Mountain Front. The trail is fairly gentle for the first half and then climbs rather steeply to the top. Since it is a short distance, the hike is worth nudging little ones to the top.

**Directions:** The trail is 10 miles west of Dupuyer. As you enter Dupuyer from the north you will see a small gravel road crossing the highway. Go right (west) on this road, which is marked as Pondera County 534 on the east side of the road. It is not well marked going west but the post office is visible and will be on your right just after you have made the turn. Follow this road for 8.5 miles, where you will come to a fork in the road. Take the left fork and go 0.5 mile to another fork. Stay left and continue on this road. When you pass a small log cabin on the right continue to a T junction in the road. Turn right at the T and go 2 miles. You will go over a cattle guard and drive to the top of a hill where there are wildlife viewing signs and a parking pullout on the right (north) side of the road. The trail starts and ends in the parking area.

**Important Information:** You are asked to stay along the viewing trail and not go onto the private land. The trail is open year-round except during hunting season from October 15 to December 1. For more information, or to check weather conditions, contact the ranch manager at 406-472-3380. It is not necessary to call ahead for permission to hike the trail.

## 232. Blackleaf Canyon Wildlife Management Area and Blackleaf Canyon Trail

Blackleaf Canyon is a good place to look for wildlife and enjoy a pleasant hike through the canyon's towering limestone cliffs. The management area's primary goal is to provide winter and spring range for elk and mule deer. Grizzly bear and black bear use the area extensively in the spring. A herd of 75 mountain goats makes the canyon their home, and you can generally see them here. If you park at the end of Blackleaf Road you can walk up the Blackleaf Canyon Trail about a mile or so and have a good chance of seeing the goats on the sheer cliffs along the way. This is an easy hike that actually begins on an old seismic road. It is marked at the parking area at the end of Blackleaf Road. (There are vault toilets here.) The walk takes you from riparian areas to the alpine ecosystem. There are a couple of small streams to cross and a nice waterfall on this trail, too. Up the canyon, the trail narrows and connects with other trails into the Bob Marshall. These trails are more difficult and are suitable for experienced hikers.

The grasslands and wet marshes in other parts of the wildlife management area provide for wonderful spring and early summer flowers. This is also a good place to see raptors such as marsh hawks, golden eagles, and prairie falcons. Antelope Butte and Reservoir are within the management area boundaries. They provide good wildlife viewing, too, though this area is a favorite spot for bears and may best be left to them.

**Directions:** Go north from Choteau on U.S. Highway 89 to Bynum. Turn left (west) onto Blackleaf Road by the grocery store. It is 16 miles to the management area. Take the road all the way to the end to get to the trailhead.

**Important Information:** Some parts of the management area are closed from spring until July 1 because of grizzly use. Note that vehicle traffic between December 1 and May 15 is prohibited within the management area borders.

Wind funnels down through the canyon so if you decide to hike up the canyon, bring a jacket and hold onto your hat! Weather patterns shift quickly in the mountains so be prepared with warm clothing even if the weather appears good when you leave for the hike. For information, contact the Montana Department of Fish, Wildlife & Parks at the Conrad Field Office, 406-278-7033, or the Choteau Field Office, 406-466-5621.

## 233. The Bynum Rock Shop

. . . . . . . . . . . . . . . . . . . . . . . . . . . . . . . . . . . .

The Rock Shop is run by Marion Brandvold, who discovered the baby Maiasaura dinosaur fossils at Egg Mountain in 1978. The shop is also known as the T-Rex Agate Shop and features fossils, rocks, and gift items. You can find information here about tours to Egg Mountain and other outfitter-run archaeological trips.

**Directions:** Look for the rock shop in an old church building along U.S. Highway 89 in Bynum. The dinosaurs painted on the side are a clue that you're there.

**Important Information:** Hours are usually 9 A.M. to 6 P.M. from sometime in April or May (depending on the weather) to sometime in October. The shop is open during the rest of the year but times vary, so it is best to contact the rock shop at 406-469-2314 for more information.

# Choteau

. . . . . . . . . . . . . . . . . . . . . . . . . . . . . . . . . . . .

Choteau, with a population of 1,800, is the largest of the small Rocky Mountain Front towns. It is a farm and ranch community with a fur trading history. There are visitor services here and the town serves as a base for those wanting to explore the dinosaur digs or head into the forest and wilderness areas along the forks of the Teton River. The Choteau County Courthouse, built in 1884, is the third oldest in the state. Contact the Choteau Chamber of Commerce for more information at 406-466-5316 or 800-823-3866.

## 234. Choteau City Park

. . . . . . . . . . . . . . . . . . . . . . . . . . . . . . . . . . . .

This small, wooded park is located by Spring Creek, a tiny creek that my kids found to be a highlight of the park. They enjoyed jumping into the refreshing shallow water and I had a hard time convincing them we should leave. A picnic here proved to be a delightful afternoon activity and a welcome diversion from traveling. There is free camping for RVs and tents here, though donations are encouraged and accepted. Also available are restrooms, picnic tables, and a children's playground.

**Directions:** From U.S. Highway 89 (Main Street), turn east at the junction with Montana Highway 221. This is at "the" flashing yellow light in town. Go about one block, over the railroad tracks, and turn right at the camping sign.

**Important Information:** Contact the Choteau Chamber of Commerce at 406-466-5316 or 800-823-3866 for information.

## 235. Choteau Lion's Club Swimming Pool

The area swimming pool is run by the Lion's Club and is close to the highway. It is a good place to stop for a refreshing swim on a hot day while exploring Choteau's varied offerings.

**Directions:** One block west of the junction of U.S. Highway 89 (Choteau's main street) and U.S. Highway 287.

**Important Information:** Daily public swim hours, except Friday, are 2 to 4:30 P.M. and 7 to 9 P.M. Cost is $1 for children and $2 for adults. Call 406-466-9919 for more information and to check hours and rates.

## 236. Teton Trail Village and Old Trail Museum

Here's a good starting point for a dinosaur journey. The Old Trail Museum houses a special dinosaur room where you can take a look at fossils and watch a video about the nearby finds. There are photos and castings of dinosaur nests from Egg Mountain, the site of the 1978 Maiasaura nests discovery and from various other digs. The museum also sponsors a two-day, hands-on family program at Egg Mountain and attendants can answer questions about the daily tours sponsored by the Museum of the Rockies. Outside are a half-dozen buildings along a boardwalk that houses shops, including one with ice cream. The Metis Traditional Cabin Exhibit is housed in one of these buildings.

## The Old North Trail

The peaks and foothills of the rugged Rocky Mountains have long held both a fascination for and importance to the human species. Today people come to the Rockies mostly for their beauty and wilderness opportunities, but, in the past, the number of animals to be found along the boundaries of plains and peaks brought people here. Running along the east slope of the Rocky Mountains, a well-worn trail tells of centuries of use. Indian travois and the feet of thousands of people followed the Old North Trail, which stretches from Canada to Helena. The tribes that passed through no doubt searched for food, but also used the route for trade. War parties must have traveled the route, preferring the shelter of the mountains over the open plains as they journeyed to battle. Remnants of this trail can be found along the Rocky Mountain Front, and displays tell of the trail in the Old Trail Museum in Choteau, as well as the Museum of the Plains Indians in Browning.

Other exhibits in the museum include the A. C. Robinson railroad collection, a firearms collection, an antique medical instruments collection, homesteader artifacts, a grizzly bear exhibit, an A. B. Guthrie, Jr. exhibit, and the Old North Trail Exhibit. The Choteau Visitor Center is located in the same complex and has restrooms and information.

**Directions:** Located at 823 North Main (U.S. Highway 89) in Choteau. The dinosaurs outside are a giveaway that you have found the museum.

**Important Information:** Admission charges are $2 for adults and 50 cents for kids ages 3 to 17. The museum is open daily, May 15 to September 15, from 9 A.M. to 6 P.M. Winter hours are 10 A.M. to 3 P.M., Tuesday through Saturday. Contact the museum at 406-466-5332.

# The Teton River Area

Some of the prettiest territory in the Rocky Mountain Front lies along the banks of the Teton River. Originating in the Bob Marshall Wilderness, the Teton River flows for nearly 200 river miles (100 air miles) down from the mountains and across the plains. The river eventually joins the Marias River just a few yards from the Marias's confluence with the Missouri River by Loma.

The river has sometimes been called the Rose River for the plentiful wild roses which are seen along its banks. Indians called the river the *Titan*, which referred to the "land without trees" through which it flows. The word *teton* is French for breasts, recalling human images in the majestic Teton mountains. A division of the Sioux tribe who were called Teton Sioux lived near the river and were responsible for the official name.

## 237. Teton River Float

Though floating the river is possible, the upper section requires intermediate skill levels and the middle section is painstakingly slow. The best family float is the final few miles, putting in at a county road bridge 5 miles east of Montana Highway 223 and taking out at the U.S. Highway 87 bridge across the Marias near Loma. This is a 12-mile stretch and makes a good four- or five-hour float.

**Directions:** Put in about 12 miles upstream from the take-out bridge near Loma at a county road bridge 5 miles east of the Montana Highway 223 bridge near Fort Benton. The county road bridge is easy to find.

# 238. Eureka Reservoir

This is a small plains reservoir where it is possible to do some rainbow trout fishing from the shore. Locals swim and jet ski in the reservoir and it is an acceptable stop for a quick break and a refreshing dip on a hot summer day. The reservoir has a small gravel beach, a boat ramp, and vault toilets, but no potable water. Camping is permitted and there is a nice view of the Rocky Mountain Front.

**Directions:** From Choteau, go north 5 miles on U.S. Highway 89. Turn left (west) onto Teton River Road and follow the road for 3 miles. Turn right (north) to the reservoir.

**Important Information:** For more information, contact the Freezout Lake Wildlife Management Area, 406-467-2488, or the Bureau of Reclamation at the Fresno Dam office, 406-265-2927.

# 239. West Fork Teton River Campground

You just can't get any closer than this to the wilderness without donning a backpack and heading up into the mountains on foot. The West Fork Teton Campground is at the end of the Teton River Road and marks the beginning of a main pathway into the Bob Marshall Wilderness. A journey in here to touch the wilderness results in a long, winding drive along the Teton River Road for 33 miles from the junction with U.S. Highway 89. Climbing over Teton Pass near Mount Lockhart, the road drops into a spectacularly scenic valley on the west side of the mountain slopes. The West Fork Teton Campground lies less than a mile from the pass. The official Bob Marshall Wilderness boundary is only a 1-mile walk away.

Looking up at the craggy peaks surrounding you in the West Fork area, it's clear that hikes into the Bob Marshall Wilderness require some upward effort. Getting into the Bob necessitates more energy than most families with young children can muster. This particular campground area provides an opportunity to enjoy wild lands by allowing families to get near enough to the wilderness to lose sight of the outside world. From here, a couple of trails will take families close to the wilderness along easy river-bottom walks. To reach the peaks requires strenuous hiking but is possible with older children who are experienced hikers.

The West Fork Teton River Campground has six tent-only sites with water, fireplaces, tables, and vault toilets. From the campground you can hike along the North Fork of the Teton Trail 107 or Blackleaf Trail 106 (see site 240). There are other, steeper trails in the area.

As you come toward the campground from US 89, you may want to stop about 18.5 miles west from US 89 up Teton River Road to read the interpretive sign explaining the story of the Old North Trail. Some scholars believe that the Rocky Mountain Front was traveled by ancient peoples from Asia who had crossed the Bering Land Bridge between Asia and Alaska more than 8,000 years ago. There is a picnic table here. About 2.5 miles farther, look for Indianhead Rock in the cliffs on the left side of the road. The rock formation resembles a human profile. Indianhead Rock is about 21 miles up Teton River Road from US 89.

**Directions:** From Choteau, go north 5 miles on US 89. Turn left (west) onto Teton River Road and follow the road for 33 miles. It is paved for the first 18 miles. Turn right into the campground at the Teton River Bridge. The campground is to the right after the bridge.

**Important Information:** Allow an hour and a half to get into the campground area from US 89, as the winding, gravel road is slow. There is no campground fee. The campground is open, as weather permits, between May 1 and November 15. Camping is normally acceptable in mid-June, but varies with the weather from year to year. Definitely avoid fording the Teton River along the North Fork trail if the water levels are high. Keep in mind that this water is exceptionally cold year-round.

Call the Lewis and Clark National Forest, Rocky Mountain District office, in Choteau at 406-466-5341 for more information and to check on weather conditions. This office is on the north end of Choteau on the west side of US 89 and is an easy stop for maps and information.

## 240. North Fork of Teton Trail 107

The North Fork of Teton Trail 107 begins with a 2.7-mile river-bottom walk. Most families can complete the hike to this point. The trail goes on to climb the mountains and dip into the South Fork of the Birch Creek drainage and also joins the Corrugate Ridge Trail. Experienced backpackers can go from these points deep into the wilderness for a two- to three-day intensive hike. Most families will want to content themselves with enjoying the first 2.7-mile stretch along the Teton or may even need to stop at the river crossing.

Pick up the trail at the trailhead located at the end of the campground bridge. The North Fork Trail follows the Teton River for 1 mile and then crosses the river by the turnoff for the East Fork–Blackleaf Trail 106. The Blackleaf Trail is not well marked, but can still be followed if you feel like exploring this direction. The river crossing here is knee-deep much of the year. Hikers need to be aware, though, that spring runoff is extensive on the Teton, multiplying the river volume as much as seven times the normal flow.

Depths may be prohibitive for crossing. Families should use caution when considering this crossing and carefully observe the river depth before helping children across. If the water is too high, don't cross!

If you do ford the river, you will come to the wilderness boundary in just a few feet. From here the trail dips in and out of the forest until it comes to the Bruce Creek Trail 152 up to Corrugate Ridge. The Bruce Creek ridge trail is steeper than most families can endure, and requires another river crossing. Most likely, this is the turnaround point for families.

**Directions:** From Choteau, go north 5 miles on U.S. Highway 89. Turn left (west) onto Teton River Road and follow the road for 35 miles. It is paved for the first 18 miles. Go over Teton Pass and, in about 1 mile, turn right into the campground at the Teton River Bridge. The North Fork of the Teton Trail 107 leaves from the road that goes to the left immediately at the end of the bridge on the campground side. This road is gated, but you will see the trailhead signs from the gate.

**Important Information:** Allow an hour and a half to get into the campground area from US 89, as the winding, gravel road is slow.

Call the Lewis and Clark National Forest, Rocky Mountain District Office in Choteau at 406-466-5341 for more information and to check on weather conditions. This office is on the north end of Choteau on the west side of US 89 and is an easy stop for maps and information.

## 241. Cave Mountain Campground and the Middle Fork of Teton River Trail 108

Cave Mountain Campground is a wooded car-camping area 23 miles, or about 40 minutes, from Choteau. It is about 10 miles farther to West Fork Teton River Campground (site 239).

The campground has 14 sites with water, fireplaces, picnic tables, and vault toilets. Some campsites are available for group reservations. There are commercial outfitters and horseback riding opportunities nearby.

As you travel west toward the campground from U.S. Highway 89, you may want to stop 18.5 miles up Teton River Road to read the interpretive sign explaining the story of the Old North Trail (see site 239). There is a picnic table here. About 2.5 miles farther, look up to the cliffs on the left side of the road for Indianhead Rock, which resembles a human profile. This is about 21 miles west up Teton River Road from US 89 on the way to the campground.

The Middle Fork of the Teton Trail is a river-bottom trail that follows the river and is mostly wooded. While there are no scenic views of the mountains from this trail, it does pass by beaver ponds and is mostly flat. The hike would make a good excursion for just getting out and walking in nature.

**Directions:** From Choteau, go north 5 miles on US 89. Turn left (west) onto Teton River Road and follow this for 23 miles. The road is paved for the first 18 miles. The campground is on the left. The signed trailhead for Trail 108 is near the end of the Cave Mountain Campground road.

**Important Information:** The campground is open from about May 15 through November 26, as weather permits. There is a $5 camping fee per night.

Call the Lewis and Clark National Forest, Rocky Mountain District office in Choteau at 406-466-5341 for more information and to check on weather conditions. This office is on the north end of Choteau on the west side of US 89 and is an easy stop for maps and information.

## 242. Ear Mountain Outstanding Natural Area and Trail

Ear Mountain was a vision quest site for the Blackfeet Indians for many centuries. Author A. B. Guthrie, Jr. felt a special affinity for this area and called the mountain his "hold on the universe." There is a 2.1-mile trail here that goes gently up and down along the open prairie lands and along what locals call Yaeger Flats. The natural area has a picnic area and vault toilet by the road. The trail begins at the fence line above the picnic area. The natural area makes a nice picnic stop and you can walk along the trail as far as you want to go. The Mill Falls hike is nearby, too.

This is prime grizzly territory and there is a chance of seeing griz, especially in early mornings and around dusk. There is no overnight camping at the picnic area, though you can camp in other parts of the natural area or at nearby Mill Falls Campground.

**Directions:** Go north of Choteau on U.S. Highway 89 for 5 miles to the Teton River Road. Turn left (west) here and follow the paved road for 17 miles. Turn left (south) onto the South Fork Teton Road 109 and you will cross the Teton River in 0.5 mile. To the right is Ear Mountain and Pine Butte Guest Ranch, a privately-owned guest facility. It is 2 miles to the Ear Mountain Outstanding Natural Area.

**Important Information:** The trailhead is open year-round but there are seasonal closures from December 15 to July 15 because of high grizzly bear use.

Contact the Bureau of Land Management, Great Falls Resource Area Office at 406-727-0503 for more information.

# 243. Mill Falls Campground and Mill Falls Trail

The Mill Falls Trail is a quick 0.1-mile hike in a wooded campground area. It follows a small creek to a little waterfall. This is a nice hike to take with young children, who will no doubt find other things to explore along the way and in the campground. The campground has four sites with fireplaces, picnic tables, and vault toilets. Bring your own drinking water.

Nearby is the Ear Mountain Outstanding Natural Area Trail (site 242), Egg Mountain (site 245), and the A. B. Guthrie, Jr. Trail (site 244).

**Directions:** From Choteau, go north 5 miles on U.S. Highway 89. Turn left (west) onto Teton River Road and follow the paved road for 17 miles, then turn left (south) onto the South Fork Teton Road 109 and you will cross the Teton River in 0.5 mile. Turn right and go another 9.5 miles to the campground sign at Mill Falls Road. The trail begins from the end of the campground road in 0.2 mile.

**Important Information:** There is no camping fee. Bring mosquito repellent, just in case.

Contact the Rocky Mountain Ranger District Office of the Lewis and Clark National Forest, 406-466-5341.

# 244. A. B. Guthrie, Jr. Memorial Trail

You're in Big Sky country now, and more than that, you're in the home territory for Pulitzer Prize-winning journalist and novelist, A. B. Guthrie, Jr. Guthrie wrote *The Big Sky* and other books in a series about Montana. This short nature walk, named in honor of the local man, goes to the top of a hill for a good view of the area. The trail is short, but steep. There is interpretive information at the kiosk along the road and signs on the hill identifying the area landmarks.

The kids will especially like the way the stones near the top have been laid to make "steps." The limber pine trees on the ridge have an average age of 350 years. These trees don't look that old, but they can help you imagine what it must be like to live here among high winds, precious little moisture, and cold temperatures. If you go through the fence at the top and follow the trail a short way west, you'll come to the Rocky Mountain Overlook which has information about Ear Mountain. This is a nice area for mid-summer wildflowers.

From the ridge, facing east, look back down toward the information kiosk and follow the fence line on the left a couple hundred yards north. The circle of stones you see there is a tepee ring used by native people hundreds of years ago. When you get back down below, you can walk out to the tepee ring, but be sure not to disturb any of it. From the ridge, you can also see the land included in the Pine Butte Swamp Preserve, a Nature Conservancy holding. This private, 18,000-acre preserve protects a variety of habitats and a multitude of animals and birds, including grizzly bears. You need permission from the preserve manager to enter this area. Tours of the preserve are given by appointment.

**Directions:** Go north of Choteau on U.S. Highway 89 for 5 miles to the Teton River Road. Turn left (west) here and follow the paved road for 17 miles. Turn left (south) onto the South Fork Teton Road 109 and you will cross the Teton River within 0.5 mile. Continue going straight for about 3.5 miles. You will see a kiosk on the left-hand side of the road. Across the road from the kiosk is the start of the trail.

An alternate route begins 1 mile south of Choteau on Montana Highway 287. Turn right (west) at the sign for Pishkun Reservoir by the Triangle Meat Packing Plant. This is Bellview Road and it is the first gravel road you will come to going south from Choteau. Go north past the white Bellview School, then take the fork to the right. You will see a sign providing interpretive information about the area and A. B. Guthrie, Jr. at a kiosk on the right (east) side of the road. If you get to Teton River Road, you have gone about 4 miles too far. It is about 17 miles, or a half-hour drive, from Choteau to the trailhead via Bellview Road.

**Important Information:** The trail is open year-round. If there is a sign saying no trespassing just past the Teton River bridge, it means that you are asked not to walk on the land between the bridge and the trail. The road is public access. For more information or to schedule a tour of Pine Butte Swamp, contact the Nature Conservancy at 406-466-5526.

## 245. Egg Mountain

What kid (of any age) isn't enthralled by dinosaurs? Egg Mountain is a chance to get into the world of these massive, mystical creatures. Located on the Willow Creek Anticline, Egg Mountain is the site of the first dinosaur egg discovery ever made in the Western Hemisphere. This discovery significantly changed long-held beliefs about the basic nature of dinosaurs.

In 1978 more than 300 specimens from nests of the duck-billed Maiasaura dinosaur were unearthed at Egg Mountain. The nesting area is about 80 million years old and the fossils are part of a geological zone called the Two Medicine formation. This area covers about 3,600 square miles in a 2,000-foot-deep layer of sandstone, mudstone, and shale. Large numbers of fossils are found throughout this formation.

# The Good Mother Lizard, Montana's State Fossil

All states have state flowers and birds, but Montana may be the only state with an official state fossil. And, for good reason! The *Maiasaura peeblesorum*, a duck-billed dinosaur, was given the title of Montana State Fossil after paleontologist Jack Horner located more than a dozen duck-billed dinosaur nests at Egg Mountain. The site was shown to him by locals John and Marian Brandvold, who operate The Rock Shop in Bynum.

The 6-foot-wide nests had the fossilized skeletons of baby dinos still in them. More than a pleasant surprise, this discovery shifted the world's thinking about dinosaurs. Previously they were believed to be cold-blooded, rather solitary creatures. This find led scientists to recognize the great beasts as warm-blooded herd animals who cared for their young after birth. The name *Maiasaura*, means "Good Mother Lizard" and the *peeblesorum* part of the name is given in honor of the Peebles family, local ranchers who owned the badlands where the *Maiasaura* eggs were found. The ranch land is now owned by The Nature Conservancy.

A daily tour of Egg Mountain is offered through the Museum of the Rockies. The Old Trail Museum (site 236), in Choteau can provide information and directions to the site, or a brochure with directions can be obtained directly from the Museum of the Rockies in Bozeman. The tour is about an hour and a half long and discusses dinosaurs, the significance of the Egg Mountain discovery, and the area's natural history.

**Directions:** To reach Egg Mountain, go south from Choteau on U.S. Highway 287. Turn right (west) at the sign for Pishkun Reservoir by the Triangle Meat Packing Plant. This is Bellview Road and is the first gravel road you will come to going south from Choteau. Continue on this road for 6 miles to a road fork. The left fork goes to Pishkun Reservoir and the right fork will get you to Egg Mountain in another 6 miles. The site is just past the second cattleguard on the right-hand side of the road.

**Important Information:** Tours run from late June to late August and leave from Egg Mountain at 2 P.M. every day. No advance reservations are necessary. Contact the Museum of the Rockies in Bozeman at 406-994-2251, or call the Old Trail Museum at 406-466-5332 for information about the tour. Wear comfortable walking shoes and bring sun protection.

# 246. Freezout Lake Wildlife Management Area

This lake and wildlife area have easy access right off U.S. Highway 89. It's a nice stop for a few minutes, or you can easily spend a few hours exploring the 12,000-acre management area. Freezout Lake wetlands often have large numbers of waterfowl present. Up to a million birds have been spotted here at peak migration times, which are from March to May and September to November. Up to 300,000 snow geese and 10,000 tundra swans have been spotted here. Ibis, herons, sandhill cranes, gulls, eagles, hawks, and owls are a few of the other birds that use the management area. Stop by the headquarters and pick up interpretive information and bird lists. Spring is the best time for observation but you will see birds all year.

There are six ponds on the road that winds through the management area on the west side of US 89. Mountain biking is good along the connecting roads between ponds.

The management area has vault toilets and picnic tables. There is camping at designated sites, with varying facilities. There is no potable water. The town of Fairfield, 12 miles south, has groceries, gas, and city parks.

**Directions:** Drive 11 miles south of Choteau on U.S. Highway 89. The office for the wildlife management area is on the right. A map of the area is

## Trumpeter Swan,
### *Cygnus buccinator*

At one time, fewer than 70 trumpeter swans could be found in the lower 48 states. The beautiful birds were heavily hunted for their feathers, meat, and delicate skin, which was a popular material for powder puffs in the 1920s and 1930s. Since 1935, the birds have been protected by federal mandate. The protection resulted in an increase in population numbers, and when the population reached 5,000 in 1968, trumpeter swans were removed from the threatened and endangered species list. In part, the formation of Red Rock Lakes National Wildlife Refuge in southwestern Montana was responsible for the birds' comeback. Montana remains one of the few states where you can find wild trumpeter swans. The Rocky Mountain Front, with its numerous wildlife management areas, provides excellent habitat for the birds and it is not unusual to see flocks of hundreds of trumpeter swans here during migration season. Best viewing times are from mid-March to early April and again in late October. The large birds are solid white with black beaks, have wingspans of 6 to 8 feet, and can weigh up to 40 pounds.

located by the headquarters and will show any areas that are closed. There are vault toilets at the first parking area west of the office.

**Important Information:** There is no camping fee or set hours. Bring water as there is no drinking water here and it does get hot in the summer. Hunting is allowed in the management area, so be aware of this in the fall if you are a non-hunter wanting to visit. Also, dogs can be brought but must be under control, especially during nesting season.

For more information, contact the Freezout Lake Wildlife Management Area headquarters office at 406-467-2646, or the Montana Department of Fish, Wildlife & Parks at 406-454-5840, which is the Regional Office in Great Falls.

## 247. Fairfield Legion Park and Pool

This shady park has a playground, picnic table, and the city swimming pool. It makes an excellent quick play-and-picnic stop when you're traveling through the area.

**Directions:** Fairfield is 32 miles south of Choteau on U.S. Highway 89 and 12 miles past Freezout Lake Wildlife Management Area. Turn into Fairfield across from the granaries, go three blocks to Main and Sixth streets and you will see the park.

**Important Information:** Pool hours may vary somewhat but it is generally open Memorial Day to Labor Day from 2 to 5:30 P.M. and 7 to 9 P.M., as weather permits. There is a minimal fee of $1 per person. Contact the Fairfield Chamber of Commerce at 406-467-2531.

## 248. Lion's Club City Park

This tiny park is right on U.S. Highway 89 in Fairfield and offers a quick stop for a picnic under the shaded shelter.

**Directions:** You can't miss the covered shelter in this park, because it is right on US 89.

# The Sun River Country

To the west of the small town of Augusta, the scenic Sun River cuts through steep canyons and sheer cliffs as it flows out from the Scapegoat Wilderness Area, part of the Bob Marshall Wilderness Complex. The area surrounding the Sun River in the Rocky Mountain Front offers some recreational activities for families interested in exploring the wilderness boundaries. There are well-maintained Forest Service trails and campgrounds here, with interpretive signs noting area features. There is also a mostly undeveloped wildlife management area.

From the mountains, the Sun River traverses the plains until it joins the Missouri River at Great Falls. Diversion dams and long distances between access sites make floating the Sun more of a challenge than most families will want to accept. It is still a delightful river to enjoy from shore, especially in the dramatic Sun River Canyon.

Along the south fork of the Sun River is the Benchmark wilderness access, the most popular entry into the Bob Marshall Wilderness Complex. A lake and a couple of easy trails in this area may be enjoyed by families.

While in the Sun River area, follow the suggested bear precautions (see page 14) as there are both grizzly and black bears. Be especially careful about following bear rules for camping if staying in bear country. Mountain lions have also been seen here, though less frequently. Remember that mountain weather changes very quickly; always have warm clothing available when hiking, even if the weather appears pleasant at the moment (see page 18).

## 249. Sun River Canyon and the South Fork Loop Drive

A nice driving loop can be made in Sun River Country that includes the Sun River Canyon and the South Fork of the Sun River. In the canyon, you can take time to enjoy the river. Go to the Gibson Reservoir Overlook, and take a peek at the petroglyphs (see site 250).

Along the South Fork, stop and take an excursion west to Wood Lake (site 255) and hike around it or perhaps go for a swim.

**Directions:** Start the loop by driving to Sun River Canyon and Gibson Reservoir. Take the Sun River Road which turns west from the main street of Augusta and goes toward Gibson Reservoir. At the road fork in 4 miles, stay to the right on Sun River Road, still heading toward Gibson Reservoir. It is about 15 more miles to the canyon (see site 250 for information about things to do in the canyon).

To continue the loop drive, head back out of the canyon and turn right (south) onto the Beaver–Willow Creek Road at the stop sign just after the Sun River bridge by the canyon entrance. The Beaver–Willow Creek Road will take you to Benchmark Road, Lewis and Clark County 235. Turn right on Benchmark if you want to explore Wood Lake (see site 255) and the trail along the South Fork of the Sun River (see site 256). Turn left here to complete the loop and return to Augusta. It is approximately 20 miles along Benchmark Road back to town.

**Important Information:** Contact the Rocky Mountain Ranger District, Lewis and Clark National Forest at 406-466-5341 for more information.

## 250. Sun River Canyon

A drive up the Sun River Canyon from Augusta provides an enjoyable excursion into nature. Visitors can drive to an overlook on the cliffs high above the Gibson Reservoir. The view will give you an appreciation of the magnitude of the canyon and the beauty of the area. The reservoir is well known for its blustery weather and the Gibson Reservoir Overlook is one of the places you will most likely experience the Sun Canyon winds. A trail along the cliffs above the reservoir is scenic, but exceedingly windy. At times it may not be safe for children.

The Gibson Reservoir was created when the Sun River was impounded to provide water for ranch and farm irrigation needs. Access to the water at the reservoir is difficult due to the cliffs which rise steeply from the water. Frequent draws for irrigation cause water level fluctuations, which also makes use of the lake somewhat difficult. Archaeological discoveries have been made along parts of the reservoir bottom that are exposed during low water. These artifacts date back as far as 10,000 years and reveal that the area was the home of primitive societies. Archaeological excavations continue to uncover more artifacts, and the Gibson Reservoir Archaeological Project has become a part of the Passport Through Time program, which brings volunteers in to help at dig sites while they learn about archaeology.

On the drive through the canyon, stop at the Sun River bridge between Home Gulch and Mortimer Gulch Campgrounds. Petroglyphs made by the early canyon residents some thousands of years ago can still be seen on rocks by the bridge. Interpretive information about the archaeological site is at the parking area just west of the bridge. There is a vault toilet here.

A private lodge, the Sun Canyon Lodge, offers cabins or tent and trailer camping. There are showers, electricity, and a cafe here, too. Two other lodges have outfitting and housing facilities in the Sun Canyon as well. Contact the Forest Service for a list of outfitters.

**Directions:** From Augusta, turn west onto the Sun River Road and go toward signs for Gibson Reservoir. In about 4 miles the road forks. Take the right fork to Gibson Reservoir along Sun River Road and go about 15 more miles to the canyon.

**Important Information:** Contact the Rocky Mountain Ranger District Office, Lewis and Clark National Forest for more information, 406-466-5341. To contact the Sun Canyon Lodge, call 406-562-3654.

## 251. Home Gulch and Mortimer Gulch Campgrounds

Sun River Canyon has two pleasant USDA Forest Service campgrounds adjoining the river. Surrounded by canyon cliffs and mountains, these campgrounds allow families to experience this rugged country with some degree of comfort. Home Gulch has 15 campsites and Mortimer Gulch has 28. Both areas have potable water, fire grates, tables, and vault toilets.

**Directions:** Follow the directions to the Sun River Canyon (site 250). Both campgrounds are on the Sun River Road. Home Gulch is 20 miles from Augusta on the left (south) side of the road and Mortimer Gulch is 26 miles from Augusta on the right (north) side.

**Important Information:** These are both fee areas. Contact the Rocky Mountain Ranger District Office, Lewis and Clark National Forest for more information, 406-466-5341.

## 252. Hannan Gulch Trail 240

The Hannan Gulch Trail is basically an old road. The first section of the trail is not steep and is a fun hike for families. The trail is 6.5 miles in length and gets steeper as it goes over the ridge and into Deep Creek. The lower areas are forested with quaking aspen. The gulch opens up to impressive views across the Sun River Canyon. Bear, deer, and bighorn sheep can be seen in this gulch.

**Directions:** The trail is 22 miles from Augusta. Follow the directions to Sun River Canyon (site 250). Turn right (north) on a gravel road at the Hannan Gulch sign. Cross the Sun River and proceed straight for 0.5 mile to a road fork. Take the right (east) fork and park at the trailhead.

**Important Information:** Contact the Rocky Mountain Ranger District Office, Lewis and Clark National Forest, at 406-466-5341.

## 253. Blacktail Creek Trail 223

Primarily a forested trail, Blacktail Creek Trail is not steep until quite a ways in when it climbs over a pass into open meadows. The 11-mile trail is part of the 28-mile South Fork Teton-Blacktail Gulch National Recreation Trail. The first section of the trail provides families with a pleasant woods walk along the river bottom. You can go in as far as your family feels like walking. **Directions:** The trail is 24 miles from Augusta. Follow the directions to Sun River Canyon (site 250). The signed trailhead is located on the right side of the road west of the bridge crossing the Sun River. There is a parking area and a cabin, owned by the K Bar L Ranch, at the trailhead.

**Important Information:** Contact the Rocky Mountain Ranger District Office, Lewis and Clark National Forest, at 406-466-5341.

## 254. Sun River Wildlife Management Area

The 20,000-acre Sun River Management Area provides winter range for Montana's largest elk population, approximately 2,000 to 3,000 elk. Bighorn sheep, mule and white-tailed deer, mountain goats, grizzly and black bears, mountain lions, and pronghorn antelope also use the management area. Numerous game birds are present, too. The reserve is closed in winter when elk populations are at their height, but you can still catch sight of elk at other times. There are a number of areas set aside for overnight camping but few have any facilities.

The rolling hills on the east side of the wildlife management area give way to the cliffs of the Sawtooth Ridge. Swazey Lake, at the entrance to the management area, is stocked with trout and is reputed to be good fishing. Swimming is possible here though there is no beach area and the bottom is muddy. There is a vault toilet and a primitive campground.

Five miles from Swayze Lake is Dickens Lake. The fishing is not as good at this lake and there are no facilities here. However, the road between the two lakes provides good hiking or mountain biking through the management area and can also be driven. Nearby are Sun River Canyon (site 250) and Wood Lake (site 255).

**Directions:** From Augusta, take the Sun River Road toward Gibson Reservoir for about 4 miles to where the road forks. Gibson Reservoir is to the right, but continue straight ahead for 15 miles. This will take you to the Sun River Wildlife Management Area and Swazey Lake. The road to Dickens Lake leaves from Swazey Lake. It is about 6 or 7 miles to Dickens on a rough, dirt road that is still passable by most family vehicles.

**Important Information:** The management area is open May 15 to December 1. Contact the Montana Department of Fish, Wildlife, & Parks at the Freezout Lake Wildlife Management Area for more information, 406-467-2488.

# 255. Wood Lake Picnic Area and Campground

Wood Lake is located near the Scapegoat Wilderness Area of the Bob Marshall Wilderness Complex. You can fish, canoe, or swim here. An 0.8-mile loop trail goes around the lake. Non-motorized boats are permitted.

The picnic area has tables, fire grates, potable water, and vault toilets. The campground has nine sites for tents or trailers. There are fireplaces, picnic tables, vault toilets, and drinking water at the campground.

Farther up the road toward the mountains are the Benchmark and South Fork campgrounds, and the Sun River Wildlife Management Area is also nearby (see sites 256 and 254).

**Directions:** From Augusta, turn right on Benchmark Road (Lewis and Clark County 235) at the sign in town. The lake is 24 miles west of Augusta. Pick up the trail around the lake in either the picnic or campground areas. At the campground, the trail begins across the road from the campground, by the lake.

**Important Information:** Wood Lake is open from June 1 to September 15. There is a campground fee. Be aware that there are leeches in the lake if you decide to swim. Contact the Rocky Mountain Ranger District Office, Lewis and Clark National Forest, at 406-466-5341.

# 256. South Fork Trail 202

This trail begins at the Benchmark access to the Bob Marshall Wilderness, the most popular access point of the wilderness system. From this trailhead, you can go either north or south. Both directions will take you through river bottoms for the first mile or two and are acceptable as family hikes for a ways.

Going north, the trail goes 1.5 miles to a ford across Deep Creek. It may not be worth the effort of crossing the creek with children, as the other side is generally pretty boggy.

**Directions:** Follow Benchmark Road, Lewis and Clark County 235, from Augusta, which is a right-hand turn off of main street. The trailhead is at the very end of the road. Benchmark and South Fork campgrounds are beyond Wood Lake, which is 24 miles from Augusta.

**Important Information:** If you decide to go for a hike a little way into the wilderness area, be aware that many people pack into the wilderness on horses from this access. Give these animals plenty of room. The trail can be exceptionally busy on weekends. Contact the Rocky Mountain Ranger District Office, Lewis and Clark National Forest, at 406-466-5341.

# THE UPPER MISSOURI RIVER COUNTRY: GREAT FALLS TO HAVRE

The Missouri River flows amiably through the plains country east of the Rocky Mountains. At Great Falls, five powerful falls have shaped the history of the city, and offer numerous recreational opportunities to residents and visitors. Fort Benton, too, was born as a river city, beginning as a hub for steamboats and the settlement of the west. To the north and east of Fort Benton, the river courses through land with spectacular beauty and has been designated a National Wild, Scenic, and Recreational River. In the plains areas, small towns support local people who share their experiences through historical museums and managed natural resource sites. Throughout the Upper Missouri River Country visitors will find a sense of community spirit and small-town comforts.

## Great Falls and the Surrounding Area

The roar of the cascading water led Captain Meriwether Lewis of the Lewis and Clark Expedition to these five falls and Giant Springs—important landmarks on the Missouri River. The town of Great Falls was literally built around the Missouri River, and in the early 1870s Great Falls became a major trade center because of it.

Great Falls is the state's second-largest city, with 68,000 people. Located near the center of the state, Great Falls operates as a regional center for trade and services. The city houses the state fairgrounds, an Air Force base, two significant art centers, and has a rookie league baseball team affiliated with the Los Angles Dodgers.

There are now five dams on the river, which still plays a significant role in the life of the city. The river provides a major source of recreation and enjoyment for the townspeople. The "great falls" have been harnessed for electrical power generation. The city has developed a delightful trail along the edge of the Missouri River. For more information, contact the Great Falls Chamber of Commerce at 406-761-4434. For information about area events, contact the City Center Association, 406-453-6151.

# 257. Broadwater Overlook: Great Falls Visitor Center

The Great Falls Visitor Center is located in a small park overlooking the Missouri River. It is fairly easy to reach from the interstate and has restrooms and picnic tables as well as plenty of city and regional information.

**Directions:** Take either the Central Avenue West or 10th Avenue South exit from Interstate 15. Go east through town and turn right onto River Road just after crossing the Missouri River. Take Upper River Road, which is immediately south of 10th Avenue South, and wind up the hill to the visitor center.

**Important Information:** The visitor center is open daily year-round. From Memorial Day to Labor Day, it is open from 8 A.M. to 8 P.M. and it is open the rest of the year from 10 A.M. to 4 P.M. Contact the visitor center at 406-771-0885.

# 258. The C. M. Russell Museum

You'll find appreciation for Charlie Russell everywhere you go in Montana and many places beyond. Known as "America's Cowboy Artist," Charlie was a native of Missouri but knew and loved his adopted state of Montana. He painted the subtle colors of the prairie landscape that only those who have lived on the prairie have seen. But Charlie saw even more, for he lived in Montana long enough to know the not-so-subtle hardships and the cherished moments of daily life on the plains. His works tell the story of the native peoples and of the true range cowboys. His eye caught even the experiences of Montana's wildlife and you'll see many Montana animals in his works.

Charlie created more than 4,000 works of art. This museum has the most complete collection of Russell works and personal objects in the world. The cowboy artist tried his hand at numerous art forms, so you will see his bronzes, oil and watercolor paintings, pen-and-ink sketches, and wood carvings. Both the Russell home and Charlie's log studio have been preserved in their original location at the museum site, too. There is a collection of illustrated letters and other interesting personal artifacts in these buildings.

The complex has seven galleries with more than 12,000 works of other artists, including O. C. Seltzer, Edward Curtis, E. E. Heikka, and Joseph Henry Sharp. The museum holds the John Browning Firearms Collection and Indian artifacts. It's easy to spend a bit of time here. There are guided tours of the museum and activities in the tepee set up on the grounds.

**Directions:** From Interstate 15 take the 10th Avenue South exit and follow 10th to 15th Street South. Go left (north) on 15th Street South to 5th Avenue

# Charlie Russell, Montana's Artist

Montana wasn't the birthplace of Charlie Russell, but if home is where the heart is, then Montana was Charlie's home. He arrived in Montana Territory from St. Louis, Missouri at age 16. It was 1880 and Charlie was just in time to experience the life of an open-range cowboy. For 11 years, he rode the range and learned about the Old West way of life. But Charlie saw life in a different light, from the perspective of an artist.

With the support of this wife, Nancy Cooper Russell, Charlie became one of the most successful artists of his time. His experiences on the range gave him great insights and material for his paintings. He had come to know and be a friend of the Native American people, whom he called "Mother Nature's Children." Charlie is well known for his accurate portrayal of their way of life.

Charlie and Nancy moved to Great Falls and built their home there in 1900. In 1903, Charlie built a log cabin studio next to his home. From here he painted, drew, and sculpted, creating much-loved works of Western art. It is said he never finished a painting anywhere else. The studio and home are designated National Historic Sites.

During Charlie's 46 years in Montana, he witnessed the end of the cowboy era. He saw the buffalo disappear and watched the fencing of the open range. But in Charlie Russell's art, the world can still see and appreciate the way of the West. Charlie died in 1926 at age 62. Before he died he wrote, "To have talent is no credit to its owner; any man that can make a living doing what he likes is lucky, and I'm that. Any time I cash in now, I win." With Charlie, we all won.

North and turn left. You will see the museum in two blocks. The address is 400 13th Street North.

**Important Information:** There is an admission charge which includes entrance to the museum and Charlie Russell's home and studio. Cost is $4 for adults, $3 for seniors and groups, and $2 for students. Children 5 and under enter free. Call the museum for current tour times. Hours from May 1 to September 30 are Monday through Saturday, 9 A.M. to 6 P.M., and Sunday from 1 to 5 P.M. The rest of the year the museum is open Tuesday through Saturday from 10 A.M. to 5 P.M., and 1 to 5 P.M. on Sundays. The museum is closed on Mondays. Contact the museum at 406-727-8787.

## 259. Paris Gibson Square Museum of Art

Paris Gibson founded Great Falls in 1870 and you'll see his namesakes and other evidence of his presence throughout the city. Paris Gibson Square, which today houses the museum of art, was dedicated in 1895 as the city's first high school. It is now on the National Register of Historic Places because of the high quality of craftsmanship in the construction. The building houses the Center for Contemporary Arts and the Cascade County Historical Society. The museum has a permanent collection of more than 50,000 objects and changing exhibits.

**Directions:** Take the Central Avenue West exit from Interstate 15 and follow this east through town to 14th Street North. Look for the museum at 1400 1st Avenue North, between 14th and 15th Streets North.

**Important Information:** There is no admission charge, though donations are welcome. Open from 10 A.M. to 5 P.M. Tuesday through Friday, and Saturday and Sunday from noon to 5 P.M. From Memorial Day through Labor Day, the museum is also open on Monday from 10 A.M. to 5 P.M., and Tuesday evenings from 7 to 9 P.M. Contact the museum at 406-727-8255.

## 260. Children's Museum of Montana

Especially designed for kids, this museum has interactive exhibits about human cultures, arts, science, wildlife, and regional features. The museum sponsors special monthly events for children.

**Directions:** The museum is located at 22 Railroad Square, behind the Civic Center in downtown Great Falls. Take the Central Avenue West exit from Interstate 15 and go east through town. Turn right (south) on Park Drive just after crossing the Missouri River and go one block. The Civic Center will be on your right. The museum is behind the Civic Center.

**Important Information:** Call 406-452-6661 for hours, fees, and information about events.

## 261. Great Falls Historic Trolley

Take a trolley ride around Great Falls and hear some of the history of the area while you see the sites of the city. The tour takes two hours. Stops include the C. M. Russell Museum and Gallery, Giant Springs State Park, Black Eagle and Rainbow falls, the Lewis and Clark National Historic Trail Interpretive Center, Gibson Park, the historic home district, and Paris Gibson Square.

**Directions:** Departs from the Great Falls Visitor Information Center (see site 257) at Broadwater Overlook Park by the flag.

**Important Information:** Tours depart at 10 A.M. and 4 P.M., Monday through Thursday, and 10 A.M., 1 P.M., and 4 P.M. on Friday, Saturday, and Sunday. Reservations are not necessary, but the trolley rides are on a first-come-first-served basis. Call 406-771-1100 for fee information or reservations.

# 262. Malmstrom Air Force Base Open Air Park

Malmstrom Air Force Base has an air park and a museum. The air park displays numerous historical aircraft including a Minuteman III Missile, a helicopter, and other post-World War II aircraft. The museum exhibits include a large model airplane collection, a World War II diorama, a mock missile capsule, history of the air base, and a uniform display.

Visitors need to stop at the main gate and obtain a pass into the air base. Once inside the gate, the museum is almost immediately to the right. There are restrooms at the office.

**Directions:** From Interstate 15, take the Central Avenue West exit and go east through town. Central Avenue becomes 1st Avenue North once you cross the Missouri River. Continue east on 1st Avenue North to 37th Street North and turn left, go one block, and turn right onto 2nd Avenue North. Follow 2nd Avenue North to its endpoint at the base. Pull into the office on the right just before the gates.

**Important Information:** You will need to check in at the office before entering the base. The air park is open during daylight hours all year from 9 A.M. to 3 P.M., Monday through Friday. For more information, contact the base at 406-731-4050.

# 263. Mitchell Park and Public Pool

The main public pool in Great Falls has two water slides, each with 160 feet of twisting and turning tubes that add some water fun to swimming. For the little ones there is water play equipment in the wading pool. There are also two other pools in Great Falls, the Jaycee Pool and the Water Tower Pool.

**Directions:** To get to Mitchell Pool, take the Central Avenue West exit from Interstate 15 and go through Great Falls, heading east. Immediately after crossing the Missouri River, turn right onto River Drive. The park will be on your left in a couple of blocks at 100 River Drive South. Jaycee Pool is located at 225 23rd Avenue Northeast, and Water Tower Pool can be found at 701 33rd Street South.

**Important Information:** Mitchell Pool hours are 1 to 8 P.M. every day from early June to late August. Cost is $1.50 for kids ages 3 to 17, and $2.50 for adults. A water slide pass is $2. The two other pools are open daily from noon to 6 P.M. and cost $1 for kids 6 to 17, and $2 for adults. For more information, contact the Great Falls City Parks and Recreation Department, 406-771-1265.

# 264. Gibson and Riverside Parks

These adjacent parks combine to make a delightful natural area in downtown Great Falls. Riverside Park borders the Missouri River, and Gibson lies just to the east of Riverside. Riverside has playgrounds, picnic areas, tennis courts, and an archery range. Gibson has a playground, flower gardens, picnic areas, and a lagoon. Restrooms can be found in both parks. A paved trail goes through both parks and can be used for walking, biking, or rollerblading. There is a food concession area and a bandstand in Gibson Park too.

**Directions:** From Interstate 15, take the Central Avenue West exit and go east on Central into town. Immediately after crossing the Missouri River, turn left onto River Drive or go to the next left, Park Drive. The parks are adjacent to Central Avenue. There are parking areas at both parks.

**Important Information:** Great Falls city parks are open from daylight to 10:30 P.M. daily. Contact the Great Falls Chamber of Commerce at 406-761-4434 for more information.

# 265. River's Edge Trail

Great Falls' River's Edge Trail has to be one of the most enjoyable, easily accessible urban recreational trails in the state. The trail is built along an old railway corridor and currently provides 7 miles of paved recreational trail along some of the prettiest spots in Great Falls—the south bank of the Missouri River. Here's an excellent place to walk, run, bike, or rollerblade. People of all ages use the trail, and the pavement makes the trail accessible for wheelchair users as well. The trail is graveled east from Rainbow Falls to Cochrane Dam.

Along the River's Edge Trail are interesting features and stops such as a small goldfish pond, interpretive displays, picnic tables, and resting benches. The Lewis and Clark Visitor Center will also be open in 1998 and is located along the trail. Ongoing community improvement efforts just keep making the trail better. Future plans call for more trail to be completed on the north side of the river, specifically from the West Bank Park to the 9th Street Bridge. A trailhead exhibit with historic photos is to be completed in 1998 in the refurbished railway car and caboose at the 19th Street North access point. The Old Milwaukee Bridge near Central Avenue West is being renovated and will become a part of the trail in the future.

The townspeople use the trail as a celebration place. A Moonlight Luminaria Walk occurs in early June. The trail is lit by 1,000 luminarias and music and refreshments are an added delight.

Currently the trail runs from 10th Avenue South past Giant Springs State Park. The city divides the trail into five areas. Interpretive signs along the trail display points of interest, mileages, and special trail features for each area. A guide to the River's Edge Trail is distributed free of charge at the Great Falls Visitor's Center at Broadwater Overlook Park (site 257) and other public areas in town.

Among the numerous access points along the trail, a couple stand out for ease of parking and access. Gibson and Riverside parks, on River Drive, have good parking and the added benefit of park facilities. The 19th Street North access area has a small parking area; east of it, the trail provides a long level stretch of scenic hiking with a view of Black Eagle Falls. The goldfish pond is less than a mile east and Giant Springs Heritage State Park is a little more than a mile from 19th Street North. Restrooms are located just beyond Black Eagle Falls and the King Railroad Bridge.

You can't go wrong with this trail. Whether you've got an afternoon or an hour, your family will enjoy the time spent here.

**Directions:** Follow the directions to Gibson and Riverside parks (site 264). There is parking at either park. To reach the 19th Street North access, get on River Drive which borders Riverside Park and the Missouri River. Follow River Drive north to 19th Street North.

**Important Information:** For more information about the trail, contact the Great Falls Chamber of Commerce at 406-761-4434.

## 266. Lewis and Clark National Historic Trail Interpretive Center

If you've ever wondered what it must have been like to be explorers in the wildlands of the West, you can find out at this interpretive center. The adventure begins at the door with a life-size diorama of five men pulling a canoe up a ravine (a two-story ravine!). An introductory video in the center theater provides background information about the Lewis and Clark Expedition. Numerous exhibits feature interpretive information about Lewis and Clark's travels through Indian country and there are displays about some of the tribes the expedition encountered. Many of the exhibits are interactive. For example, you can find out what it is like to pull a boat upstream by tugging on a rope hooked to a gauge that tells you how many miles you would make in a day depending on how hard you pull on the rope! Another especially interesting exhibit is a walk-in Mandan Indian lodge.

Future plans call for a Lewis and Clark History Walk, a 1.5-mile trail between Giant Springs Heritage State Park and the Lewis and Clark National Historic Trail Interpretive Center. The trail is scheduled to open in

# Lewis and Clark and the Corps of Discovery

• • • • • • • • • • • • • • • • • • • • • • • • • • • • • • • • • • • • • • • • • • • • •

In 1803, the United States Congress appropriated money to send a military expedition to explore and map the unknown lands west of the Mississippi River, which had recently been purchased from France. This uncharted territory was a mystery that would unfold to settlers through the fascinating adventures of the Corps of Discovery, the Lewis and Clark Expedition.

The three-year exploration took a group of 33 people across the open plains and through the rugged Rocky Mountains of what would become Montana Territory. The explorers would find and note the path of the mighty Missouri River through plains and mountains. They would climb through miles of massive peaks and discover passes through the rugged terrain. The newcomers would meet the inhabitants of the land and learn of their way of life. But most importantly, the Corps of Discovery would lead the way west for homesteaders, miners, trappers, and traders. The journey of the Lewis and Clark Expedition brought the beginning of a new era to the people and places on their historic route.

1999 and will have interpretive information displayed along its path by the river. There will also be a living history site here where people in period costumes provide interpretive information through dramatic presentations.

The center is situated along the River's Edge Trail and has a wonderful view of the river. Within a few miles are numerous family activities. Walk along the River's Edge Trail (site 265) as far as you like, or go down the road and look at wildlife exhibits in the Montana Department of Fish, Wildlife & Parks Visitor Center (site 267). Just beyond is Giant Springs Heritage State Park and the fish hatchery (site 268). This part of Great Falls is more than a one-day experience—it's great area for family fun!

**Directions:** The facility is located within Giant Springs Heritage State Park lands and sits near the state park turnoff from River Drive. Take the Central Avenue West exit from Interstate 15. Follow Central Avenue east through town and, after crossing the Missouri River, turn left immediately onto River Drive. Follow River Drive for 3.7 miles to a sign for Giant Springs Heritage State Park. The center is within a few hundred feet on the left.

**Important Information:** The interpretive center is open daily from Memorial Day to Labor Day, 9 A.M. to 8 P.M., and Tuesday through Saturday, 9 A.M. to 5 P.M. the rest of the year. Admission is $5 for adults, $4 for seniors, $2 for children 6 through 17, and free for kids 5 and under. Group rates are available for groups of 20 or more, but reservations must be made in advance. Family passes are $40 per year or $20 per year for individual passes. Contact the center at 406-727-8733.

# 267. Montana Department of Fish, Wildlife & Parks Visitor Center

• • • • • • • • • • • • • • • • • • • • • • • • • • • • • • • • • •

There are lots of interesting things to see here, including animal track castings and mounts of black and grizzly bears, lynx, porcupines, and various birds. There is interpretive information on pocket gophers, with a display showing a cross-section of their elaborate home structure. Videos on natural and cultural resources are shown regularly in a small theater. The center has restrooms and picnic tables.

**Directions:** Take the Central Avenue West exit from Interstate 15. After crossing to the east side of the Missouri River, take an immediate left onto River Drive. Follow River Drive 3.7 miles and you will see a sign for Giant Springs Heritage State Park. Turn left and drive 1 mile. Turn right into the parking area for the visitor center.

**Important Information:** Visitor center hours from May 1 to September 30 are 8 A.M. to 7 P.M., Monday through Friday, and 10 A.M. to 7 P.M. on weekends. Winter hours are 8 A.M. to 5 P.M., Monday through Friday. Fishing licenses may be purchased here during regular business hours. Contact the Montana Department of Fish, Wildlife & Parks at 406-454-5840 for more information.

# 268. Giant Springs Heritage State Park

• • • • • • • • • • • • • • • • • • • • • • • • • • • • • • • • • •

This urban park combines a couple of kids' delights, fish and water. A short, but sweet, self-guided tour through the hatchery includes a large outdoor pond where you can feed 8- to 12-pound rainbow trout. The giant springs here are reported to be the largest freshwater springs in the U.S. Nearly 7.9 million gallons of water flows through the springs per hour, or about 134,000 gallons a minute! The spring was discovered by Lewis and Clark in 1805. Lewis wrote that it was the "largest fountain I ever saw, and doubt if it is not the largest in America." The Roe River flows for 206 feet from the spring to the Missouri, and is documented in the Guinness Book of World Records as the shortest river in the world.

The park has picnic tables and restrooms, but no camping. The 218-acre facility includes the springs, hatchery, and the regional headquarters and visitor center for the Montana Department of Fish, Wildlife & Parks (site 267), which is across the street. This center has interpretive displays and a mini-theater which shows wildlife videos.

The Lewis and Clark National Historic Trail Interpretive Center (site 266) is nearby. From here you can get on the River's Edge Trail (site 265) and go east or west.

**Directions:** Take the Central Avenue West exit from Interstate 15. Follow Central Avenue through town and, after crossing the Missouri River, turn left immediately onto River Drive. Follow River Drive for 3.7 miles to a sign for Giant Springs Heritage State Park. Turn left at the sign and drive 1.1 miles to the marked left-hand turn into the state park.

**Important Information:** There is a fee for entrance to the spring and hatchery. The cost is $1 per person age 6 and over or $4 per vehicle. Annual statewide park passes are available here for $20 per year, with a $10 fee for a second vehicle. Giant Springs hours are 8 A.M. to 8 P.M. weekdays and 10 A.M. to 8 P.M. on weekends, from Memorial Day to Labor Day. Hours the rest of the year are 8 A.M. to 5 P.M., Monday through Friday. The springs are wheelchair accessible. Contact the Montana Department of Fish, Wildlife & Parks at 406-454-5840 for more information.

## 269. Lewis and Clark Overlook and the Cochrane Dam Trail

This overlook gives visitors a view of Crooked Falls, the only falls on the Missouri River that have not been dammed. There is interpretive information here about Lewis and Clark and the falls. The overlook has a parking area and a vault toilet.

The trail to Cochrane Dam begins from the parking lot. This is a dirt trail and is not suitable for rollerblades or wheelchairs, though mountain bikers and hikers use it. The trail is 3 miles long and steep in some parts.

**Directions:** The overlook and trailhead is 1.2 miles downstream from Giant Springs Heritage State Park (see directions for site 268).

**Important Information:** The trail can get muddy in wet weather. For more information, contact the Great Falls Chamber of Commerce at 406-761-4434.

## 270. Benton Lake National Wildlife Refuge

This wildlife refuge has a ten-stop, 9-mile auto tour along Prairie Marsh Wildlife Drive. Plan on spending an hour to an hour and a half on the drive. The refuge covers 12,300 acres and encourages waterfowl production and the preservation of 175 species of birds and land animals.

A wheelchair-accessible boardwalk near marsh unit 2 has interpretive information and ends at a platform over the water, which makes this a nice spot to get out of the car and have another view of the marsh.

There is no camping at the refuge though there are wheelchair-accessible vault toilets at the headquarters. During April and May the refuge has an observation blind, the "grouse house," which may be reserved for very early morning sharptail grouse viewing of their spring courtship dancing ritual. Call the refuge for reservations.

**Directions:** Take the Central Avenue West exit from Interstate 15 and go east through town to 15th Street North. Turn left (north) and cross the bridge. Continue 1 mile and turn left (north) onto Bootlegger Trail Road where you will see a small sign for the refuge. Follow this road 12 miles to the refuge entrance on the left. You actually enter the refuge shortly before you reach the headquarters. Note that the Montana state highway map shows access from Interstate 15. This route is not feasible for most vehicles.

**Important Information:** The refuge is open during daylight hours all year. It is open for game bird hunting season beginning with the opening of the state waterfowl season. Contact the U.S. Fish and Wildlife Service at 406-727-7400 for more information.

## 271. Ryan Dam and Falls Overlook and Picnic Area

This day-use area is within 15 minutes of Great Falls and has an excellent picnic area. It's a nice spot for an afternoon or evening away from home. The park is located on Ryan Island and is operated by Montana Power Company. The fun begins with a walk across a suspension bridge to the island. Once at the park, there is a short walk to Ryan Falls Overlook. A historical marker explains the history of the area. There are flush toilets, picnic tables, and a covered picnic area here.

**Directions:** Take the Central Avenue West exit from Interstate 15 and go east through town to 15th Street North. Turn left and cross the Missouri River. Drive 3.8 miles on what is now Montana Highway 87, and turn right at the sign for Ryan and Morony Dam. Follow this road for 7 miles and turn right again at the sign for Ryan Dam. It is 1.8 miles to the parking area for the park.

**Important Information:** You'll want to keep track of little ones both on the suspension bridge and at the overlook. The park area is fenced. The entire park is wheelchair accessible, including the suspension bridge. For more information, call the Great Falls Chamber of Commerce at 406-761-4434.

## 272. Mehmke's Steam Engine Museum

The Mehmke Steam Engine Museum has the largest private collection of steam engines in Montana. The ones on display here actually run. Plenty of other antique farm machinery is on display too.

**Directions:** This museum is about 10 miles east of Great Falls on U.S. Highway 89/87. It is right on the highway and you'll see a tractor by the museum sign.

**Important Information:** Open during daylight hours, weather permitting. Fee is $2 for those over 12. Call 406-452-6571 for more information.

## Bison, *Bison bison*

The largest land animal in North America, bison, also incorrectly called buffalo, once roamed the plains in numbers estimated as high as 30 million. The woolly beasts are 5 to 6 feet tall at the hump and can weigh anywhere from 800 to 2,000 pounds. Bison graze on grasses, leaves, shrubs, greenery, and twigs. The herding animals at one time roamed the plains freely. Each year in April or May, one calf is born to most adult females.

## 273. Ulm Pishkun State Park Buffalo Jump and Visitor Center

This mile-long buffalo jump is thought to be the largest *pishkun* in the country. Thousands of buffalo were driven over these tall cliffs by native American tribes who then processed the meat for food. The word *pishkun* comes from the Blackfeet language and means "deep blood kettle." Other parts of the animal were used for tools, clothing, tepee covers, and utensils. Arrowheads, knives, drills, hide scrapers, chippers, hammers, and pottery have all been found in the area.

A visitor center, scheduled to open in the summer of 1999, is located below the jump and has a great view of the cliffs. The center has archaeological information and displays on the Indians and their relationship to the buffalo. You can drive to the top of the cliffs and walk down into the jump area on a short trail. There is also a great view of the surrounding land, including Square Butte, from the top of the pishkun. The jump site has picnic tables, shelters, vault toilets, and fire grates.

An interesting feature of the park is the prairie dog town at the entrance to the top of the jump site. Stop here and read the interpretive plaques about prairie dog social life.

**Directions:** Take Interstate 15 south of Great Falls 10 miles to Ulm. Take the Ulm exit and go north on Ulm-Vaughn Road. At the T intersection, take a left and stay on this main road for about 3 or 4 miles. You will see the visitor center on your left. To get to the top of the site drive beyond the visitor center and turn left at the sign for the jump. Follow this road to the top.

**Important Information:** The last 0.4-mile ascent to the top of the buffalo jump is quite steep. This is not a problem for cars, but motor homes may have a bit of a struggle. The park is open from dawn until dusk. There is no admission charge. Contact the Montana Department of Fish, Wildlife & Parks at 406-454-5840 for visitor center hours and other information.

# The Upper Missouri River National Wild, Scenic, and Recreational Floats

Once more the Missouri River creates magic along its banks. So much so, that the 149-mile stretch from Fort Benton to the James Kipp Recreation Area is designated a National Wild, Scenic, and Recreational River. This distinguished river is an excellent family float in canoes or rafts. It is also open to motorized boats. The Missouri flows gently past varied scenery which, in some sections, is spectacular. Floating down the river creates a sense of timelessness for travelers. Away from the hustle of daily life, visitors here can enter into the peaceful flow of life on the river. One can imagine the experiences of the Lewis and Clark expedition as they pushed upstream on their legendary journey, or consider the challenges a homesteader must have faced on the spacious, but lonely, plains. The rugged breaks and limestone canyons that border the waterway lure floaters from the river to make discoveries on land.

The riparian areas offer habitat to a variety of creatures. Deer, antelope, rabbits, foxes, coyotes, beavers, muskrats, otters, and other wildlife may be seen along the riverbanks or on the adjoining land. The white pelican, great blue heron, eagle, meadowlark, and various species of hawk are among the birds frequently observed along the river. Rattlesnakes are also a part of the landscape in this part of Montana and floaters should be careful of them (see page 16).

The Missouri River flows at a rate between 3 and 5 miles per hour. Floaters can make 20 to 25 miles in a day with a minimum of paddling and a few stops to explore the banks—that is, unless the wind picks up. As you may have noticed, wind and eastern Montana are nearly synonymous terms. When the winds blow downstream, you get a little boost on your floating time. But when it blows upstream, as it sometimes does, floaters may have to do some serious paddling to get downriver. Sometimes the wind is so fast and furious that you have to quickly paddle to shore, as the waves that kick up can be hazardous. There are no rapids on the river, however, only an occasional riffle which can be easily avoided.

Four access points conveniently divide the Wild, Scenic, and Recreational River into 3 sections, each between 40 and 60 miles long. These sections can be floated in 2 to 3 days each. The entire 149-mile stretch takes 5 to 7 days to float. For planning purposes, make sure you add in adequate vehicle shuttle time, as the road system that connects access points can be slow. Shuttle service and canoe rentals are available in Fort Benton and Virgelle. A list of outfitters is available from the Bureau of Land Management and they have excellent, detailed maps for sale. Ask for the water-resistant Upper Missouri River National Wild and Scenic River maps. There is a fee of $8 for the set of two maps.

The Upper Missouri River Visitor Center in Fort Benton (site 278) provides maps and information about river floats, regulations, and history. Near the center is a river access point. Bureau of Land Management (BLM) personnel are available to assist floaters at Judith Landing and James Kipp Recreation Area. These sites, and also Coal Banks Landing, have camping facilities with vault toilets, picnic tables, cooking and warming units, and potable water. There is a camping fee at Kipp, but at present, there are no fees at the other sites.

Camping on the river is at designated public land areas, noted with small campground signs. There is no potable water at these areas except for Hole-In-the-Wall. The larger river campsites have vault toilets. Floaters are expected to pack out their garbage. Assistance at the Fort Benton landing can be obtained from visitor center staff.

Currently floaters are asked to register with the BLM at their put-in location and to notify BLM staff when they leave the river. In recent years, the National Wild, Scenic, and Recreational sections of the Missouri River have become increasingly popular. It is now common to see many people on the river and sometimes there are rather crowded conditions at the shared campsites. Floaters should contact the BLM for information about permits when planning a Missouri River float in case high use requires a limit on the number of floaters. For more information, contact the Lewistown Resource Area Office of the Bureau of Land Management, 406-538-7461.

## 274. Fort Benton to Coal Banks Landing Float

This section of the Missouri, designated a recreational river, slowly sheds signs of civilization as it leaves the town of Fort Benton and heads toward relatively undisturbed river plains and ranch land. The river banks rise gently from the water's edge to form canyon walls or open landscapes. It is

41 miles to Coal Banks Landing. Private land borders most of this segment of the river.

**Directions:** Take any of the three Fort Benton exits from U.S. Highway 87. Turn onto St. Charles Street and go toward town. Turn toward the river on 13th and go 5 blocks to Front Street. Go left and in three blocks the street ends by the Old Fort Park. The center and landing are by the park.

To reach Coal Banks Landing, take U.S. Highway 87 to either of two signed turns between Big Sandy and Loma. Turn south and it is 8 miles by either all-weather gravel road to Coal Banks.

**Important Information:** Make sure you are well supplied with water, food, and emergency items as there are no takeout points before the next landing. Pack out your garbage. Contact the Bureau of Land Management, Lewistown Resource Area Office at 406-538-7461 for more information.

# River Otter, *Lutra canadensis*

Playful, cute, and clever, the personality of the river otter makes this sleek creature a fun animal to catch sight of along its riverbank home. The otter seems to feel its role in life is to play. It's not unusual to see one of these skinny 20-pound fellas simply playing with a pebble or piece of wood for long periods of time. Sometimes the whole otter family will join in a game of keep-away, hide-and-seek, or follow-the-leader. Even eating becomes fun as the otter chases its lunch of fish or floats on its back while feasting. Otters seem to especially enjoy sliding down a mud bank or an icy hill using their bodies as sleds. What a life!

## 275. Coal Banks Landing to Judith Landing Float

White limestone cliffs, molded and shaped by weather and time, create intriguing shapes and figures along this float, which offers the most distinctive landscape of the wild and scenic river. Lewis and Clark noted in their journals that the spires and cliffs along this stretch vary from 2 to 300 feet in height. Eye of the Needle, Citadel Rock, Labarge Rock, and Hole-in-the-Wall are notable natural landforms that stand watch high above the river and function as travel landmarks today in the same way they did a hundred years ago for steamboat captains. Take time to stop along this stretch and hike into the narrow limestone canyons or among the rock formations that border the river. Keep in mind that natural landmarks such as these are public, protected resources. Recent vandalism to the Eye

# White Pelican,
## *Pelecanus erythrorhynchos*

One of the joys of floating the Missouri River is the sight of these large white birds with black wing patches gliding up the river. The bird has a 9-foot wingspan and can be seen slowly and gracefully flying along the river in search of food. The long yellow bill hides a large pouch which is used to scoop up fish. White pelicans have been around as a species for some 60 million years and are one of the most ancient birds alive today. They average 15 pounds and are one of the largest birds on earth. Females lay one to two eggs each year between April and June. Pelicans can frequently be seen on large lakes and especially along the Missouri River, a favorite nesting spot.

of the Needle demonstrates the loss to future generations when resources are not treated with respect.

Located near Coal Banks Landing is the town of Virgelle which consists mostly of the Virgelle Mercantile. This is the location of the Missouri River Canoe Company, one of the outfitters that will rent canoes, guide river trips, and do vehicle shuttles for river floaters. Call early to reserve canoes, 800-426-2926, or contact the Bureau of Land Management for a list of area outfitters. Virgelle also has rental cabins and a bed and breakfast.

**Directions:** To reach Coal Banks Landing, take U.S. Highway 87 to either of two signed turns south between Big Sandy and Loma. It is 8 miles by either all-weather gravel road to Coal Banks.

Judith Landing is 42 miles southeast of Big Sandy, which is located on US 87, 38 miles north of Fort Benton. The all-weather gravel road begins at a signed turn in Big Sandy.

**Important Information:** Make sure you are well supplied with water, food, and emergency items as there are no takeout points before the next landing. Pack out your garbage. Contact the BLM, Lewistown Resource Area Office at 406-538-7461 for more information.

## 276. Judith Landing to Fred Robinson Bridge

Montana breaks country is just that—land broken with coulees and ravines into an intricate landscape of folds and cuts. This badlands area borders the river for most of the 40 miles between Judith Landing and Cow Island, the location where Chief Joseph and the Nez Perce crossed the

Missouri on their famous journey toward freedom (see page 188). From there, the land opens into a broader and more gentle valley for the last 20 river miles of this segment, which includes about 10 miles of floating through the western edge of the Charles M. Russell National Wildlife Refuge (site 371). Floaters take out at the James Kipp Recreation Area (site 372), which is downstream from the Fred Robinson Bridge where U.S. Highway 191 crosses the river.

The James Kipp Recreation Area has picnic tables, vault toilets, and a large campground area that accommodates RVs. It does not have electricity. There is a pay phone here. A special camping area is designated for floaters and there is a kiosk with interpretive information and maps. Future plans include a half-mile interpretive trail from Kipp to Armells Creek.

**Directions:** Judith Landing is 42 miles southeast of Big Sandy, which is located on U.S. Highway 87, 38 miles north of Fort Benton. The all-weather gravel road begins at a signed turn in Big Sandy.

To reach the James Kipp Recreation Area go 90 miles east of Fort Benton on Montana Highway 81, then go north on U.S. Highway 191 for 69 miles to the bridge. The recreation area is next to the bridge. If you are driving from Judith Landing, cross the Judith bridge and stay on this road, Choteau County 236, for 49 miles south to Hilger. Follow US 191 for 64 miles to the recreation area.

**Important Information:** Make sure you are well supplied with water, food, and emergency items as there are no takeout points before the next landing. Pack out your garbage. The Kipp Recreation Area is a fee area. Contact the Lewistown Resource Area Office of the Bureau of Land Management, 406-538-7461, for more information.

# Fort Benton

Fort Benton is known as the birthplace of Montana. Steamboats sailed to the "port" of Fort Benton, which is strategically located on the Missouri River. During the westward expansion era, the town became one of three main routes used to reach the wild frontier. Determined homesteaders with belongings piled high in their wagons rolled into the town en route to a new life. Then, at the peak of the Gold Rush era, the steamboats hauled freight and hopeful miners as far as Fort Benton. Until the railway arrived in 1887 and expanded the travel and trade routes, Fort Benton was the most important town in Montana Territory.

The town was known in frontier times for having the "bloodiest block in the west." Fort Benton served as the southern end for the "Whoop-Up Trail," a whiskey-runners route between Fort Benton and Alberta. It's hard

# The Story of Shep

Dogs have long been recognized for their dedication to their owners; many are loyal to the very end. Shep, a famous Fort Benton dog, was loyal long past the end. In fact, for five-and-a-half years after his master died in 1936, this admirable dog demonstrated his loyalty. Shep had anxiously watched as his owner's body was loaded onto a passenger train for burial in Ohio. Not understanding why his owner had left, the sheep dog dutifully returned to the train station every day and met all of the passenger trains that came through, hoping to be reunited with his owner. He watched as the passengers disembarked and then returned for the next train.

The dog slept beneath one of the wooden platforms at the depot and wore a mile-long trail to the Missouri River, where he would go for water. The railroad employees determined what had happened and began feeding the homeless dog. When his story was published, Shep became famous. Railroad passengers routed their trip through Fort Benton just to see Shep and the dog got so much fan mail that the station master had to appoint a secretary to handle it!

The dog's owner, of course, never returned, and one snowy day Shep slipped on the icy tracks and fell beneath the wheels of a train. To recognize the loyal dog's amazing dedication, the town gave Shep a funeral service and buried him on top of a nearby hill. Hundreds of people attended the service, the boy scouts carried his casket, a eulogy was given, and "Taps" was played. The Great Northern Railroad erected a statue of Shep, in honor of his faithfulness and loyalty. It stands by the levee on Front Street in Fort Benton.

to imagine that this quiet little town once had 24-hour saloons and brothels, complete with gun fights and poker games. But yet another era for the town brought wealthy merchants, sophisticated bankers, and eager cattlemen in from long distances to the mercantile capital of the region, Fort Benton.

Today, history brings visitors to the town to explore its museums and walk its historic, quiet streets. Some come to view the steamboats and Lewis and Clark landmarks. Others come to venture onto the mighty Missouri River for a real-life exploration of the plains and breaks along its banks. You will enjoy the town. For information, contact the Fort Benton Chamber of Commerce at 406-622-3864 or call city hall at 406-622-5494.

## 277. Old Fort Park

An adobe blockhouse is all that remains from the early days of Fort Benton. You can go inside the blockhouse and also see the re-created layout of the fort at the interpretive signs at this park. This building at Old Fort Park is thought to be the oldest standing building in the state.

The shady recreational complex has a swimming pool, lighted tennis courts, horseshoe pits, picnic area, and playground.

**Directions:** Take any of the three Fort Benton exits from U.S. Highway 87. Turn onto St. Charles Street and go toward town. Turn toward the river on 13th and go five blocks to Front Street. Turn left and go to the end of Front Street.

**Important Information:** Pool hours are 1 to 5 P.M. daily. Rates are $2 for those 18 and over and $1.50 for ages 6 to 17. Ages 5 and under are admitted free. Contact the pool at 406-622-9943.

## 278. The Upper Missouri River Visitor Center

Here's the place to find out about the Missouri River, both from a historical perspective and for information about floating the river. The center's interpretive displays set the scene of the Lewis and Clark journey with a short slide program, a diorama, and a map of Lewis and Clark's campsites. The center has information for floaters on campgrounds, historic trails, river hazards, rattlesnakes, and weather. They also sell river maps and other interpretive material. The center is next to Old Fort Benton Park and the historical artifacts along the steamboat levee.

**Directions:** Take any of the three Fort Benton exits from U.S. Highway 87. Turn onto St. Charles Street and go toward town. Turn toward the river on 13th and go 5 blocks to Front Street. Turn left and in three blocks the street ends by the visitor center, 1718 Front Street.

**Important Information:** The center is open seven days a week, generally from 8 A.M. to 5 P.M. from the weekend before Memorial Day to the weekend after Labor Day. For more information, contact the visitor center at 406-622-5185 or call the Bureau of Land Management at the Lewistown Resource Area Office, 406-538-7461.

## 279. Museum of the Upper Missouri

Steamboats, wagon trains, saloons, whiskey-running, homesteaders, and the railroad are among the elements that shaped the rich and colorful history of Fort Benton, depicted through dioramas, photos, and artifacts in this museum. The museum also displays the rifle Nez Perce leader Chief Joseph surrendered to Colonel Nelson Miles at the Bear's Paw battlefield.

**Directions:** Take any of the Fort Benton exits from U.S. Highway 87. Turn onto St. Charles Street and go toward town. Turn toward the river on 13th and go five blocks to Front Street. Go left and in three blocks the street ends by the museum at 1718 Front Street.

**Important Information:** Open daily Memorial Day through October 1, from 10 A.M. to 5 P.M. Admission is $3 for adults and $1 for kids. There are reduced rates for school and tour groups. Admission also includes entry to the Montana Agricultural Museum (site 280). Contact city hall for information at 406-622-5494.

## 280. Museum of the Northern Great Plains and Montana Agricultural Center

This is the state's largest agriculture museum and exhibits here trace farming history. Displays include the Hornaday Buffalo and a variety of antique machinery. The Old Fort Park (site 277) and the Museum of the Upper Missouri (site 279) are four blocks north on 20th, toward the river.

**Directions:** Take any of the Fort Benton exits from U.S. Highway 87. Turn onto St. Charles Street and go toward town. Follow St. Charles Street to 20th Street and turn toward the river. The center is within a block at 1205 20th Street. It is four blocks from the Old Fort Park and next to the high school playing field.

**Important Information:** The museum is open from Memorial Day to Labor Day from 10 A.M. to 5 P.M. The admission fee, which also includes entry to the Museum of the Upper Missouri, is $3 for adults and $1 for kids. Call the museum directly at 406-622-5316 or call city hall at 406-622-5494.

# Loma

Loma is a small farm and ranch community located 11 miles north of Fort Benton on U.S. Highway 87. Surprisingly, you'll find several unusual museums in this small community.

## 281. House of One Thousand Dolls

This unusual little museum houses not only dolls but lots of toys from the early 1800s. Most of the dolls here are pre-1970s vintage, and there is a great variety. Kids will enjoy seeing what used to be popular and comparing it to the current craze.

**Directions:** Take U.S. Highway 87 to Loma. Turn east from US 87 onto 2nd Avenue, go three blocks, and turn south on 1st Street. This private museum is one block from the Earth Science Museum (site 283), at 106 1st Street.

**Important Information:** Open from June 1 to October 15, depending on weather. Hours are 10 A.M. to 6 P.M., Monday through Wednesday. Admission charge is 50¢ for adults and 25¢ for children. Contact the museum at 406-739-4338.

## 282. Earth Science Museum

Here's a collection of rocks, fossils, and minerals that everyone will find interesting. Some of this museum is hands-off to youngsters, but there are specimens that kids can pick up and get a close look at.

**Directions:** Take U.S. Highway 87 to Loma. Turn east from US 87 on 2nd Avenue, go two blocks, and turn south on Main Street. This private museum is one block from the House of One Thousand Dolls (site 281), at 106 Main Street.

**Important Information:** Open daily from May 15 through Labor Day. Hours are 10 A.M. to 5 P.M and other times by appointment. Admission charge is $2 for adults and $1 for kids 12 and under. Contact the museum at 406-739-4224.

## 283. Richard Wood Watchable Wildlife Area

This is a small wildlife viewing area that has easy access to the main highway. It is nestled in the cottonwoods along the Marias River and is a pleasant place to walk, fish, or enjoy the river. Look for turtles, beavers, muskrats, and waterfowl along shoreline areas. You are likely to see pelicans and geese along the river, too.

**Directions:** Take U.S. 87 to Loma, and turn at the signed dirt road a short ways upriver from the Marias Bridge. The wildlife area is on the south side of the river. Once off the highway, turn down the fishing access road. There is a sign here telling about the area.

**Important Information:** The refuge is open year-round.

# Big Sandy

You can pick up supplies in this small ranching community or stop for a travel break. A museum and city park make for pleasant, if brief, family outings.

# 284. Big Sandy Historical Society and Museum

This museum, housed in the old railroad depot, focuses on cultural displays of Big Sandy history. Homestead history is featured and there are numerous artifacts, including a horse and carriage, period clothing, and household items. Photos of past Big Sandy residents hang in a large room of the depot.

**Directions:** Take U.S. Highway 87 to Big Sandy. Turn into the town of Big Sandy across from the bank. Go one block to the main street and you will see the depot along this street.

**Important Information:** Open Memorial Day to Labor Day from 2 P.M. to 5 P.M. There is no fee. Contact the museum at 406-378-2640.

# 286. Big Sandy City Park

This city park is right on U.S. Highway 87 and is an official state rest stop. It has a picnic shelter with tables, barbecue pits, and water. There are restrooms and overnight camping.

**Directions:** The city park is on U.S. Highway 87 at Big Sandy, across from the bank.

**Important Information:** There is no camping fee.

### Lewistown and the Judith Basin Area
Central Montana Historical Association Museum
Lewistown Art Center
Hanson Creek Recreation Area
Crystal Lake
Hidden Basin Wildlife Trail
Kendall and Maiden Ghost Town
Big Spring State Fish Hatchery
Gigantic Warm Spring
Judith Peak Recreational Area
Judith River Wildlife Management Area
Judith Basin Museum
Ackley Lake State Park
Sod Busters Museum
MSU Central Agricultural Research Center
Highwood Mountains
Square Butte
Thain Creek

### White Sulphur Springs
Castle Mansion and Meagher County Museum
Spa Hot Springs
Castle Ghost Town
Crystal Lake Shoreline Loop Trail
King's Hill National Scenic Byway
Memorial Falls
Newlan Creek Reservoir
Smith River State Park
Fort Logan

### Harlowtown
Upper Musselshell Museum
E-57B Engine Park

### Martinsdale
Charles M. Bair Family Museum
Martinsdale Reservoir

# YELLOWSTONE COUNTRY

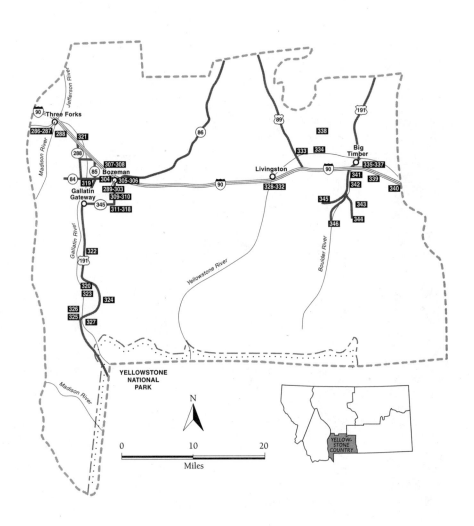

# Yellowstone Country

Yellowstone Country draws to it outdoor enthusiasts who revel in the bountiful natural resources of this dynamic area. Numerous blue-ribbon trout rivers have created an angler's paradise. At the same time, these rivers offer both wild whitewater excitement and pleasant, easy, floating adventures. In this country, it's tough to choose a favorite hiking or camping area because the region has some of Montana's most spectacular mountain ranges. The Madison, Gallatin, Bridger, Absaroka, Beartooth, and Crazy mountains blend together to form a prominent section of the Rocky Mountains famous for magnificence.

Interstate 90 divides the region with state and federal highways branching north and south to provide access to wild lands in the south and Montana small towns to the north. Frontier and railway history, and the traditions of the Shoshone and Crow people, provide a rich portrait of human experience. Wildlife in Yellowstone Country is as bountiful as the natural resources. Together, the land and people form a way of life that is rugged, vibrant, and thoroughly charming.

## MISSOURI RIVER CONFLUENCE

Rivers have figured prominently in the life and development of the town of Three Forks and the area surrounding the confluence of the Madison, Jefferson, and Gallatin rivers. Historically, these three tributaries of the Missouri have brought people of various cultures together. The Indians came together at this spot because it was a converging point for wildlife and a crossroads of hunting trails. Fur traders found these river junctions an excellent trading location. Today a museum and state park preserve the history of this confluence of people and rivers.

### Three Forks and the Surrounding Area

Explore the cultural and natural resources this small Montana town at the headwaters of the Missouri River has to offer. Two state parks and a fine museum make Three Forks an excellent place for family adventure. Food, gas, restaurants, and gift shops can be found in the town. For more information, contact the Three Forks Chamber of Commerce at 406-285-3198.

# 286. Headwaters Heritage Museum

Historical artifacts document the history of Three Forks at this museum. Displays vary from historical photographs to a barbed wire collection. Upstairs are replicas of a turn-of-the-century village including a kitchen, bedroom, and school room. Across the street is the Sacajawea Inn, listed on the National Register of Historic Places. Five miles away is the Missouri Headwaters State Park (site 287).

**Directions:** Take the Three Forks Exit 278 from Interstate 90 and go toward town on Montana Highway 2. It is 1.4 miles to the museum, which is on the right side of Main Street, on the corner of Cedar Street and Main.

**Important Information:** The museum is open from Memorial Day to Labor Day from 9 A.M. to 5 P.M., Monday through Saturday and 1 to 5 P.M. on Sunday. Donations are accepted. Contact the museum for more information at 406-285-4778.

# 287. Missouri Headwaters State Park

Three wild rivers tumble from rugged mountains and converge near Three Forks into one mighty force, the Missouri River. The area around this confluence was long a special site for Indians who found prolific wildlife here. The Corps of Discovery, led by Meriwether Lewis and William Clark, was justifiably taken by the numerous animal species they observed here. The explorers perused the headwaters and surrounding land for some time, naming the rivers the Jefferson, Madison, and Gallatin after the current President of the United States, the Secretary of State, and the Secretary of the Treasury.

Today, the site has recreational opportunities where visitors can picnic, camp, hike, appreciate wildlife, and learn more about the area's history through interpretive displays. As you drive into the park, you will find a parking lot to the right, as well as an interpretive area that outlines the park facilities and the lay of the surrounding land. Here, too, is an old building, a remnant of Gallatin City, from an era long gone. Farther up the park road is a picnic area and several short interpretive trails. Look for access points to the Missouri River on the left as you drive through the park. Across from the picnic area one such pullout has a trail leading over a bridge to a river island.

By the picnic area is a 0.5-mile hike around Fort Rock which provides viewpoints of the surrounding area. Along this trail hikers pass by the grave of a homesteader's child, bringing home the severity of the challenges that faced Montana pioneers. Inside the picnic shelter is interpretive information about early residents. There are restrooms, picnic tables, and grills at the picnic area.

# Sacagawea

By the birthplace of the Missouri River at Three Forks, a young Indian girl named Sacagawea was taken away from her own tribe, the Shoshones, by an Indian tribe passing through the area. She was raised by this tribe. As a teenager, Sacagawea married an explorer named Charbonneau who was hired to assist Lewis and Clark and the Corps of Discovery on their famous expedition. Sacagawea was also made part of the expedition, and her influence and guidance would prove invaluable to the explorers. The trip also brought Sacagawea the opportunity to reconnect with her people. At Camp Fortunate, 20 miles south of the present-day city of Dillon, the explorers would come upon a camp of Shoshone Indians. Wanting to trade with the amiable tribe for horses, Sacagawea, Lewis, and Clark approached the Indians to discover that the chief, Cam-e-ah-wah, was Sacagawea's brother.

The headwaters offer good fishing and more than 90 species of birds have been observed here in the mixed river bottom and rocky upland habitats.

**Directions:** Take Exit 278 from Interstate 90 near Three Forks. Go 1.8 miles east from the exit and turn left onto Montana Highway 286 at the sign for the park. Follow the highway 1.7 miles to a right turn into the park information area and interpretive display. The campground is on the left across from this turn. From this point it is 1.5 miles on the main park road to the picnic area and the Missouri River access pullouts.

**Important Information:** The park is open year-round. There is a day-use fee of $4 per vehicle or $1 per person, whichever is less. Keep your eyes open for rattlesnakes (see page 16). Camping is $4 to $8 per night. Contact the Bozeman Region 3 office of the Montana Department of Fish, Wildlife & Parks at 406-994-4042 for more information.

## 288. Madison Buffalo Jump State Park

As recently as 200 years ago, Indians used the sheer cliffs at this *pishkun*—a place where they would force summer-fattened buffalo to stampede over the edge to their death below. This was a common method of hunting buffalo before the introduction of horses allowed the Indians to outmaneuver the herds. The Madison Buffalo Jump is one of the larger pishkuns, also called buffalo jumps, in Montana. Piles of buffalo bones, up to 60 inches deep, and tepee rings on the plateau, reveal that the site was used as far back as 2,000 years ago. Though different tribes came here to hunt, the Northern Shoshone came most frequently.

The bluffs form a semicircular bowl shape. At the base of the cliffs is the area the Indians used for processing the massive animals for food and other necessities once they were killed. Visitors can drive to an overlook across from the buffalo jump for a view of the cliffs and land below. There is also a picturesque view of the Madison Valley and Tobacco Root Mountains from the overlook. An interpretive display explains the process of the hunt and points out the different areas used by native people at the site. Visitors can walk along the top of the plateau or even venture down into the area below the cliffs. There are no marked or maintained trails, though there are some indistinct pathways where previous visitors have explored. It is a ways down to the base of the cliffs, but this could be an interesting adventure that would extend appreciation for the land and lifestyle of the Indians. Fossils of plants and animals have been found here that date back 80 million years. Keep in mind that any artifacts found in the area should not be removed.

There is a vault toilet, picnic site, and potable water at the park.

**Directions:** Go east of Three Forks and take Exit 283 from Interstate 90. This exit is signed for Logan and the state park. Go 4 miles south from the exit and turn left onto Buffalo Jump Road, which is signed for the park. Continue 2.6 miles on this road to a left turn into the park. The interpretive area is 0.5 mile up the hill. The drive takes about 10 minutes from the highway exit.

**Important Information:** The park is open for day use only. Keep your eyes open for rattlesnakes (see page 16). There is a user fee for non-residents. Contact the Montana Department of Fish, Wildlife & Parks, Bozeman Regional Office, at 406-994-4042 for more information.

# BOZEMAN AND THE SURROUNDING AREA

Five mountain ranges, each spectacular in its own right, surround the city of Bozeman and make this area of Montana a recreational paradise. Within Bozeman the influence of Montana State University and an active arts community provides unique and interesting family entertainment. Plan to spend some time in Bozeman!

## City of Bozeman

If one could sum up the spirit of Bozeman, it would be to say that the town reflects the same sense of adventure that the city's namesake, John Bozeman, demonstrated (see page 241). The community has developed many recreational sites both within the city and in the outlying areas. Parks and hiking areas have been developed with thought to providing nature experiences for young, old, and people using wheelchairs. An extensive urban trail system crisscrosses the city and is used for hiking and biking. Biking enthusiasts have created bike trails in outlying areas, too. Local shops rent mountain bikes by the hour, day, or week. A map of city and nearby trails is available from the Gallatin Valley Land Trust, 406-587-8404.

Bozeman is home to Montana State University, which has about 11,000 students. The university is a leader in agricultural research, is actively involved with regional paleontology research, and assists in support of the outstanding Museum of the Rockies. The city has a complement of art galleries and museums, as well as an active arts center.

The lively Bozeman community has much to offer its residents and share with visitors. For more information about Bozeman, contact the Chamber of Commerce at 406-586-5421 or 800-228-4224.

## 289. American Computer Museum

If you want your kids to understand just how much change there has been in technology in recent years, this museum will help. Just know that you'll be dating yourself when you actually recognize some of the early computers and items in pre-computer exhibits. There are more than 4,000 years of computer-related artifacts on display here, beginning with ancient adding tools. An eight-minute Disney video, *Disney Computers: Where They Come from and How They Work*, is good for explaining some basic computer concepts to kids of all ages.

Included in the displays is the original Apollo Spacecraft Guidance Computer and other computerized tools used by astronauts, and one of the 1,000-pound mainframe computers used in the mid-1960s. A short tour is available and there are some interactive displays. As someone commented in the guest book: "We enjoyed every 'bit.'"

**Directions:** Take the Main Street Exit 309 from Interstate 90 and head west through Bozeman or take the North 19th Avenue Exit 305, follow 19th south to Main, and go east on Main. Turn south from Main onto Wilson Avenue, go one block and turn left (east) on Babcock Street. You will find the museum on the right-hand side of Babcock between Bozeman Avenue and Rouse Avenue in four blocks.

**Important Information:** Hours in June, July, and August are 10 A.M. to 4 P.M. every day. From September through May, the museum is open Tuesday, Wednesday, Friday, and Saturday from noon to 4 P.M. Admission is $3 for adults and children over 13, $2 for children ages 6 to 12, and free for kids under 6. Call 406-587-7545 for more information.

## 290. Gallatin County Pioneer Museum

Besides the interesting historical perspective visitors get from viewing this former county jail, the facility has a varied collection of artifacts to enjoy. A self-guided tour brochure leads visitors through the exhibits, detailing how the different rooms were used when the building was a jail and explaining the displays. Among the items are buffalo head trophies and Indian artifacts, early farm and ranch tools, a model of Fort Ellis, and a historical display of the Bozeman Trail.

Visitors can walk into a 12-by-14-foot hand-hewn log cabin and imagine living in it with an entire family. Or go into the jailhouse isolation chambers, and envision having to stay there. In the sheriff's room are items collected from prisoners, an old whiskey still, and an actual gallows! The museum is only a few blocks from the American Computer Museum (site 290).

**Directions:** The museum is at 317 West Main Street, next to the county courthouse. It sits between North 5th and North 3rd avenues. Though the address is West Main, because of the way the streets are numbered, the museum is actually on the east side of town. To reach the museum, take the North 19th Avenue Exit 305 from Interstate 90 and go east on Main Street to North 5th, or take the Main Street Exit 309 and go west.

**Important Information:** There is no charge for the museum. It is open weekdays from Memorial Day through Labor Day, 10 A.M. to 4:30 P.M., and Saturdays from 1 to 4 P.M. Winter hours are Tuesday through Friday from 11 A.M. to 4 P.M. and Saturday from 1 to 4 P.M. Call the museum at 406-582-3195 for more information.

## 291. Emerson Cultural Center

This community center for visual and performing arts also houses a number of artist studios, many of which welcome visitors. The galleries rotate exhibits regularly with a variety of contemporary, Native American, and local artists' works. Wednesdays from 11:30 A.M. to 1:30 P.M., between July 1 and the end of August, the center provides a Lunch on the Lawn concert series featuring local musicians. The center sponsors other arts-related activities as well.

**Directions:** From Main Street, go south two blocks on Grand Avenue to 111 South Grand Avenue. The facility is a full city block so you can't miss it!

**Important Information:** The free gallery is open from 10 A.M. to 5 P.M., Tuesday through Saturday. Contact the center at 406-587-9797 for information or a schedule of events.

## 292. Beall Art Center and Park

The Beall Art Center is housed in a historic building made of cobblestones that sits in wooded Beall Park. The art center features changing exhibits of contemporary, traditional, and folk artists. The 2.2-acre park has restrooms, picnic tables, grills, a playground, a basketball court, and a winter ice rink. **Directions:** The center is at 409 North Bozeman Avenue. Take the Main Street Exit 309 and go west on Main Street. Turn north on Wilson Avenue and go four blocks to Villard. Turn right on Villard and go three blocks to Bozeman Avenue.
**Important Information:** Contact the art center at 406-587-3970.

## 293. Museum of the Rockies

The world of dinosaurs comes to life in this renowned museum that features the most complete displays in the state about the massive, mysterious beasts that once roamed many areas of the Big Sky country. Montana State University is actively involved in paleontological research of dinosaurs along the Rocky Mountain front. The museum, sponsored in part by the university, presents a display of fossils from the landmark Egg Mountain discovery (see site 245). This exhibit is set up as a re-created nesting colony of the *Maiasaura peeblesorum*. Other dinosaur displays include nearly complete dinosaur skeletons and a view into a real lab involved in processing paleontological finds. Changing exhibits bring other aspects of dinosaur natural history to life.

The museum has outstanding exhibits on a variety of other topics too. An interesting and comprehensive exhibit entitled *Enduring Peoples: Native Cultures of the Northern Rockies and Plains* has numerous artifacts and dioramas depicting 11,000 years of native history. A permanent exhibit, *Landforms and Lifeforms*, describes regional natural history. Among the hands-on exhibits is a pinball game about extinction and an interactive "space station." The Martin Discovery Room is a children's interactive playroom with dinosaur themes. Outside the museum, the *Living History Farm* portrays the lifestyle of a Montana pioneer family. The museum presents traveling exhibits on a wide spectrum of topics, too.

Taylor Planetarium is located in the museum. The planetarium has a 40-foot domed multimedia theater with daily presentations. A laser computer graphics system can simulate 3-D effects and spaceflight and offers periodic laser shows.

There is a small picnic area and summertime food service outdoors. A gift shop in the museum offers fun, educational items. The museum also offers a wide variety of educational lectures and programs year-round, including on-site paleontological field courses at Egg Mountain.

**Directions:** From Interstate 90, take the North 19th Avenue Exit 305 (MSU) and follow 19th Avenue south through town. Turn left (east) on Kagy Boulevard and go about one mile to the museum entrance on the right side of the road. The museum is on the MSU campus at 600 West Kagy.

**Important Information:** Open daily 8 A.M. to 8 P.M. from Memorial Day weekend through Labor Day weekend. Off-season hours are Monday through Saturday from 9 A.M. to 5 P.M. and Sunday from 12:30 to 5 P.M. The Taylor Planetarium is open during regular summer hours. Off-season the planetarium is open regular hours plus Friday night from 6:30 to 9 P.M. The *Living History* exhibit is open daily from 9 A.M. to 4 P.M. during the summer, but closed in winter.

Museum admission for two days is $6 for adults, $4 for kids 5 to 18, and free for children under 5. Planetarium admission is $2.50 and laser shows are $4. The planetarium recommends that children under 6 not be taken into the regular planetarium shows. However, there is a Saturday morning children's program specially designed for these little ones. Contact the museum at 406-994-DINO for a recorded message of current exhibits or the museum office at 406-994-2251.

## 294. Kirk Hill

Go exploring on Kirk Hill and you will find marshy meadows, picturesque aspen groves, and ridge-top sage and juniper habitat on 10 miles of self-guided trails. You can pick from different trails, including loop trails that are 1.5 miles, 1.9 miles, and 1.3 miles in length. Along the trails are interpretive signs. Trail maps are located at the entrance. More than 70 species of birds have been noted here. The area is managed by the Museum of the Rockies.

**Directions:** Take the North 19th Avenue Exit 305 from Interstate 90 and go south on 19th for 5.7 miles. Kirk Hill is on the left where the road takes a sharp curve to the right. Be ready to turn into the parking area immediately after the turn.

**Important Information:** This is a free-use area. No dogs, horses, or bicycles. Contact the Museum of the Rockies education department at 406-994-5257 for information.

# John Bozeman: Wagons, ho!

It took pioneers a lot of stamina to survive the hardships of westward migration, and a fair amount of courage too. And it required a certain kind of person to lead others on the long, arduous, and sometimes dangerous trails to the west. John Bozeman, a Georgian who had grown tired of fruitless days of prospecting in Montana Territory, became one of these leaders. In fact, he and his partner, John Jacobs, decided that the journey north to Montana could be easier if a new and shorter route could be developed. So, in 1863, they founded a northern spur route from the Oregon Trail, leading through Wyoming to the heart of Montana mining fever, Virginia City. The Bozeman Trail was indeed an easier travel route but it turned out not to be safe. The trail ran right through the midst of hunting grounds for the Sioux and Cheyenne tribes, Indians who were not at all pleased with the intrusion of white people onto their lands.

Still, the wagon master persevered, and when the gold boom kept growing in southwestern Montana, he obtained government support for protection along the trail. Literally seeing the pot of gold at the end of the trail, the government built three forts to protect settlers and miners traveling on the Bozeman Trail. They even met with Indian tribes to make treaties providing for safe passage along the trail. It seems that they met with the wrong Indians, however, so the situation got worse, not better. Finally, in 1868, after several skirmishes with the Indians, the government withdrew their troops from the forts. Within a short time, the Indians burned all three forts to the ground.

Remnants of the Bozeman Trail can still be found. As for John Bozeman, he was found murdered on the banks of the Yellowstone River. Who killed the wagon master is still a mystery. Today, around southern Montana, you will frequently see the name of this adventurous pioneer.

## 295. Lindley Park

This park is convenient for passers-through since it is situated just off Main Street, a short distance from Interstate 90. The park has restrooms, grills, picnic tables, and a playground.

**Directions:** Take Exit 309, the Main Street exit, from Interstate 90 and go west into town. The park is on the left (south) side of Main Street, just west of the Blue Sky Motel about a mile from the exit. Turn south from Main onto Buttonwood Street, next to Sunset Hills Cemetery, to get to the park.

**Important Information:** For more information contact the City of Bozeman, Division of Parks, 406-582-3200.

# 296. Bogert Park and City Pool

One of Bozeman's two city pools is associated with this nicely shaded park that has restrooms, picnic tables, and grills. It also has a band shell with frequent summer music events, plus tennis and basketball courts. Nearby is Peets' Hill (see site 298), where you can climb a short distance up to a low ridge that overlooks the city or take a longer walking trail. The Gallagator Linear Park (site 297) trailhead begins a couple blocks south of the park.

**Directions:** The park is on the east side of Bozeman, just south of Main Street. Take Exit 309, the Main Street exit, from Interstate 90, and go west into town. Turn left (south) onto South Church Avenue, just one block before the Montana Highway 86 junction. The park is on the right side of Church Avenue, 0.5 mile south of Main Street, at 325 South Church Avenue.

**Important Information:** The outdoor pool is open mid-June to late August. Recreational swims are from 1 to 8 P.M. Monday through Thursday, and Friday from 1 to 9:30 P.M. On Saturdays and Sundays the pool is open from 1 to 6 P.M. Family swims are from 5 to 8:30 P.M. on Wednesdays and Fridays. Admission is $2.75 for adults, $1.75 for kids up to age 17 and seniors, and free for kids 3 and under. Family swims are $4.50. For more information, contact the Bozeman Recreation Department at 406-587-4724 or call the pool directly at 406-587-9995.

# 297. Gallagator Linear Park and Trail

Want to go for a walk away from traffic, or are you looking for a good place to bike? The Gallagator Linear Trail provides plenty of urban trail through the city of Bozeman on what was originally the Gallatin Valley Electric Railroad right-of-way. The trail begins on the north end of town by Bogert Park and goes about a mile and a half south to the Museum of the Rockies. A 0.5-mile extension trail goes around the museum and continues south past Morningstar School to South 3rd Avenue by Sacajewea Middle School. There are occasional gaps in the trail where it is necessary to cross the roadway, but signs lead you to the next trailhead. It is also possible to hook up with other Bozeman urban trails via the Gallagator.

**Directions:** To get to the South Church Avenue trailhead by Bogert Park, take the Main Street Exit 309 into Bozeman from Interstate 90. Follow Main Street west toward town and turn left (south) on South Church Avenue. Go three blocks, past Bogert Park, to where the trail starts on the right by Story Street.

You could also start the trail by the Museum of the Rockies (site 292), and go north to Bogert Park or south on the Morningstar extension trail. The south end of Morningstar Trail can be found at the north edge of Sacajewea Middle School on 3rd Avenue South.

**Important Information:** For more information contact the Bozeman Division of Parks at 406-582-3200. A Bozeman city trails map is available from the Gallatin Valley Land Trust, 406-587-8404.

## 298. Peets' Hill and the Highland Ridge Trail

From atop Peets' Hill you can look out over the city of Bozeman and to the scenic peaks of five mountain ranges. A very short but steep trail leads from the parking area on South Church Avenue to the top of Peets' Hill. Don't worry, this hill isn't big enough to be considered a deterrent to taking young children onto the ridge.

The hilltop is a good place to see wildflowers, and the Gallatin Valley Land Trust provides a list of flowers you might see here. There are no picnic facilities but you could pack a lunch up to the top and eat at the resting benches. Bogert Park (site 296) is within a couple of blocks and the Gallagator Linear Trail (site 297) begins across the street from the base of the hill.

The Highland Ridge Trail goes 2.3 miles from Peets' Hill to Kagy Boulevard. The trail follows the ridge on top of Peets' Hill and drops down, via two routes, onto access points on Kagy Boulevard. The east route connects to the Painted Hills Trail (site 300) via the Kagy Connector Trail along Kagy Boulevard. The west route joins the Simkins Spur Trail at Kagy Boulevard and Sourdough Road.

**Directions:** The trail is on the east side of Bozeman, just south of Main Street. Take Exit 309, the Main Street exit, from Interstate 90, and go west into town. Turn south from Main Street onto South Church Avenue. A small parking lot by the Peets' Hill trail is at the corner of South Church and Story Street.

**Important Information:** For more information contact the Gallatin Valley Land Trust at 406-587-8404 or the City of Bozeman, Division of Parks, 406-582-3200. The land trust has maps of Bozeman city trails.

## 299. Sourdough Trail

Here's another great Bozeman city trail. This packed dirt trail goes from Kagy Boulevard to Goldenstein Lane. The hike follows a tree-lined creek much of the way, though at times it is in open meadow areas. There are access spots to the creek where children can play.

The Sourdough Trail connects with the Sundance Trail at the south end for some extra hiking miles. At the end of the Sundance Trail is McLeod Park, an undeveloped park.

**Directions:** Because of parking problems on the north end, it is best to start at the south trailhead. Take 19th Avenue south from Main Street (take the North 19th Avenue Exit 305 if you are coming from Interstate 90), and go to Goldenstein Lane. Turn left and pull off the road where Goldenstein crosses Sourdough Creek. The trail starts here. If you want to start at the north end, get the Gallatin Valley Land Trust map and directions, as you can start from the Gallagator Linear Trail and, with some road crossings, get to the Sourdough Trail from the north.

**Important Information:** For more information contact the Bozeman Division of Parks at 406-582-3200 or the Gallatin Valley Land Trust, 406-587-8404.

# 300. Painted Hills Trail

On the outskirts of Bozeman is the Painted Hills Trail, a packed dirt trail which goes through a gully area. The 1.25-mile trail goes up and down somewhat and crosses the creek several times.

The trail begins on Kagy Boulevard and heads south. At the writing of this book, only a short section of private land blocked the trail from connecting with the Triple Tree Trail (site 301). Negotiations are ongoing for permission to allow hikers to cross the private land and go on to the Triple Tree Trail if they desire. Unless negotiations are complete, you must stop at the fenceline that marks the private land and return the same way you came. However, the 2.5-mile round-trip hike of Painted Hills Trail is worth the walk in itself and may be as far as families want to go anyway.

The Kagy Connector, a short trail at the northern trailhead, connects Painted Hills to the Highland Ridge Trail (site 298) by following Kagy Boulevard west. From the junction with the Highland Ridge Trail you can go up and follow Highland Ridge, explore Peets' Hill, or connect to the Sourdough or Gallagator Linear trails.

**Directions:** To reach the Painted Hills trailhead, take the Main Street Exit 309 off Interstate 90 and follow Main Street west toward town about a mile. Go south from Main Street onto South Church Avenue. You will pass Bogert Park and Peets' Hill. Continue south to Kagy Boulevard. Turn left (east) on Kagy and go 0.7 mile to a righthand turn into a small parking area. You can also reach this site by going south on 19th Avenue from Main Street on the west side of town. Turn left on Kagy Boulevard and go east, past the Museum of the Rockies, to the Kagy and South Church Avenue intersection. From here, continue on Kagy 0.7 mile to the parking area.

**Important Information:** Contact the Gallatin Valley Land Trust, 406-587-8404, for a map of Bozeman trails.

# 301. Triple Tree Trail

Triple Tree Trail takes hikers on a wooded course from Bozeman toward the mountains. The packed dirt trail has some climbing to it, especially on the state land loop. The trail, about 6 miles long, goes east from Sourdough Road across a meadowed ridge, along a forested hillside, across a creek, and then along a fenceline to the ridgetop.

**Directions:** The trail begins about 2 miles south of the intersection of Kagy Boulevard and Sourdough Road. From Interstate 90, take the North 19th Avenue Exit 309 and go south through town on 19th to Kagy Boulevard. Turn left (east) onto Kagy and follow this to Sourdough Road. Turn right (south) and look for the trailhead on the left side of the road in about 2 miles. The trail begins past the Triple Tree Development. You will see a small parking lot on the left several hundred feet beyond the development turnoff. Follow the trail markers once on the trail.

**Important Information:** Contact the USDA Forest Service, Bozeman Ranger District, at 406-587-6920. A Bozeman city trails map is available from the Gallatin Valley Land Trust, 406-587-8404.

# 302. City of Bozeman Recreation Center

This year-round facility offers an indoor 50-meter pool, fitness equipment, a hot tub, and a variety of classes.

**Directions:** The center is at 1211 West Main Street, just west of Bozeman High School. Take the North 19th Avenue Exit 309 from Interstate 90 and go south on 19th to Main. Turn left on Main.

**Important Information:** The pool is open year-round. Summer hours begin mid-June and run until late August. Hours are 1 to 8 P.M., Monday through Friday, and 1 to 6 P.M. on Saturdays. This pool is closed Sundays in the summer, though Bogert Pool (site 296) is open. Summer admission is $2.75 for adults, $1.75 for kids up to age 17 and seniors, and free for kids 3 and under. Family swims are from 5 to 8 P.M., Wednesdays and Fridays, and cost $4.50.

Winter hours are 5:30 to 8:30 P.M., Monday through Thursday, 3:30 to 9 P.M. on Fridays, and noon to 6 P.M. on Saturdays. The pool is open on Sundays from 1 to 6 P.M. Winter rates are $1.50 for kids and seniors, $2.50 for adults, and free for kids 3 and under. Families can swim for $4. For more information, contact the center at 406-587-4724.

# 303. Bozeman Pond

Even though this is a tiny pond, you can enjoy playtime here with a picnic, fishing, or even swimming. The site has a beach and a trail that goes most of the way around the pond. There is a large shelter, picnic facilities, and a vault toilet. Since the pond is stocked, it's pretty easy to pull out rainbow, brook, or brown trout as well as perch. Kayaks and canoes are allowed, but no motorized craft.

**Directions:** Exit into Bozeman from Interstate 90 on the North 19th Avenue Exit 309 and follow 19th south to Main Street. Turn right (west). The entrance to Bozeman Pond is on Fowler Avenue, which is a right (north) turn west of the Mountain Mall and adjacent to the State Capitol Employees Credit Union.

**Important Information:** There is no lifeguard at the pond. A fishing license is required. Contact the Bozeman Division of Parks at 406-582-3200 for more information.

# 304. The East Gallatin Recreation Area and Trail

The 300-foot beach along manmade Glen Lake at this recreation area is a refreshing and entertaining summer activity site. And if swimming and fishing aren't energizing enough, there is a trail from the lake through the fields to fishing along the East Gallatin River. The recreation area has picnic shelters, a vault toilet, and grills. The facility is wheelchair accessible, including the fishing dock.

The trail to the river is about 1.5 miles, including a loop through the park and around the lake.

**Directions:** From Main Street in Bozeman, go north on Rouse Avenue, Montana Highway 86, 1.3 miles to the T intersection at Griffin Drive. Turn left (west) onto Griffin and go 0.4 mile to Manley Road. Turn right on Manley, go 0.6 mile, and turn right again at the signed entrance by a farmhouse. The trail starts from the north end of the lake by the fence.

From Interstate 90, take the North 7th Avenue Exit 306 and go north from the exit. Turn right on Griffin Drive, which is Mandeville Lane to the left, and then go left onto Manley Road. Turn right at the signed entrance by the farmhouse.

**Important Information:** A day-use fee of $2 supports the facility. No dogs or camping permitted. Watch for logs, rocks, and sudden dropoffs in the lake. There is no lifeguard at the site. For more information contact the City of Bozeman, Division of Parks, 406-582-3200.

# The Bridger Canyon and Mountain Range

When the first wagon train made its way through the canyon toward what is now Bozeman, frontiersman Jim Bridger was leading the way. The canyon, mountain range, and area trails now bear his name. Hiking in this area is delightful and scenic. The Bridger Bowl Ski Area takes advantage of the configuration of the sedimentary Bridger Mountains for its excellent ski slopes.

## 305. Bozeman Fish Technology Center

This hatchery has outdoor fish runs and other exhibits where visitors can observe a full complement of hatchery trout in various stages of development. You'll also see some albino trout at this center.

A short nature trail leaves from the end of the parking lot and goes over the hill and around the back of the hatchery to the fish runs. There is a map of the trail on the interpretive display in the parking lot. The trail is a little vague in places but it would be tough to get lost. In the summer, a tepee is set up on the lawn. Families can picnic on the grounds. Across the road is the "M" trail (site 306).

**Directions:** From Interstate 90, take the North 7th Avenue Exit 306 and go north from the exit. Turn right on Griffin Drive, which is Mandeville Lane to the left, and then left onto Bridger Drive which becomes Bridger Canyon Road, Montana Highway 86. Follow this road about 4 miles, then turn right onto Fish Hatchery Road. From Bozeman, take Rouse Avenue north from East Main Street. Follow Rouse and veer right to Bridger Drive which becomes Bridger Canyon Road. The hatchery is located at mile marker 4 at 4050 Bridger Canyon Road. You will see a large painted "M" on the hill across the road from the center.

**Important Information:** Contact the fish technology center at 406-587-9265.

## 306. The "M" Trail

In the college tradition, Montana State University students have created a huge hilltop letter "M" to honor their school. Two trails lead up to the "M" from the trailhead on Bridger Canyon Road for a great view toward Bozeman. There is a quick and steep trail to the right. The trail that goes to the left is easier, though the numerous switchbacks make it longer. The Bridger Foothills National Recreation Trail, which also begins here, goes nearly 21 miles to the Fairy Lake Campground.

At the "M" trailhead is a very small picnic area with two tables and a vault toilet tucked into a corner of a very small parking lot. You may want to find a nice spot along the trail to picnic. There is no potable water at the trailhead. Across the road is the Bozeman Fish Technology Center (site 306). **Directions:** From Interstate 90, take the North 7th Avenue Exit 306 and go north from the exit. Turn right on Griffin Drive, which is Mandeville Lane to the left, and then turn left onto Bridger Drive, Montana Highway 86, which later becomes Bridger Canyon Road. Follow this road about 4 miles. The "M" trailhead is just across from the Bozeman Fish Technology Center 0.1 mile farther up Bridger Canyon Road.

From Bozeman, take Rouse Avenue, marked as Montana Highway 86, north from East Main Street. Continue on Rouse up to the T intersection, then veer right, following MT 86 as it becomes Bridger Drive, and then Bridger Canyon Road. The trailhead will be on the left side of the road. **Important Information:** Open all year. No fee. Bring your own water. For more information contact the USDA Forest Service, Bozeman Ranger District, at 406-587-6920.

## 307. Fairy Lake and Campground

This pretty little alpine lake makes a nice fishing spot and has a nine-unit campground, too. A 0.25-mile trail goes to the lake from the parking area and there is a fishing path around the lake. The campground has potable water, picnic tables, and vault toilets.

**Directions:** From Interstate 90, take the North 7th Avenue Exit 306 and go north from the exit. Turn right on Griffin Drive, which is Mandeville Lane to the left, and then turn left onto Bridger Drive, Montana Highway 86, which later becomes Bridger Canyon Road. Go north of Bozeman for 22 miles on MT 86. You will go past the Bridger Bowl Ski Area and the Battle Ridge campground turnoff. About 2 miles beyond the Battle Ridge Campground sign, turn left (west) at the sign for Fairy Lake Campground. **Important Information:** There is no campground or day-use fee. The road gets rough toward the end and can become severely washboarded, especially in late summer. Leave time to go slowly on the graveled section of the road. For more information, contact the USDA Forest Service, Bozeman Ranger District, at 406-587-6920.

# 308. Sacajawea Peak

If your kids have been initiated into the world of hiking, you can use this trip as a graduating ceremony to more difficult hikes. The ascent to the top of Sacajawea Peak is a 2-mile uphill grade that gains 2,000 feet of elevation. That's not bad considering that when you get to the top, at 9,666 feet, you are at the top of the highest peak in the Bridger Range. At the end of the trail it seems you can see forever. The trail goes up a saddle between Sacajawea Peak and Hardscrabble Peak and then goes left on a winding trail to the top.

**Directions:** From Interstate 90 take the North 7th Avenue Exit 306 and go north from the exit. Turn right on Griffin Drive, which is Mandeville Lane to the left, and then turn left onto Bridger Drive, Montana Highway 86, which later becomes Bridger Canyon Road. Go past the Bridger Bowl Ski Area, about 20 miles north. Continue past the Battle Ridge Campground. About 2 miles beyond the campground, turn left (west) on the road to Fairy Lake Campground. Follow the campground road about 7 miles. Turn right toward the end of the campground and go about 200 yards to the trailhead parking area.

**Important Information:** Bring plenty of water as there is none here. The road gets rough toward the end and can become severely washboarded, especially in late summer. Leave time to go slowly on the graveled section of the road. Also note that this trail gets a fair amount of use, so expect other hikers, many of them families. For more information, contact the USDA Forest Service, Bozeman Ranger District, 406-587-6920.

# South Canyons

As the city flatlands give way to mountain foothills south of Bozeman, canyons wind into the Gallatin Mountains. From the city's edge it is possible to explore biking and hiking trails in several canyons, including Sourdough, Leverich, and Hyalite, and the Cottonwood Drainage. The Hyalite has been extensively managed for recreation while most of the other canyons have some housing developments in relatively undisturbed Forest Service land. There are hiking trails to be found on the Forest Service land, and bike trails have been developed in some of these areas, too.

# 309. South Cottonwood Trail 422

This is a very easy trail that is relatively flat for the first 7 or 8 miles as it goes up the South Cottonwood Creek drainage. Beyond this, the trail climbs rather steeply up a ridge. Log bridges across the South Cottonwood Creek make a hike along this trail feasible for families, as the creek is too swift and deep in places for families to wade across. The trail provides some variety of scenery as it goes alternately through wooded creek bottoms and open meadow areas. This is not a loop trail, so go in only as far as you feel the kids can handle hiking back. Creekside play can make the hike more memorable for children.

**Directions:** Take the North 19th Avenue Exit 305 from Interstate 90 and go south on 19th Avenue for 8.3 miles. It will become South 19th Road. Turn left onto Cottonwood Road, which is the first main county road after the Hyalite Canyon Road. Go 2.1 miles to Cottonwood Canyon Road and turn left again. The signed trailhead is at the end of this road in 2.2 miles.

**Important Information:** Contact the USDA Forest Service, Bozeman Ranger District, at 406-587-6920 for more information.

# 310. Mystic Lake

The mystery of this lake for families may be wondering what it looks like. The small man-made reservoir is 10 miles in and most families won't get that far. The hike is in a pretty area, however, and is close to town, making this a pleasant summer evening or afternoon walk. It receives regular use by families, hikers, and mountain bikers.

The trail, mostly an old road bed on the lower portions, is wide and alternates between level areas and very gradual uphill sections. The trail follows the Bozeman-Sourdough Creek, sometimes quite high above the creek and sometimes at the same level. The creek was dammed at Mystic Lake and used as a reservoir for the City of Bozeman water supply some time ago. The dam has since been let go, but a small, good fishing lake still exists. Not too far from the trailhead, you will pass a small reservoir which the city now uses.

**Directions:** From Interstate 90, take the North 19th Avenue Exit 305. Follow 19th Avenue south through town to Kagy Boulevard. Turn left and follow Kagy to Sourdough Road, then turn right (south). Follow this road for 3.7 miles. It is paved until the last 0.5 mile. At Nash Road turn right (west) and go 0.2 mile, turning left onto Sourdough Canyon Road. You will be at the trailhead in 1 mile.

**Important Information:** Remember that mountain weather changes very quickly. Always have warm clothing available when hiking, even if the weather appears pleasant at the moment (see page 18). Contact the USDA Forest Service, Bozeman Ranger District, at 406-587-6920 for more information.

# Hyalite Canyon

Hyalite Canyon is a beautiful area with easy access and varied recreational opportunities. Care has been taken to preserve the pristine nature of the resource. The Gallatin Empire Lion's Club, the Forest Service, and other community organizations cooperated to create the Hyalite Challenge Project. This successful joint effort has made a number of sites accessible to all people including those with disabilities, families with small children, and senior citizens. The offerings include four wheelchair-accessible trails and accessible picnic tables and toilets. The Hyalite Challenge Dedication Park is located 2 miles up Hyalite Canyon Road. The park has a pullout and an area map (unless vandals have removed it) showing accessible Hyalite Canyon sites, a sitting bench, and a local artist's sculpture.

The canyon campgrounds and hikes are an easy half-hour from Bozeman. A creek, a reservoir, numerous waterfalls, and several hikes provide diverse recreational opportunities. Hyalite Canyon is an area families can take a week to explore or a place they can visit frequently for an afternoon or day of outdoor fun. The close proximity to the city means that a Hyalite Canyon nature experience will be shared with numerous other people. Weekend camping spaces are at a premium, so come early, have an alternate plan, or make reservations for your campsite with the Forest Service. A first-night prepayment of the $8-per-night camping fee, plus a $4 reservation charge, must be made 10 days in advance if you want to reserve a campsite. Contact the Gallatin Canyon Campgrounds, 406-587-9054, for a reservation. However you choose to explore the canyon, it can certainly be a positive outdoor family experience.

## 311. Langohr Campground and Hyalite Creek Recreation Trail

Nestled along Hyalite Creek, near the beginning of Hyalite Canyon, is the Langohr Campground. There are 12 campsites here, as well as group picnic areas, wheelchair-accessible toilets, and potable water.

The Hyalite Creek Recreation Trail is a 0.3-mile paved trail located at the north end of the campground. Aside from being a pleasant and easy walk along the creek, it connects to fishing access points along the way.

**Directions:** Take the North 19th Exit 305 from Interstate 90 and go south through town on 19th. From Main Street and 19th, it is 7.5 miles to Hyalite Canyon Road, Forest Road 62. Turn left (south) at the signed turn for Hyalite Canyon Road and go 5.5 miles to Langohr Campground which will be on the right.

**Important Information:** There is a camping fee of $8 per night. See information on campsite reservations in the Hyalite Canyon description (see page 251). Call the Gallatin Canyon Campgrounds at 406-587-9054 for reservation information. The campground is open from late May to mid-September, weather permitting. For more information, contact the USDA Forest Service, Bozeman Ranger District, at 406-587-6920.

## 312. History Rock Trail 424

History and hiking mix on this 1.2-mile trail that goes to a large rock where early pioneers carved their names and the dates they were there. Unfortunately, local graffiti artists have since covered the historical markings with more recent writings. Still, the trail is a nice, short hike and the rock provides a destination point. Though this is an easy, hard-packed dirt trail, it is not wheelchair accessible. After passing the rock, the trail continues west to the South Cottonwood Creek drainage.

**Directions:** Take the North 19th Exit 305 from Interstate 90 and go south through town on 19th. From Main Street and 19th, it is 7.5 miles to Hyalite Canyon Road, Forest Road 62. Turn left, south, at the signed turn for Hyalite Canyon Road and go 9.7 miles to the History Rock turnoff on the right (west) side of the road. The turnoff is 1 mile north of Hyalite Reservoir.

**Important Information:** Contact the USDA Forest Service, Bozeman Ranger District, at 406-587-6920 for more information.

## 313. Hyalite Reservoir

After driving up the winding road through the first 10 miles of picturesque Hyalite Canyon, visitors find the Hyalite Reservoir. An agricultural dam constructed in the late 1940s, Hyalite Reservoir provides water for Bozeman farms and ranches. The manmade reservoir also provides recreational opportunities in this appealing environment. Cutthroat trout and arctic grayling keep anglers busy on the lake. Small motor boats, canoes, and sailboats are allowed, though there is a "no-wake" rule, so only low-speed trolling is permitted for motorboats.

Chisholm and Hood Creek campgrounds, on the east side of the lake, provide campsites, picnic areas, outhouses, potable water, and a boat ramp. Hood Creek has 18 sites and Chisholm has nine. The boat ramp is located in the Hood Creek Campground. There is also a boat ramp at Blackmore Recreation Area (site 314). Both boat ramps can be steep in late summer, and at other times when the water is low, but are acceptable most of the year. The Hood Creek boat ramp is the least steep.

**Directions:** Take the South 19th exit from Interstate 90 and go south through town on 19th. From Main Street and 19th, it is 7.5 miles to Hyalite Canyon Road, Forest Road 62. Turn left (south) at the signed turn and follow Hyalite Canyon Road 10.5 miles to the reservoir. Continue around the reservoir to the campgrounds, which are within a mile of each other.

**Important Information:** The reservoir is subject to water-level fluctuation. For more information, contact the USDA Forest Service, Bozeman Ranger District at 406-587-6920.

## 314. Blackmore Recreation Area

A nice place along Hyalite reservoir to play, fish, picnic, or go for a short hike can be found at the Blackmore Recreation Area. Located at the north end of the reservoir, this recreation site has wheelchair-accessible vault toilets and picnic sites, a boat ramp, and potable water. The West Shore Trail and Crescent Lake Trail (site 315) are accessed here.

**Directions:** Take the North 19th Exit 305 from Interstate 90 and go south through town on 19th. From Main Street and 19th, it is 7.5 miles to Hyalite Canyon Road, Forest Road 62. Turn left, south, at the signed turn and follow Hyalite Canyon Road for 10.5 miles to the Hyalite Reservoir.

**Important Information:** There is no use fee. For more information, contact the USDA Forest Service, Bozeman Ranger District, at 406-587-6920.

## 315. West Shore Trail 431 and Crescent Lake Trail 213

The West Shore Trail is a hard gravel surface, accessible by wheelchair users. This 0.5-mile trail from Blackmore Recreation Area (site 314) leads to a scenic overlook of the Hyalite Reservoir.

Near the overlook, the trail connects with the Crescent Lake Trail, a packed-dirt trail (not wheelchair-accessible) that makes the hike a 2.5-mile loop trail back to Blackmore Recreation Area. Crescent is a small lake right next to the trail. It does not have fish.

**Directions:** The trail starts from the parking area of Blackmore Recreation Area (site 315).

**Important Information:** For more information, contact the USDA Forest Service, Bozeman Ranger District, at 406-587-6920.

## 316. Palisade Falls National Recreation Trail

A scenic woodland trail leads visitors 0.6 mile to a picturesque falls on Palisade Mountain. The paved trail is wheelchair accessible though it is a 30 percent grade, making the hike a moderately difficult trip for wheelchair users. There are interpretive signs along the trail explaining aspects of the natural ecosystem. The falls are good-sized and the mountain cliff the water tumbles over is impressive. Because the trail is paved, it makes a nice hike for very young children. However, anyone will enjoy this pleasant hike and the vigorous falls.

Look for pikas and even marmots in the rock slide area near the falls. The cliffs of Palisade Mountain have golden eagle nests. And of course, keep an eye out for dippers in the creek. The tall columns of rock, characteristic of Palisade Mountain, are columnar basalt. There are wheelchair-accessible picnic tables and a vault toilet in the parking area, but no potable water.

**Directions:** Take the North 19th Avenue Exit 305 from Interstate 90 and go south through town on 19th. From Main Street and 19th, it is 7.5 miles to Hyalite Canyon Road, Forest Road 62. Turn left (south) at the signed turn and follow Hyalite Canyon Road for about 12 miles to the East Fork junction, a short distance past Chisholm Campground. Turn left on the East Fork Road. In 1 mile you will see a sign on the left for the Palisade Falls parking area.

**Important Information:** For more information, contact the USDA Forest Service, Bozeman Ranger District, at 406-587-6920.

## 317. Grotto Falls and Hyalite Creek Trail 427

This trail gives families the option of making the 1.25-mile hike to see Grotto Falls the focus of a family outing, or getting involved in a more extensive journey by continuing beyond the falls toward Hyalite Lake. The lake is another 4 miles down Hyalite Creek Trail, so going all the way to the lake would make this a 10-mile excursion round trip. However, along the trail are nine more falls to enjoy, so there are rewards for walking at least a short distance past Grotto Falls. The first 3 miles beyond Grotto Falls is a moderately easy trail but the final mile gets steep, which could make a journey to the lake even more discouraging with little children. If you do go the full 5 miles from the trailhead to the alpine lake, you'll find yourself surrounded by craggy peaks and wonderful seasonal wildflowers. As you drive into the parking area you get a taste of what's in store up the trail, for you can see the massive cliffs of the canyon you will ultimately go through.

The trail is a hard gravel surface as far as Grotto Falls. There is no potable water but there is a vault toilet and a picnic site in the trailhead parking area.

**Directions:** Take the North 19th Exit 305 from Interstate 90 and go south through town on 19th. From Main Street and 19th, it is 7.5 miles to Hyalite Canyon Road, Forest Road 62. Turn left (south) at the signed turn and follow Hyalite Canyon Road for about 12 miles to the East Fork junction, a short distance past Chisholm Campground. Stay to the right on the West Fork Road at this junction. The junction sign directs you to Hyalite Creek Trail in 2.5 miles. Go to the end of the road where there is a large parking area for the falls trail.

**Important Information:** Bring drinking water. For more information, contact the USDA Forest Service, Bozeman Ranger District, at 406-587-6920.

## 318. Horsetail Falls via the Emerald Lake Trail 434

If your family is feeling energetic and you don't mind some uphill hiking, take a walk into Horsetail Falls. It is 1.5 mostly uphill miles to the tumbling falls on Hyalite Creek. Another 4.5 miles of steady elevation gain brings hikers to Emerald Lake, a pretty alpine lake with mountain whitefish, arctic grayling, and various species of trout.

**Directions:** Follow the directions for Palisade Falls (site 316). Go beyond the entrance to the falls parking lot and all the way to the end of the East Fork Road where you will find the trailhead.

**Important Information:** Most years it is best to wait until July to hike this trail as the snow here sometimes lasts a while. Call the Bozeman Ranger District of the Gallatin National Forest at 406-587-6920 for more information.

# GALLATIN GATEWAY: U.S. HIGHWAY 191

The Gallatin Valley is a particularly beautiful Montana mountain area where U.S. Highway 191 meanders between the prominent Madison and Gallatin Mountains toward Yellowstone National Park. The picturesque landforms on either side of the highway are evidence of volcanic action. These tall spires and rugged cliffs are common to the Gallatin Canyon. The rugged rocks are softened by the greenery of the forests and colorful splashes of plentiful wildflowers in the country Indians called the "land of the flowers."

Though the Gallatin Valley is considered a gateway to Yellowstone National Park, which lies 90 miles south of Bozeman, the Gallatin is a thoroughly enticing destination in its own right. The Gallatin River offers good fishing and exciting whitewater, and there are numerous hikes into the mountains and associated wilderness areas for the adventurous.

Many people have discovered the Gallatin and visit frequently. Others stop on their way to Yellowstone National Park. There are five Forest Service campgrounds along US 191; these are most often full, even past Labor Day. If you plan on camping in the Gallatin come early, have an alternate plan, or make reservations for your campsite with the Forest Service. A first-night prepayment of the $8-per-night camping fee, plus a $4 reservation charge, must be made 10 days in advance if you want to reserve a campsite. Contact the Gallatin Canyon Campgrounds, 406-587-9054, for a reservation.

A diverse and interesting trip can be made by following US 191 south from Interstate 90 at Bozeman through the Gallatin Valley and into the northwest corner of Yellowstone National Park. Heading northwest from the junction with U.S. Highway 287 takes visitors through Ennis and Virginia City (see "Gold West Country") before returning to I-90 west of Bozeman.

For more information about the Gallatin Gateway, contact the Bozeman Chamber of Commerce at 406-586-5421 or 800-228-4224. Much of the valley is on Gallatin National Forest land, managed by the Bozeman Ranger District. Contact the district office at 406-587-6920.

# North Gallatin Valley

Families will find interesting activities to augment fun time in Bozeman or the Gallatin Valley, in the 20 miles of foothills just beyond Bozeman. Between the city and the boundaries of the National Forest and wilderness areas are hot springs, wildlife watching, and the scenic Gallatin River.

## 319. Bozeman Hot Springs

Settle in to a relaxing soak at Bozeman Hot Springs after traveling or hiking. You can pick your preferred water temperature here, as four indoor pools range in temperature from 90 to 106 degrees F and a fifth pool offers a cooling-off temperature of 59 degrees F. An outside pool runs about 94 degrees F in the summer and 100 degrees F in the winter. If you forget your swimsuit or towel, you can rent them at the hot springs, so there's no excuse for not going in!

**Directions:** Take Main Street, which is also U.S. Highway 191, west from Bozeman. Continue west to the junction of Montana Highways 85 and 84, about 6 miles west of the Main Mall. Follow US 191 as it turns left, south, toward the Gallatin Gateway. The hot springs facility is on the right side of the highway about 1.5 miles from the junction.

**Important Information:** The hot springs are open Monday through Thursday from 7 A.M. to 10 P.M., and Friday from 7 A.M. to sunset. The facility is open on Saturday from sunset till midnight in the summer and sunset till 11 P.M. in the winter. Sunday hours are 8 A.M. to 10 P.M., year round. Rates are $5 for adults and kids over age 12, $4 for kids 5 to 11 years old and seniors 60 and over, and $2 for little ones under age 4. There is an MSU student rate of $3 with MSU identification cards. Contact the springs at 406-586-6492.

## 320. Flying D Ranch: Bison Viewing Area

The Flying D Ranch has a long history of cattle and horse ranching, but media mogul Ted Turner, who bought the 130,000-acre ranch in 1980, raises bison there now. He has had as many as 5,000 bison on the ranch. The ranch is not open to the public and there are no guarantees that you'll see Turner's bison herd as you drive along the Spanish Creek Road, but even if you don't, the scenery will be worth the drive.

**Directions:** Take Main Street, U.S. Highway 191, west from Bozeman. Continue west to the junction of Montana Highway 85 and 84, about 6 miles west of the Main Mall. Stay on US 191 as it turns left (south) toward the Gallatin Gateway. After entering Gallatin Canyon, look for the Spanish Creek Road, Forest Road 982, turnoff to the right. This is a public road that winds through the ranch and goes up to the Spanish Creek Picnic Area and trailhead. Spanish Creek Road is 21 miles south of Bozeman.

**Important Information:** Keep in mind that the ranch is private property and you may observe bison from the road only.

## 321. Gallatin River

Here's a river with spirit! The West Gallatin waters converge from the Madison and Gallatin mountains and run a wild course for 90 miles to join the East Gallatin River and then on to the Missouri River confluence with the Madison and Jefferson rivers at Three Forks. The river's passage through the sentinel cliffs of Gallatin Canyon is rough and rowdy. The river was featured in the film, *A River Runs Through It*. This is a whitewater river for experienced floaters only, although there are guided whitewater trips specifically designed for families—an energizing experience to remember! Contact the Bozeman Chamber of Commerce at 406-586-5421 or 800-228-4224 for names of river guides.

As you pass by the river on U.S. Highway 191, take advantage of pullouts where you can observe, and perhaps fish, the Gallatin. The major rapids are in the 15-mile section north of the Big Sky Ski and Summer Resort. One of these, the galloping "House Rock Rapids," is visible from the highway and is a popular river observation location. The Gallatin is a blue-ribbon fishing river that does have its calmer, deep fishin' holes, and there are nearby feeder streams to fish too.

The only section of this river that is floatable by beginners is a 12-mile stretch from the Gallatin Forks Fishing Access Site, where the East and West Gallatin rivers join, to the river's confluence with the Missouri. Take out at the Missouri River Headwaters State Park.

**Directions:** You can get to the Gallatin Forks fishing access site by turning north from Interstate 90 at the town of Manhattan (milepost 288) onto Nixon Gulch Road. Follow Nixon Gulch Road 2 miles north. The access site permits camping and has a canoe launch area. For a longer float, begin at Central Park, a small access site that goes under the Interstate 90 bridge east of Manhattan.

**Important Information:** This is a full-day, 19-mile float.

# Madison and Gallatin Mountains

Like a great stone wall, the Madison and Gallatin ranges extend south from Bozeman through the Yellowstone National Park area. Within these rugged mountains is the particularly spectacular Spanish Peaks Management Area, a unit of the Lee Metcalf Wilderness Area. Going farther south, the narrow valley between the two ranges offers scenic hiking, fishing, and camping opportunities. The Forest Service manages these lands and may be contacted at the Bozeman Ranger District, 406-587-6920, for more information.

## 322. Golden Trout Lakes Trail 83

The lure of golden trout calls you up to this small, but nicely stocked lake in the Gallatin Mountains. There are actually three Golden Trout Lakes, but only the first has any fish. Cutthroat can also be hooked out of this alpine lake.

The 2.5-mile trail to Golden Trout Lakes is an easy to moderate hike with some climbing. The trail is a bit rocky, so when picking family activities, consider both your kids' uphill stamina and their trail tenacity before selecting this trail. The forested trail gains 1,200 feet of elevation. The views here are not as spectacular as some hikes, but, since you can't eat scenery and you can eat trout, this hike might be just the thing for anglers!

**Directions:** Take Main Street, which is also U.S. Highway 191, west from Bozeman. Continue west to the junction of Montana Highways 85 and 84, about 6 miles west of the Main Mall. Stay on US 191 as it turns left (south) toward the Gallatin Gateway. Follow US 191 south of Bozeman for 16 miles to Portal Creek Road. Turn left (east) and follow Portal Creek Road for 6 miles to the parking lot by the trailhead.

**Important Information:** For more information, contact the USDA Forest Service, Bozeman Ranger District, at 406-587-6920.

## 323. South Fork of Spanish Creek Trail 407

A glimpse of the Spanish Peaks provides numerous reasons you might want to hike this trail. The Spanish Peaks Management Area is a unit of the Lee Metcalf Wilderness Area, which is nationally acclaimed for magnificent scenery. Though the lower portions of the South Fork of Spanish Creek Trail don't enter into the wilderness at all, the hike does provide some scenic vistas of these spectacular mountains.

The Spanish Peaks Trail is a 26-mile loop that takes serious hikers to a number of pristine alpine lakes at the edge of the prominent mountains. Fortunately for families, you can hike for a considerable distance along the creek bottom at the beginning of the trail without stressing little ones' hiking capabilities. The first 8 miles is gentle hiking, which is farther than most families would consider going anyway, since you have to go back out, too. The trail follows the wooded creek bottom part of the time and some of the hiking is through open meadow areas. This hike can be a hot one, but there are plenty of access points to the creek where a little water play will cool you down in rising temperatures or allow some fishing time.

**Directions:** Go 21 miles south of Bozeman on U.S. Highway 191. Turn right (west) onto Spanish Creek Road, Forest Road 982. The trailhead and picnic area are located at the end of Spanish Creek Road, 9.5 miles from the highway.

**Important Information:** Bring water or fill water bottles at the picnic area if you plan to hike, as the parasite *Giardia lamblia* may be present in the stream (see page 17). Since the trail can be hot, you will definitely want plenty of water.

This trail is one of the most popular in Montana, so be aware that it can be heavily used, especially on weekends. For more information, contact the USDA Forest Service, Bozeman Ranger District, at 406-587-6920.

# Indian Paintbrush, *Castilleja spp.*

It looks like you could pick these flowers and paint yourself a landscape on canvas with them. The colorful plants are generally about a foot high and have a couple of inches of brilliant color atop them, like a freshly dipped brush. These bright splashes of color range from red to orange to yellow and even white. But the colorful "brushes" aren't really the flowers; they are bracts, or leaves, which look somewhat like petals, especially in these delightful colors. Small green flowers are tucked in between the bracts.

The plant is actually a root parasite, which gathers nutrients from other plants by tapping into the roots of neighboring plants. Look for plants close to the paintbrush, which are probably host plants for the wildflowers.

## 324. Swan Creek Campground and Swan Creek Trail 186

If you're camping at Swan Creek and want a short family outing, or if you just want to take a little hike in the area, the Swan Creek Trail is an easy 2-mile (one-way) hike along the creek bottom. A beaver dam and pond make a fun stop about half a mile up the trail. The rocky trail sometimes goes along the side of the narrow drainage, providing a good view of the creek below. Look for summer flowers here, especially wild roses. There are also plenty of wild berries. The trail ultimately goes to Hyalite Peak.

You will be reminded that this was a logging area as you see some clearcut areas and cross logging roads. For additional adventures, you can follow the logging roads up side drainages.

The Swan Creek Campground has 11 units and potable water.

**Directions:** Go 32 miles south of Bozeman on U.S. Highway 191, then turn left (east) at the sign for the Swan Creek Campground, Forest Road 186, and go 1 mile. Follow the campground road 0.5 mile to the parking area at the end of the road.

**Important Information:** Parts of the trail have been damaged from flooding in 1997, but you can still find the trail.

The campground is open Memorial Day through Labor Day, and there is an $8-per-night camping fee. As this is a high use area, campsites are at a premium. See information on campsite reservations in the Gallatin Gateway description (see page 255). To reserve a campsite, contact the Gallatin Canyon Campgrounds, 406-587-9054.

# 325. Big Sky Ski and Summer Resort

• • • • • • • • • • • • • • • • • • • • • • • • • • • • • • • • • •

The Big Sky Ski and Summer Resort sits peacefully below towering 11,166-foot Lone Peak. The facility is located in the midst of the Madison Range, tucked between two outstanding units of the Lee Metcalf Wilderness Area. The late newscaster and Montana native Chet Huntley purchased the resort with other investors in 1969.

Summer activities at the resort include horseback riding, golfing, mountain biking, hiking, and rock climbing. Guides and equipment are available on site as needed. A lift ride up Lone Peak is an enjoyable way to appreciate the splendid mountain scenery. Winter activities include—you guessed it—skiing. This is one of the finest ski areas in the state.

**Directions:** Take U.S. Highway 191 south of Bozeman for 34 miles to the turnoff for the Big Sky Ski and Summer Resort on the right (west) side of the highway. Drive 9 miles to the Mountain Village Resort, turning left into the resort area.

**Important Information:** For more information, contact the resort office at 406-995-5000 or 800-548-4486.

# 326. Beehive Basin Trail 40

• • • • • • • • • • • • • • • • • • • • • • • • • • • • • • • • • •

Beehive Basin is cradled in the spectacular Spanish Peaks Management Area, a unit of the Lee Metcalf Wilderness Area. The presence of Big Sky Ski and Summer Resort allows hikers to drive to within 4 miles of the basin and hike this delightful trail. The hike takes visitors up the ridge and over the edge into the basin where little Beehive Lake and an alpine meadow can be explored. There are trout in the lake, and when we hiked the trail, we saw a moose in the distance. Look for bighorn sheep and mountain goats on the cliffs above the lake. Wildflowers are numerous and a pleasure to look at along the trail.

The hike goes gradually uphill for most of the way with a short, steep pitch at the basin's edge. The round-trip hike is 8 miles. Despite the distance and uphill sections, the hike is a favorite for families. We saw several kids along the trail and at the lake who were definitely enjoying the day's events.

There are two choices for starting the trail. The lower trailhead makes the hike a 10-mile, round-trip hike. It may be best to start at the upper trailhead, which cuts off a mile of trail each way, so you can get to the lake with less wear and tear.

**Directions:** Take U.S. Highway 191 south of Bozeman for 34 miles to the turnoff for the Big Sky Ski and Summer Resort. Drive 9 miles to the Mountain

Village Resort but don't go into the resort. Instead, turn to the right at the entrance (the resort entrance road goes left over the causeway across a tiny lake). Go 1.1 miles to Moonlight Basin Ranch subdivision and turn right just before the gate. Follow this road for 1.7 miles, staying on the main roadway. The first trailhead parking lot is at the bottom of a steep downhill grade. It is marked with a parking sign. The trail here leads through beautiful wildflowers in season, but is an extra mile farther from the lake than the second trailhead.

To start the hike farther up the trail, continue past the first parking area about a mile. Stay to the left to find this trailhead. There is no trailhead parking area, just wide spots in the road. A pullout right by the trail is located where the road turns to the right and goes up a hill. An additional pullout is located 0.2 mile before this. The trailhead is marked by a mileage sign and leaves from the left side of the road.

**Important Information:** For more information, contact the USDA Forest Service, Bozeman Ranger Station, 406-587-6920.

## 327. Porcupine Creek Trail 34

This easy 4.5-mile loop trail through a creek bottom and along low ridges makes a nice family jaunt. An optional trail can shorten the loop. On the Porcupine Creek Trail you'll go though some dry, open, sagebrush areas that have nice views of the Gallatin Mountains. The area does get some use by folks on horseback, too.

The gravel bars and shallow areas of Porcupine Creek make for fun water play. Look for petrified wood in the creek and along the banks. You'll recognize these strange rocks by the grain and wood rings you can see in them.

**Directions:** Take U.S. Highway 191 south of Bozeman for 34 miles to Big Sky Ski and Summer Resort and drive 2.6 miles beyond the resort. Turn left after the Ophir School and cross the Gallatin River. The trailhead is 0.25 mile past the river.

Walk by the closed gate and, after you pass the last cabin, cross the log bridge over Porcupine Creek to the start of the trail. Take the trail to the right at the trailhead; this is the primary trail that goes into the Porcupine Elk Preserve. Once on the trail, two route options present themselves about 1 mile in.

For the longer route, take either fork at the first Y in the trail. If you stay left, then at the second fork, the left trail, which goes straight ahead, will commit you to the 4.5-mile loop, while the right fork allows you, farther up the trail, to take the longer option or the shortcut.

To take the shorter trail option, stay to the right at either the first or second forks in the trail. The return trail is about a mile up either of these right-hand trails, which join together to make a shorter loop. The connecting point is by a small creek in the meadow. Look across the creek when you get to this point and you will see a post marking the shortcut route back to the trailhead.

**Important Information:** Contact the USDA Forest Service, Bozeman Ranger District, at 406-587-6920, for more information. Because of the high horse usage, there are horse trails leading off from the main trail which may be confusing. Stay on the main trail. Forest Service plans call for improved trail signage in the future.

# THE WEST YELLOWSTONE AND BOULDER RIVER AREA

Here's where the Big Sky begins. As the magnificent mountain ranges of southern Montana give way to the plains here, the ecosystems around Livingston and Big Timber are transformed from timbered mountain forest to drier prairie hills and flatlands. The sky opens up to wide blue expanses and the land turns to golden fields and plains. Yet, Livingston and Big Timber are still fairly close to the mountains. The Absaroka-Beartooth Wilderness Area to the south provides spectacular mountain recreation. However, much of the recreational emphasis in these towns is on the renowned blue-ribbon trout fishing along the Yellowstone and Boulder Rivers and numerous feeder streams. In addition to a variety of natural resources, the active community enthusiastically shares its history, arts, and culture with those who come to explore this part of Big Sky Country.

## Livingston

In the early 1800s, Livingston was a bustling railroad town with a supply store and a locomotive repair shop. Today, serious farming and ranching support the local economy, and the townspeople have developed interesting pastimes. Next to the feed store in Livingston you just may find one of several art galleries featuring fine art, western art, and local and regional art. This town probably has more art galleries per resident than any other town in the West. No doubt, it has more real cowboys, too. The town also claims more restaurants per capita than any other Montana town, so you won't go hungry in Livingston!

One has only to look around to be impressed by the natural setting of the town. The impressive Absaroka-Beartooth Mountains rise to the east, while the equally beautiful Gallatin Range marks the western horizon. Meandering on the edge of town is the Yellowstone River, and not far away, the blue-ribbon Boulder River flows amiably through mountains and prairie lands, luring in avid fly-fishing enthusiasts.

For more information about this intriguing Montana town, contact the Livingston Chamber of Commerce at 406-222-0850. The chamber has a tourist information center located at 208 West Park Street. Here you can find information about the area, including the brochure, *What to Do When Your Spouse Is Fishing*.

## 328. Sacajawea Park

This peaceful city park has all the elements needed to keep kids entertained for a while. The Yellowstone River meanders along the boundary and a small lagoon attracts ducks and geese while offering visitors a place to fish. The park has a covered picnic area, potable water, picnic tables, and barbecue pits. A playground, the city swimming pool, and vault toilets round out family needs. There are also tennis courts and horseshoe pits.

A path along the Yellowstone River has benches for resting while viewing the river. The Livingston Civic Center is also at the park. The indoor scenes from Robert Redford's movie *A River Runs Though It* were filmed in the Civic Center. **Directions:** Take the Yellowstone Park Exit 333 from Interstate 90 and go north into town on U.S. Highway 89. Turn right (south) onto Yellowstone Street, two blocks west of the Depot Center. Take Yellowstone Street five blocks to the park.

**Important Information:** For information, contact the Civic Center at 406-222-8155 or the Livingston Chamber of Commerce at 406-222-0850.

## 329. International Fly Fishing Center

If you want to see what all the fly-fishing fuss is about and find out more about the art of the sport, the International Fly Fishing Center is a good stop. It is the nation's only fly-fishing center, sponsored by the Federation of Fly Fishers. The facility provides information about the how and why of the sport and has interesting exhibits about fish and water ecology.

In the center you'll find live game fish with explanations about fish habits and habitats. A coldwater fish room has a tank of Yellowstone cutthroat trout that blends into an 18-by-17-foot mural of the ecosystem inhabited by these fish. The technically accurate mural was painted by local artist Bob Spannring. There is also a trout-hatching display and additional fish tanks. A warmwater fish room has aquarium displays with bass, sturgeon, and other warmwater fish. The center brings in new exhibits regularly.

Other informative displays feature flies and other fly-fishing tackle, and the history of fly fishing. You can also appreciate angler art, explore the fly-fishing library, or stop by the gift shop. Summer programs and clinics include youth fly-fishing classes, and the center offers free fly-casting instruction a couple evenings a week for those who want some practical know-how. If your kids are into fish (and what kid isn't?), this center will be a delight for you!

**Directions:** Take the Yellowstone Park Exit 333 from Interstate 90 and go north into town on U.S. Highway 89. Turn right (south) onto B Street one block past the Depot Center museum (site 330). Go two blocks on B and turn left (east) onto Lewis Street. The fly-fishing center is in the old school building on the left side of the street at 215 East Lewis.

**Important Information:** Center hours are 10 A.M. to 6 P.M. daily, from June 15 to September 15. The center may actually be open earlier and later in the year, so check it if you come through town before or after these dates. Admission is $3 for adults, $1 for children 7 to 14, and free for kids under 7. For more information, contact the center at 406-222-9369.

## 330. Livingston Depot Center

The old railway depot now holds a historic record of railroading in the Pacific Northwest and Montana. Artifacts and photographs tell the story of the people, jobs, and accomplishments of one of America's most important industries. There are hands-on displays for kids, and a children's mezzanine where kids can actually run a little train. Each summer a different traveling exhibit is displayed.

The Montana Rockies Rail Tours offer Montana tours that go though Livingston and to various points of interest in Montana and Yellowstone National Park.

**Directions:** The depot is located at 200 West Park Street which is right on U.S. Highway 89. Take the Yellowstone Park Exit 333 from Interstate 90 and go into Livingston on US 89. Look for the depot on the left.

**Important Information:** Open daily from late May to the end of September from 9 A.M. to 5 P.M. Monday through Saturday, and 1 to 5 P.M. on Sunday. The museum is also open on the evenings when the tour train is in town. Admission to the museum is $3 for adults, $2 for seniors and children ages 6 to 12, and free for kids under 6. Contact the center at 406-222-2300.

## 331. Park County Museum

This museum features pioneer artifacts, archaeological finds, and displays of Yellowstone National Park early explorers. A real-life, original stagecoach, a caboose from the 1890s, and a covered wagon help define life in early Montana. The facility houses a room of railroad memorabilia and re-created pioneer structures: an old-time schoolhouse, turn-of-the-century rooms, and a blacksmith shop. The archaeology display includes a rendition of a Shoshone bison kill site and camp.

**Directions:** Take the Yellowstone Park Exit 333 from Interstate 90 and go north into town on U.S. Highway 89. Turn left (north) one block east of the Depot Center, at Main Street. This road goes under the train trestle. Go two blocks north and then turn left (west) on Chinook Street. The museum is in this block at 118 West Chinook.

**Important Information:** Museum hours, June 1 through September 1, are from noon to 5 P.M. and 7 to 9 P.M. daily. Contact the museum at 406-222-4184.

## The Western Meadowlark: Singing Montana's Song

Listen carefully! The western meadowlark (*sturnella neglecta*) is singing Montana's song. The bubbly trill of Montana's state bird can be heard around the state in nearly any meadowlike area. Prairies, fields, and pastures are home to the bird with the brown and tan, grassy-looking back. Its bright yellow front has a distinctive black "v" collar. The bird's song is a long call that seems to bubble upwards, joyfully telling prairie stories. The male bird sings this song to warn rivals to stay out of his territory. Protective birds, the females keep their ground nests well hidden. In fact, a female will never fly directly to her nest. Instead, she lands 20 to 50 feet away and walks to the nest! She walks away from it when she leaves, too, before taking flight.

## The Yellowstone River

The *Roche Jaune*, or yellow-rock river, as French trappers called the Yellowstone, is one of Montana's best-loved waterways. The river gets a high degree of respect from anglers and floaters who appreciate the unusual circumstances that led to the river's pristine waters and productive fishing. And the river doesn't lack for scenic beauty, either.

The longest free-flowing river in the lower 48 states, the Yellowstone begins as a mountain stream in a Wyoming wilderness south of Yellowstone National Park. The pristine quality of this river's beginnings keeps the waters clear and pure, leading to a high volume of aquatic "bugs"—and ample trout food! As it flows through the park, the river adds greatly to the visitor's appreciation of this natural wonderland.

From Yellowstone National Park, the rollicking river gains volume and vigor in 20 miles of impressive rapids north of Gardiner. When the mighty river makes the "Big Bend" near Livingston and turns east, the waters begin to slow and flatten out, and the character of the river changes. The trend continues from Livingston to the Yellowstone's confluence with the Missouri River in North Dakota, where the waterway takes on a meandering, lazy-river quality.

The Yellowstone gets worldwide acclaim as an extraordinary fishery, for both high density of fish and large size of the much sought-after trout. Densities as high as 500 trout per 1,000 feet of stream have been determined in the upper section between Gardiner and Livingston. Some of the largest trout ever captured have come from this river. Dan Bailey's Fly Shop in Livingston, at 209 West Park Street, provides proof of dubious fish tales with a "Wall of Fame" where outlines of monster fish can be viewed. Even when the fish change from coldwater to warmwater species around the Laurel-Billings area, the fishing is still applauded.

Wildlife flock to the river as much as people do. Beavers, muskrats, deer, antelope, elk, geese, and a multitude of water birds appreciate the river's habitat and can be seen along its banks. Indians called the Yellowstone the Elk River, and Lewis and Clark were speechless at both the numbers and variety of animal species seen here.

For those who don't fish, the river provides floating experiences that vary from whitewater canyon rafting trips to lazy floats in the meandering sections. Those who wish to experience the spirit of the Yellowstone by floating it can find numerous guides in the Gardiner area. Each year, locals sponsor a public boat float that goes from Livingston 110 miles downstream to Laurel.

Beginners can handle floating the sections below Livingston on their own, although first-time floaters may want to pick a slower river for a maiden voyage. The pamphlet *Montana Afloat #12, The Yellowstone River*, available from the Montana Department of Fish, Wildlife & Parks, provides plentiful information on appropriate float areas. If you choose to float any of the Yellowstone River sections listed here on your own, keep your eyes open for weirs and diversion dams. Be aware, too, that if the wind decides to blow upstream, any of these floats could become hard work.

## 332. Mayor's Landing to Sheep Mountain Fishing Access Site Float

This is an enjoyable 10-mile, half-day float. The river can run 3 or 4 miles per hour on this stretch though there are no rapids. Be aware that the river, especially early in the season when water is high, is braided and may have multiple channels. Keep your eyes open for downed trees.

**Directions:** Mayor's Landing is in Livingston. From Depot Center (site 330), on U.S. Highway 89, Park Street, go east for about a mile. Then turn right onto H Street and go south 0.5 mile to the county fairgrounds. Turn left at the T intersection and you will be at the river access in 0.5 mile. The landing has toilets and a picnic area.

## 333. Sheep Mountain Fishing Access Site to Springdale Bridge Float

This is a pleasant 10-mile Yellowstone float that will be 3 to 4 hours to Springdale Bridge, depending on the time of year and water levels.

**Directions:** The Sheep Mountain Fishing Access Site can be reached by going 4 miles east of Livingston on Interstate 90. Take the exit at milepost 340 and go north on U.S. Highway 89 for 2 miles. After you cross the river on the US 89 bridge, you will come to a signed gravel road. Turn right (east) and follow this road for about 4 miles. This site has toilets and camping.

## 334. Springdale Bridge to Gray Bear Fishing Access Site Float

This is a nice family float. The 8- or 9-mile stretch is somewhat slower than the other segments mentioned here and would take three to four hours of floating time.

**Directions:** To find the Springdale Bridge take Interstate 90 from Livingston and drive for 22 miles, heading east. Take the Springdale Exit. Then go north 1 mile on a county road toward the Springdale Bridge. To find the Gray Bear Fishing Access Site, go 5 miles west of Livingston on the north frontage, then turn right (north) at the gravel road, signed for Gray Bear. Go 0.4 mile and turn left onto a sandy road into the access site. At Gray Bear there is a campground, toilets, and potable water. The boat ramp is on the opposite side of the road from the campground.

# Big Timber

When Lewis and Clark came through this part of Montana, William Clark was impressed with the immense size of the cottonwood trees lining the banks of the Yellowstone River. Big Timber received its name from William Clark in appreciation of these trees.

Big Timber is cattle country today and has one of the largest Norwegian settlements in Montana. A visitor center is located on the west end of town on old U.S. Highway 10 at the Interstate 90 interchange off of Exit 367. For more information about the area, contact the Big Timber Chamber of Commerce at 406-932-5131.

## 335. Crazy Mountains Museum

The museum features historical exhibits of Sweet Grass County and the surrounding area. A special display at the museum is a model of Big Timber as it stood in 1907. The replica contains 184 buildings and took 6 years to research and build. Other exhibits feature information about rodeos, a sheep and wool industry display, a pioneer memorial display, and an exhibit depicting the effects of a fire that destroyed a third of the town in 1908. There is also a Norwegian storehouse, called a *stabbur*. These traditional Norwegian buildings have sod roofs that often grow flowers and even small trees. A pioneer schoolhouse is under construction.

**Directions:** To reach the museum, take the Big Timber Exit 367 from Interstate 90. Turn left at the stop sign just off the exit and take another immediate left onto the cemetery road. The museum is on this road.

**Important Information:** The museum is open Memorial Day to Labor Day, from 1 to 4:30 P.M., Tuesday through Sunday. Closed Monday. There is no admission fee but donations are accepted. Contact the museum at 406-932-5126.

## 336. Lion's Club Park

This shady picnic area also houses the town swimming pool.

**Directions:** Exit Interstate 90 at either Big Timber exit and go through town on U.S. Highway 191. Turn south on McLeod Street. The park is on McLeod and East 8th Avenue.

**Important Information:** The pool is generally open from 1 to 4 P.M. The pool is open for some evening swims, too. Contact the Big Timber Chamber of Commerce, 406-932-5131, for specific hours.

## 337. Yellowstone River Trout Hatchery

Here's where many of Montana's famous Yellowstone cutthroat trout come from. Visitors are welcome to stop by this small hatchery during normal business hours and the manager will show you around.

**Directions:** Exit from Interstate 90 at one of the two Big Timber exits and go through town on U.S. Highway 191. Turn north on McLeod Street and cross the tracks. Continue on McLeod down a short, steep hill and on your left is the trout hatchery.

**Important Information:** The hatchery business hours are 8 A.M. to 4:30 P.M., seven days a week. The hatchery is closed daily for lunch between 12 P.M. and 12:30 P.M. For more information, contact the hatchery at 406-932-4434.

# What Makes the Crazy Mountains So Crazy?

Once you've been into these mountains, you might think the reason for the name is that you're crazy if you don't go into this area. Certainly this is beautiful country, and having been there once, you'll be crazy about going back. But there are other theories about why these mountains might be crazy.

Geologists think these mountains are crazy because they haven't been able to explain the geologic history to their satisfaction. There was a lava upthrust in recent (geologically speaking) years that created some of the mountain formations. But other, older rocks tell another story that doesn't seem to jibe with the rest of the picture. It's crazy.

Indian artifacts from the mountains date back some 11,500 years. The Crow and Shoshone Indians inhabited the area most recently and the Crow called this range the "Blue Bird Mountains." One theory says that Indians gave the peaks the name "Mad Mountains" because of the crazy sound made by the haunting winds that blow down through the steep canyon walls.

Local folklore tells a story of a pioneer family that stopped along the Musselshell River for wagon repairs and decided to stay and rest a bit. Unfortunately, a group of Blackfeet braves came upon the family and killed all but the mother, who, upon finding the grisly massacre scene, went crazy and managed to kill four of the Indians with an ax before the rest took off. They say she never left the area and never quite returned to her senses. When she died, local Crow Indians buried her near her loved ones. Some say that the Crazy Mountains were named for this poor woman who went crazy from her grief.

## 338. Half Moon Campground and Upper Big Timber Falls

If you are crazy about mountains, the Half Moon Campground in the Crazy Mountains is a place you'll be glad you visited. The campground is located up Big Timber Canyon, and serves as a trailhead area for backpackers headed up into the glacier-sculpted peaks. Though most backcountry trails in the Crazies are fairly difficult hiking, families can go along the Big Timber Canyon Trail about a half a mile to this pretty cascading waterfall on Big Timber Creek. This is a great family hike. The campground has eight sites, toilets, and potable water. There's fishing here, too.

**Directions:** Take U.S. Highway 89 north of Interstate 90 and Big Timber. Go 11 miles on US 89, then turn west on Big Timber Canyon Road and go 12 miles to the campground. The Big Timber Canyon Trail begins at the campground.

**Important Information:** The road access to Half Moon Campground crosses a considerable amount of private land. It is essential that visitors be respectful of private landowners and be careful not to trespass. This is a sensitive issue in the Crazy Mountains.

The campground does not have a good turn-around site or adequate parking for motor homes. However, the campground will be going through renovations, and improvements will make this area more accessible to RVs. You may want to call the Forest Service before going into the area, due to possible closures during renovation. Contact the USDA Forest Service at the Big Timber District Office, 406-932-5155.

## 339. Greycliff Prairie Dog Town State Park

This town is home of the black-tailed prairie dog and at this Watchable Wildlife site, you have an opportunity to watch these furry little critters in their natural habitat. The Montana Department of Fish, Wildlife & Parks provides interpretive information about prairie dog lifestyles at the site. Look for western meadowlarks, western bluebirds, and hawks here, too.

There is a picnic area with wind shelters at the site. Restrooms are 1 mile east. The Big Timber Waterslide (site 340) is 1 mile away.

**Directions:** Take Interstate 90 to the Greycliff Exit 377, about 7 miles east of Big Timber. The state park is only 0.1 mile from the exit and is signed.

**Important Information:** There is a self-pay user fee of $4 per vehicle or $1 per person, whichever is less. For more information, contact the Montana Department of Fish, Wildlife & Parks in Billings at 406-247-2940.

# Prairie Dog Talk (and Walk)

If you've ever wanted to be able to understand animals, these cute little fellas are a good place to start. Since the furry little critters make a tasty meal for a number of mammals and raptors, communication is an essential survival tactic for prairie dogs (*Cynomys ludovicianus*). Consequently, one of the most important prairie dog body language messages is the danger posture. When the prairie dogs sense danger, they lift their heads high and hold very still, sometimes standing on their hind legs to check out the scene. Another important body language message is the greeting ceremony between prairie dogs from the same family. In this gesture, the dogs touch teeth, an act which is usually followed by a considerable amount of mutual grooming. The dogs have 11 different auditory messages, too. A short, nasal *yip* indicates a danger call while *whee-oo* means the coast is clear.

The dogs are just about as elaborate in their homebuilding, too. Neat little critters, prairie dogs build a burrow that has different chambers for different purposes, including a separate toilet room! A listening room is at the top of the burrow so the dogs can listen for safety signals before coming out in the open. Each burrow may have 15 to 40 entrances per acre with tunnels from 15 to 25 feet long between them. The burrow entrances have mounds of excavated soil around them which can be 2 feet high, providing a great lookout.

Ranchers don't like the dangerous holes the dogs leave, or the little animals' voracious appetite for food that livestock eat, too. However, some areas have been set aside to protect these social creatures. The black-tailed dog, found at Greycliff Prairie Dog Town State Park, is the most common of the five North American prairie dog species.

## 340. Big Timber Waterslide

After a day of summer hiking or traveling in the car, a pool can look pretty good, and a pool with a waterslide looks even better. The Big Timber Waterslide has several slides, a rapids ride, a junior Olympic-sized pool, and a kiddie pool. There is a picnic area and deli too. Next door is a KOA Campground with shaded sites, a pool and hot tub, a playground, and nightly hayrides. KOA campers get a waterslide entrance discount.

**Directions:** Take Exit 377 from Interstate 90, 7 miles east of Big Timber. The waterslides are visible from the Interstate. A mile west is the Greycliff Prairie Dog Town State Park (site 339).

**Important Information:** The waterslide is open from early June through Labor Day, 10 A.M. to 7 P.M. every day, weather permitting. There is an admission charge. For more information contact 406-932-6570.

# Boulder River Valley

The Boulder River Valley, known for its good fishing, has six campgrounds with easy fishing access. The river begins in the Absaroka-Beartooth Wilderness, a 906,000-acre wilderness made up of two mountain ranges which parallel one another. The Absaroka Range is steep, with forested valleys and craggy peaks, while the Beartooth Mountains have high plateaus and numerous lakes. The biggest mountains in Montana are in this wilderness, including the state's highest mountain, Granite Peak, at 12,799 feet. The Boulder River campgrounds provide access to some of these wilderness areas via backcountry trails. Be aware that these areas have both grizzly and black bears (see page 14).

While families may not want to scale the steep peaks in this area, it is possible for kids to thoroughly enjoy fishing on the river and hiking some of the lower elevation trails, and they will appreciate the pristine environment.

As you drive through the valley, look for the Baby's Face rock formation about 23 miles south of Big Timber on the west side of U.S. Highway 289.

## 341. Big Rock Fishing Access Site

If you just want to get out on the Boulder River and fish, or want a place to walk along the river, this fishing access site will work well. The site has toilets, but no water. People are allowed to camp here. A roadway follows the river for about a half a mile.

**Directions:** Exit Interstate 90 at Exit 367 and go through Big Timber on U.S. Highway 191. Turn south on the Boulder River Road about 3.5 miles from the edge of town. You will cross the river on a bridge just after you turn. At the opposite side of the bridge turn right into the access area.

**Important Information:** For more information contact the Montana Department of Fish, Wildlife & Parks office in Billings at 406-247-2940.

## 342. Spring Creek Camp and Trout Ranch

Here is an easy way to appreciate fishing around Big Timber. This private recreation area is fully set up with stocked trout ponds and access to the Boulder River. You can rent cabins or camp, and there are RV hookups.

**Directions:** Exit Interstate 90 at one of the two Big Timber exits and go through town on U.S. Highway 191. Turn south onto the main street of town, McLeod Street, which later becomes Montana Highway 298. There is a sign at the turn from US 191 indicating that this is where to turn if you wish to get to the town of McLeod. From the edge of town, the camp is about 2.5 miles. Turn left at the sign for Spring Creek Camp and go to the end of the road.

**Important Information:** For more information, call 406-932-4387.

## 343. McLeod Road Kill Cafe

This is a restaurant with a Montana sense of humor. Road kill, or critters hit by cars, are unfortunately a common roadway sight in Montana. The Road Kill Cafe motto, "from your grill to ours" states one obvious solution to wasted road kill. Fortunately they aren't serious, but the menu is funny and they do have great lunches.

The cafe is a bit out of town, but since it is on the way to the Natural Bridge Picnic Area (site 346), it can be an interesting stop as part of an outing to the natural bridge. Check out the restaurant's fun T-shirts, too.

**Directions:** Take either of the two Interstate 90 exits to Big Timber and drive into town on U.S. Highway 191. Go south onto the main street of town, McLeod Street, which later becomes Montana Highway 298. There is a sign at the turn from US 191 indicating that this is where to turn if you wish to get to the town of McLeod. Follow the road for 16 miles. The restaurant is on the left.

**Important information:** Hours for this cafe vary considerably, but it is generally open for lunch from Memorial Day to Labor Day at noon. Closing hours have been described as "whenever," meaning they close when everybody's gone. Hours the rest of the year vary even more. Call ahead to make sure they are open, at 406-932-6174.

## 344. East Fork Boulder River Trail 27

If you're after some fishin' on the Boulder River, you can add a little hiking and walk 3.5 miles up the East Fork trail to a bridge that crosses the trout-filled stream. There is a picnic area at the log bridge, which many day hikers make their destination. This trail is a gradual uphill climb that starts on what used to be an old wagon road. This is a hiking and horse trail only as the trail enters the Absaroka-Beartooth Wilderness in about a half a mile from the trailhead. Ultimately, this trail goes to the Lake Plateau, an alpine plateau dotted with lakes. The trail gets a fair amount of use.

**Directions:** Take either of the two Big Timber exits from Interstate 90 and go into town on U.S. Highway 191. Turn south onto the main street, McLeod Street, which later becomes Montana Highway 298. There is a sign at the turn from US 191 indicating that this is where to turn if you wish to get to the town of McLeod. Stay on MT 298 for 19 miles, then turn left onto the East Boulder Road. From here, the Box Canyon Trailhead, where Trail 27 starts, is 6 miles farther on the bumpy gravel road. The trailhead is past the Ricks Park Campground and Upsidedown Creek Trailhead and is well signed.
**Important Information:** There is no gas along the way, so fill up before you leave town. Be careful about trespassing in this area as a part of the trail does go through private land.

Follow the suggested bear precautions (see page 14) as this area has grizzly bears. Be aware of the presence of the parasite *Giardia lamblia* in the river and bring your own drinking water. When hiking, be sure to bring warm clothing as mountain weather changes quickly.

Contact the USDA Forest Service, Big Timber Ranger District, at 406-932-5155, for more information.

## 345. West Boulder Campground and West Boulder Trail 41

• • • • • • • • • • • • • • • • • • • • • • • • • • • • • • • • •

This easy trail is a relatively gentle grade that ultimately goes 16 miles to Mill Creek Pass. The trail gets high use on the lower section, and is a cattle-grazing area so you may share the trail with cows, too. The trail pretty much follows the river but don't start fishing until you reach the wilderness boundary sign, as some of the land before this is private property.

The West Boulder Campground has ten sites, a vault toilet, and potable water. The West Boulder Cabin, a Forest Service rental, is here and can be reserved by contacting the Forest Service.
**Directions:** From either of the Big Timber exits off Interstate 90, take U.S. Highway 191 into town. Turn south onto the main street of town, McLeod Street, which later becomes Montana Highway 298. There is a sign at the turn from US 191 indicating that this is where to turn if you wish to get to the town of McLeod. Go 16 miles south of Big Timber on this road toward McLeod, then turn right onto Sweetgrass County 35 and go 6.5 miles west. Stay left at the next major road fork and go 8 miles farther on West Boulder Road to the signed campground turn. To get to the trailhead, continue straight at the campground entrance, rather than turning into the campground. You will see the signed trailhead in a few hundred feet.
**Important Information:** There is no gas along the way, so fill up before you leave town. The trail can be wet and boggy in sections.

Follow the suggested bear precautions (see page 14), as this area has grizzly bears. Be aware of the presence of the parasite *Giardia lamblia* in the river and bring your own drinking water. When hiking, be sure to bring warm clothing as mountain weather changes quickly. For more information, contact the USDA Forest Service, Big Timber Ranger District, at 406-932-5155.

## 346. Natural Bridge Falls and Picnic Area

The Boulder River makes an impressive falls over 100-foot cliffs at this picnic area. When the water is low, the river seems to disappear as it flows underneath the limestone and comes back out through a hole in the cliff, cascading 80 feet to the water below. The natural rock bridge that once spanned the river tumbled down in 1988 and is no longer visible.

An asphalt trail leads from the parking area to an overlook near the cliff's edge. Short spur trails from here allow visitors to explore the area. Interpretive signs provide information about the park's natural features. Be careful to hang on to small children and dogs as the cliffs are steep throughout the park. Across a foot bridge over the river is the Green Mountain Trail, a moderately difficult hike that heads up into the mountains.

Picnic facilities and toilets are available and there are two campgrounds up the road, Falls Creek and Aspen campgrounds. These are located just outside the boundaries of the Absaroka-Beartooth Wilderness. Both campgrounds have eight units, toilets, and potable water.

**Directions:** Take either of the two Big Timber exits from Interstate 90 and drive into town in U.S. Highway 191. Turn south onto the main street of town, McLeod Street, which later becomes Montana Highway 298. There is a sign at the turn from US 191 indicating that this is where to turn if you wish to get to the town of McLeod. The Natural Bridge Picnic Area is 27 miles south on MT 298.

**Important Information:** Follow the suggested bear precautions (see page 14), as this area has grizzly bears. Be aware of the possible presence of the parasite *Giardia lamblia* in the river and bring your own drinking water. When hiking, be sure to bring warm clothing as mountain weather changes quickly. For more information, contact the USDA Forest Service, Big Timber Ranger District, at 406-932-5155.

**Paradise Valley**
Dailey Lake
Chico Hot Springs
Spring Creek Hatchery
Pine Creek Trail
Gallatin Petrified Forest

**US. Highway 89 North of Livingston**
Cottonwood Reservoir
Shields River

**Columbus**
Itch-kep-pe Park
Museum of the Beartooths
Halfbreed National Wildlife Refuge
Hailstone National Wildlife Refuge

**Red Lodge**
Carbon County Historical Museum
Meeteetse Trail
Crazy Creek
Beartooth Nature Center
Cooney State Park
Broadwater Lake

**Beartooth Mountains**
Sioux Charley Lake
East Rosebud Lake
Elk Lake
Slough Lake
Mystic Lake
Beauty Lake

**Cooke City**
Lady of the Lake
Rock Island Lake

# MISSOURI RIVER COUNTRY

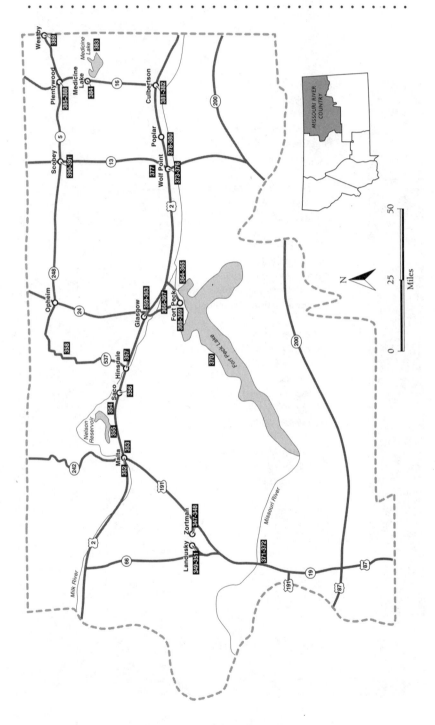

# Missouri River Country

Missouri River Country is a great place to learn about the legends of the West. This is truly Big Sky Country, and the people who inhabit its harsh landscape have a strong sense of community and of the past. When you visit the small towns and wide open spaces of Missouri River Country, be sure to see a rodeo or powwow—an easy task in this area since both are plentiful here. Cowboys still ride the range in this timeless prarieland, and the history of the pioneers who settled this region is on display in the many area museums. Both the Sioux and Assiniboine Indian Tribes inhabit this region, and their presence gives an opportunity to glimpse the culture of Montana's native peoples.

## THE LITTLE ROCKIES

The Little Rockies rise from the plains at the southern edge of what is today the Fort Belknap Indian Reservation. The mountains have held many secrets in the past, from hiding renegades like Kid Curry and his gang to hiding a great wealth of gold beneath their rugged surface. Despite the intensive mining in parts of the Little Rockies, there is still much to appreciate here and you can even try your hand at a little gold panning, too.

### The Zortman-Landusky Area

The little towns of Zortman and Landusky grew up in the early 1900s around the Ruby Mine, at one time the second largest producer of gold in Montana. From 1904 to 1920, when the mine burned, it produced 5 million dollars in gold. The small towns and surrounding area make interesting territory for exploration. Though they are officially considered ghost towns, Zortman actually has some thriving businesses. You can try your hand at panning for gold here and also get an enlightened perspective on the environmental costs of mining. The gold-mining companies that once thrived here, but are not currently in operation, used a cyanide-leaching method of mining in which cyanide is poured over rocks containing gold flakes. The cyanide leaches out the small flecks of gold, but the waste water from the process contaminates both the creeks and groundwater. If you explore the area near the town of Landusky you will see beautiful, clear streams with signs warning visitors not to drink or get in the water. You can also see how the mine has eaten up the mountain. It's an easy place to explore and you will find interesting rock formations in these pretty mountains.

## 347. Zortman

This town is listed in some sources as a ghost town, but we saw a lot more people there than ghosts. The mining industry was active here in recent years, but the mines are closed now, and even the roads to the large Ruby Mine have been blocked. However, gold panning can be done safely in area streams. The Zortman Garage and Motel rents pans, explains how to use them, and provides directions to area sites. They can tell you how to find the town's old school, the church, and the old jail, too. The view from the church is impressive and worth the climb up the hill.

Other local excursions include a picnic at Buffington Picnic Area, camping at the Camp Creek Campground (site 348), and taking a look through the old Zortman cemetery. Numerous crosses and worn headstones are reminders of pre-1900s Zortman. Nearby, on the Fort Belknap reservation, is an interesting land feature, a natural bridge, and an old mission building.

**Directions:** From Malta, take U.S. Highway 191 southwest for 48 miles, then turn right (north) onto a paved county road signed for Zortman. Go 7 miles up this road, then turn left into town at a paved crossroads. The Zortman Garage and Motel is on this road, which goes through the town. To reach the cemetery, go straight at the paved crossroads instead of turning left into town, then turn left onto a grassy road 0.2 mile from the crossroads. The cemetery is 0.3 mile down this dirt road.

**Important Information:** The town has a small store. John and Candy Kalal operate the Zortman Garage and Motel; you can reach them at 406-673-3160, or see them at http://www.huntersmall.com/zort.htm on the Internet.

## 348. Camp Creek Campground and Buffington Picnic Area

Camp Creek is a pleasant campground in a pretty mountain setting. It provides a good base for exploring Zortman and the nearby area. Here you will find picnic tables, restrooms, and tent sites. Buffington Picnic Area has picnic tables, shelters, water, fire pits, and vault toilets.

**Directions:** From U.S. Highway 191, take the Zortman turn and drive north about 6 miles on the paved road. At the paved crossroads where the road goes left to the town of Zortman, go straight and continue 1.5 miles to the campground and picnic area.

**Important Information:** Fee for camping is $5 per night. For general information about the campground and picnic area, contact the U.S. Bureau of Land Management at the Malta Resource Area office at 406-654-1240.

## 349. Landusky

This historic ghost town has several old buildings and some inhabited houses and cabins. There are no conveniences or commercial enterprises here. Nearby is the Montana Gulch Campground (site 350) and the Landusky Cemetery (site 351).

**Directions:** To reach the town, take U.S. Highway 191 south 55 miles from Malta to the junction with Montana Highway 66. Go north and watch for the graveled road which turns to the right (east). Follow this road all the way to Landusky, about 5 or 6 miles.

**Important Information:** Keep in mind that the town is private land and visitors need to be respectful of property rights.

## 350. Montana Gulch Campground

This primitive campground is in a pretty woodland area along a creek. There are grills, picnic tables, and vault toilets, but the water is not potable, so bring your own.

# Kid Curry and Pike Landusky

The notorious outlaw Curry brothers lived in the Little Rocky Mountains and surrounding area for somewhere between 10 and 15 years in the 1880s and 1890s. They were well known in the mining camps here, and the feisty outlaws could lay claim to a variety of shenanigans. Once they decided to play pool in a local saloon while still on horseback. One horse broke through the floor, dropping both horse and rider into the cellar. Then one Christmas, at a Landusky dance, they got a little out of hand and shot up the town, including the piano. The Curry brothers' escapades came to a head after Kid Curry shot and killed a saloon keeper named Pike Landusky. The Kid and his family band reportedly left the area after the murder, though some folks said they did see him again in town. The Curry brothers eventually topped off their activities with a daring train robbery which earned them about $30,000 in unsigned currency.

**Directions:** Take Montana Highway 66 north from U.S. Highway 191, 55 miles south of Malta. Turn right toward Landusky and the campground road will be on the left-hand side of the road. It is signed.

**Important Information:** Contact the U.S. Bureau of Land Management at the Malta Resource Area office at 406-654-1240.

### 351. Landusky Cemetery

The Landusky cemetery reportedly holds the graves of notorious outlaw Kid Curry's brother John, and Pike Landusky, the rough character for whom the town is named. We couldn't find either of these graves, but the cemetery was still interesting to walk through.

**Directions:** Take the Montana Gulch Campground road (see site 350) and head toward the campground. Before you reach the campground you will see another dirt road turn off to the left. There is a cattleguard and fence here. This is the road to the cemetery. It is unsigned but is the dirt road closest to the campground turnoff. You can also reach the cemetery from the campground by walking along the campground road and looking toward the fields at the edge of the campground. From there you can see some of the headstones in the open areas.

# THE HI-LINE: MALTA TO GLASGOW

Nicknamed the "Hi-Line," U.S. Highway 2 spans the width of Montana, parallel to the Great Northern Railroad, which gave birth to many of the towns along the route. The highway rolls through mile after mile of plains, with small towns dotting the open landscape. The townspeople here have a strong sense of community, bonding together to withstand the challenges of living in this landscape. You'll find that northeastern Montana is about Big Sky prairie and tough-spirited people.

## Malta

This railway town is located at the crossroads of U.S. Highway 2 and U.S. Highway 191. It was once the cowboy entertainment capital of the region. For more information about this community, contact the Malta Chamber of Commerce at 406-654-1776.

## 352. Phillips County Museum

The museum, in a building which once served the community as a library and is now on the National Register of Historic Places, chronicles the development of Malta from the time it was Siding 54 on the Great Northern Railroad to the present. Other exhibits of interest are the dinosaur display, a special Civil War weapons section, and Indian artifacts.

**Directions:** The address of the museum is 133 1st Street West. Most anyone can point it out to you.

**Important Information:** Open from 10 A.M. to noon and 1 to 5 P.M., Tuesday through Saturday, from Memorial Day to Labor Day. Contact the museum at 406-654-1037.

# The Sleeping Buffalo Area

On the crest of a ridge near a place where the Cree Indians frequently crossed the Milk River, a herd of buffalo appears to rest quietly—only they never seem to move! The "herd" is really a group of glacial boulders that from a distance resembles a group of sleeping buffalo. A prehistoric sculptor tried to further the resemblance to bison with crude carvings on the boulder at the Sleeping Buffalo Rock National Historic Monument, near the Sleeping Buffalo Resort turnoff on U.S. Highway 2. An interpretive sign explains that the Sleeping Buffalo boulders were held sacred by the Indians. Long before the white settlers moved into the area, the natives sacrificed possessions to the Sleeping Buffalo Rock. Located in this area now is a hot springs resort as well as an undeveloped campground area by Nelson Reservoir. Not far away is the Bowdoin National Wildlife Refuge.

## 353. Bowdoin National Wildlife Refuge

This wildlife refuge is in the central flyway of waterfowl migration from Canada to Mexico and is a great place to watch the multitude of birds that pass overhead and pause here during their travels. The 15,500-acre Bowdoin National Wildlife Refuge accommodates more than 200 different varieties of birds. Every year more than 100,000 ducks alone migrate through the refuge. White pelicans, terns, gulls, cormorants, and blue herons nest at Bowdoin, some flocking there by the hundreds. Visitors may also see ibis, black-crowned herons, bitterns, grebes, and various mammals. The best bird-viewing seasons are early fall or late spring. Early morning and dusk are the most likely times of day to catch sight of four-footed wildlife. But you're guaranteed to see birds here at any time of day.

The refuge is a pleasant canoeing spot and there is a boat ramp located just north of the headquarters building. Beyond this building, on the right, is a short trail leading to Strater Pond, a good place to see birds at midday. The trail is actually an old service road and is marked as such. There is another short trail around a pond across from the headquarters building. This pond is on your right as you come in the refuge entrance, and there are nearly always ducks and other waterfowl enjoying it.

A self-guided auto tour encircles Lake Bowdoin and is open at all times, except when weather creates poor driving conditions. A brochure for the 15-mile auto tour and a bird list are available at the office, where the auto tour begins. There are 11 stops along the route, including a tepee ring at stop 4. Here, the ring of rocks still remains where Indians placed stones around the edges of the tepee to keep them down. There is a good view of the refuge from this site, too.

**Directions:** There are two entry points for the refuge. Take U.S. Highway 2 from Malta and go 1 mile east. Turn right (south) at the signed blacktop road. Follow the blacktop about 6 miles from US 2. After the initial turn the road will bend eastward. Stay on blacktop road all the way to the refuge. At the refuge boundary you will cross a cattleguard.

An alternate route to the refuge begins by turning south off US 2 just west of Sleeping Buffalo Hot Springs. Just west of the hot springs is a hill. The signed gravel road to the refuge is immediately to the left at the crest of the hill, so be watching for it. Follow the gravel road 2 miles and turn right at the Bowdoin sign. The refuge is 9 miles from this turn.

**Important Information:** The refuge is open from dawn to dusk. Restrooms are open at all times. No camping or fires are allowed. For information, contact the refuge at 406-654-2863.

## 354. Sleeping Buffalo Hot Springs

You might be surprised to find these hot springs out on the high plains, but it is a pleasant discovery. There are three pools here, including one at 106 degrees F. A water slide makes the outdoor pool even more exciting for kids of all ages. The high mineral content of the water is purported to be healthful for skin disorders, gastric disorders, ulcers, and other maladies.

The resort also has cabins for rent, camping, golfing, fishing, dancing, a lounge, a picnic area, and laundry facilities. Though not a luxury resort, the facilities are clean and adequate and a dip in the pools is a treat. Butte native Robbie Knievel, son of daredevil Evil Knievel, once flew over 20 covered wagons on his motorcycle here—a distance of 125 feet.

**Directions:** Take U.S. Highway 2 east out of Malta for 17 miles or west out of Saco for 11 miles. Turn north around mile marker 489 at the sign for the resort. It is 1 mile to the resort.

**Important Information:** Cost for using the pools is $2 for children ages 1 to 5, $4 for kids 6 to 11, and $5 for everyone 12 and over. The water slide is $4 extra per person. The resort is open year-round. Pools are open from 8 A.M. to 10 P.M. in the summer. Winter pool hours are 9 A.M. to 9 P.M. weekdays, and to 10 P.M. on weekends. Call 406-527-3370 for information.

## 355. Nelson Reservoir Fishing Access Site

This irrigation reservoir offers locals and visitors a chance to camp, fish, swim, or picnic in a prairie setting. The warm waters and sandy beach provide a place to enjoy a swim on a hot day. Chances of seeing waterfowl are excellent. Anglers find the fishing for sauger, pike, walleye, and perch rewarding. This is a low-maintenance primitive area that has a minimum of facilities: toilets, picnic tables, and a boat ramp.

**Directions:** The reservoir is off of U.S. Highway 2, 17 miles east of Malta. Turn north at the sign for the reservoir and Sleeping Buffalo Hot Springs around mile marker 489. It is 1.5 miles to the reservoir. Take the first left past the first cattleguard you come to after the resort.

**Important Information:** Contact the Montana Department of Fish, Wildlife & Parks at 406-228-9347 for information.

## 356. Huntley School

The late, renowned newscaster Chet Huntley actually went to school as a kid in this one-room schoolhouse at Saco. The building has been restored and is open to the public.

**Directions:** The schoolhouse is on U.S. Highway 2, at the east end of the town of Saco.

**Important Information:** The school is open from Memorial Day to Labor Day. Hours vary. Contact the Saco Chamber of Commerce for more information, 406-527-3312.

# Hinsdale

Nestled by the winding Milk River among cottonwoods and willows is the town of Hinsdale. The shady greenery is enjoyed not only by the town's population, but also by the large number of mule deer, white-tailed deer, and other wild game that roam from Hinsdale through the prairies north to Canada. The town celebrates Milk River Days every Fourth of July with one of the best rodeos in northeastern Montana.

## 357. Hinsdale Park on the Milk River

Here's a chance to play by the slow-moving Milk River. This park has a campground, electrical hookups, a picnic shelter, tables, barbecue grills, restrooms, and boat ramp. In the summer there is a dock by the boat ramp. The park is a favorite swimming place for locals. The bank is somewhat steep and the water would be over the heads of little ones, so bring life jackets for them. Many people boat from here to Vandalia Dam, 7 miles downstream. Canoeing is possible, although you'd want to watch out for all the water-skiers! (It's true—people water-ski on the Milk River.) Look for deer, beavers, and birds, especially great blue herons, along the river. There are also large concentrations of waterfowl during migration seasons. Fishing is pretty good here, too.

**Directions:** To get to the Hinsdale Park on the Milk River, turn into Hinsdale from U.S. Highway 2 on Montana Street. Go straight to the end of the street, turn right, and then take the first left. The park is by the school yard.

**Important Information:** Watch your kids if they go in the river as there are no lifeguards here. Also, watch for mosquitoes, as they seem to like the Milk River, too, and can be found here in good numbers during June and July. The river can run high during spring runoff. There is no fee for camping, though there is a fee for power.

# The Milk River

The murky water of the Milk River prompted Lewis and Clark to give it its descriptive name. The color can be attributed to the heavy sediment load of fine sand the winding river picks up in the 100-mile stretch that flows through Canada. Locals joke that the water is so thick during the spring runoff that you can walk across it. The river does offer good fishing. In fact, the Milk hosts 42 species of fish, including walleye, sauger, catfish, northern pike, and the highly unusual paddlefish. The stretch of river from Dodson to Vandalia Dam is listed by the Montana Department of Fish, Wildlife & Parks as one of the best walleye streams in the state.

# 358. Bitter Creek Badlands

There are no trails here but the open-country hiking is easy and there is little chance of getting lost. This is a designated wildlife viewing area. Watch especially for sharp-tailed and sage grouse.

**Directions:** Drive west of Glasgow on U.S. Highway 2 and turn north on Britsch Road, opposite Vandalia Road, about 5 miles west of Hinsdale. Follow graveled Britsch Road north for 17 miles. You will see signs for the wildlife viewing area. Park to the side of the road.

**Important Information:** Take along plenty of water, and in the summer months plan to hike early in the day to avoid the hot sun. The road is impassable when wet. Call the Glasgow office of the U.S. Bureau of Land Management, 406-228-4316, for information.

# Glasgow

This town was born along the tracks of the Great Northern Railroad in 1887. It was named after Glasgow, Scotland, by the numerous Scots that came to work on the railroad. As you come into town from the west, watch for the large sculptures on the left. You'll see more than one dinosaur, a bear, a coyote, and an eagle. The sculptures were locally hand-crafted by Buck Samuelson and donated to the community.

If you've ever wondered what people do here in the winter, one guess would be that they play a popular card game called whist—just as residents have since the homesteading days. Glasgow claims to be the whist capital of the world, bringing in international contestants for a two-day tournament in November and also in late January. For more information about Glasgow, contact the Chamber of Commerce at 406-228-2222.

## 359. Valley County Pioneer Museum and Bundy Park

This is one of eastern Montana's best museums, so don't miss it. The museum advertises that you can see everything from dinosaur bones to items brought back from moon walks, and chances are you will be able to find something to interest everyone. Kids will enjoy the dioramas, an Indian tepee and other artifacts, and the full-sized, old-time-town displays. The Stan Kalinski Wildlife Collection includes 300 mounted animals including such oddities as an albino skunk, two-headed calves, an 18-foot boa constrictor, and an eight-legged lamb. No less impressive is the second largest buffalo fish in the United States. The 62-pound monster was hauled out of Fort Peck Lake in 1980. Other interesting tidbits here include the world's tiniest workable violin, made by Glaswegian Frank Lafournaise and listed in *Ripley's Believe It or Not.*

Just behind the museum is Bundy Park, a pleasant picnic location with a children's play area and restrooms. The picnic tables here have shelter from the sun.

**Directions:** The museum is located on U.S. Highway 2. Look for it on the left as you enter Glasgow from the west. Bundy Park is on adjacent land.

**Important Information:** The museum is open daily Memorial Day through Labor Day from 11 A.M. to 8 P.M., except Sundays, when hours are 1 to 5 P.M. There is no charge. Contact the museum at 406-228-8692.

## 360. Candy Cane Park

This small park is only six blocks from the Valley County Pioneer Museum (site 359) and makes a great outdoor stop before or after your museum visit. The park has some interesting playground equipment for little tots. It is fenced and has picnic tables but no restrooms.

**Directions:** From U.S. Highway 2 by the Valley County Pioneer Museum, go one block east to 7th Avenue North and turn left. Go four blocks and turn left again. The park is one block ahead on Park Street.

## 361. Baker's Jewelry

This long-standing Glasgow jewelry store has some wonderful examples of Montana agates on display. Many are found in only one area of eastern Montana. The jewelers are happy to share their interesting collection. Agates come in varied forms. Some have patterns that look like landscapes, ocean waves, or whatever else your imagination can conceive. This is a great place to play "what do you see?"

**Directions:** The jewelry store is located at 530 2nd Avenue South. From U.S. Highway 2, take the turn south to Montana Highway 24 that crosses the railroad tracks. Go straight to 2nd Avenue South, turn left, and go one block to the corner at 5th Street South.

## 362. Hoyt Park and the Glasgow Civic Center

Hoyt Park has an Olympic-sized swimming pool, a picnic table with a shelter, and a playground. It's a nice place to refresh your family on a hot day before going on across the plains. The park is near the Milk River. The nearby Civic Center has an extensive program of activities for youth.

**Directions:** The park is located at 319 3rd Street South. From U.S. Highway 2, take the turn south to Montana Highway 24 across the railroad tracks and follow this road east. Turn right on 3rd Street South and you will see the Civic Center on your left in four blocks.

**Important Information:** The pool is open June through August and costs $1.25 for 1-hour-and-45-minute sessions. Call 406-228-8341 for information.

## 363. Alumni Park

This park is right on U.S. Highway 2 and makes a quick and easy picnic stop. There are picnic tables but no restrooms here.

**Directions:** Follow US 2 into Glasgow. Just past the fairgrounds you will see the Rustic Lodge on your left. The park is behind the Lodge at 701 1st Avenue North.

# THE MISSOURI RIVER

From James Kipp Recreation Area to North Dakota, the Missouri River flows through isolated country, alternating rugged breaks with more gentle woodland riparian areas. The damming of the Missouri at Fort Peck has created some interesting recreational opportunities. Wildlife abounds along the river here, and there are easily reachable locations from which to enjoy the mighty Missouri.

# Fort Peck Dam and Lake

The damming of the Missouri River at Fort Peck created the fifth largest reservoir in the world. Fort Peck Lake is 134 miles long, with 1,520 miles of shoreline, more shoreline than the state of California. A drive across the top of the dam to the power plant and museum brings home the immensity of the project.

Fort Peck Lake, like most reservoirs, is easiest to appreciate via power boat, but there are still numerous activities of interest to families without boats. Because of the fluctuating water levels, it is not possible to maintain many swimming beaches, though there is shoreline access with beaches at the Dredge Cuts. Canoeing is possible throughout the reservoir, but because of the long stretches of open water, winds can kick up good-sized waves. Boat ramps are available.

Of course, fishing is big here, and there are some 40 species of fish in the lake, among them sauger, northern pike, catfish, lake trout, and small-mouth bass. An annual Governor's Cup Walleye Tournament brings in hundreds of anglers every third weekend in July.

The Charles M. Russell National Wildlife Refuge surrounds the reservoir and has 13 recreation areas located around the lake. Access to some of these areas requires long drives on dirt roads. Listed here are two easy-access sites. Most of these recreation areas are primitive sites with limited facilities.

The town of Fort Peck, with a population of 300, retains many original buildings now listed on the National Register of Historic Places. The town has shopping and dining. The Fort Peck Theater is well known for its live summer theater.

Every year the locals sponsor a dam run including races across the dam and 10K, 5K, and 1-mile races. The festivities end up at the Downstream Campground day-use area for food and fun. Call the Glasgow Chamber of Commerce for more information, 406-228-2222.

## The Building of a Dam

Some said it couldn't be done. Others raised eyebrows at the anticipated expense. But the 4-mile-long, 250-foot-high, earth-filled Fort Peck dam was indeed constructed to block the mighty Missouri River. The project was a part of President Franklin D. Roosevelt's Public Works Program during the Great Depression. More than 11,000 people found work on site construction during the Depression, and the dam has since provided the area with flood control, irrigation, power generation, and jobs. Eighteen towns were constructed to accommodate workers and families. Although the Fort Peck Dam cost $150 million to build, it has more than paid for itself.

## 364. Power Plant and Museum

If you have never seen the inner workings of a dam facility, this is a good one to tour. The massiveness of the structure and the hustle and bustle of dam operation will keep even the little ones entertained. There is a small museum inside the power house with displays on dam history and 400 dinosaur speci-mens found in the area, including a *Triceratops* skull. The Fort Peck area is well known for fossils and petrified wood. Near the power house is Flat Lake and the spillway, an engineering marvel.

**Directions:** From U.S. Highway 2, take Montana Highway 24 south from Glasgow. MT 24 will take you across the top of the dam. Turn left immedi-ately after you have crossed the dam. This leads to the power plant parking lot. The museum is 2 miles from the town of Fort Peck.

**Important Information:** Daily free guided tours are offered from Memorial Day through Labor Day on the hour between 9 A.M. and 5 P.M. For informa-tion, call the power plant office at 406-526-3431 and ask for administration.

## 365. Flat Lake

This little lake has primitive camping spots, a picnic area, restrooms, and a trout pond stocked with rainbows. A boat dock and ramp provide access to adjoining Fort Peck Lake.

**Directions:** Follow the directions to the power plant and museum but con-tinue on Montana Highway 24 past the power plant turn. The lake is just before the spillway. It is 4 miles from the town of Fort Peck.

**Important Information:** Contact the U.S. Army Corps of Engineers at 406-526-3411 for information.

## 366. Leo Coleman Wildlife Exhibition Pasture

If you've not been lucky enough to see plains buffalo, elk, antelope, or deer, this 250-acre wildlife pasture can afford your family the opportunity. The en-closure has a one-way road all the way around it and you'll no doubt see some critters there. There may even be a curious antelope at the fence. You can park anywhere along the road and get out to stand by the fence, but visitors are not allowed inside the enclosure. An adjoining enclosure holds longhorn steers.

**Directions:** From U.S. Highway 2, take Montana Highway 24 south and then go north on the Montana Highway 117 fork that goes around the town of Fort Peck. The pasture road starts on the other side of town from MT 24 and is signed.

**Important Information:** Be sure not to get inside the pasture area and be aware that bull elk can be dangerous. Contact the U.S. Army Corps of Engi-neers at 406-526-3411 for information.

# Paddlefish, *Polyodon spathula*

This creature takes the prize for most unusual Montana creature. Also called the spoonbill catfish, the paddlefish is a "living fossil," having existed for at least 135 million years. Individual fish have 30-year lifespans, which gives them plenty of time to grow to lengths of 5 to 6 feet. While paddlefish average 40 pounds, some weighing as much as 140 pounds have been found. Scientists aren't sure how the long, paddle-shaped snout functions for the creature, though they guess that it may be a sensory organ for locating food. Another paddlefish oddity is the fact that it has no true bones, only a cartilage skeleton.

Each spring and summer, these monstrous creatures make an annual spawning run up the Yellowstone River and the Missouri River upstream from Fort Peck. Catching a paddlefish is considered a challenge. Since they feed on microscopic plankton and won't bite on a worm, paddlefish must be snagged. Snagging involves the use of a hefty rod, such as a saltwater rod, and a large-spooled reel fitted with a palm-sized hook. The hook is dropped to the river bottom in hopes of coming upon a paddlefish. The line is jerked soundly to snag the hook into the tough skin of the fish. Once snagged, the powerful monster must then be dragged in, and it can be quite a fight! The light inner meat is said to be tasty, and some folks eat the paddlefish eggs as a caviar.

## 367. Dredge Cuts Swim Beach

Three locations at the Dredge Cuts have a swimming beach, but the best place for families is the area closest to the town of Fort Peck on the west side of Montana Highway 117. This beach has restrooms, a changing facility, potable water, and picnic tables. Fishing is pretty good here, and even includes a chance at the unusual paddlefish. These ponds have quiet waters nice for canoeing.

**Directions:** Take MT 117 from Montana Highway 24 and go 1 mile past the town of Fort Peck. Look for the first sign on the left for Dredge Cuts.

**Important Information:** The swim areas are not supervised. Call 406-526-3411 for more information.

## 368. Downstream Campground and Day-Use Area

This developed campground has picnic tables, campfire grills, water, showers, electrical hookups, and restrooms. The park area by the entrance, once called Kiwanis Park, is a free day-use recreation area with plenty of shade trees, horseshoe pits, playground equipment, restrooms, and charcoal grills. The Beaver Creek Nature Trail (site 370) goes through the campground area. Nearby are two free fishing ponds: one for youth that is stocked with trout, and another, stocked with perch, that is open for use by all.

**Directions:** Two miles west of Glasgow on U.S. Highway 2, go south on Montana Highway 24 for 15 miles. You can then turn left (north) onto Montana Highway 117 either before or after crossing the Fort Peck Dam. The campground and park will be on the right 1 mile north of the town of Fort Peck.

**Important Information:** There is a $6 per night fee, with an additional charge for electrical hookup. Reservations may be made for an additional $3 fee. Note that July usage is extremely high due to well-attended fishing tournaments. Call 406-526-3411 for more information.

## 369. Beaver Creek Nature Trail

This pretty, self-guided interpretive trail is a level, 1-mile trail that goes through the Downstream Campground area (site 368) and passes by the river on its travels. An interpretive brochure is available.

**Directions:** The trail begins by the playground near the dam site administration building in Fort Peck.

**Important Information:** Future plans call for paving the trail to allow for rollerblading, biking, and wheelchair access. It will also eventually loop back via the trout ponds. Contact 406-526-3411 for more information.

## 370. The Pines Recreation Area

The tall ponderosa pine trees at this recreation area make this Fort Peck Lake campground a unique eastern Montana site. The pines were the first evergreen trees that Lewis and Clark saw in this area. This is a primitive camping area which has a shelter building with a fire grill, potable water, toilets, a picnic area, and a boat ramp. There are no developed beaches but the shoreline can be accessed.

**Directions:** From the town of Fort Peck, follow Montana Highway 24 north for about 5 miles to a signed turnoff. Turn left (west) and go 26 miles on this road. All turns are well marked.

**Important Information:** Contact the U.S. Army Corps of Engineers at 406-526-3411.

# 371. Charles M. Russell National Wildlife Refuge

This wildlife haven consists of more than 1 million acres of prairies, badlands, and rolling hills surrounding Fort Peck Lake and parts of the Missouri River. The third-largest contiguous wildlife refuge in the United States, it is named in honor of Montana's famed cowboy-artist, whose paintings portrayed the richness and beauty of the Montana landscape. Originally established as a national game range in 1936, the national wildlife refuge boundaries were determined in 1976. The refuge extends 150 miles up the impounded Missouri River, Fort Peck Lake. There are 13 recreation areas in the refuge, many with launch sites and campgrounds. Some of these areas are managed by the U.S. Army Corps of Engineers or private concessionaires. Access by vehicle to some of the recreation areas requires long-distance drives.

You will find wildlife abundant here. Look for some of the 230-plus species of birds that have been identified on the refuge since the early 1900s. Included are great blue heron, golden eagle, osprey, red-tailed hawk, sharp-tailed grouse, great horned owl, and prairie falcon. Visitors can see double-crested cormorants on the islands. The nation's largest remaining prairie elk herd—nearly 1,000 animals—also resides here. You will see them along the Missouri River, especially in the southern part of the tour route. They are especially prominent in September, during the mating season.

Additional activities on the refuge include hiking and horseback riding. You can hike nearly anywhere. There are no designated trails.

A wildlife auto tour along a scenic 20-mile-loop requires about two hours to complete. It begins at an information kiosk north of the James Kipp Recreation Area (site 372). There are 13 stops along the way with natural and cultural information provided on the tour brochure. Bird lists and refuge brochures can most often be found at the kiosk, although it is best to call and have one mailed to you before you visit so you are sure to get it.

**Directions:** The easiest refuge access is at Fort Peck Lake and James Kipp Recreation Area. To get to the kiosk at the beginning of the loop tour, go 1 mile north of James Kipp Recreation Area on U.S. Highway 191. Look for the kiosk on the right (east) side of the highway.

**Important Information:** If you choose to drive through the refuge area, take any signs about road conditions seriously. The soil here contains large amounts of bentonite and creates what locals call "gumbo." With even a slight amount of moisture, the dusty roads become slick, unforgiving mud! Also, take plenty of drinking water with you on the refuge as it is extremely scarce there.

To shorten the tour length to one hour, the U.S. Fish and Wildlife Service suggests going to stop number 6 and returning via the same route. For more information, contact the U.S. Fish and Wildlife Service, Charles M. Russell National Wildlife Refuge Office, Box 110, Airport Road, Lewistown, Montana 59457, or call 406-538-8706.

## 372. James Kipp Recreation Area

This recreation area on the Missouri River has picnic tables, a boat ramp, camping facilities, and bathrooms. It is a good place to stop and enjoy the river. From here you can explore the Charles M. Russell National Wildlife Refuge (site 371) and the Little Rockies.

**Directions:** The recreation area is located where U.S. Highway 191 crosses the Missouri River, on the south side of the Fred Robinson Bridge.

**Important Information:** Contact the U.S. Bureau of Land Management office in Lewistown at 406-538-7461.

# FORT PECK INDIAN RESERVATION: ASSINIBOINE AND SIOUX TRIBES

The Fort Peck Indian Reservation has 10,000 enrolled members with descendants of six of the 33 bands of Assiniboine Tribe and representatives of all divisions of the Dakota Sioux. About 6,800 tribal members live on more than 2 million acres of reservation land.

# Wolf Point

This small reservation town enthusiastically advertises its Wild Horse Stampede, an annual event held the second weekend in July. The event actually began at the turn of the century as an Indian day for riding and celebrating. But it wasn't too long before the local cowboys joined in, riding untamed horses wildly through the town's streets for sport. The word rodeo wasn't even in use yet but Wolf Point had created its own! Today the Stampede is a top professional rodeo and still features a Wild Horse Race. There are parades, a carnival, music, and lots more. Contact the Chamber of Commerce for more information at 406-653-2012.

# Wolf Point: What's in a name?

Though there are several versions of how Wolf Point got its name, this particular story seems to be a favorite. The town is in an area that was a favorite hunting spot for the Assiniboine and Sioux people and for fur trappers, too. It was also the halfway point for steamboats traveling between Fort Benton and Bismarck, North Dakota, during fur-trading days. The place became a frequent stopping point and a good spot to stock up on wood for the next half of the journey. Well, one year, trappers bagged several hundred wolves, a bigger number than usual. They hauled the carcasses to the river, but, before they could get to skinning them, winter took hold and froze them solid, and there was nothing to do but stack the bodies and wait till spring thaw. So, all winter long there sat this huge pile of wolf carcasses—so tall that the point became a landmark to talk about. Ever after that, the point was called Wolf Point.

## 373. Nellie Park

This shaded picnic park makes a great quick stop for lunch on a hot summer day. It's set up for easy access off the highway, and there are fast-food places across the street. The park does have playground equipment.

**Directions:** The park is on the north side of U.S. Highway 2 about halfway through Wolf Point.

## 374. Wolf Point Museum

This small museum, run by the Wolf Point Area Historical Society, displays artifacts from early-day white settlers and their Native American predecessors in the area. There is also a life-sized statue of cowboy-artist Charles M. Russell. The historical society members seem quite knowledgeable about the area, so this is a good place to hear stories and history! The museum is only a couple of blocks from a nice, shaded picnic area: Sherman Park and Shumway Gazebo (site 375). Across the street from the park is the Swap Shop, where you can stop in to see examples of star blankets.

**Directions:** The museum is located in the basement of the local library at 200 Second Avenue South. Turn south from U.S. Highway 2 onto Third Avenue South and go under the railway bridge. Turn left (east) on Main Street at the first light, go one block and then veer to the right onto Second Avenue South. You'll see the library in one block.

# Star Blankets

A functional art form, these beautiful blankets have a large, colorful star quilted in the center. The women of the reservation began making these blankets back in the 1920s when Nina First, of Fort Kipp, Montana, introduced this quilting style. Star blankets require great artistry. They have become a Fort Peck Reservation tradition and are given as gifts to friends and family members as an expression of love or thanks. Newborn babies are wrapped in these blankets, visiting dignitaries are honored with them, caskets are draped with them, and loved ones are buried with them. Examples of star blankets can be seen at the Poplar Museum (site 379) and in Wolf Point at the Swap Shop which is across from Sherman Park (site 375).

**Important Information:** The museum is open 10 A.M. to 5 P.M., Monday through Friday, during June, July, and August. Call 406-653-1912 for information. The phone number is not in service during the off-season.

## 375. Sherman Park and Shumway Gazebo

A good-sized facility, Sherman Park has picnic tables and plenty of shade trees. The Shumway Gazebo is dedicated to a local family. You can find memorial flags and historical information about the Shumways inside. Across the street is the Swap Shop, which has examples of Star Blankets. The Wolf Point Museum (site 374) is within two blocks.

**Directions:** Turn south from U.S. Highway 2 into Wolf Point onto Third Avenue South and go under the railway bridge. Turn left (east) on Main Street at the first light and you will see the park on your left within two blocks. Main Street becomes Anaconda Street as you travel.

## 376. Borge Park and Pool

A local favorite family park because of the pool and playground, Borge Park also has athletic fields and restrooms. It is only 11 blocks off U.S. Highway 2 and offers a shady picnic spot.

**Directions:** From US 2, turn north into Wolf Point onto Sixth Avenue and follow this 11 blocks to North G Street. The park is on your left.

**Important Information:** The pool is open daily from 1 to 4 P.M. mid-June through mid-August. Evening hours vary. Cost has been $2 per visit, but may be subject to change. Call 406-653-1650 for more information. The phone number is not in service during the off-season.

## 377. Toav's John Deere Tractor Collection and Museum

Louis Toav has collected more than 500 John Deere tractors and invites visitors to stop by and see them. This is the largest known collection of tractors in the country. Toav also has a number of Lincoln Continentals and a collection of toy tractors.

**Directions:** Take U.S. Highway 2 west of Wolf Point 1 mile and turn north on Volt Road, an oiled road. There is a sign in town noting the turn. The tractor collection is 15 miles up this road—you can't miss it.

**Important Information:** Call ahead at 406-392-5224 to make sure someone is there to direct you to the best exhibits. No charge.

# Poplar

For the Indians, Poplar has always been a center of activity. It was an Indian winter camp long before fur traders built a post here. The U.S. Army ran a military post, Camp Poplar River, at the site for a time, too. Today, Poplar is the center of the Fort Peck Assiniboine and Sioux tribal government.

## 378. Fort Peck Assiniboine and Sioux Tribal Museum

The tribal museum has a very small collection of artifacts of the Assiniboine and Sioux tribes. Though not large, the collection is certainly authentic and worth a quick stop.

**Directions:** The museum is located in the Tribal Cultural Center in Poplar on U.S. Highway 2 at 605 Indian Avenue. Look for it on the north side of the highway as you go through Poplar.

**Important Information:** Open year-round, Monday through Friday, from 8:30 A.M. to 4:30 P.M. Call 406-768-5155 for more information.

# 379. Poplar Museum

The Poplar Museum is housed in the 1920 jailhouse, a building with an important place in the history of the town. The museum is surrounded with artifacts that further reveal the town's varied past. In the yard is the *Poplar Pride*, a ferryboat that made crossings over the Missouri River from 1949 to 1969. The large, weathered bell by the museum's entrance at one time directed children back to the Indian Boarding School in the late 1800s. Inside are Indian artifacts and paintings by local artists that depict the life of the Plains Indians. Impressive Indian beadwork and colorful star quilts display the talent and culture of the Sioux and Assiniboine tribes. This small museum has the best display of Indian culture to be found on the Fort Peck Reservation.

**Directions:** The Poplar Museum is across the street from the Fort Peck Assiniboine and Sioux Tribal Museum, located in the Tribal Cultural Center. Look for it on the south side of U.S. Highway 2 on the east end of town.

**Important Information:** The museum is open daily June through August, from 11 A.M. to 5 P.M. There is no fee for the museum.

# 380. A and S Tribal Industries

The Assiniboine and Sioux Indian tribes own and operate this industrial manufacturing plant, which produces various items on contract. The plant employs up to 500 people during contract projects, and is one of Montana's largest employers. The Fort Peck Tribes have created a variety of products including camouflage netting used in Desert Storm, hydraulic presses, computer-controlled punch presses, medical chests, and other items. Guided tours are available during work hours.

**Directions:** To reach the industrial park, go through Poplar on U.S. Highway 2. Three blocks east of the cemetery, turn south at a sign for the industrial park. You will see the industrial park on the right hand side, just after crossing the railroad tracks. Go to the far west end of the building, and enter at the personnel sign.

**Important Information:** Open Monday through Friday from 9 A.M. to 4 P.M. Call ahead, 406-768-5151, to set up a tour time.

# THE HI-LINE: CULBERTSON

Nicknamed the "Hi-Line," U.S. Highway 2 spans the width of Montana, parallel to the Great Northern Railroad, which gave birth to many of the towns along the route. The highway rolls through mile after mile of plains, with small towns dotting the open landscape. The townspeople here have a strong sense of community, bonding together to withstand the trials of living in this harsh landscape. You'll find that northeastern Montana is about Big Sky prairie and tough-spirited people.

## Culbertson

Culbertson is a farm and ranch community. Folks here seem to enjoy hunting, fishing, and playing along the river in their spare time.

### 381. Culbertson County Historical Museum and State Visitor Information Center

The nine historical rooms at this museum offer a view into pioneer homestead days. The rooms are set up to represent an early chapel, school, general store, kitchen, doctor's office, and a barber and beauty shop.

**Directions:** The museum is 1 mile east of town on U.S. Highway 2.

**Important Information:** Open from May to September from 9 A.M. to 5 P.M. and 1 to 5 P.M. on Sundays. Admission is free and there is wheelchair access. Contact 406-787-6320 during the months when the museum is open.

### 382. Culbertson Centennial Park and Campground

This park has picnic tables, restrooms, and camping spots and offers visitors a good place to stretch their legs or eat lunch.

**Directions:** The park is located on Highway 16 at 3rd Avenue East, about two blocks from where Highway 16 meets U.S. Highway 2.

**Important Information:** No camping fee. Contact the town hall at 406-787-5271 for more information.

# SHERIDAN AND DANIELS COUNTIES

Tucked away in the far northeast reaches of Montana are several towns and interesting sites within Sheridan and Daniels counties. The area was among the last places settled in Montana and remained free-range ranch land until the early 1900s. This is a farming and ranching community, which for a couple of years during World War I was a major shipping point for wheat out of northeast Montana. The area enjoyed a brief oil boom, too. Today, the locals enjoy the peacefulness of prairie living.

## Medicine Lake

The national wildlife refuge one mile south of town provides outdoor recreation here. Rumor has it that this area has some great pheasant hunting, too. The town of 350 people has full visitor services.

### 383. Medicine Lake National Wildlife Refuge

This U.S. Fish and Wildlife refuge has more than 31,000 acres of lakes, wetlands, and shortgrass prairie. The land is glaciated rolling plains and is part of the prairie pothole region that covers southern Canada, the Dakotas, and western Minnesota. It is home to a multitude of birds as well as deer, antelope, skunks, raccoons, foxes, and other small mammals. The refuge protects one of the largest populations of white pelicans in the United States. More than 3,000 white pelicans nest on the refuge. Thousands of sandhill cranes pass through the refuge area in late October. While at the refuge, also look for blue herons, grebes, California gulls, cormorants, and numerous others, including 100,000 ducks and geese that enjoy a stop at the refuge during annual migrations. Though you will see wildlife year-round, May and October are the heaviest migration times.

Kids will enjoy the 18-mile auto tour which takes only about an hour if driven straight through. However, you can stop and walk anywhere along the route, and doing so makes the experience more enjoyable. Ten stops are noted on the tour brochure, available at the refuge office. The brochure gives history and points out special features.

Native Americans passed through this area to collect medicinal plants. The alkaline water in the lake might have served a medicinal purpose also.

Supporting this are the numerous tepee rings on the hills around the refuge, some of which date back at least 4,000 years. You can check one of these tepee rings out at site 6 by climbing to the top of the little hill.

If you get out and walk to the water by site 9, it's easy to spend a fair amount of time just enjoying the beach. Though the best times to see the most wildlife are May and October, you will certainly see birds at other times of the year. We saw hundreds of pelicans at site 9 in early June. A wheelchair-accessible platform has been constructed near the end of the auto tour route. The Pelican Overlook Observation Platform has two mounted binocular stands which allow observation of the pelicans without disturbing them. Look for a signed turn to the platform on the right side of the road. The platform is about 2 miles from the turn.

One of the favorite features at the refuge for kids is the 100-foot viewing tower by the refuge office. The tower is kept locked but a key may be obtained from the refuge office. If you aren't worried about heights, the view from the top is superb. Be sure you accompany children up the tower, however. During the winter months, the tower is closed due to ice on the steps.

The headquarters office has information about the refuge offerings and some bird mounts and displays. There are picnic facilities at the west end of the refuge and next to Montana Highway 16 about 0.5 mile south of the signed turn for the refuge.

Fishing is permitted from November 15 through September 15. Certain areas are excluded and there are no motorized boats allowed. There are various fishing access trails throughout the refuge. No motorboats are allowed on the lake, but the canoeing is excellent.

**Directions:** Go 25 miles north of U.S. Highway 2 on MT 16. Turn east on North Shore Road at the sign for the refuge and go 2 miles to the refuge headquarters. The town of Medicine Lake lies just 1 mile north.

**Important Information:** The refuge headquarters office is open from 7:30 A.M. to 3:30 P.M., Monday through Friday. The refuge is open sunrise to sunset every day of the week and visitors are welcome to stop and explore. The auto tour route is open from May 1 until the opening of waterfowl season, which is usually in late September. Call 406-789-2305 for information.

# 384. Medicine Lake City Park and Swimming Pool

This city park has picnic tables, a playground, shade trees, and barbecue grills. Restrooms are on the north side of the swimming pool building.

This is a good spot to rest from eastern Montana heat, which, by the way, was at its hottest recorded temperature—117 degrees F—right here at Medicine Lake on July 5, 1937.

**Directions:** Turn into town on Main Street, go 1 block west, then turn north and go one block. The park is located at 113 6th Avenue North.

**Important Information:** The pool is open every afternoon from Memorial Day to Labor Day from 1 to 5 P.M. and evenings from 6:30 to 8:00 P.M. Monday, Wednesday, Friday, and Sunday. Admission is $1.25 a day. Call City Hall at 406-789-2422 for more information.

# Plentywood

Here's a town with spirit and creativity. What began as a one-family town grew rapidly during World War I when good rains brought plentiful grain crops and shipping grain became a boomtown activity. The town fell into rivalry with neighboring Scobey over baseball. Plentywood solved its baseball problems by hiring members of the Chicago Black Sox, blackballed baseball players who rigged the 1919 World Series. Guess who won that game!

Plentywood has survived radical politics, the Depression, an oil boom, and drought. Today the town has around 2,000 residents and is busy turning its creativity to improving life on the prairie. Among their latest endeavors are construction of a community town square and organization of an annual Hot Air Balloon Rally in August, sponsored by the Elks. The Plentywood Chamber of Commerce has an answering service at 406-765-1607 and the City Hall can answer some questions at 406-765-1700.

## 385. Sherwood Park and Municipal Swimming Pool

The town park has restrooms, camping, a playground, a pool, and picnic tables. There are also horseshoe pits, basketball courts, tennis courts, and a refreshment stand. This park makes a good stop to get out of the car and play or have a picnic.

**Directions:** From Montana Highway 16 (First Avenue) turn right (north) onto Carroll Street and go two blocks to Laurel Avenue. The park will be on your right.

**Important Information:** Pool hours are 1 to 5 P.M. and some evenings (varies) from Memorial Day to Labor Day. Cost is $1 a day. No camping fee. Contact City Hall at 406-765-1700.

# 386. Sheridan County Museum

The museum is dedicated to the preservation of Montana's pioneer heritage and contains artifacts from every aspect of Montana life during the early part of the 20th century. Here you will find the state's longest mural, painted by Bob Sutherland on 74 feet of continuous canvas. It took Bob three months to paint the mural and it required 15 men to move it to its present location. The artwork depicts the history of the county through Indian plainsmen, fur traders, cowboys, homesteaders, the oil boom days, and up to present times. While you're at the museum, take a peek at the Old Tractor Club collection of threshing machines and tractors at the fairgrounds. There are 30 threshers and more than 80 tractors with plows, wagons, and other antique farming equipment.

Next to the museum is the Sitting Bull Surrender Monument. Sitting Bull was a great Sioux chief who called together the Sioux, Cheyenne, and Arapaho tribes to defeat General George Armstrong Custer at the famous Battle of the Little Bighorn in July of 1876. Sitting Bull led his people into Canada after the battle but surrendered with his tribe in 1881 at the site where Plentywood now stands.

Just a few steps from the museum is a rest stop which Plentywood residents have landscaped with interesting geologic and historical features. Large boulders have been hauled in to outline the grounds. There is a buffalo rubbing rock here; these were used by buffalo as "scratching posts" when they freely roamed the plains. A mock Indian tepee ring artistically serves as a flower bed for 20 species of native plants. Water and restrooms are available here.

## The Outlaw Trail

If it looks like you could get lost out here in Big Sky country, you're right. In fact, that's just what a bunch of pretty wild varmints did back around the turn of the century. The outlaw Butch Cassidy and a variety of other lawless fellows organized a series of trails from Canada all the way to Mexico that stretched through this area. They planned the trails through areas where they could get "lost" and, more specifically, lose sight of the law! The Outlaw Trail had stations set up about every 15 miles where they could grab fresh horses and supplies. The plan worked, for Cassidy and his "Wild Bunch" were considered the most elusive outlaw band in the West. In Sheridan County there are apparently still caves that offered these outlaws shelter. There are bits and pieces of outlaw history throughout Missouri River Country, from killings near Landusky, to train robberies near Malta, and hideouts in Plentywood. You can find out more about the Outlaw Trail at the Sheridan County Museum (site 386).

**Directions:** The museum is located on the east edge of town on Montana Highway 16, at the entrance to the Sheridan County Fairgrounds.

**Important Information:** The museum is free and is open from 1 to 5 P.M. Tuesday through Sunday, Memorial Day to Labor Day. Call 406-765-2219 for more information.

## 387. Box Elder Reservoir and Bolster Dam

There's good fishin' for walleye and pike here! There are also camping and picnic facilities. The campground includes water and electricity hookups. There are vault toilets and potable water too. There are no swimming beaches, but there is a dock for fishing, if you don't have a boat.

**Directions:** To get to the campground take Montana Highway 16 (First Avenue) and turn right (north) on Monroe Street. Follow the road when it jogs to the right as it crosses Box Elder Creek, then make an immediate left onto Box Elder Street. Follow this to a left-hand turn to the campground, boat launch, and dock.

To reach the picnic area, turn right (north) at Jefferson Street. In two blocks Jefferson jogs slightly and becomes Sheridan Street. Follow Sheridan until you come to a right-hand turn marked for the dam and picnic area. The picnic area and vault toilets are on the hill.

**Important Information:** No camping fee. For information, contact City Hall at 406-765-1700.

## 388. Montana Ostrich Ranch

No, these 7-foot-tall, 350-pound critters aren't native to the area, but you can catch a tour and see them at this ranch. They are raised for their high-protein, low-cholesterol meat, their feathers, and soft leather. The ranch has about ten ostrich adults with plenty of chicks in the spring.

**Directions:** The ranch is within city limits at the edge of town. Call for directions.

**Important Information:** Contact the ranch owners at 406-765-1897.

# Westby

Westby sits on the border of Montana and North Dakota. It's a hotspot for birdwatching, and the prairielands have many unique plants; among the more colorful are the *Echinacea, Psoralea,* and *Anemone* varieties. People here raise crops for a living. The town has necessary visitor services and Onstad Memorial Park offers camping.

## 389. Rolling Hills Llamas and Exotics

Have you ever seen a Muntjac deer or a Tennessee fainting goat? Well, now's your chance, for Sheridan County seems to have an unusually high percentage of ranchers who delight in raising unusual animals. In fact, the Mon-Dak Game Breeders Association, headquartered in Plentywood, offers support to this kind of activity. The Rolling Hills ranch welcomes visitors at their ranch. They are also distinguished as the most northeastern ranch in Montana.
**Directions:** To get to Rolling Hills Llamas and Exotics, you'll have to go 8 miles north of Westby to within 1 mile of North Dakota and 3 miles of Canada.
**Important Information:** Contact the ranch at 406-385-2597.

# Scobey

If you make it out this far, you'll be delighted at the attention paid to history here, where the 1,300 townspeople have spent time and effort to create a realistic Pioneer Town. Chamber of Commerce messages are taken at the library, 406-487-5502, or you can call the City of Scobey at 406-487-5581.

## 390. Roseland Park and Municipal Swimming Pool

This park is right in the middle of town and has sheltered picnic tables, playground, trees, water, and restrooms.
**Directions:** The park is located in the 300 block of Park Street.
**Important Information:** The pool is open from 1 to 5 P.M. and 7 to 9 P.M. every night. Prices are minimal. Contact City Hall at 406-487-5581.

## 391. Daniels County Museum and Pioneer Town

This museum is a re-created, 42-building frontier town, complete with all the trimmings. Its 20-acres also has early farm equipment and more than 50 restored, antique automobiles. The visitor center has additional displays. The Rex Theater provides regular shows in the summer. Each year a special Pioneer Days event is held in Pioneer Town for two days at the end of June. This celebration features community activities and an authentic re-creation of what the legendary American Frontier was like. Included is a performance by the famous Dirty Shame dance-hall girls, who once entertained President Bush. There is great Dixieland music here, as well.

**Directions:** The museum is at 7 County Road, located on the west edge of town. You can easily reach the museum by turning west from "the" stoplight.

**Important Information:** Open 7 days a week with tours between 1 and 4:30 P.M., from Memorial Day through Labor Day. Admission is $3 for adults, $1.50 for children, and free for kids under 6. There are group tours and group rates available. Call the museum for information at 406-487-5965.

**Bainville**
Fort Union Trading Post
Bainville Historical Association Museum

**Fairview**
Snowden Bridge

**Sidney**
Mon-Dak Heritage Center

**Fort Peck**
Hell Creek State Park
Devils Creek Recreation Area
Snow Creek Recreation Area

**Circle**
McCone County and Circle Museum
Montana Sheepherders Hall of Fame
The Gladstone Hotel National Historic Site

**Jordan**
Garfield County Museum

# Custer Country

This region is named for Lieutenant General George Armstrong Custer, who was known to the local Indians as "Yellow-hair." The area has been shaped by the historical events surrounding the Indian-settler conflicts of the late 1870s, and the Battle of the Little Bighorn, also known as Custer's Last Stand, figures prominently in area history and activities.

The land in Custer Country has much for all people to appreciate. The Yellowstone River flows boldly through the plains with massive cottonwoods gracing the banks. Wildlife and people flock to the river to enjoy its peace, beauty, and excellent fishing. Bordering the river in places are towering sandstone cliffs such as the prominent Rimrocks formation in Billings. To the south, the unique Pryor Mountains and Bighorn Canyon add to the magic of the Crow Indian Reservation.

The Indian cultures of the Crow and Cheyenne tribes reach far past the two reservations that these people now call home. Indian legends, history, arts, and traditions are visible throughout the widespread Custer Country lands these people once inhabited. Crow Chief Arapooish echoed the attitude of the Indians when he said, "The Crow country is good country. The Great Spirit has put it in exactly the right place; while you are in it you fare well; whenever you go out of it, whichever way you travel, you fare worse." After exploring Custer Country you'll agree that this land is good country.

## BILLINGS AND THE SURROUNDING AREA

The Yellowstone River, once the riverboat highway of trade and transportation, is now bordered by the interstate highway which brings people through the vast southeastern portion of Montana and into North Dakota. From Billings, another interstate leads through the Crow Indian reservation south into Wyoming. Along these major transportation routes visitors will find a wealth of cultural and natural resources to enjoy.

# CUSTER COUNTRY

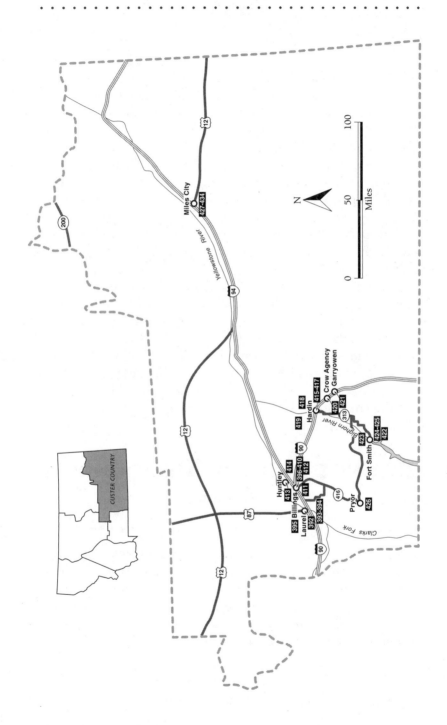

310

# Laurel

· · · · · · · · · · · · · · · · · · · · · · · · · · · · · · · · · · · ·

The community of Laurel is only 16 miles from Billings and its numerous offerings, so Laurel residents have focused less on recreational developments and more on their own community activities. Laurel boasts the biggest 4th of July fireworks show in the state, celebrates a late summer Mountain Man Rendezvous, enjoys a fall Herbstfest modeled after the German Oktoberfest, and sponsors a special Winter Rodeo, just to name a few events. For more information about the following fun sites to visit in Laurel or the town's community events, contact the Chamber of Commerce at 406-628-8105.

## 392. Fireman's Park

· · · · · · · · · · · · · · · · · · · · · · · · · · · · · · · · · · · ·

If you've wandered into Laurel and want a place to picnic or rest, Fireman's Park in downtown Laurel will provide a shady respite. The Chamber of Commerce plans to move to the log building at the highway convergence near the park in 1998, so there will be a handy place to gather information about the area from this picnic spot.

**Directions:** From Interstate 90, take Exit 434 onto 1st Avenue (U.S. Highway 212), or Exit 437 onto Main Street (U.S. Highway 10). Follow either through town to the junction of Main and 1st.

**Important Information:** For more information, contact the Laurel Chamber of Commerce at 406-628-8105.

## 393. Riverside Park and Campground

· · · · · · · · · · · · · · · · · · · · · · · · · · · · · · · · · · · ·

Riverside Park offers a place to picnic in the shade and fish along the Yellowstone River. The facility has a pleasant picnic area by the river, boat ramps, restrooms with showers, potable water, and overnight camping. Swimming isn't really possible here in the fast-moving Yellowstone River, but you can enjoy the presence of this scenic river. The large campground has 100 sites with some RV hookups available. The park houses numerous community facilities and is the site of various Laurel events.

**Directions:** From Laurel, take U.S. Highway 212 (1st Avenue) south of town and continue south of the interstate. Just beyond the interstate is a signed left-hand turn into the park. The park is 2 miles south of downtown Laurel.

**Important Information:** There is no cost for day use of the park but there is an overnight camping fee that ranges from $10 to $15 depending on hook-ups used. For more information, contact the Laurel Chamber of Commerce at 406-628-8105.

## 394. Altman Tract Fishing Access Site

Nestled between the Clark Fork and the Yellowstone rivers is this 400-acre tract of land set up as an undeveloped fishing access and recreation area. Wildlife here includes a large population of pheasants. The nonprofit organization Pheasants Forever is a part of the cooperative management of the area with the Bureau of Land Management. Look for bald eagles and raptors, deer, and other critters in this prolific wildlife habitat.

Fishing is good and the undeveloped site lends itself to exploring if you just want to be out in an untamed riparian area. Walk along the riverbanks and appreciate these rivers. Keep in mind that there are no developed facilities here, so you will have to create your own interest in the natural surroundings. There is an access road into the recreation area and a vault toilet.

**Directions:** From Laurel, go south on U.S. Highway 212 (1st Avenue in Laurel). As soon as you cross the Yellowstone River bridge, go left on Thiel Road. Follow this for 2 miles to the signed entrance for the recreation area.

**Important Information:** There is no overnight camping. The area is open dawn to dusk. Contact the Bureau of Land Management, Billings Resource Area at 406-238-1540 for more information.

## 395. Canyon Creek Battlefield Site

The Canyon Creek Battlefield was the site of a skirmish between the U.S. Cavalry and the Nez Perce Indians when they were on their famous 1,300-mile flight toward freedom in Canada (see page 188). Currently (as of 1998) there is only a marker at the site, but plans call for the development of a sheltered picnic area with displays interpreting the battle. Just east of the battleground is one of the last known homesites of Calamity Jane, though no structure remains.

**Directions:** The battlefield site is 7 miles north of Laurel. From Interstate 90 take Exit 434 to get onto 1st Avenue. Take 1st Avenue, U.S. Highway 212, north from downtown Laurel.

# Calamity Jane

Martha Jane Canary came to Montana as a child during the gold rush in 1864. Her nickname was said to have been given to her in the gold camps where she grew up. She seemed to be one of the first at the scene of any calamity, always ready to lend a hand to others. Calamity Jane's desire to help others and her adventurous nature led her to jobs as stagecoach driver, a bullwhacker and an army scout for Lieutenant Colonel Custer. She acquired some fame for being able to ride and shoot better than any man, yet was renowned for being a saintly nurse when calamity struck. She said she was once married to Wild Bill Hickock, and some credit her with having had 12 husbands.

As the years and experiences mounted, Calamity Jane developed a different kind of reputation. When she toured with Buffalo Bill Cody on his Wild West Show, the saintly legend was hard to recognize in the tobacco-chewing, swearing, cigar-smoking woman who had a tendency to drink too much. Calamity Jane had lost her renowned abilities, had become fairly cantankerous, and was sometimes reputed to be the cause of calamity. She settled for a time in the Canyon Creek area north of Laurel.

In 1903, as the legend and the woman herself were dying, Calamity Jane boarded a train for South Dakota, headed to Deadwood where she wanted to be buried next to Wild Bill. Martha Jane Canary had no money for this final train ticket, so compassionate passengers took up a collection and paid her fare. Calamity Jane died in Deadwood and was buried near her friend, Wild Bill Hickock.

# City of Billings

With a nickname like the Magic City, a town has a reputation to live up to! Billings grew so fast when it was founded that people said it seemed to have almost magically appeared from nowhere. Today, visitors can find magic in the city and its surroundings. Prominent and colorful sandstone cliffs rise from the Yellowstone River at the north and east edges of the city. From atop the Rimrocks, as the locals call these bluffs, one can see dramatic views of the Yellowstone Valley.

The Northern Pacific Railroad decided in 1881 to create a main railway connection in the southeastern Montana plains area and selected this location for the town they named Billings. Settlers, eager to buy in to what was sure to be a bustling city, bought 5,000 lots in the new town during the first month of land sales. By mid-year there were 124 homes in Billings, with tents and shacks sprouting up all over the town. Within 20 years the city had 10,000 residents. Present-day Billings is Montana's largest city, with a population of about 86,000.

The Yellowstone Valley was once the center of Crow Indian country. The Crows called the site where Billings now stands *Ammalapashkuua* or "place where we cut wood." The name Billings came from Frederick Billings, a millionaire entrepreneur who was president of Northern Pacific Railroad for nine years and promoted the development of the town. The founding father was well known for his generosity and it was his son, Parmly, who built the town library which now houses the Western Heritage Center.

Billings became a transportation center linking Montana to Wyoming, North Dakota, and the rest of the world. Soon the city was a busy trading center. Cattle, wool, oil, and sugar beets evolved into industries that are important to the city today. Manufacturing has become a mainstay of the Billings economy with over 200 manufacturing companies operating in the city. Two colleges, Rocky Mountain College and Montana State University-Billings are located here. Peoples of various cultural heritages have been drawn to Billings by its many industries. One finds a potpourri of cultures in the town, evident in the large number of ethnic choices in its 150-plus restaurants. Billings also serves as a gateway to the scenic Beartooth Highway, Yellowstone National Park, and the historic Little Bighorn Battlefield area.

For information, contact the Billings Chamber of Commerce at 800-735-2635 or 406-245-4111.

# 396. Riverfront Park

This extensive 400-acre, wooded, river-bottom park adjoins the Yellowstone River and has four picnic shelters, vault toilets, and a small lake. Josephine Lake was named after a sternwheeler that set the steamboat record for reaching the highest point upstream on the river in 1875. Around this pleasant lake is a trail that is just over a mile long and is paved about two-thirds of the way around. Plans call for complete paving by the end of 1998. The paved portion is wheelchair accessible.

The park also has separate equestrian trails. There is no boat ramp or swimming. Bring your own water, too, as there is no potable water here. Take the concrete walk under South Billings Road from the west end of the park and you will cross Wendalls Bridge to Norm Schoenthal Island where you can fish and explore the small river island on marked trails. The path to Wendalls Bridge is wheelchair accessible and the first 0.5-mile section of the island trail will be accessible by the end of 1998.

**Directions:** From Interstate 90, take Exit 447, the Chief Plenty Coups exit, and go south on South Billings Boulevard for 0.8 mile. Turn left (east) into the park.

**Important Information:** Open daily from 5 A.M. to 10 P.M. Contact the City of Billings Parks and Recreation Department at 406-657-8372 for more information.

# 397. Big Splash Waterpark

Cool off from the hot summer sun on water slides and inner tube rides. Picnic facilities are available at the slide. There is something for everyone here, including a "tad" pool for little ones. Picnic facilities are available at the slide.

**Directions:** Take the King Avenue Exit 446 from Interstate 90 and look for the waterpark across from the Holiday Inn.

**Important Information:** An all-day ticket at the waterpark is $11.95 for those 42 inches and taller and $5.95 for kids under 42 inches. Anybody 36 inches and under are free with a paid adult admission. Seniors are $7.95 and there is a $2.95 charge for non-sliders. The hours are from 10:30 A.M. to 7:30 P.M. Memorial Day to Labor Day. Contact the waterpark at 406-256-5543.

# 398. ZooMontana

Wildlife viewing takes on a new meaning in this 70-acre zoo designed with natural habitat exhibits. Temperate-climate, northern-latitude animals are highlighted at ZooMontana; both regional species and some exotic animals from various northern climate zones are included. One such exhibit houses two Siberian tigers in a habitat designed to simulate their natural environment.

The zoo's displays are situated along a 1-mile-loop nature trail. Canyon Creek flows through the area and along its banks you can see water birds like great blue herons and kingfishers plus river mink, beavers, and muskrats. There is a waterfowl wetlands area, too. For the visually impaired and wheelchair users, a sensory botanical garden makes this pleasant nature experience accessible. Kids particularly enjoy the Montana homestead exhibit, which includes a farm animal petting area. The Discovery Center has hands-on exhibits, and there is also an amphitheater for interpretive nature programs.

The zoo has a picnic area with a shelter, restrooms, potable water, and concessions. A variety of special summer events are scheduled; call for information.

**Directions:** There are numerous signs for the zoo on the roads leading to it. From Interstate 90, take the King Avenue West Exit 446 and go north on King, following it left when the road comes to a T intersection. Turn left (south) on Shiloh Road and you will come to the zoo in 0.5 mile.

**Important Information:** Admission is $4 for adults, $3 for seniors, $2 for kids ages 3 to 15, free for kids under 3. Hours from April 1 to October 1 are 10 A.M. to 5 P.M. daily. The zoo is open from 10 A.M. to 4 P.M. daily in winter except for Christmas Day. Most of the exhibits are outdoors, so bring appropriate clothing. Concessions are not open in the winter. Call 406-652-8100 for more information.

# 399. Rose Park

Slide away a hot summer day on the 165-foot-long waterslide at the city-owned Rose Park. The slide funnels into a large pool. There is a wading pool and picnic tables at the park, too.

**Directions:** From Interstate 90 take South 27th Exit 450 and go north on 27th. Turn left (west) on 6th Avenue which becomes Grand Avenue. The park will be on your right between 21st Street West and Avenue C.

**Important Information:** Cost for the pool is $2 for adults 18 and over, and $1 for kids. The charge for a full day's use of the waterslide is $3 for kids and $4 for adults. The pool opens the second week in June and closes the third week in September. Hours are noon to 8 P.M. daily. Contact the City of Billings Parks and Recreation Department at 406-657-8372 for more information.

# 400. P. B. Moss Mansion

This stately mansion is a monument to turn-of-the-century Montana wealth. The three-story home was built in 1902 for a cost of $105,000. At that time, the average home cost $3,000. The exterior is imported red sandstone from Lake Superior. The mansion contains many of the original furnishings of the Preston B. Moss family. A Billings banker, Moss was one of Montana's wealthiest men. Tours are offered regularly at this spectacular mansion, listed on the National Register of Historic Places. The mansion grounds have well-kept gardens with perennials, annuals, and specialty roses. Visitors are welcome to tour the grounds.

**Directions:** The mansion is located at 914 Division Street. Take the South 27th Exit 450 from Interstate 90 and go north on 27th Street. Turn left (west) on 1st Avenue North, go seven blocks, and then go right (north) on Division Street. It is one block to the mansion.

**Important Information:** Hour-long public tours are offered daily, from early June to the end of August. They run on the half-hour beginning at 10 A.M. and ending by closing time at 4 P.M., Monday through Saturday, and from 1 to 3 P.M. on Sunday. Wednesday evenings there is a 7 P.M. tour. In the winter, there are daily tours at 1, 2, and 3 P.M. The mansion is closed Christmas Day, New Years Day, and Thanksgiving Day. Admission is $6 for adults, $5 for seniors, $3 for kids ages 12 and under, and free for kids under 5. Contact the mansion for more information at 406-256-5100.

# 401. Western Heritage Center

Regional history comes alive through displays and interactive exhibits at the Western Heritage Center. You can get a good idea of what the Frontier West looked like as you view a large collection of historic photographs. Memorabilia and artifacts invite you to stretch your imagination and appreciate what life was and is like in the farming and ranching business. Rotating exhibits here feature topics such as saddle making, steam power, quilts, and western art. Relief maps and other regional displays give an overview of the region's natural landforms. Kids will enjoy the interactive exhibits where they can go into a tepee, open an irrigation headgate, visit a post office, and use touch-screen computers to learn more about the area.

The center itself is a piece of history, being housed in an impressive two-story stone building constructed in 1901 as the town library.

**Directions:** Take the South 27th Exit 450 from Interstate 90 and go north on 27th Street to Minnesota Avenue. Turn left on Minnesota and you will see the museum on your right in one block at 2822 Montana Avenue

**Important Information:** The museum is free. It is open Tuesday through Saturday from 10 A.M. to 5 P.M. It is closed Sunday, Monday, and legal holidays. For more information call the center at 406-256-6809.

# 402. Yellowstone Art Museum

The Yellowstone Art Museum is the leading museum of contemporary art in the state. The facility has over 1,900 pieces of art by 100 different artists including Charlie Russell, John Buck, Diane Butterfield, and Will James. Housed partly in the county's old jail and partly in a new addition, the building has some historical interest as well.

The museum education department sponsors art classes for kids and free family fun days. There is a museum store.

**Directions:** Take the South 27th Exit 450 from Interstate 90 and go north on 27th Street toward the airport. The museum will be on your right at the corner of 27th Street and 4th Avenue North.

**Important Information:** The museum is open from 10 A.M. to 5 P.M. every day except Monday, between Memorial Day and Labor Day. Thursday nights it stays open until 8 P.M. In the winter the museum opens at 11 A.M., but otherwise hours remain the same. Admission is $3 for adults, $2 for seniors and students through high school, and $1 for children under school-age. Contact the art museum for information and event schedules at 406-256-6804.

# Will James

Will James is remembered by many as a writer of popular Western romance books. Others may remember that his children's book, *Smoky*, received the Newbery Award for best book of children's literature. All told, he wrote 24 books.

Will was born in Quebec but ran away at age 15 to become a cowboy. Since his real name, Ernest Duffault, didn't make him sound much like a cowboy, he adopted the name of Will James, claimed he was born in the back of a wagon in Montana, and reported that he spent his childhood among cowboys and trappers. In 1927, Will purchased a ranch south of Billings where he wrote his books and did his illustrations. Alcoholism cost him his ranch, and at age 50 he died. In honor of its long-time resident, the city changed the name of the street where he had a home in Billings to Smoky Lane.

## 403. Athletic Park and the Mustangs Baseball Team

Here's the place to catch a rookie-league baseball game! This park holds the city's baseball stadium at Cobb Field, which features baseball games by the Mustangs, Billings's rookie-league team affiliated with the Cincinnati Reds. The team runs a short season from mid-June through the first of September. Athletic Park also has a large swimming pool and a couple of picnic tables. **Directions:** The park is located across from the Deaconess Medical Center. From Interstate 90, take South 27th Exit 450 and go north on 27th Street to 9th Avenue North. The field and park will be on your right on 27th between 9th and 10th Avenue North.

**Important Information:** Cost for the pool is $2 for adults 18 and over, and $1 for kids. The pool opens the second week in June and closes the third week in September. Pool hours are from noon to 6 P.M. daily. Contact the City of Billings Parks and Recreation Department at 406-657-8372 for more information. To find out about the baseball games, call the Mustangs team at 406-252-1241.

## 404. J. K. Ralston Cabin

J. K. Ralston was a Montana cowboy-turned-artist. Raised in the mining camps around Alder Gulch in the late 1890s, Ralston later moved to Sidney and worked as a cowboy for a while. His enjoyment of painting landed him a job painting gasoline pumps for Yale Oil in Billings, but he eventually gave that up to paint on canvas. Ralston became a well-known regional artist documenting the history of the Old West. He is especially known for his oil paintings and murals. The 1940s mural of Dr. Frank Bell making the first airplane flight in Billings is on display at the city's Logan International Airport. Another Ralston mural hangs at the Little Bighorn Battlefield National Monument. This 8-by-18-foot painting portrays the battle scene at Custer's Last Stand after the fighting had stopped. In 1978 Ralston was inducted into the National Cowboy Hall of Fame of Great Westerners. He died at the age of 91 in the late 1980s.

The famed artist's restored home and studio were donated as a museum by his family. The hand-hewn log cabin was built by Ralston and his son. Displays in the historic building provide information about Ralston and exhibit his cowboy gear and art materials. An art gallery features Ralston's paintings of the west, and a 15-minute video entitled *The West of J. K. Ralston* can be viewed.

**Directions:** From Interstate 90, take South 27th Exit 450 and go north on 27th Street all the way through town. Turn left onto Rimrock Road by Montana State University and continue to Rocky Mountain College. The cabin is located at the north end of the Rocky Mountain College campus at 1426 Rimrock Road between 13th and 17th streets.

**Important Information:** Entrance to the cabin is free; donations are appreciated. The facility is open from the first week of June to mid-October. Though hours vary, it is generally open Wednesday through Sunday, from noon to 4 P.M. Call for more information at 406-254-0959.

# 405. Peter Yegen Jr. Yellowstone County Museum

Overlooking the Yellowstone Valley from atop the Billings Rimrocks is the museum that preserves the history of Yellowstone County. The exhibits are partially housed in a log cabin, originally the community social center in Billings. The structure was built by pioneer Paul McCormick in 1893 and later moved to its current site. The museum is named after Peter Yegen, Jr., who was one of the area's early merchants.

Inside the cabin and in the basement exhibit area are displays that document western life at the turn of the century. These include both settler history and an extensive collection of Native American artifacts and history. Outside is a coal-fired steam engine. An observation deck overlooks the Yellowstone Valley and houses more exhibits below. An art gallery is located in an attached log building.

There are picnic facilities and restrooms at the site. Kids seem to be fascinated by the two-headed calf on display, so keep your eyes open for it!

**Directions:** The museum is located on the north Rimrocks just south of Logan International Airport and across from the airport parking lot. From Interstate 90, take South 27th Exit 450 and go north on 27th Street through town toward the airport. This road leads directly onto Terminal Circle at the junction of Montana Highway 3. After crossing MT 3, follow the circle by staying to the left to get to the museum at 1950 Terminal Circle. There are signs.

**Important Information:** No admission charge. Open Monday through Friday from 10:30 A.M. to 5 P.M. and from 10:30 A.M. to 3 P.M. on Saturday. Closed Sunday. Contact the museum at 406-256-6811.

## 406. Black Otter Trail Scenic Drive

Drive to the top of the Rimrocks for a piece of Billings history and some peace with a view of the Yellowstone Valley. This short but scenic drive is named after the renowned Crow chief, Black Otter. The bumpy dirt road follows the Rimrocks for a couple of miles to Boothill Cemetery. A 0.75-mile side road climbs Kelly Mountain and goes by the grave of Yellowstone Kelly, a famous frontier scout who asked to be buried overlooking the Yellowstone River.

Boothill Cemetery is located just off Black Otter Trail on the east end of the road. This cemetery was the burial site for the 1880s town of Coulson. The cemetery has been significantly vandalized, and is no longer maintained, but an interpretive sign explains some of the history of the town and cemetery. The grave of Muggins Taylor, a civilian scout who carried the news of Custer's Last Stand to the world, is buried here, and his gravemarker remains. Taylor was a deputy in Coulson when he was mortally wounded by a drunken townsman.

Near the west end of the road is a scenic overlook. The evening view of the city is particularly enchanting.

**Directions:** From Interstate 90 take South 27th Exit 450 and go north through town toward the airport. At the T intersection by the airport, turn right (east) and follow Montana Highway 3 heading east. The Black Otter Trail is a right-hand turn from MT 3. When Black Otter Trail comes to a T intersection, turn right to get to Boothill Cemetery (which will be on your left a few yards past the turn), or turn left to rejoin MT 3.

## 407. Lake Elmo State Park

Cool off from the hot Montana sun at manmade Lake Elmo in the Billings Heights area. This well-maintained Montana Department of Fish, Wildlife

& Parks site also has the best beach in town. Lifeguards are on duty during the summer high-use times. There is also some good fishing here and a biking and hiking trail that is partly wheelchair accessible. This 1.3-mile interpretive trail goes around the lake and then onto a road where visitors can stop by the Fish, Wildlife & Parks office to view wildlife mounts and a display on area fisheries and mammals before returning to the lake.

Wind surfing is big here, and you can also rent surfboards or even have lessons. Fishing at Lake Elmo can land you catfish, crappie, yellow perch, or large mouth bass. For deep fishing access, Roger's Pier on the south side of the lake gets you out onto the lake. The park has a boat ramp, restrooms, showers, potable water, and concessions, but no overnight camping.

**Directions:** From Interstate 90 take Montana Highway 87 Exit 452 and go north toward town. Turn right (east) at the junction onto MT 87, toward Roundup. Follow this street and turn left onto Pemberton Lane which converges with Lake Elmo Drive. Follow the signs once you are on Lake Elmo Drive. You will see the Montana Department of Fish, Wildlife & Parks building at 2300 Lake Elmo Drive, and about 0.6 mile around the lake is the Lake Elmo parking area and the main beach. Across the lake from the beach is the less-developed recreation area where Roger's Pier is located. The lake is less than 5 miles from the interstate.

**Important Information:** The Montana Department of Fish, Wildlife & Parks office is open from 8 A.M. to 5 P.M., Monday through Friday. Park beach hours, and hours when a lifeguard is on duty, are 11 A.M. to 8 P.M. weekdays, and 10 A.M. to 9 P.M. on weekends, from the first week in June through the third week in August. The rest of the park is open sunrise to sunset.

Pets are not allowed on the beach and must be on a leash in the undeveloped south side of the lake by the pier. Cost for using the park is $1 for anyone over 6 (school age), children under 6 enter free. A Montana Department of Fish, Wildlife & Parks annual pass permits free entry for up to 6 people. Contact the park office at 406-247-2940 for more information.

## 408. The Heights-MetraPark Bike Trail

For biking, hiking, or rollerblading, this is the trail to use in Billings. The old railroad right-of-way has been converted to a wide, paved path that goes along the northeastern edge of Billings. Locals have expanded the trail, which is currently 5 miles long, and plans call for ongoing extensions. The 2-mile Heights portion goes from Mary Street in Billings Heights to Yellowstone River Road where the MetraPark portion continues another 3 miles to Coulson Park (this section to be completed in the summer of 1998).

**Directions:** To reach the Mary Street access, take Interstate 90 Exit 452 for Montana Highway 87 and go north toward Roundup. Turn right (east) at the intersection onto MT 87. Follow MT 87 and turn right on Mary Street at the junction of U.S. Highway 10 and MT 87. MT 87 goes left, US 10 is straight ahead, and Mary Street makes a hard right turn by the junction. Follow Mary Street to the sign for the trailhead.

You can also pick up the trail at the Yellowstone River Road access near Two Moon Park (site 409). Turn right (east) from MT 87 onto Hilltop Road and then go left on Yellowstone River Road.

**Important Information:** Contact the City of Billings Parks and Recreation Department at 406-657-8372 for more information.

## 409. Two Moon Park

You can see more than 200 species of birds at this 150-acre park along the Yellowstone River. The river-bottom habitat has shady cottonwood trees, dense underbrush, and marshy areas along backwater sloughs. There are great views and a large gravel bar at the river. Be careful of the river here as the flow is fairly fast. Look for geese and pelicans along the river. You may see bald eagles in the spring and winter.

There is a signed nature trail with a self-guiding brochure. The entire trail makes a 3-mile loop which goes to a point on the Yellowstone River. A shorter hike can be made along the trail, so check out the map at the kiosk by the trailhead which shows the trail options. There are other unmarked trails

## Sacrifice Cliff

A Crow legend tells the story of this Yellowstone River cliff near the edge of present-day Billings by the fairgrounds. Apparently a teenage Crow Indian returned to camp to find that smallpox, brought to the tribe by the white man, had killed his sweetheart. In anguish, the brave declared that he would ride to the "Other Side Camp." His best friend agreed to accompany him and the two blindfolded their horses and plunged over the 60-foot cliff. Another story says that a Crow war party returned to their village to find it decimated by the dread disease and rode off the cliff in despair.

This cliff was also a vision quest site for Crow warriors, where the boys who were coming of age would seek meditative time to receive guidance for their adulthood. They would go without food or water for four days while awaiting the dream that would guide their lives and help ensure the survival of their people.

Sacrifice Cliff is part of the Rimrocks south of the Yellowstone River and opposite Boothill Cemetery. It is not marked but it is near the county fairgrounds.

to explore in the park, which also has picnic tables. Toilets and potable water will be added by 1999.

**Directions:** From Interstate 90 take Montana Highway 87 Exit 452 and go north toward town. Turn right (east) at the junction onto MT 87, toward Roundup. Follow MT 87 and, at the stoplight past the county fairgrounds entrance, Lake Elmo Drive turns left and Bench Boulevard goes right. Turn right onto Bench Boulevard and follow the signs to the park, which is very close. The park entrance is at the bottom of a hill.

**Important Information:** The park is open from half an hour before sunrise to 10 P.M. Contact Yellowstone County Parks at 406-256-2701 for more information.

# 410. Coulson Park

The town of Coulson almost made it big, but today little remains of the Yellowstone River town that was overshadowed when the railroad chose to develop the Magic City of Billings as a depot center. Politics were hot on this issue. The railroad could have just as easily gone through the existing town of Coulson, but land sales for a new town made starting a new center more profitable. So Billings, within easy view of Coulson, was founded and the town of Coulson died a quick death.

Though Coulson was only around from 1877 to 1884, the town had a colorful seven-year history. One tale reveals some of the character of Coulson. It's reported that the Miles City sheriff asked Coulson's sheriff, the infamous mountain man "Liver-Eating" Johnson, why he made so few arrests. Sheriff Johnson replied that, since he didn't have a jail, he just "whomped" the trouble-makers and let them go!

Today Coulson Park commemorates the town with 80 acres of grassy open areas where the town used to be. There is a nice view of the Yellowstone River and cliffs across the waterway. The park is undeveloped except for a couple of picnic tables. If you want a quiet, undeveloped spot by the river, this park may be your choice.

**Directions:** From South 27th Exit 450, go south on 27th Street, away from town. Take the first left and go north on Garden Avenue. Follow this road to a T intersection. Turn left (west) here (Belknap Avenue) and then turn immediately right (north) onto Charlene Street. Follow this road 1.1 miles past the Montana Power Company coal yard and you'll see a road sign for the park on the right.

**Important Information:** The park is open from 5 A.M. to 10 P.M. daily. Contact the City of Billings Parks and Recreation Department at 406-657-8372 for more information.

# 411. Pictograph Caves State Park

Imagine living in a sandstone cave by a bubbling creek when you visit this park. The three large caves, carved by wind and water over eons of time, have no doubt seen numerous peoples come and go. One cave was used as a burial place and rock paintings are located on the back wall of another, the Pictograph Cave. These paintings have been dated back 4,500 years and are thought to have been made by ancient peoples who lived in the area before the Crow Indians arrived. Over 100 pictographs, painted in red, white, and black, tell stories of battles, celebrations, and wildlife. Many of these have been vandalized and others are hard to see, but visitors can still view some of them. Archaeologists unearthed over 30,000 artifacts from the site, some of which can be seen at the Peter Yegen Jr. Yellowstone County Museum in Billings (site 406).

A self-guided, paved, wheelchair-accessible trail goes by the sandstone canvases. The 1,000-foot trail is somewhat steep in places. An interpretive brochure is available at the trailhead. At the park are wheelchair-accessible picnic tables, a drinking fountain, and vault toilets. There is no camping.

**Directions:** Take Interstate 90 to Exit 452 in Billings. Go south from the exit and turn right (west) onto Coburn Road at the sign for the pictographs. Follow the signs on the road for almost 5 miles to the state park.

**Important Information:** Binoculars are nice to have to enhance the view of the pictographs. Be alert for rattlesnakes at the edge of the trail. There is a use fee of $4 per car or $1 each for walk-ins, bicyclists, or motorcyclists. An annual state parks pass gets visitors in free. The facility is open from May 1 to October 15 from 8 A.M. to sundown. Call Montana Department of Fish, Wildlife & Parks at 406-247-2940 for more information.

# 412. Yellowstone River

The Yellowstone River is another one of Montana's remarkable rivers. Tumbling from the high mountains of Wyoming, the river courses through Yellowstone National Park and goes north to Livingston where it turns east and becomes the prairie river one sees around Billings. Cottonwoods grace its shores and wildlife is abundant. Fishing, even in the plains area, is excellent. Diversion dams cause floaters concern and must be avoided. Two short floats near Billings make pleasant family activities.

Riverfront Park to Two Moon Park requires only an hour and a half or so on the river. The Yellowstone can move rapidly here, depending on the time of year, but there are no rapids or dams. Combining this pleasant float with a picnic in one of the parks makes an excellent family outing.

Gritty Stone Fishing Access Site to Pompeys Pillar National Landmark is about a 7-mile float that takes only a couple of hours and provides the opportunity to explore Pompeys Pillar (site 414) at the end.

**Directions:** See sites 397 and 410 for directions to Riverfront and Two Moon parks. To get to Gritty Stone Fishing Access Site and Pompeys Pillar National Landmark, take Montana Highway 312 Exit 6 to Huntley from Interstate 94 east of Billings. Stay on MT 312 almost to Worden. Turn left (north) onto Yellowstone County 14. A large dairy farm sits at the turn. Go north on CR 14 to the sign for the fishing access.

**Important Information:** For more information, contact the Montana Department of Fish, Wildlife & Parks at 406-247-2940 or the Bureau of Land Management, Billings Resource Area, 406-238-1540. Be sure to come prepared for family river floating with food, water, and extra clothing.

# Huntley

This town is on its second life, having died out once in 1862 when the railway came through Billings. That's when Huntley's role as head of navigation on the Yellowstone River ended. But in 1904, when the U.S. Bureau of Reclamation decided to construct a major irrigation system, and selected Huntley as the center of construction, the town was revived and has since become a thriving small town focused on farming. The town is 12 miles west of Pompeys Pillar National Landmark (site 414) along U.S. Highway 312 or slightly less along Interstate 94.

## 413. Huntley Project Museum of Irrigated Agriculture

This turn-of-the-century homestead museum has a large collection of homestead and farm machinery. Included is various machinery used in the sugar beet industry. There are also homestead buildings, including a schoolhouse, homestead house, and various outbuildings. The museum itself has over 5,000 homestead artifacts used from 1880 to 1940, such as homemade toys, saddles, kitchen items, and much more. The Montana Antique Tractor Club holds its annual threshing bee here the third weekend of August. Huntley Homesteader Days also happens here the third weekend of July.

The museum is in the east part of the Lion's Club Homesteader Park on the main canal for the irrigation project. The park has picnic tables, toilets, and a walking and jogging trail.

# What Was That? The Pronghorn Antelope, *Antilocapra americana*

What was that streaking by at 50 miles an hour? Well, if it was reddish-brown and white with short, curved horns, and you saw it in eastern Montana, it was probably a pronghorn antelope. These prairie animals are the fastest land animal in all of North America. The grazers have even been clocked at 84 miles an hour for a short distance!

These speedy critters are not large animals, usually only 3.5 feet tall at the shoulder. They generally weigh between 75 and 140 pounds. Common in eastern Montana, pronghorns are most often seen grazing in herds in open areas.

A Blackfeet legend says the Creator, "Old Man," made the pronghorn from dirt in the mountains. But when he set the animal down, it ran so fast that it tripped over the mountain rocks. So, Old Man took the pronghorn to the prairie where it could run free and it has lived there ever since.

**Directions:** Take Interstate 90 east of Billings and get onto Interstate 94. Take Exit 6 onto Montana Highway 312 to Huntley. Go through town and 3 miles east you will find the museum across the railroad tracks by the Montana State University Experiment Station. Look for the signed turn to the museum. Continue east on MT 312 to get to Pompeys Pillar.

**Important Information:** There is no charge, but donations are accepted. The museum is open daily from 9 A.M. to 4 P.M. between Memorial Day and Labor Day. Call for museum information at 406-967-2881.

## 414. Pompeys Pillar National Landmark

Rising 150 feet from the Yellowstone River, the prominent butte called Pompeys Pillar has long been a river landmark. It was also a rendezvous point for early travelers. On July 25, 1806, explorer William Clark carved his name on the sandstone monolith. This graffiti is the only remaining physical evidence along the trail of the famous Lewis and Clark expedition. Clark named the pillar in honor of Sacagawea's son, whom he called "my little Pomp." *Pomp* is slang in the Shoshone language for little chief. The boy's real name was Jean Baptiste Charbonneau. He was born to Sacagawea at the Mandan village during the expedition's winter stay there in 1804. Jean Baptiste was 18 months old when the corps reached the pillar. Pompeys Pillar was called "Where the Mountain Lion Lies" by the Crow people.

The pillar is an excellent place for a family jaunt. If you are ready for a strenuous 220-step climb, a stairway will take you to the top of the pillar for a spectacular view of the surrounding area. Your kids will probably want to go up, and will probably beat you there too! Halfway up, visitors can view Clark's signature on the rock. Tours are available during the high point of the season when Bureau of Land Management staff are available to provide interpretive information. A visitor center includes several displays, including maps of the Lewis and Clark journey. There is a scenic picnic area by the Yellowstone River. People can fish here, though the river is not conducive to swimming. The site has vault toilets. Bottled water is available at the visitor center, and there is a souvenir shop.

**Directions:** From Billings, take Interstate 90 east of town and get on Interstate 94. Take Exit 23, located 30 miles east of Billings and follow the signs 0.5 mile north to the recreation area.

**Important Information:** The site is open from Memorial Day through the first Sunday in October. Through Labor Day the visitor center and souvenir shop are open from 8 A.M. to 8 P.M., and after Labor Day it is open from 8 A.M. to 5 P.M. Visitors may still go past the closed gate during the off-season and walk the 1-mile distance to the pillar. Contact the Pompeys Pillar Visitor Center at 406-875-2233 or the Bureau of Land Management, Billings Resource Area at 406-238-1540 for more information.

# Hardin

• • • • • • • • • • • • • • • • • • • • • • • • • • • • • • • •

The farm and ranch community of Hardin is located 46 miles east of Billings, just outside the boundary of the Crow Indian reservation. The community avidly celebrates both homestead and Indian history during its Little Big Horn Days around the third week in June. For more information contact the Hardin Chamber of Commerce at 406-665-1672.

## 415. Bighorn County Historical Museum and Centennial Park

• • • • • • • • • • • • • • • • • • • • • • • • • • • • • • • •

Visit the displays in the museum building and then take the kids outside to explore the tepees set up on the grounds, as well as the 14 historical buildings located around Centennial Park. Here you will find an authentic old school building, church, store, farmhouse, doctor's office, blacksmith shop, barn, service station, and train depot. The buildings surround Centennial Park, which has a shaded picnic area that is a welcome respite in hot summer months. Restrooms and drinking water are available. The museum has a gift shop and visitor information. The Little Bighorn National Battlefield Monument (site 420) is not far from this museum.

**Directions:** Take Exit 497 into Hardin from Interstate 90 and go toward town. The museum will be on your right immediately off the interstate before you get to town.

**Important Information:** The museum is free. It is open May 1 through September 30, from 8 A.M. to 8 P.M., Monday through Sunday, and the rest of the year from 9 A.M. to 5 P.M., Monday through Saturday. Call the museum at 406-665-1671 for information.

## 416. Kids World Playground and Custer Park

Kids World Playground is a fun stop for kids. Adults will have a chance to relax here while kids enjoy the unique play area. Custer Park is one block west and has a picnic table, restrooms, and shade.

**Directions:** Take Exit 497 from Interstate 90 and go toward town following U.S. Highway 87. Continue on US 87 (3rd Street) for 0.8 mile and you will find the playground on the left by Cody Avenue. Custer Park is one block west.

**Important Information:** Contact the Hardin Chamber of Commerce at 406-665-1672 for more information.

## 417. Hardin Community Activity Center

Hardin's community center has an indoor pool—three pools, in fact. There is one Olympic-sized pool, a lap pool, and a junior pool, plus a hot tub.

**Directions:** The pool is located at Mitchell and 8th by the high school. Take Exit 497 from Interstate 90 and go toward town on U.S. Highway 87. Stay right on US 87 (3rd Street). Take this to Mitchell, the 4-way stop, and turn right. The pool is at Mitchell and 8th.

**Important Information:** Open swim hours are 7 A.M. to 8:45 P.M., Monday through Thursday, and 1 to 4 P.M. Friday through Sunday. Cost is $1.50 for adults, $1.25 for kids, and 50 cents for kids 5 and under. Contact the pool at 406-665-2346.

## 418. Arapooish Pond and Fishing Access Site

If you want to explore the Bighorn River, this undeveloped river-bottom access site will give you a place to do so. Both the river and a fair-size manmade pond offer good fishing. The access site has a boat ramp too. Unmarked trails and a wide roadbed provide a pathway through the riparian habitat to enjoy nature and look for wildlife. A great blue heron rookery offers bird-watching opportunities; numerous birds and animals can be seen here. There are picnic tables by the pond where you can also appreciate a symphony of crickets during cooler times of day.

**Directions:** The access site is located 2 miles from the Bighorn County Historical Museum (site 415). Go south from the museum across the Interstate 90 Exit 497 overpass and take the frontage road left just beyond the overpass. Follow this road, which will turn sharply to the right and become Bighorn County 307A. Follow CR 307A until it takes a sharp turn left, but go right instead onto Bighorn County 236. In 1.3 miles you will be at the Arapooish Fishing Access and Recreation facility. An alternate route is to take Exit 495 from the interstate onto Montana Highway 47. Go north on MT 47 and in about a mile is a sign for the site. Turn here and follow the signs to the site.

**Important Information:** No overnight camping. Only non-motorized craft are allowed on the pond. For more information contact the Montana Department of Fish, Wildlife & Parks in Billings at 406-247-2940.

## 419. Grant Marsh Wildlife Management Area

Look for birds in this small but accessible river-bottom area along the Bighorn River. Check out the cattail marsh across from the entrance and look

# The Coyote: Music on the Plains

The concert starts when the lights go down—and also when they come back up. The coyote concert, that is, will usually be heard at dawn or dusk.

The coyote (*Canis latrams*) is one of the most vocal animals on the prairie. Coyotes talk to one another over long distances with howls and yips. Though the howls may seem mournful, the animals' sounds warn of danger, let others know about a food source, and sometimes ask for help. And sometimes they just seem to want to visit or know that another coyote is out there. Once one starts, others usually join in the chorus and their voices ring from every direction. In the spring you can hear adult coyotes teaching their young to howl and yip and the sound of the high, tiny voices may be somewhat comical. For those who have heard coyote music, the delightful sound of the coyote is as much a part of the plains as the big sky.

along the river, too. You have a good chance of seeing ducks, red-winged blackbirds, flickers, and downy woodpeckers, plus a number of different kinds of song birds. There are also great blue herons, muskrats, and beavers along the river. Bald eagles are common in winter.

**Directions:** Take Interstate 90 south of Billings to Hardin and then take Montana Highway 47 Exit 495. Go north on MT 47. Turn right (east) at the sign for Grant Marsh. Follow this gravel road for 1 mile to the wildlife management area entrance.

**Important Information:** For more information contact the Montana Department of Fish, Wildlife & Parks in Billings at 406-247-2940.

# CROW RESERVATION

When speaking of the *Apsalooke* people in sign language, an Indian translator would flap his arms like a bird. The word *Apsalooke*, or *Absarokee* in the language of the Hidatsa tribe of which the Crow were a part, translated to English literally as the Children of the Large-Beaked Bird. White people named this tribe the Crow.

The Crow Indians have traditionally been friendly with the "white intruders," some even acting as scouts for military leaders, including Lieutenant Colonel Custer. Though the Crow were originally deeded 35 million acres of land through the Fort Laramie Treaty of 1851, the Crow reservation was ultimately whittled down to the 2.2 million acres it is today. About 6,300 of the 9,311 tribal members live on the reservation. The majority of the Crow tribe, 85 percent of the current residents, speak Crow as a first language, a much higher percentage than most Indian tribes.

The Crow Fair is the largest celebration of the tribe. This powwow is held on the third weekend of August in the "tepee capital of the world," Crow Agency. For more information about the Crow reservation, contact the Crow Tribal Office at 406-638-2601.

## Little Bighorn Battlefield Area

Along the Bighorn River of eastern Montana, the Sioux and Cheyenne Indians fought one of the final great battles in the Indian Wars of the 1870s. The tribes vigorously resisted relinquishing their traditional way of living for the sedentary life on the government-issue reservations. But the expanding forces of the U.S. government fought with determination to claim management and ownership of the land they claimed as the land of the free for their people. The Cheyenne and Sioux Indians had a resounding triumph at Custer's Last Stand in 1876. But ultimately the tribes succumbed to the powerful and plentiful newcomers and were forced to abandon claim to traditional lands and lifestyles. In the battlefield area you will find excellent opportunities to explore this important aspect of cultural history.

If you are in the area during the week closest to the battle's anniversary date of June 25th, there are two re-enactments of the Battle of the Little Bighorn. Both the National Park Service and the Hardin Chamber of Commerce sponsor re-enactments around this time. Between 200 and 300 actors in full regalia portray the military defeat in performances acclaimed for accuracy. The hour-long presentations sponsored by the Hardin Chamber of Commerce are repeated five times in a field 6 miles from Hardin. The National Park Service sponsors an equally impressive re-enactment at the battle site. For more information about the re-enactments, contact the Hardin Chamber of Commerce at 406-665-1672, or the National Park Service at the Little Bighorn Battlefield, 406-638-2621. A private re-enactment is also held later in the year at Sitting Bull's encampment.

## 420. Little Bighorn Battlefield National Monument

In the Battle of the Little Bighorn, 260 soldiers and military personnel of the Seventh Cavalry, under the command of Lieutenant Colonel George Armstrong Custer, were killed. An additional 99 men under the command of majors Reno and Benteen, lost their lives. Somewhere between 60 to 100 of the several thousand Sioux and Cheyenne that fought in the battle were killed.

The Little Bighorn Battlefield National Monument presents a thorough account of this historic conflict. A museum and visitor center provide exhibits explaining historical aspects of the battle while artifacts and authentic re-creations detail the scene and give visitors insights into the experiences of the combatants. The National Park Service has an extensive interpretive program including guided tours of the battlefield, informative films, living history dramatizations, and programs covering a multitude of related topics. Visitors can drive to the Reno battlefield site and walk along a 0.75-mile interpretive trail. A guided bus tour of the battlefield is available. There is a self-guided trail through the military cemetery. The National Park Service offers a Junior Ranger program for kids.

**Directions:** From Billings, take Interstate 90 southeast to Hardin and continue 15 miles beyond Hardin to Exit 510 (61 miles from Billings). The battlefield is just off the interstate; follow the signs.

**Important Information:** The park is open Memorial Day to Labor Day from 8 A.M. to 8 P.M. daily, and in spring and fall from 8 A.M. to 6 P.M. Winter hours are 8 A.M. to 4:30 P.M. Change of season dates vary, depending on weather. The self-guided tour road closes one half hour before the park closes. Entrance fees are $6 per vehicle, and $3 per bike and motorcycle.

There is no camping or picnicking at the facility. Pets are not allowed outside of vehicles at the national monument. For more information contact the National Park Service at 406-638-2621.

## 421. Custer Battlefield Museum and Tomb of the Unknown Soldier

The Battle of the Little Bighorn actually began at this location where Chief Sitting Bull's camp was located. Visitors can stop and find out specifics about Custer's Last Stand at this private museum. The facility also houses rotating art exhibits plus the D. E. Barry collection of photographs of participants in the battle.

In front of the museum is a tomb of an unknown soldier, a man thought to be one of Major Reno's troops, who was found by a road construction crew in 1926. On the 50th anniversary of the Battle of the Little Bighorn, a pistol and a hatchet were ceremoniously buried in the tomb with the soldier. General Godfrey, who actually fought in the battle, and Sioux Indian White Bull shook hands over the tomb to symbolize the metaphorical "burying of the hatchet" between cultures.

There is a trading post gift shop, restroom, and picnic area by the fort-style museum.

**Directions:** From Interstate 90, take Exit 514. The museum is right by the exit at Garryowen. The Little Bighorn Battlefield is 4 miles north.

**Important Information:** Cost of the museum is $3 for adults, and $2 for seniors and kids 12 and over; kids under 12 enter free. The museum is open daily during the summer from 8 A.M. to 9 P.M., and in the winter from 9 A.M. to 5 P.M. daily. For more information contact the museum at 406-638-2000.

# Bighorn Canyon National Recreation Area

The third largest canyon in the country is found in this remote area of Montana. Yellowtail Dam is perched between the rugged walls of Bighorn Canyon and has created 71-mile-long Bighorn Lake. Canyon cliffs over 1,000 feet in height rise dramatically above the lake. The recreation area is managed by the National Park Service which operates facilities at the northern district by Fort Smith and the southern district near Lovell, Wyoming.

The northern district facilities at Yellowtail Dam are accessible from the Crow Reservation towns along Interstate 90 in Montana, and from Hardin and Pryor. Bighorn Lake has excellent fishing for yellow perch, ling cod, crappie, catfish, carp, and walleye. Anglers can come away from the blue-ribbon trout fishery on the Bighorn River below Afterbay Dam with plentiful rainbow and brown trout. The Ok-A-Beh Marina, 406-665-2216, rents motorboats, pontoon boats, and fishing gear. It has food, a picnic area, and a swimming beach. Boat tours of the lake are available on a limited basis but must be reserved by calling 406-252-0733. There are two camping facilities in the northern district at Afterbay Lake. The National Park Service has a visitor center and provides a variety of interpretive and campfire programs as well as a tour of the dam. Nearby Fort Smith has motels, a restaurant, gas, and groceries.

The recreation area extends into Wyoming where the southern district lands have a variety of offerings at Horseshoe Bend and Barry's Landing. These include fishing, picnicking, swimming, hiking, historic sites, and a campground. Bighorn sheep and wild mustangs are an interesting wildlife draw in the southern district. The Bighorn Canyon Visitor Center is located southwest of Lovell at the junction of U.S. Highway 310 and U.S. Highway 14A. The southern district facilities must be approached from Lovell or Sheridan, Wyoming along US 14A, or via boat along Bighorn Lake from the north. There is no road connecting the northern and southern districts. The southern district is a frequent stop for travelers en route to Yellowstone National Park.

Most of the Crow Indian reservation lands are closed to visitors. Generally, paved roads are open to visitors but most unpaved roads are closed. Bicycling is permitted only on established public roads. There are no designated bike paths, and park roads are narrow and winding, which may make bicycling difficult. Pets must be leashed in the recreation area. Be aware that summer thunder and lightning storms are common on the lake and may come up quickly. The winds associated with these storms can be dangerous to small craft. Watch for snakes in rocky places, particularly in the evening. There are black bears in the recreation area and proper food storage methods should be followed (see page 14).

Entrance into the recreation area is $5 per car or $2.50 if one of the passengers holds a Golden Age or Golden Access pass. For information about the northern district area, contact the National Park Service at 406-666-2412. The southern district office in Wyoming can be reached at 306-548-2251.

# 422. Yellowtail Dam Visitor Center and Power Plant

• • • • • • • • • • • • • • • • • • • • • • • • • • • • • • • •

The visitor center is named for Crow Indian Robert Yellowtail, who was an influential tribal leader throughout the 1900s; the massive dam along the Bighorn River was also named in his honor. The dam is 525 feet tall and spans 1,480 feet across Bighorn Canyon at the top of the dam. The National Park Service visitor center at Yellowtail Dam provides information about the dam and how it was built. There are good views of the dam through large windows at the center and the National Park Service provides regular tours of the facility. At the visitor center, a fly-fishing exhibit compares man-made fly-fishing flies with their natural counterparts.

**Directions:** To get to the dam, take Bureau of Indian Affairs Road 313 from Hardin to Fort Smith and go 3 miles south to the dam. This is about a 45-minute drive.

**Important Information:** The visitor center is open from 9 A.M. to 6 P.M. from Memorial Day through Labor Day. Tours of the power plant are given twice daily. Contact the visitor center for information during summer operation hours at 406-666-3234, or call the National Park Service office at other times at 406-666-2412.

# 423. Afterbay Campground and Bighorn Headgate Trail

• • • • • • • • • • • • • • • • • • • • • • • • • • • • • • • •

Afterbay is a 2-mile-long body of water below Yellowtail Dam, created by the small Afterbay Dam. This site has good fishing, a short hike, and a couple of campgrounds. Families can appreciate the 0.1-mile trail to the stone and mortar headgate built by the Crow Indians near the turn of the century. There is access at Afterbay to the section of Bighorn River between Bighorn Lake and Afterbay.

The Afterbay Campground has 30 sites with some RV facilities, vault toilets, picnic tables, and potable water. There is a boat ramp and fishing dock. Though anglers need a boat to fish on the Bighorn River or Bighorn Lake, fishing can be successful from shore or the fishing dock at Afterbay. An added treat at Afterbay is good birdwatching. The water draws thousands of migrating birds. Up to 20,000 mallards winter at Afterbay and along nearby Bighorn River. Among the 47 species of birds found on the river in summer are teals, mallards, goldeneyes, swans, pelicans, loons, cranes, and mergansers. Visitors may also see eagles, hawks, falcons, and other raptors.

**Directions:** Take Bureau of Indian Affairs Road 313 from Hardin to Fort Smith (about a 45-minute drive) and go south about 3 miles. There are campgrounds on the north and south shore of Afterbay. For birdwatching, the Afterbay waters can be viewed by crossing the river at the Afterbay Dam to the north side, or from the southside road and campground. The Headgate Trail begins from the west end of the Afterbay Campground parking area.

**Important Information:** The Afterbay Campground is open all year, weather permitting. The park entrance fee includes overnight camping. Note that the coldness of the water in Afterbay and the Bighorn River makes swimming inadvisable. Contact the National Park Service at 406-666-2412 for information.

## 424. Ok-A-Beh Marina and Swim Beach

Ok-A-Beh is a privately owned marina that rents motorboats, pontoon boats, and fishing gear. There is a boat ramp here and a small swim beach serviced by a lifeguard. Though the fluctuating water levels don't allow for a smooth beach area, the opportunity to jump into the clear, cold lake on a hot summer's day is a refreshing treat. Food, restrooms, and potable water are available at the marina.

**Directions:** Take Bureau of Indian Affairs Road 313 from Hardin to Fort Smith and go south to the left-hand signed turn to the marina. It is 10 miles to the marina. It takes about an hour to reach Ok-A-Beh Marina from Hardin.

**Important Information:** The National Park Service provides lifeguard service Monday through Friday from mid-June to Labor Day. Contact the marina at 406-665-2216 for more information.

## 425. Om-Ne-A Trail

This rim-top trail gives hikers a chance to view the dramatic Bighorn Canyon. The 3-mile trail starts at Yellowtail Dam and goes to Ok-A-Beh Marina. If you have a shuttle vehicle, you can hike it one way, or you could just hike part way and return via the same route to keep the hike a reasonable distance for kids. The trail is steep for 0.25 mile up to the rim and also on the way back down again at the other end of the trail. Though it is not regularly maintained, the trail gets frequent use.

**Directions:** Take Bureau of Indian Affairs Road 313 from Hardin to Fort Smith (about a 45-minute drive) and go south from Fort Smith about 3 miles. The trail begins at the south end of the parking area at Yellowtail Dam.

**Important Information:** Contact the National Park Service at 406-666-2412 for information.

# Pryor

On the southeastern edge of the Crow Indian Reservation are the intriguing Pryor Mountains and the small town of Pryor. The mountains were created by an upward geological thrust of limestone rock. Eroded by rain and snow, the limestone was shaped into a maze of caverns and canyons fascinating to explore. South of the reservation is a section of the Pryors managed by the Custer National Forest, and the Pryor Mountains National Wild Horse Range. Access to these natural areas is difficult, and a four-wheel-drive vehicle is recommended. However, one can appreciate the beauty of the Pryor Mountains by viewing them from the town of Pryor. Here the Chief Plenty Coups Memorial State Park offers an interesting museum and a peaceful picnic area.

## 426. Chief Plenty Coups Memorial State Park

The Crow people never appointed another tribal chief after Chief Plenty Coups passed away. The Crow chief had a long and rich life and remains the tribe's most revered leader. By age 26 he was considered a valiant warrior and had 80 feathers on his coup stick to prove it. He led scouts under General Cook in the late 1800s. In 1904, *Aleck-chea-ahoosh*, meaning Many Achievements, was named chief of the Crows.

The chief was a man of vision. In fact, at age 9, Plenty Coups had two important visions that would guide his life and leadership. In one vision he saw the buffalo falling into a hole and being replaced by spotted buffalo, foretelling the coming of white man's cattle. In another vision, he saw himself as an old man sitting by a creek near a two-story log home. Beyond was a spectacular mountain range. Later, Chief Plenty Coups recognized Pryor Creek and mountains as the place in his dream and built his homestead at this site.

The man of prophetic dreams believed that his people would need to change their lifestyle if they were to survive the conquering white regime and the loss of the buffalo. So Chief Plenty Coups built a two-story log home, farmed his land, and opened a store. He encouraged the education of the Crow Indians in the style of the white man, telling his people, "With an education you are white man's equal. Without it, you are his victim."

Chief Plenty Coups was known and respected by white leaders as well. He was selected to represent all American Indians at the dedication ceremony for the Tomb of the Unknown Soldier at Arlington National Cemetery in 1924. In the ceremony, Chief Plenty Coups laid his war bonnet and coup stick upon the memorial and prayed for peace for all people.

Chief Plenty Coups donated his homestead to all humankind as a token of his friendship for the people of every race. The Chief died at age 84 in 1932. His home became a state park in 1965. The park now houses a circular museum, designed to symbolize a tepee. Exhibits there document the life of Chief Plenty Coups, explain the history of the Crow Indians, and provide descriptions of the Crow people's renowned hunting techniques, the role of women in the matrilineal culture, and other aspects of Crow life. A short walk east of the museum leads to the two-story log home of Chief Plenty Coups and the log cabin he used as a store. The chief is buried with his two wives and an adopted daughter at the homestead site by the springs he believed held good medicine.

There is a wooded picnic area with tables, potable water, and vault toilets at the park. The museum has restrooms and a gift shop.

**Directions:** From Interstate 90 in Billings, take Exit 445 and go south for 0.5 mile. Turn right onto Old Pryor Road, Bighorn County 416, and follow this road for 10 miles. At the junction of CR 416 and Pryor Road, turn right (south) and go 23 miles to Pryor. Turn right at the stop sign and go 0.75 mile west to the state park. Though the park is 35 miles south of Billings, allow extra time to travel as the road can be slow.

**Important Information:** The park is open May 1 through September 30 from 8 A.M. to 8 P.M. Museum hours are from 10 A.M. to 5 P.M. daily. Tours through the Chief's home are given at 1:30 P.M. The gift shop is open 9 A.M. to 5 P.M. daily. The park entrance fee is $3 per carload or 50¢ per walk-in. Montana Department of Fish, Wildlife & Parks family passports provide free entrance. For more information, contact the museum at 406-252-1289.

# LOWER YELLOWSTONE AREA

The multi-faceted Yellowstone River takes on a lazy character in the lower stretch from Billings to the North Dakota border. Along the way it passes through a number of small Montana towns, which thrive on its presence. The surrounding prairie lands have supported these communities with agriculture and coal. A unique find here are the moss and plume agates which are fairly plentiful in graveled areas of the river and surrounding hills. History here revolves around the frontier West and you'll find the life of the cowboy is a common theme. The Cheyenne, Crow, and Sioux tribes have an even longer history in this region.

# Miles City

If you've ever wanted to buy a bucking horse, you can actually do so in Miles City. Each year during the third full weekend in May, the city puts on the Bucking Horse Sale, with a rodeo, bull riding, wild horse races, and much more. If this isn't your thing, come back during the fourth weekend in June for the Balloon Roundup and enjoy the sight of hundreds of balloons above the prairie. You'll find plenty to do in this spirited town along the Yellowstone River. The folks here seem to have a knack for inventing fun activities. The town considers itself Montana's Cowboy Capital and prides itself on having plenty of town characters. This town of about 8,500 people maintains its dime store lunch counter and doesn't believe in parking meters.

Miles City has been around since 1877. It was actually named after Colonel Nelson A. Miles, the cavalry colonel to whom Chief Joseph surrendered the Nez Perce tribe at the Bear's Paw Battlefield. Miles set up a cantonment near the Tongue River after the battle with the Nez Perce and the Cedar Creek battle he fought with Sitting Bull just 509 miles to the north. These temporary quarters served soldiers awaiting the completion of Fort Keogh; the encampment later became Miles City. For a while it was called Milestown, and sometimes, the Town of Miles.

For more information about Miles City, contact the Chamber of Commerce at 406-232-2890. The chamber is open Monday through Friday from 9 A.M. to noon and 1 to 5 P.M.

## 427. Range Riders Museum

Here's a tribute to life in the westward migration. The Range Riders Museum has grown in its 55-year history to include nine buildings which house thousands of artifacts that portray the lives of men and women during pioneer times. Pictures, cowboy memorabilia, homestead artifacts, and a re-created frontier town are among the exhibits here. There is also a miniature Indian village replicating a village of Chief Lame Deer, plus Indian artifacts from the Sioux, Cheyenne, and Crow tribes. A recent addition is the Charles Russell Gallery with prints of Montana's favorite artist's works. If you want to get a great perspective on the history of the cowboy hat, you can explore the museum's collection of nearly 1,000.

**Directions:** The museum is at the west end of Main Street, just across the Tongue River Bridge. From Interstate 94, take Exit 138 and go north into town on Main Street. It veers left (west) and goes through town. Just after you cross the Tongue River, look to your right to see the museum.

**Important Information:** The museum is open from April 1 to October 31 from 8 A.M. to 8 P.M. every day. Admission is $3.50 for adults, $3 for seniors, $1 for older students and 50 cents for grade school students. For more information contact the museum at 406-232-4483.

## 428. Custer County Art Center

This art center is touted as one of Montana's best and you'll understand why when you see the creative presentations here. A visit to the art center has an interesting beginning as the entrance is through a huge culvert. This makes sense when you find out that the facility housing the county art center was once the water treatment plant for Miles City. The building is listed in the National Register of Historic Places and has been wonderfully remodeled to house two large galleries featuring art in a wide variety of media. Included in the permanent collection are some of the historic American Indian photos taken by Edward S. Curtis. Kids will enjoy the unusual entrance, the variety of works, and the tepee outside. There is an extensive children's summer workshop program.

The center is next to Pumping Plant Park, a 2.5-acre park that has restrooms, a picnic area, and playground equipment. Camping is allowed at this city park at no charge.

**Directions:** From Interstate 94, take Exit 138 and go north into town on Main Street. It veers left (west) and goes through town. After you cross the Tongue River, just beyond the Range Riders Museum, turn right on Waterplant Road, which takes you to the art center in 0.5 mile.

**Important Information:** The museum is open from 1 to 5 P.M. Tuesday through Sunday year-round, but closed in January. Admission is free. For more information, contact the art center at 406-232-0635.

## 429. Ursuline Convent of the Sacred Heart

The "lady Black Robes" or the Ursuline Sisters, came to this area in 1884 and the convent was built between 1889 and 1902. This was the first convent in the Rocky Mountains. The first facility was destroyed by fire in 1897, but the community came forward and built a three-story brick-and-stone structure. The facility was used as an academy and then was leased as a mental health center in 1978. In 1991, the facility was rescued from demolition by community advocates who called themselves the "Convent Keepers." Today the building is on the National Register of Historic Places and is used for community meetings. Tours by appointment.

**Directions:** Take Exit 138 from Interstate 94 and go into town on Main Street. Follow Main where it veers to the left and continue several blocks. Turn right onto Montana Avenue just beyond the U.S. Highway 12 turnoff. Go three blocks to Leighton and turn left. The convent is on this block at 1411 Leighton Boulevard.

**Important Information:** There is a minimal charge for the tour. Contact the convent at 406-232-4146 before visiting.

## 430. Fort Keogh Livestock and Range Laboratory

Once the largest military post in Montana, this fort is now an agricultural research station. The fort was built in 1877 during the Indian Wars but closed in 1908. Fort Keogh was named in honor of Captain Myles Keogh who died in the Battle of the Little Bighorn. Several of the original fort buildings still stand and have been incorporated into the research facility. The station operates in conjunction with Montana State University and focuses on beef research. It is one of the largest research ranges in the world with 50,000 acres of grassland, 1,000 acres of irrigated cropland, and 4,000 acres of irrigated pasture. The range supports a herd of 1,200 cows, 40 working horses, and a staff of more than 40 people. The research station's mission is to develop ecologically and economically sound range livestock production tactics for the Northen Great Plains. The scientists there study range ecology, range animal nutrition, beef cattle genetics and physiology, and integrated research management. Tours of the agricultural research center are given on weekdays by appointment.

The early history of the fort is still present on the site as well, and every year Mile City townsfolk relive the encampment of the 5th Infantry Regiment at Fort Keogh. The group portrays the unit that built Fort Keogh and founded Miles City in the late 1870s. There are numerous activities over this weekend, generally the last weekend in June. These include shooting contests, guided tours of the camp, and a mock skirmish.

**Directions:** Take Exit 135 from Interstate 94 and go north from the Interstate. Within a mile there is a signed turn to the left for Fort Keogh. The laboratory is less than a mile on this road.

**Important Information:** Contact the laboratory at 406-232-4970.

## 431. Riverside Park and Oasis Swimming Lake

The area surrounding the town's pool also has nice park facilities, including plenty of trees, picnic tables, and restrooms. The park is by the Tongue River, which actually fills the natural pool. The water is then filtered and chlorinated for public use. There is a sandy beach and shady cottonwoods. On the west side of the swimming lake there are tennis courts and a ballpark.

**Directions:** Take Exit 135 from Interstate 94 and go east on Main Street. Just after you cross the Tongue River you will see the park and pool on the right.

**Important Information:** Daily cost for the swimming lake is $1 for kids 12 and under, $1.50 for teens 13 to 17, and $2 for anyone 18 or over. Hours are Monday through Friday from 2 to 8 P.M., and weekends noon to 8 P.M. Contact the city at 406-232-3462 for more information.

## 432. Wibaux Park

If you have little ones 7 or younger, this is the pool to go to. Designed specifically for this age group, the wading pool has fun little-kid slides and in the park are picnic tables, a shelter, and playground equipment.

# As Pretty as a Picture: Montana Agates

It looks like a tree, or maybe a scene along the banks of the Yellowstone, or perhaps a mountain? Montana agates look like many things and no two are alike. Within the translucent material that makes up agates are discolorations that have grown in such a way that they look like scenes intentionally drawn in the rocks. They are often called moss or plume agates and are famous for their variegated designs. A little imagination goes a long way in looking at these stones.

Agate hunting is a popular activity in the eastern area of Montana near Miles City. The attractive gemstones are found along the Yellowstone River from the city of Custer to Sidney, 300 miles downstream. A good time to look for them is after high water has receded and exposed new stones. Rockhounds gather around gravel bars and islands looking for these intriguing rocks. Another good place to look is in the gravel of hills and creeks. But you have to know what to look for because, although the stones are translucent, they have a rough outer shell and can be hard for an amateur rockhound to spot unless a broken place reveals the translucent material. Look for rocks that have a rough skin and are gray, tan, or brown. They are often shaped like potatoes. Some are small, but the largest can weigh as much as 10 pounds.

People have been hunting for agates in this area since prehistoric times. Indians used the stones to make arrowheads and scrapers. Many people today walk along the Yellowstone in search of this treasure and some take the opportunity to float the river and look for the stones at gravel bars along the way. There are actually guided agate-hunting boat tours in Glendive. Contact the Miles City Chamber of Commerce for more information about agate hunting. Don't worry if you're not lucky enough to find any of these treasures; you can always find rough agates for sale in this region.

**Directions:** The park is by the VA hospital. Take Exit 138 into Miles City on Main Street. Just after the road veers to the left, turn left onto Winchester Street. The park is one block south.

**Important Information:** There is no charge for the use of this pool. Contact the city at 406-232-3462 for more information.

## 433. Lower Yellowstone River

• • • • • • • • • • • • • • • • • • • • • • • • • • • • • • • • •

The Lower Yellowstone is a smooth-flowing river from Hysham to Miles City. This area is blessed with an abundance of fishing access sites that make selecting a stretch to float difficult because you have so many choices of where to put in and take out. It's been a determination of the Montana Department of Fish, Wildlife & Parks to have an access site every 12 miles and they must be pretty close.

Among the floats to be recommended to families is the Roche Jaune to Kinsey Bridge fishing access site. This is about a 10-mile float, which could be three to four hours on this slow-moving part of the Yellowstone. Both sites have only a boat ramp.

The Montana Department of Fish, Wildlife & Parks has an excellent publication on floating the Yellowstone from Billings to the North Dakota border. It is called *Treasure of Gold* and can be purchased from the state organization at most regional offices. Contact the Miles City office at 406-232-4365.

The lower section here has 45 species of fish, including a couple of ancient species: shovel-nosed sturgeon and paddlefish. You'll also find prolific waterfowl and other unusual species such as white pelicans, eared grebes, and double-crested cormorants.

**Directions:** You can get to the Roche Jaune access site by following Main Street from Exit 138 off of Interstate 94 to U.S. Highway 59. Before you cross the Yellowstone, go straight on 6th Street where the highway veers left. Follow this two blocks to Truscott Street and you will see the access site. To get to Kinsey Bridge, take Exit 11 and turn right onto U.S. Highway 12. Shortly you will see a signed gravel road that gets you to the bridge, which you can see from the turnoff, in about half a mile.

**Important Information:** Though the river is slow here, keep in mind the safety factors for river floating. For information contact the Montana Department of Fish, Wildlife & Parks at 406-232-4365.

# 434. Pirogue Island State Park

A Yellowstone River island, this park is a haven for waterfowl, eagles, beavers, and white-tailed and mule deer who appreciate the densely wooded areas and the contrasting open sections of the 269-acre park. There's also a good chance of seeing kingbirds, pheasants, woodpeckers, and great blue herons. It's also a good spot for fishing and has a boat ramp if you want to float the river. Moss agate hunting is pretty good too. A dirt road meaders through the island and makes a great hiking road for families. It's best to park your car at the entrance and walk this road. There are no facilities at this undeveloped recreation area.
**Directions:** Go north from Miles City on Montana Highway 212 for 1 mile. Turn right (east) onto Kinsey Road and follow this 1.5 miles to a marked turnoff. It is another 1.6 miles along this county road to the island park.
**Important Information:** Call the Montana Department of Fish, Wildlife & Parks at 406-232-4365 for more information.

**Roundup**
CowBelle Campground
Lake Mason National Wildlife Refuge
Musselshell Valley Historical Museum
Western and Wildlife Museum

**Ryegate**
Deadmans Basin

**Forsyth**
Rosebud State Recreation Area
Rosebud County Pioneer Museum

**Terry**
Terry Badlands
Cameron Gallery
Prairie County Museum

**Glendive**
Frontier Gateway Museum
Makoshika State Park
Intake Recreation Area
Moss Agate Hunting

**Wibaux**
Beaver Creek Pond
Pierre Wibaux Museum

**Baker**
Baker Lake
Sandstone Reservoir
Medicine Rocks State Park
O'Fallon Historical Museum

**Ekalaka**
Chalk Buttes
Capitol Rock National Natural Landmark
Carter County Museum
Ekalaka Park
MacNab Pond Campground

**Broadus**
Reynold's Battlefield National Monument
Powder River Historical Museum
Mac's Museum
Powder River Taxidermy Wildlife Museum

**Otter**
Cow Creek Campground

**Decker**
Tongue River Reservoir

**Ashland**
Red Shale Campground
St. Labre Indian Mission and School
Cheyenne Indian Museum

**Busby**
Rosebud Creek Battlefield
Two Moon Monument

**Colstrip**
Castle Rock Lake

# Appendix: Important Phone Numbers, Addresses, and Websites

Knowing what's in store for you on a trip is a good way to be prepared and make the most out of your time. Contact numbers are listed for each site in the book. Here's a quick reference list for management agencies and tourist information sources in Montana.

**Travel Montana**
This program is operated by the Montana Department of Commerce with the goal of promotion and development of Montana's tourism industry.
It is not directly related to local chambers of commerce. The organization provides information to visitors about Montana and is a good resource. Ask for their Montana Travel Planner and Montana Vacation Guide.

Website: http://www.travel.mt.gov
406-444-2654 or 800-VISIT MT (800-847-4868)

**Regional Tourism Offices**
These offices can provide you with helpful travel planners or recreation guides for their respective tourism regions.

Glacier Country, Bigfork
406-837-6211 or 800-338-5072

Yellowstone Country, Red Lodge
406-446-1005 or 800-736-5276

Gold West Country, Deer Lodge
406-846-1943 or 800-879-1159

Missouri River Country, Wolf Point
406-653-1319 or 800-653-1319

Russell Country, Great Falls
406-761-5036 or 800-527-5348

Custer Country, Hardin
406-655-1671 or 800-346-1876

**Montana Department of Fish, Wildlife & Parks**
Website: http://www.fwp.state.mt.us
On-Line Computer Bulletin Board
800-962-1729 (in-state)
406-444-5648 (out of state)

Regional Offices:
Billings             406-247-2940
Bozeman          406-994-4042

| Glasgow | 406-228-3700 |
| Great Falls | 406-454-5840 |
| Helena | 406-444-3750 |
| Kalispell | 406-752-5501 |
| Missoula | 406-542-5500 |
| Miles City | 406-232-4365 |

## Montana Chamber of Commerce

Most cities have an active chamber of commerce. To obtain general state information or phone numbers for a particular city office call the state office in Helena at 406-444-2406.

## Museum Association of Montana

Many Montana museums are members of this association. For information about a specific museum or to get a contact phone number for a museum, call the Helena office at 406-444-4710.

## Montana Wilderness Association

This statewide organization sponsors annual summer hikes led by various knowledgeable members. Some of these are excellent family hikes. Contact them for their current hike schedule at 406-443-7350.

## USDA Forest Service

Listed below are headquarters offices for each forest service region. Contact them for specific information in their particular forest region or for phone numbers of district offices. Website: http://www.fs.fed.us/r1/

Northern Region Headquarters, Missoula
406-329-3511

Beaverhead-Deer Lodge National Forest, Dillon
406-683-3900

Bitterroot National Forest, Hamilton
406-363-3131

Custer National Forest, Billings
406-248-9885

Flathead National Forest, Kalispell
406-755-5401

Gallatin National Forest, Bozeman
406-587-6701

Helena National Forest, Helena
406-449-5201

Kootenai National Forest, Libby
406-293-6211

Lewis and Clark National Forest, Great Falls
406-791-7700

Lolo National Forest, Missoula
406-329-3750

## U.S. Department of the Interior, National Park Service
Bear's Paw Battleground National Monument, Chinook
There is no phone on site; contact the Blaine County Museum for information,
406-357-2590.

Bighorn Canyon National Recreation Area, Fort Smith
406-666-2412

Glacier National Park, West Glacier
Website: http://www.nps.gov/glac
406-888-7800

Grant Kohrs Ranch National Historic Site, Deer Lodge
Website: http://www.nps.gov/grko
406-846-2070

Little Bighorn Battlefield National Monument, Crow Agency
406-638-2621

Yellowstone National Park, Wyoming
307-344-7381

## U.S. Bureau of Land Management
Montana State Office, Billings: 406-255-2904
Website: http://www.wb.mt.blm.gov/

| | |
|---|---|
| Billings Field Office | 406-238-1540 |
| Butte Field Office | 406-494-5059 |
| Dillon Field Office | 406-683-2337 |
| Garnet Field Office | 406-329-3914 |
| Great Falls Field Office | 406-727-0503 |
| Havre Field Station | 406-265-5891 |
| Lewistown Field Office | 406-538-7461 |
| Headwaters Field Office | 406-494-5059 |
| Miles City Field Office | 406-232-4333 |
| Phillips Field Office | 406-654-1240 |
| Valley Field Station | 406-228-4316 |

## U.S. Bureau of Reclamation
Montana Area Office, Billings
Website: http://www.gp.usbr.gov/www/mtaosum1.htm
406-247-7295

## Indian Reservation Headquarters

Blackfeet Nation, Browning
406-338-7276

Crow Reservation, Crow Agency
406-638-2601

Flathead Reservation-Confederated
Salish and Kootenai Tribes, Pablo
406-675-2700

Fort Belknap Reservation, Harlem
406-353-2205

Fort Peck Reservation, Poplar
406-768-5155

Northern Cheyenne Reservation,
Lame Deer
406-477-6284

Rocky Boy's Reservation, Box Elder
406-395-4282

## Montana Road Conditions
Website: http://www.mdt.mt.gov
406-444-6339 or 800-226-ROAD/7623

## Montana Weather Reports
| Billings | 406-652-1916 |
| Glasgow | 406-228-9625 |
| Great Falls | 406-453-5469 |
| Helena | 406-443-5151 |
| Kalispell | 406-755-4829 |
| Missoula | 406-721-3939 |

# INDEX

· · · · · · · · · · · · · · · · · · · · · · · · · · · · · · · · · · · · · · · ·

# ABOUT THE AUTHOR

Chris Boyd (formerly Brewer) is an educational trainer and the author of seven educational books. Her dedication to children and families prompted her to write this book about Montana. Raised in Washington state, Chris lived in and explored Montana for 20 years. She is an outdoor enthusiast who believes that nature experiences are an especially important part of family life.